SUCCESSFUL Biblical YOUTH WORK by Elmer L. Towns

impact books
Nashville, Tennessee

TABLE OF CONTENTS

FOREWORD

Hello!

I love to be with teenagers and I have great trust in Christian youth. They are the life of the church today. All too often we relegate them to next year and say, "Teenagers are the future of the church." Yes, but more important, they are the *today* of the church. They have needs that should be met now, or there will be no tomorrow for them in the church.

Do you like teens? How do you feel as one adult, sitting around and talking with three or four young people? Most adults feel uncomfortable in the teen subculture. From this uneasy position they like to "handle" the teens like children. It may be threatening to accept a youth as an equal. I hope this book develops your love for the "offbeat generation."

One of the problems we youth workers face is: what to call the youth. A number of names could be used: teens, youth, adolescents, young people, hippies, kids, teenagers, students, guys and gals, the gang, etc. When I'm in a youth rally or camp, I usually call them "kids," or to a group I say, "Let's go, gang." Other than first names, titles seem impersonal to me. I'll not criticize you for your teenage "handle" if you'll allow me to call them as I choose. However, when writing I use all the titles from kids to teenagers and they don't like the latter title. (I probably use many titles for youth as a journalistic technique to keep from being repetitious.)

The purpose of SUCCESSFUL BIBLICAL YOUTH WORK is to help the average lay person in the church work with teenagers. I have tried to think in terms of the total needs of young people and the total program of the church. The word "total" is a very inclusive term. All needs of young people are not mentioned in this book—but a *total* overall program is suggested. As this program is implemented, principles will affect the *total* area of the local church.

You who read this book will learn very little unless you *work*. The questions at the end of each section are designed to cause you to dig. The questions should cause you to reflect upon and assimilate truths already known. There are practical applications for you. Work through each one of the "check charts." Also, make sure you work through the practical project at the end of each section.

This book is directed at youth work in the local church. Today, many organizations are working to win young people to Christ and to build them up in the faith. These purposes are good, but I am dedicated to the ministry of the local church. This book is geared to help you work with youth in the church.

"No man is an island," said John Donne, and I find this true. So, no man is a product of his own making. This book is not a *new contribution* from me to the world. My writings are the sum total of life's impressions.

Dr. Howard Hendricks made a great contribution to my thinking as I sat in his class on youth work, spring 1956 at Dallas Theological Seminary. His stirring lectures on "ivory tower" wisdom and "grass root" realism captured my thinking. Some of the phrases such as "independent decency" and "compartmentalized Christianity" are his. In my early teaching I found his ever-present influence, as was found in the first edition of this book. There are footnotes in this volume showing Dr. Hendricks as a source. I express deep appreciation for his permission to use these.

Roscoe Brewer, then youth director at Tulsa Baptist Temple, invited me to speak at a youth clinic, April 1967. This introduced me to the Baptist Bible Fellowship, which in turn influenced my thinking about youth work. Churches belonging to this group have some of the most successful youth groups in our country. This second edition of *Successful Youth Work* is edited to include principles from these large, fast-growing churches. I am indebted to Roscoe Brewer for his influence on my thinking regarding youth ministry.

As I go to press with this book, my three teens are in the youth department at the Thomas Road Baptist Church, Lynchburg, Virginia. Dr. Jerry Falwell has built the fastest growing church in America; I have seen attendance grow from 2,618 to over 7,000 in Sunday School. This experience has proven to me that God can not only transform the life of a youth, but that multitudes of teens can be attracted to a local church.

I must express affection to my wife for her encouragement and help. She was my partner in working with youth in Savannah, Georgia; Columbia, South Carolina; Minneapolis, Minnesota; and Dallas, Texas. Today, she is a counselor in the high school department at Thomas Road Baptist Church.

When I first wrote parts of this book, I was a young married youth minister and my children were not born. I had never heard of "identity crisis" nor had I thought of sophisticated methods of counseling. This book was first printed when my children were approaching adolescence. Now as I rewrite this book, all three of my children are in high school. My basic approach to youth work has not changed. I believe methodology should be based on the Word of God, hence our message and method does not change. Also, human nature has not changed; God's laws for governing the world have not changed. But as I have watched my children grow into teens, I realize the world has changed, knowledge has spiraled, sex perversion has moved from the back alleys to our TVs, and our youth-oriented society has swung the pendulum to the left. So I ask the question, "Do I change my method of reaching youth?" Many in the evangelical world are changing to a relevant ministry. Preaching is thrown out in favor of dialogue. Super-aggressive soul-winning is replaced with sharing. The church is evacuated for the "Jesus people" commune or coffee house. When I see these new trends I ask, Where are the results? God wants us to be fruitful and our fruit should remain. My answer to the trends is clear. "I do not change, because God's methods do not change." But I learn all I can to make my preaching up to date, but I do not give up preaching. I study "identity crises" and other developments in our youth society to better understand their needs, but salvation still is their answer and aggressive soul-winning is the method to meet their need. I observe teens' disillusionment with dead traditional churches, and I share their perplexity, but I don't desert the church to join the street people and become a "Jesus freak." I would find a dynamic New Testament church because God's method centers in a local church. My methods have not changed in 22 years since I started working with young people. They have become sharper with understanding and clearer with learning. When I am around youth workers, I try to learn as much as possible to reach modern youth. But I gauge new ideas by the criteria of Scripture and the purpose of the church. There are many new fads in youth work that will ultimately pull a program away from its New Testament goal, but at the same time there are new ideas that will help youth workers accomplish New Testament aims. My methods remain unchanged—centered in the local church and grounded in the Word of God.

I must also mention all the young people with whom I worked—those I helped and those I didn't. Thank you for your confidence. You taught me much about youth, as we sought the Lord together.

Finally, I must acknowledge the help of my college and seminary students. We were together in St. Louis, Missouri; Winnipeg, Canada; Deerfield, Illinois, and Lynchburg. Thank you for your questions in class and your criticism of the mimeographed copy of this book. Your term papers and projects have challenged me to be creative and thorough. I trust you have learned as much as I have about youth as we have lived through many educational experiences.

May this book carry forward the investment that so many have made in it.

Sincerely yours in Christ,
ELMER TOWNS

SECTION ONE

SETTING THE SCENE

Why are youth problems more different than ever before?

Why are teens religious, yet they reject the traditional church?

Why do churches (and youth groups) die, and what can be done to stop the process?

Where do individuals go who leave deteriorating churches?

Why are fundamental churches growing larger and faster than evangelical churches?

What are the unique features of youth programs in fundamental churches?

1

THE CONTEMPORARY YOUTH CULTURE

"**T**he NOW generation" is a phrase that characterizes contemporary young people between the ages of 12 and 24 in our American society. The NOW generation of teens reflects an orientation of the 70's towards experience-centered lives, spontaneous reaction to stimuli and relevant morality. The term *now* shows the difference between former generations of teenagers and today's adolescents. Also, *now* reflects a difference between adults and teens, sometimes called the "generation gap." Sociologists refer to this gap as an "intergenerational conflict." In the late 40's the term *teenager* was invented and the phrase "juvenile delinquent" was coined. The popular press revealed that America was moving toward a youth society. Even as more attention was focused on teens, many magazines predicted that emphasis on youth was a fad and eventually interest would shift away from the youth society; as Kenneth Keniston has been quoted as saying in 1962, there is "Little likelihood of American students ever playing a radical role, much less a revolutionary one in our society." [1] Obviously, our culture has greatly changed since that time. The youth society has proven itself more than a fad, the youth culture reflects an ideology or way of life based on definite philosophical assumptions.

The youth culture, described as a "hang-loose ethic," has produced

---

[1] Robert J. Bartel, "Campus Tensions and Evangelical Response," *Christianity Today*, XIII (June 6, 1969), p. 12.

tension between the older generation and young people. This tension was reflected during the summer of 1972 in the National Democratic Convention and the ensuing jockeying for political power by many young people who have been previously denied a voice in American politics. The tension is also reflected in the American home where teen-agers have definite ideas and lifestyles, many times conflicting with their parents. Family tension is not restricted to non-Christians or to a certain segment of the country; family tension seems to be prevalent in all of society. The tension is also seen in local churches. Adults yearn for the "good ole days," while young people want their religion to be up to date. The boy asks, "What's wrong with long hair?" and backs up his argument: "Jesus had long hair." The mini-skirt, bikini craze is a repudiation of the Puritan ethic by which parents were reared. Tension is manufactured when they want their children to continue the past life-style. Rock music is an existential expression of the Now generation and cannot be correctly understood apart from the youthful experience-oriented society. Kids want rock music in the church. Adults do not because they are irritated by its constant stacatto beat and loud, blaring sounds. The tension created over youth work in local churches is real and not an illusion; it exists at the subliminal area. Both youth and adults feel deeply about the other's lifestyle.

The fact remains, the youth culture is decidedly different from the past youth culture as adults know it and it is distinctive from the lifestyle of the older generations in the church today. This tension raises the first major issue in youth work—"To fight 'em or join 'em." Those who minister to young people have two alternatives: First, to adapt their principles and techniques to the youth culture, to reach them for Christ, hence becoming relevant; or second, hold onto the traditional approach, communicating to teens the values of the past, then reinforcing the desired way of life, so youth will think and act differently from those around them. Campus Crusade for Christ, San Bernardino, California, and Campus Life (Youth for Christ), Wheaton, Illinois, have adapted to the youth culture, incorporating relevance into their ministry whereby their leaders identify with youth in language and dress, and soften their standards on common youth practices such as dancing, movies and dress. Leaders of these organizations point out that they are still committed to conservative doctrine while their methodology has changed. The second alternative: youth workers can structure a ministry that is traditional and/or authoritarian in approach. Relevancy is rejected as an operative principle. Young people are admonished to "Come out from among the world and be ye separate," so that the teen neither looks, acts, or thinks like the world. Thus the demand for holy living is reflected in the "clean-cut" young man and "modest" (nonexposure of the body) attire of the girls. Internal discipline is taught whereby the young person submits himself to external authority and reverences authority figures such as pastors, parents and Sunday School teachers.

Actually, an absolute choice does not exist. Young people must live in the youth culture and any church program can never completely isolate them from the influence and pressures of the youth world. But at the same time, a true Christian position is authoritarian by design and demand; discipline is the natural outgrowth of the Scriptures. The Christian must live in the world and not withdraw from it; therefore, the minister to young people must understand the youth culture, first to reach into that culture and win young people to Christ, and second, to equip each Christian young person to return to that culture as a witness for Jesus Christ.

Therefore, before we begin a study of the psychology of adolescents, we must begin by an examination of the youth culture where the young person lives. The purpose of this chapter is to understand today's student culture by summarizing a portion of the vast amount of recent literature on youth.

The Youth Culture

The Now generation is *experience-oriented,* just as the Puritan ethic was future-oriented. They have been reared on television which has cultivated a new standard of valuing people and things in terms of action and relevancy. It was thought when they were children that their vicarious identification with television would produce a passive generation. Rather, young people have seen that sex, murder, action and travel can be packaged by the style-setting media, all for the purpose of providing a new experience to stimulate the audience. Instead of being passive, they want to become part of all they see. Television has taught them that *Mission Impossible* is attainable. As a result, the young people feel they can do . . . be anything they desire. But their desires are not tempered, they want it *now.*

> No longer does the young person want to know what's happening, he *wants to be* what's happening. This desire to be involved in the movement and the total environment accounts for the attractiveness of the *psychedelia* to those without authentic Christian experience. He does not want to be controlled by his environment . . . but to be free to create the setting in which he is to be immersed.[2]

Even the beer advertisements capitalize on the Now theme: "You

---

[2] Evan Adams, "Contemporary Student Thinking: As Related to the Missionary Enterprise" (unpublished paper presented to the Missions Executive Retreat, 1967). p. 4.

only go around once in life; grab all the gusto you can." The knowledge explosion has given young people a vast amount of historical data, yet the past has little hold upon their lives. Professor Erik Erickson, the social psychologist, known for his writings on identity crisis, suggests three reasons why young people are *now-oriented*.

> First, the past grows increasingly distant from the present . . . the past grows progressively more different from the present in fact, and seems more remote and irrelevant psychologically. Second, the future, too, grows more remote and uncertain. Because the future directions of social change are virtually unpredictable, today's young men and women are growing into a world that is more unknowable than that confronted by any previous generation. . . . Third, the present assumes a new significance as the one time in which environment is relevant, immediate and knowable. The past's solution to life's problems are not necessarily relevant to the here-and-now, and no one can know whether what is decided today will remain valid in tomorrow's world; hence, the present assumes an autonomy unknown in more static societies.[3]

Since the past has little influence and the future is remote, the Now generation would not be inclined to explore historic Christianity for answers to their questions. Inasmuch as the Bible is a Book of history (His story), the church and historic Christianity have little appeal to the contemporary youth culture. But youth have gone one step beyond ignoring Christianity; the young person finds himself in active opposition to tradition. One of the fundamental characteristics of youth culture is *irreverence*. Simmons and Winograd describe the irreverence of the youth culture, "It repudiates or at least questions such cornerstones of conventional society as Christianity. 'My country, right or wrong,' the sanctity of marriage and premarital chastity, civil obedience, the accumulation of wealth, the right and even competence of parents, the schools, and the government to take and make decisions for everyone—in sum, the establishment." [4] The three institutions set up by God—the home, government, and the church—are not only ignored, but also challenged and defied. Simmons and Winograd summarize the rebellion as: "Youth culture is an attempt to live a life relatively independent of conventional society" [5] Many church young people are caught up in antiestablishment feelings, which are reinforced by television, movies, magazines and even school textbooks. Inasmuch as young people are blind to their society, because they are a part of it, the adult who attempts to minister to young people will

---

[3] Erik Erickson, *Youth, Change and Challenge* (New York: Basic Books, Inc., 1962), p. 168.
[4] Simmons, J.H. and Barry Winograd, *It's Happening,* (Santa Barbara: Marc-Laird, 1966), p. 12,13.
[5] *Ibid.*

have to give reasons for demanding youth's allegiance to historic Christianity. He cannot reach them by simply belittling fads of teen-agers.

Pervasive humanism is another basic foundation of youth culture. They place great store in the value of human beings and human life. Teenage humanism is not the same as philosophic humanism, which is a proclamation of the inherent goodness and the rationality of men. Hippie communities put great value upon man being a human and his becoming a full and complete person. They reflect adolescent human-ism, which places emphasis on personhood. Most literature concern-ing adolescents minimizes the contribution of adults to young people, especially pointing out the detrimental influence of authority figures such as parents, ministers and teachers. Larry Richards asks, "Will we grant young people equality of personhood—will we respect them, listen to them, and share ourselves with them as we ask them to listen to us and share themselves with us? Again, the true Christian's re-sponse must be to extend true personhood to youth, to accept their differences and value them, and to extend to each the freedom to find his personal authority in God." [6] The average high school student is asked to make decisions without appealing to any authority other than himself. As a result, many young people have grown to believe that their opinion is impeccable; hence, they argue with mother, teachers, police, and political figures. Adolescent humanism leads to rationalism whereby the young person appeals only to his mental processes to make decisions and/or determine a lifestyle.

Robert Bartel cites Richard Flacks, sociologist at the University of Chicago, as asserting that the value system of the youth is essentially humanistic, with an emphasis on individual development and self-expression, along with a genuine social and humanitarian concern.[7] Youth are very impatient with institutions that seem to perpetuate in-justice, inequality or are simply unresponsive to human needs. Teens see the traditional American church as dead and hypocritical. Many times the church is governed by a board of deacons who are insensitive to human needs and they tend to hold onto the past rather than follow the New Testament command. For the most part, the youth's disgust with the traditional American church is valid—many of the American churches are dead.

Humanism reflects itself in many adolescent viewpoints, such as opposition to the Vietnam war, concern for ethnic and racial minori-ties, pragmatic ethics, and relevant Christianity. At the present time,

[6] Lawrence O. Richards, *Youth Ministry*, (Grand Rapids: Zondervan Publishing House, 1972), p. 31.
[7] Bartel, *op. cit.*, p. 14, 15.

adolescent humanism, combined with irreverence, produces a passive resistance toward the establishment rather than active rebellion. However, the mood in the future may shift as circumstances vary.

Many adolescents feel adults are the cause of society's problems and, from the point of view of the "hang-loose ethic," adults represent people and social forces which put other people down and hang them up, which teach people to be stolid and dignified, rather than swinging —self-righteous and moralistic rather than responsible, dutiful rather than devoted. The young people feel adults are villains who pass their own hangups to others, thus propagating sickness "for your own good." [8] While adults charge youth with being immoral, irresponsible and irreverent, youth make countercharges against adult hypocrisy, some of which charges are true.

> Look at you blowing up whole countries for the sake of some crazy ideologies that you don't live up to anyway. Look at you . . . kids getting a revolving charge account and buying your junk. (Who's a junkie?) Look at you, needing a couple of stiff drinks . . . to talk to another human being. Look at you, making it with your neighbor's wife on the sly just to try and prove that you're really alive. Look at you, hooked on *your* cafeteria of pills, and making up dirty names for anybody who isn't in your bag, and . . . calling this nowhere scene the Great Society! AND YOU'RE GONNA TELL US HOW TO LIVE? C'mon, man, you've got to be kidding![9]

The pursuit of experience is another characteristic of the Now generation. The young person seeks experience, first as a thing in itself, and second, as a means of learning and growing. Experience entails a heightened attention to the present ongoing movement and far less concern with the past or future. "If I can't feel it, it must not be real," is the motto of young people. Their experience-oriented life involves a mistrust of dogmas and propositional truth which they feel obscures the richness of life. Spontaneity is a highly valued personal trait, as is tolerance. They do what they want to do, when they want to do it and have tolerance for others to "do their own thing." The idea is to do whatever you want to do, so long as you don't interfere with other people. The average young person chafes at virtually all restrictions because he sees laws as a limitation of the growth and development of people.[10]

Young people passionately demand honesty and are impatient with forms having no content. Youth reject the doctrine that truth is to be found by a ritualistic study of the legacy of the past. The Now gen-

---

[8] Simmons and Winograd, *op. cit.*, p. 19.
[9] *Ibid.*, p. 28.
[10] *Ibid.*, p. 14–16.

eration feels that knowledge is not something to be learned and stored up for future use, but must serve an immediate end and practical purpose.

The young people also are a searching generation characterized as "liberated" and "skeptical." Young people are acutely aware that the major problems of society have not been solved by the talk and action of adults; therefore, young people are reluctant to join adult organizations or to adopt adult customs. They want to join groups and movements that are consistent with their own values. Allen J. Moore draws the following conclusion:

> Almost all observers of the youth and young adult culture agree that in their eyes the adult empire with its institutions has fallen. Young adults are more aware than any previous generation of the inconsistencies of adults, the insincerity that has characterized much of their public performance, and the sheer inability of adult leaders to deal creatively with the problems of the age. With the loss of respect has come the downfall of authority . . . an adult deserves respect, not because he holds a position of authority, but because he as an individual has demonstrated his worth as a person and his competence in his position.[11]

What else has eroded adolescents' respect for authority? Perhaps it is more than adult incompetence that has destroyed the teenager's confidence in adults. Perhaps it is adult success in communicating to young people their desires and visions. Adults have long preached excellence and competence to the young people and now these young people are taking adult advice at its face value and attempting to fashion an ideal world. Simmons and Winograd agree with the above conclusion:

> America is now, in a sense, confronted by a legion of youths who are trying in their own fumbling way to practice what generations of fatuous graduation speakers have been preaching. This emerging ethos which seems so heretical at first is partly a restatement of some of the highest ideals and values which the great middle classes struggled for during the Industrial Revolution and which have since served all too often as a covering rationalization for self-seeking exploitation; the ideals we learn to bend and compromise in the process of "growing up" and "learning the ropes" and becoming "mature." The irony is not that Americans have failed to teach the upcoming generation but that they have been perhaps too successful in their training and must now confront their fervent pupils.[12]

We have attempted to refrain from using the phrase *generation gap* because it has become a clichè which is suggested as the only

---

[11] Allen J. Moore, *The Young Adult Generation* (New York: Abingdon Press, 1969), p. 94–95.
[12] Simmons and Winograd, *op. cit.,* p. 30.

cause for youth-adult problems. Even though there is tension between the generations, youth and adults are similar in many ways. Many studies reveal young people have the same moral values as their parents, they just practice them differently, probably because they are aware of the inconsistencies they have observed. Honesty requires telling a teacher that his course is stupid, and love demands personal expression in a kind of naive romanticism. The internalized Protestant value system built on the worth of the individual, is found in both parents and adolescents. However, on top of this Protestant value are the newly created middle-class values found in suburbia, "sociality, materialism and status." These were not originally found in the Protestant values, while young people have adopted the values of "individual differences, interpersonal relations and personal experience." Even though youth and adults are similar in outlook, their cultural expressions are different in reality.[13]

Robert Michaelson observes that the present generation shows a definite and remarkable interest in the study of religion.[14] This interest is a result of a significant amount of personal probing and searching; they want to know themselves, and the religious side of man is unknown. However, most of the religious interest is noninstitutional and, many times, anti-institutional in nature. This is reflected in the phenomenal success of *Jesus Christ, Superstar* and the growth of the "Jesus People" movement outside of the local church. Also, the growth in interdenominational agencies among evangelicals is related to the anti-institutional religious search by young people. Teens are told Biblical answers to their questions and a relationship to God can be found outside the local church. Interdenominational agencies claim their ministry is relevant, whereas the church has failed. Contrary to popular opinion, teenage interest in religion is far more serious than casual. Far from being apathetic, they are interested in issues and decisions about the problems that are vital to them.

Paul Goodman agrees and explains that it is wrong to say students aren't interested in religion, that they are agnostic. He feels agnosticism thrives in a stable world and we do not have that! He sees the current search into Zen, Yoga, Love feasts, drugs, occult worship, and astrology as a religious desire on the part of students. He feels their religion is intensely intellectual and there is no definite line between their religious experiments and their moral and political behavior.[15]

The new religious search by young people is increasingly secular

---

[13] *Moore, op. cit.,* pp. 35-38, 45.
[14] Robert Michaelson, "The Study of Religion. A Quiet Revolution in American Universities," *Religious Studies in Public Universities,* edited by Milton D. McClean (Carbondale, Ill.: Central Publications, Southern Illinois Unversity, 1967), p. 9.
[15] Paul Goodman, *Growing Up Absurd* (New York: Vintage Books, 1956), chapter 7.

in nature; they look to the natural world and to this present age for a context and orientation for human life. There is a collapse of "folk religion," where religious beliefs are woven into family, community, and national life. Their religious tenets are derived more from psychology, psychiatry and mental hygiene than from historic Christianity. Gordon Allport believes that in spite of the rejection of former religion on the part of the young people, there remains at this time in life a strong disposition towards the religious, perhaps because the teen is searching for his identity by giving himself to a cause greater than himself. He sees this as a normal growth pattern of "moving from the egocentricity of adolescence to the allocentricity of adulthood."

Today the religious alternatives include Playboyism (neo-hedonism), Ayn Rand's Objectivism (religion of selfishness), the Diggers (the hippie cult of poverty), Timothy Leary's Neo-Americanism church (drug cult), Zen Buddhism (spiritual exercises), Maharishi Mahesh Yogi's Spiritual Regeneration Movement (transcendental meditation), and humanistic psychologism (self-discovery and expression) . . . You might say that we are experiencing a recovery of religion outside the structures of traditional Christianity.[16]

Young people go on drugs both as an escape and a search. They are escaping from the reality of this world, and other times they are searching for a new thrill or a new experience. For most, drugs are a kick. However, Simmons and Winograd feel peer pressure is a significant influence on the teen who tries drugs. The following statement by a young coed demonstrates the place peer pressure has in drug use.

With an air of "how could I have ever thought otherwise," a pretty university sophomore declared, "Well, they looked like they were enjoying it. We'd had the standard lecture and talks in high school, where they were always supposed to be doing bad things; then I got here and found them smoking and talking and taking lovely walks under the stars and having fun and just not hurting anybody—even themselves. Y'know, the grades didn't go down the tubes or anything like that. They said why didn't I try it so I did and I kept on with it. I mean, should I give up a good thing, something that if it's doing anything it certainly isn't hurting me, just because some freak in the state capitol says it's illegal?" [17]

Other significant factors associated with drug usage are "permissive child-rearing techniques" and "a blind rebellion against restrictive parental proclamations." Marijuana has become an "in" action with teenagers. The youth, by and large, are convinced that it is no more harmful to smoke marijuana than it is to drink alcohol.[18]

[16] Moore, *op. cit.*, pp. 78, 83.
[17] Simmons and Winograd, *op. cit.*, p. 91.
[18] *Ibid.*

The new music of teenagers is more direct in its sensuality, protest and chagrin than the tunes of young people of the immediate past. Their music boldly depicts the confusion of the modern scene. The major emphasis is to lay aside preoccupation and hangups, by becoming immersed in an all-encompassing sound. Another theme is that of a stranger moving through an alien environment; the invitation is to join the "seekers" searching for meaningful values and a new world appropriate for the modern spirit. Many who believe the music is an accurate expression of their attitude and emotions, do not deny that the music itself is suggestive and sexually arousing.[19]

There is a shift in teenage morality taking place from traditional standards to a more liberal, humanistic ethic, based on the behavioral sciences. Moral practices tend to be immediate, workable solutions rather than principles basic for all men. Most young people are openly rejecting traditional morality which has been under attack since the end of World War II. According to Moore, "Young people are not engaging in sex more than previous generations did, but they are apparently enjoying it more. The revolution in sexual relations is an attitude and not a practice." Empirical studies show that promiscuity has declined; at least half the non-virgins have slept only with the man they plan to marry. Also, premarital intercourse tends to take place in a meaningful relationship with persons who intend to marry.[20]

The traditional distance between sexes has decreased among teenagers; they see each other much more under a greater variety of circumstances. Sex has lost its sacred character to the young person; it is simply becoming another human activity to them. They view married life as a swinging affair, based on mutual involvement and fulfillment. The idea of executing a solemn vow at marriage is remote; few want to include the word "obey" in their ceremony. There is an emphasis on communication and companionship as preliminaries to sexual intimacies.

The sex ethic is not changed as drastically as many believe. The majority of females still consider intercourse as the supreme treasure; a girl is extremely careful in selecting a bedmate, thinking she will find reward in sex if she is not free with her body. But, clearly, sex is no longer a thing to be saved until formal marriage vows are executed. Most young people feel that sex is fine so long as it is not promiscuous. Most females tend to believe that their bed-partner will become their husband if circumstances permit.[21]

Bruno Bettelheim, professor of psychology and psychiatry at the

[19] *Ibid.*, pp. 155–165.
[20] Moore, *op. cit.*, pp. 87–91.
[21] Simmons and Winograd, *op. cit.*, pp. 105–110, 112-114.

University of Chicago, examines "youth revolt" and concludes that, basically, young people are subject to an inner revolution, from which tensions are discharged into acts of violence. He believes that issues like Vietnam, the bomb, impersonal college education are used as a screen for what really ails them: their feelings of being obsolete, socially irrelevant and, as persons, insignificant. He goes on to indicate, that is why there is no student revolt in the emerging nations (and Russia). There, young people know that their energies are needed to help build the future.[22]

Other young people are not activists nor do they fight the adult system. Some are apathetic; most of these are antintellectual (read little, belittle research); because they do not trust man's intellect to get us out of the technologically caused impasse they turn their hopes to personal relationships and feel that Martin Buber has personified their feelings in I-Thou encounter. These young people pin their hopes on personal relationships because it gives them the feeling that, at least while the interaction lasts, they are important to someone.

Another reason for teenage rebellion is the fact that our society keeps the next generation too long dependent in terms of mature responsibilities. We do not let them have independence, nor are they accountable for their actions. "Independence occurs only among the affluent, and it can be widespread only in the modern, industrial state, since it is the only one where economics permit large numbers of young people to be taken care of by others long after puberty. As long as students are in school they cannot be economically independent and often are emotionally dependent as well. Many have been pushed to go to university when they personally haven't wanted to; some aren't ready to face the result of intellectual and self-discovery which is the essence of a university education. Some won't find self-discovery through intellectual pursuits. Thus deprived of self-mastery, their immature ego projects its hatred on those they can blame for their predicament. Rather than face and fight against his inner turmoil of ambivolence to dependents, he creates turmoil in the outside world and tries to fight it there.[23]

This then is today's youth, a floating person in a floating world. He lives in a world created by adults that the adults now repudiate, a world the teen doesn't want to surrender. It is a culture that places him at the center, feeds his desires and allows him to develop according to an internal pattern, called "individual differences" by psychologists, but titled "selfish egotism" by church leaders. The teen world is

---

[22] Bruno Bettelheim, "Redundant Youth." Realites, 241 (December 1970), 38–42, 98.

tied to relevancy and the password to enter its sanctuary is *now*. Inside the youth culture, we see teens searching for a pursuit that teens have never sought before, because youth culture has created the kind of teen that has never existed before—they are searching for self-identity. Identity crisis is a product of our decade and the "Who Am I" question has roots in cultural alienation, pervasive humanism, and existential philosophy. The question remains to be explored, Are teens searching for something that doesn't exist? They are trying to find self-identity, but perhaps that identity is not something to be found but something to be developed.

Teens are skeptical of adult authority, attempting to live co-equal with adults, while at the same time they don't have the facilities to do so. We think of the youth as a has-been-child or a becoming-adult. He is neither child nor adult. He is a young person.

Where Do We Go from Here?

Are we to fashion a ministry to youth based on existentialism, attempting to make life meaningful and relevant? Are we to design our programs on an experience-based curriculum, because youth culture has produced young people who guide their life through experience? Are we to accept humanism as the foundation for our philosophy of youth work, because this is "where they are"? Are we to construct a non-institutional religious program because there is an erosion of respect for the establishment? Is "personhood" our answer to their search for identity? Do we rule out traditional Christianity because young people are irreverent to established traditions and reject authority figures such as parents, teachers and law enforcement officials? [24]

The answer to the above questions, of course, is no!

Young people need an objective answer to their needs and the Word of God is the only source for an ultimate answer. Our ministry should be grounded on the Scripture because it is the Word of God that produces regeneration (I Peter 1:23), that causes teens to grow (I Peter 2:2), that keeps youth from sin (Psalm 119:9,11), that meets their need (Phil. 4:19). The Bible is an absolute that will satisfy the desires of youth who live in a variable world. This volume takes

---

[24] I do not ignore the issues of the youth culture, nor am I saying there is no truth found in their ideology. Existentialism is not completely false. Man must have meaning, but meaning is found in objective Christianity, not a subjective search for purpose. Also, I don't reject experience, because conversion is an experience affecting intellect, emotions and the will. However, I reject their experience-based lifestyle; experience must be based on the Word of God. I reject humanism as a philosophy and way of life, but I do feel the youth are correct in their sensitivity to persons, and their desire to help the culturally deprived. Man is the highest created being, made in the image of God, and every human has such great value that God gave His Son for him. Teens should become a person (see chapter 2 on Identity Crisis) but phenomenology does not have the answer to teens' search. I believe we should understand the teenager and his culture, but the basis of our ministry is the Word of God.

the position that both the *message* to communicate to teens and the *methods* used in the youth program should be based on the Scriptures.

Perhaps one of the reasons for the decline of Christian influence among the youth culture is the lack of allegiance Christians give to the church.[25] Christ founded the church: "I will build my church" (Matthew 16:18), and it is next to His heart. "Christ loved the church and gave himself for it" (Eph. 5:25*b*). The New Testament gives priority to the gathering of believers and the local assembly was the only basis for ministry in the pages of Scripture. The closer you come in the ministry to the model of the New Testament church, the more you will experience the blessings of God. An interdenominational agency can have a ministry on a personal level, but the farther it departs from the local church, the less likely it has the full blessing of God.

When interchurch agencies close down for the summer, the local church continues its weekly ministry to teens. A youth can disagree with his leader or get his feelings hurt at a Christian club and quit, but there is no scriptural basis for leaving a church, unless it dies.

There is a devilish attack on the three institutions founded by God: the home, government and the church. Those who believe in the inspiration of Scripture must place themselves under its absolute authority and recognize the place of the home, the government and the church. A Christian teenager should be under authority: (1) to his father and mother, because God placed him in that family, (2) to his local government, because God constituted municipal authority, and (3) to his local church, because a lost world needs disciplined witnesses (disciples) and the Christian teen needs a place to grow.

When a teen accepts Christ, the first thing he must do is to be baptized, then be instructed in "all things whatsoever I have commanded you" (Matthew 28:19-20). Then the young person should join in the church's program of evangelism, worship and fellowship. Strong New Testament churches produce strong Christians, not *vice versa*.

However, you cannot have a strong church without strong Christians. Contemporary teens need the church more than in any other generation, because they need to be obedient to the total commands of Scripture. The total ministry of the New Testament is not offered in nonchurch agencies, no matter how good their program.

Teens complain about dead churches. Their gripe is valid, for many churches have departed from the New Testament form. Other

---

[25] A church is a group of baptized believers, in whom Christ dwells, under the discipline of the Word of God, organized for evangelism, education, worship, fellowship and the administration of the ordinances.

youth are fed up with the bureaucracy of some churches or politics found in other ecclesiastical groups. True, many churches are bogged down with institutionalism, and are more concerned with the *form* of a church, than fulfilling the *function* of a church (evangelism, education, worship and fellowship). These pseudo-churches are not the groups that deserve the loyalty of dedicated teens. This author is disgusted with traditional dead American churches. We need to return to New Testament churches; teens need such a church.

Finally, this volume places emphasis on leadership. The current emphasis on small groups and dialogue, is an extension of the youth culture's humanism and irreverence for traditionalism. Youth feel they have equal stature with adults; so why give allegiance to traditional authority-persons. The youth is a person, granted, and should be accepted on an equal basis with adults. However, the Scriptures teach that certain men are "called" to be leaders (prophets, pastors, teachers) and these men are given abilities to carry out their God-given tasks. Therefore, a biblical youth ministry will be built on biblical leadership. (See chapter on adult leadership.)

This volume is not another how-to-do-it handbook for youth work, although principles of youth work along with practical points are included. This volume attempts to examine the root-causes for the teen culture, along with an examination of identity-crisis. It is felt that when you understand the causes of a movement, you can better work in its context.

A distinction is made between youth work in fundamental churches and evangelical churches. (See chapter 12, 13.) The closer you come to fundamentalism, the closer you are to a correct biblical ministry. However, some of the methodology employed in evangelical churches is found in this volume (see chapter 13). Some youth leaders will find themselves with a youth group in an evangelical church and the only course of action is an institutional ministry.

When Goals Become Problems

If you are going to work with young people, expect problems. There is no easy place to serve Christ, and this is especially true in youth work. But with every problem is a challenge. Don't view your young people's group as a headache but as a challenge. Place every gift and capacity in the work, and trust God for results.

There are certain ways in which we can meet the challenge of modern youth. These few basic principles will leave their imprint over and over again in this book:

1. *By taking a trip into the real but unseen world of adolescents.*

You must understand the Bible before you can teach it. Just so, you must understand an adolescent before you can teach him. Adolescence is one of the hardest areas of life to understand. Many people think that they understand the teenage period of life, just because they were teenagers once. This is not so. The person who went through adolescence five years ago is five years outdated. Times are changing, and if we are going to minister to young people, we must change, even though the gospel never changes.

You probably won't like what you learn about adolescents. However, your feelings are not important—the feelings of your youth are. You must understand why teenagers feel as they do, how they think, and who they are. Only by understanding adolescents can you help them.

The purpose of this book is to take you on a trip through the world of adolescents. Be prepared to study, think, observe and reflect.

2. *By giving you a road map of your destination.* Aims—goals—procedures—methods—philosophy; these are important to help you help teenagers. Many youth leaders want to work with youth but they have no basic direction. The youth leader who knows where he is going, goes some place. Your road map may be a philosophy for working with young people or basic opinions on how youth work should be carried out. First, you must have a road map. Second, your road map must be accurate.

This book will be like a road map, pointing you in the right direction and giving you principles of operation. This book will not be a handbook of programs. The handbook-of-programs approach is like the ready-mix cake. All you have to do is open the box and pour out the Sunday evening program. This book is intended to be like a recipe, which can be used many times. Every church, youth group, and neighborhood will have different ingredients, but the principles of working with young people are the same.

3. *By using up-to-date methods and materials.* Never before in the history of the church have there been so many materials and methods with which to work. You have helps, books, youth kits, and resources not available to the leaders of a generation ago. Today the larger churches have their youth workers on salaries. Volunteers are well trained. Most denominations furnish curriculum and resources for their youth workers. Christian education objectives and curriculums are on sale in any bookstore. At many Sunday School conventions you may find outlines of long-range strategy for reaching and keeping young people. Also you find at your disposal short-term plans and techniques for capturing the attention of youth. Teacher-training classes

and workshops are available. Avail yourself of all these advantages in youth work.

These up-to-date materials will not compensate for the working of the Holy Spirit in your young people. However, God does not delight in ignorance. The Spirit works most effectually through organized, well-prepared biblical content that is interesting and meets the needs of young people.

Some of the latest materials and methods will be presented in this book. Try many of them in your youth group. The latest up-to-date method may accomplish an old-fashioned result.

4. *By "nailing together" the Bible and life.* The Bible was written to meet the needs of young people. Remember, we work with people not programs, with lives not lines. When we become "people-centered" in our interest and application, we truly become basically "Bible-centered."

Some youth leaders become "completely Bible-centered." They become so "Bible-centered" that the young people are forgotten; the youth are manipulated and treated as objects rather than people. The young people's worker who does this is neither Bible-centered nor Christ-centered. The youth leader who is Bible-centered and Christ-centered will be youth-centered.

This text is unashamed in acceptance of the Word of God as the final authority for belief and practice. The thrust of this book will be to "Get teens into the Bible and the Bible into teens." Young people seek answers to life, and these are found only in God's inspired revelation, the Bible. The Word of God will be appealed to as the final authority and directive for working with teens.

2

TRENDS IN CHURCH YOUTH WORK [1]

The world of youth is changing and this is nowhere more apparent than in the youth meeting. Some youth groups still have kids sit in a circle and discuss the "youth quarterly." Other youth groups still have a speaker "preach" to the kids. Some youth groups produce educational programs, while still others have evolved to the "way out" fads: sensitivity groupings, psycho-drama, group dynamics, poetry, creative sessions or some other new experiment.

Why do some youth groups have "preaching," while others attempt to be relevant? The answer is not simple, but actions are usually based on principles. Youth groups are different because their principles are different, and these organizations change when their principles change. All change is not good; sometimes a fundamentalist church that is organized aggressively to evangelize its community slowly erodes into a liberal-dead church. Obviously, church buildings or organizations do not depart from the faith; people give up the faith. When people change, the church changes. Inasmuch as the youth group is an extension of the local church, any change in the church is reflected among the young people.

The largest churches in America are unashamedly fundamentalist

---

[1] The content of this chapter was given in Christian Education Lecture at Philadelphia (Pa.) College of the Bible, 1970, under the title "Changing Faces of Youth Work." Part of this chapter appears in *America's Fastest Growing Churches* (Impact Books: Nashville, 1972). The material is there applied to Sunday School, whereas here it is applied to youth work.

in doctrine. The fastest-growing religious movement, the Baptist Bible Fellowship of Springfield, Missouri, now has over 2,000 churches, whereas there were only 13 churches at its founding twenty-two years ago. Youth Groups in fundamentalist churches appear to be large and vibrant. When I originally wrote *Successful Youth Work,* I was deeply involved in the National Sunday School Association and reflected an evangelical approach in the methodology of youth work. During 1967-68 I was exposed to a number of youth groups in the Baptist Bible Fellowship. These young people deeply impressed me. They were aggressively reaching non-Christian teens and their active program attracted teens—all kinds. I was impressed with the clean Christian lives of the young people and many young people were going into full-time Christian service. I had never before seen 400 young people gather for a Sunday evening program nor had I ever heard of a group sending 200 high schoolers to Mexico for summer missionary training in evangelism. I saw a vitality in these groups that I had not seen in the evangelical youth groups in and around Chicago, considered the center of Evangelicalism. I began asking "Why are they different?" and "What makes them more successful than most evangelical works?"

In two of my previous books, *The Ten Largest Sunday Schools* and *America's Fastest Growing Churches,* I described twenty churches that have had rapid growth in the present and should continue to expand in the future because they have overcome barriers to expansion. Each one is now a flaming witness for God, they have large youth groups and many young people are going into full-time ministry. But sometime in the distant future these churches will deteriorate. However, their decline of attendance will probably not come with the present pastor or the next. Even these fundamental churches will erode into liberal edifices in the next 100 to 200 years. Members of these churches will vehemently deny that their church will grow liberal, yet death is as inevitable to a church as to every newborn babe. The purpose of this chapter is first to examine those factors that cause churches and youth groups to grow and, secondly, to determine what causes deterioration.

Youth groups grow because of an inner strength, not because of organizational techniques. Youth groups and churches reflect the growth dynamic that is found at the beginning stage of the religious movement known as the sociological cycle of church growth. The churches of which I have written show a dynamic growth that comes at the beginning of the cycle. America is witnessing general church decline and youth are leaving mainline denominational churches; yet fundamentalist churches are growing, and many of them register monthly growth. Teenagers organize to go out and witness to the lost; they bring their unsaved friends to hear the Word of God, many of them receiving Jesus Christ. The power of narcotics is broken in lives, and purposeless young people are given new direction in life. When these young people are saved, they remain in a church, causing attendance to grow. Then they join in the task of evangelizing other teenagers. As a result the church and youth group continue to grow. However, after a period of time the purpose of the youth group slowly changes, causing the church to progress around the cycle. Natural growth based on religious factors becomes more difficult.

The process of deterioration from a high peak of revival to the low valley of sin is noted in the Scripture.

And the people served the Lord all the days of Joshua, and all the days of the elders that outlived Joshua, who had seen all the great works of the Lord, that he did for Israel. And Joshua the son of Nun, the servant of the Lord, died being an hundred and ten years old . . . . And also that generation were gathered unto their fathers: and there arose another generation after them, which knew not the Lord, nor yet the works he had done for Israel. And the children of Israel did evil in the sight of the Lord, and served Baalim (Judges 2:8-11).

Dr. Lee Roberson, pastor, Highland Park Baptist Church, Chattanooga, Tennessee, has often said, "Everything rises and falls with leadership." This is nowhere more evident than in youth work. The youth program in a church drifts naturally until God raises up a man who can lead young people back to a point of spiritual devotion. Just as God worked through men in the Scriptures, so he works through men today. The more abilities a youth worker has, the more God is able to work through him into the lives of young people. (See chapter on the Position of Youth Director.)

Richard Niebuhr, the religious sociologist, set forth the rags-to-riches-to-rags cycle that takes place in religious families. Although he did not use the term *fundamentalist,* the cycle is obviously there.

Children born into families of first-generation sect members begin to change the sect into a church even before they reach adulthood. With their coming, the sect must become an educational and disciplinary institution in order to make the new generation conform to its ideas and customs. The second generation holds its convictions less fervently than pioneers of the sects, whose convictions were formed in the heat of conflict and sometimes at the threat of martyrdom. With each succeeding generation, isolation from the world becomes more difficult.[2]

The thesis of this chapter is that youth groups reflect the theological and sociological posture of the churchs' position on the sociological cycle. (1) Fundamentalist churches have the capacity for the fastest numerical growth and the largest youth groups, although not all fundamentalist churches have growing youth groups. (2) Evangelical churches have capacity for growth, although their size and growth is not as fast as fundamentalism. Also, many evangelical churches have shifted their emphasis to a quality ministry away from a quantity outreach, hence are not growing. (3) Liberalism or mainline denominationalism does not have the New Testament dynamic to naturally attract young people. When attendance at denominational-type youth groups climbs, it does so for extraneous reasons such as humanitarian, social or entertainment motives. Most denominational-type youth groups are not successful (see Factors of Successful Youth Programs) because they apply no external motivation for outreach or their spiritual life is void, hence they have no internal dynamic for growth.

After studying the ten largest Sunday Schools in America, I maintained that those churches which were the largest in America had sectarian-type characteristics or were closely identified with characteristics of fundamentalism. Ernst Troeltsch, the German philosopher-sociologist, wrote that churches evolve from a sect status to *ecclesia* or a denominational stage.[3] The following cycle is an elaboration of Troeltsch's position to show the church's sociological cycle. A church begins as a sect and moves to the second stage of the cycle, an institution. The third stage on the cycle is a fully organized denomination, and the final stage is deterioration. In this chapter the sect will be associated with the theological position called *fundamentalism*. The second stage of the cycle called the *institution* will be identified with evangelicalism.[4] *Denominationalism* will be associated with the mainline denominations and/or the positions of theological liberalism.[5]

---

[2] R. Richard Niebuhr, *The Social Sources of Denominationalism* (Hamden, Connecticut: Shoe String Press, 1954), pp. 19–21.

[3] Ernst Troeltsch, *The Social Teaching of the Christian Churches*, trans. by Olive Wyan (London: George Allen and Unwin, 1931), 2 Vols. An outstanding analysis of the factors that cause deterioration in churches.

[4] The term *evangelical* is generally synonymous with *neo-evangelical*.

[5] I have often been asked to evaluate and place the Southern Baptist Convention on the sociological cycle. I find Southern Baptist churches at each stage of sociological development. In reference to the sociological cycle, Southern Baptists do not usually classify themselves by the label *fundamentalist* or *evangelical*. Rather they tend to use the label *conservative* or *liberal*, leaving out the midpoint designation of evangelicalism or institutionalizationism.

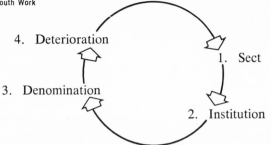

4. Deterioration

1. Sect

3. Denomination

2. Institution

David Moberg, the church sociologist from Marquette University, had designed the cycle as "a process by which cults originate, develop into sects, and then change into denominations, perhaps finally to emerge from the process as churches." [6] Harvey Cox in his controversial book, *The Secular City,* explains the development of churches in relationship to the socio-economic factors of society. He sees the cycle as: (1) the tribe, (2) the town, (3) metropolis, and (4) megalopolis.[7] His cycle has many parallel factors to Moberg's and Troeltsch's cycles.

The sociological cycle can also be described; (1) man, (2) movement, (3) machine, and (4) monument.

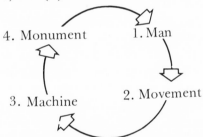

4. Monument   1. Man

3. Machine   2. Movement

A youth organization will begin with a *man,* called of God. He has a burden for teens and is willing to sacrifice time and enegry to win youth to Christ. This man may minister in a youth program of a local church or an inter-church agency. The second stage occurs when the efforts of the leader results in a *movement.* When his efforts become successful hundreds of teens are reached for Christ. Then others join him with like enthusiasm and like methods. After a period of time the original catalyst of the founding youth worker no longer permeates the movement, the founder is too old to relate to youth or the movement becomes so large he can't communicate to all his followers. When an organization is needed to accomplish the original aims, the movement becomes a *machine.* When the original purpose flounders the machine

[6] David O. Moberg, *The Church or a Social Institution,* (Englewood Cliffs, N. J.: Prentice-Hall, Inc., 1962), p. 100.
[7] Harvey Cox, *The Secular City* (New York: The Macmillan Co., 1965), pp. 1–13. When Cox sees the bankruptcy of American denominations he suggests we advance to a religionless society, where God is dead, as an answer. When I see the same bankruptcy, I maintain we must return to the origination, the sect-fundamentalist church.

turns into a *monument*. Some youth organizations live in the past but have no present-day ministry to youth.

An Examination of Sects/Fundamentalism

Webster defines the sect as "A class, order, or kind of men; a group having in common a leader or a distinctive doctrine; a following; a school, as of philosophy; a group holding similar views; a party. The term comes from the root word 'one's own.' In religion: (1) a party dissenting from an established or parent church; a body of sectaries, (b) one of the organized bodies of Christians." [8] The sects have theological beliefs that fall within the context of historic Christianity. A youth group in a sectarian/fundamentalist church is made up of those who believe and practice the same way.

The evangelical and/or fundamentalist movement, arising in this country since the turn of the century took its name from the magazine, *The Fundamentals,* which was a rallying point for theologically conservative individuals. However, the term *fundamentalist* that once reflected a conservative enlightened position, no longer has that connotation in the perspective of others. In the minds of many, the term *fundamentalist* today implies a negative connotation. But those who are fundamentalist are proud to wear this label.

Carl F. H. Henry, past editor of *Christianity Today,* is a severe critic of fundamentalism, indicating that it is more than a doctrinal position, that fundamentalism has a lifestyle or methodology all its own. "Historically fundamentalism was a theological position; only gradually did the movement come to signify a mood and disposition as well." [9] Later, Henry went on to describe fundamentalism both theologically and methodologically:

> Fundamentalism is considered a summary term for theological pugnaciousness, ecumenic disruptiveness, also unprogressiveness, scientific obliviousness, and/or anti-intellectual inexcusableness. By others, fundamentalism is equated with extreme dispensationalism, pulpit sensationalism, accepted emotionalism, social withdrawal, and bawdy church music.[10]

Fundamentalists and sects have similar characteristics and these will be developed in this chapter. Some fundamentalists may resent being called a sect. However, Christianity was a sect in its beginning (Acts

[8] Webster's *Third New International Dictionary* (Springfield, Mass., 1963).
[9] Carl F. H. Henry, "Dare We Renew The Controversy?", *Christianity Today,* June 24, 1957, pp. 23f.
[10] Carl F. H. Henry, "What Is Fundamentalism?", *United Evangelical Action,* July 16, 1966, p. 303. I find Henry's evaluation of fundamentalism an example of an uneducated name-calling bias, without documentation. He has the same weakness he criticizes in the fundamentalists.

4:5, 28:22), as were the Pharisees (Acts 5:17, 15:5, 26:5). Hence, the title *sect* in the Scriptures is a religious title.

Arnold Hearn, writing in the *Christian Century,* 1958, in an article entitled "Fundamentalist Renaissance," describes a "revival" (his term) going on among fundamentalists concerning scholarship and scientific investigation.[11] (We are not sure whether Hearn was referring to fundamentalists or evangelicals as a group; he probably was referring to all church groups to the theological right of the neo-orthodox position.)

William Hordern recognizes a division in the right wing of the theological world in a chapter entitled "The New Face of Conservatism," written for *New Directions in Theology Today,* claiming many in the church thought:

> Fundamentalism was pronounced dead, and it was assumed that it would soon disappear from its sanctuaries in the hinterlands. To those who were writing the obituaries of fundamentalism, there were disturbing signs.[12]

Hordern indicates the strength of fundamentalism is growth in church attendance, higher per capita giving them liberal congregations, and the fact that these fundamentalists were providing far more than their share of candidates for the ministry.[13] These facts are reflected in a survey of the 100 largest Sunday Schools in America.[14] Hordern was teaching at Garrett Theological Seminary, Evanston, Illinois, where he observed the conservative churches of Chicago changing in nature from the fundamentalist to the evangelical camp. He characterizes these churches:

> During the fifties, however, a group of young scholars arose from the fundamentalist circles to forge a new theology. These scholars rejected the term "fundamentalist" because they felt it had become a term of abuse and not a meaningful description of a theological position. Furthermore, they were conscious of the shortcomings of their theological fathers and wished to remold the tradition. They were as concerned as the liberals of an earlier day were to make Christianity relevant to the modern age, but they were determined not to repeat what they saw as the errors of liberalism. Although most of these young men came from fundamentalist seminaries and colleges, they began taking graduate degrees at nonfundamentalist institutions. They returned to their denominations and seminaries to revitalize the theology that had hardened during the fundamentalist-modernist controversy. There is no agreed name . . . They prefer the name "evangelical" or "new evangelical."[15]

---

11 Arnold Hearn, "Fundamentalist Renaissance," *Christian Century,* April 30, 1958, p. 528.
12 William Hordern, *New Directions in Theology Today,* Vol. I., *Introduction* (Philadelphia: The Westminster Press, 1966), p. 75.
13 *Ibid.*
14 "The 100 Largest Sunday Schools in America," an annual listing appearing in the Ocotber issue of *Christian Life* Magazine, showing that most of the large churches in America are fundamental in nature.
15 Hordern, *op. cit.,* p. 76.

The categories for a sect that was developed by Troeltsch are perhaps the best outline to use in this chapter to describe fundamentalism.[16]

1. *Sects/Fundamentalism is comparatively small.* Troeltsch lived in Germany where the Lutheran state church was large and sects were small. However, in Protestant America, sect-type churches are rapidly growing and are numbered among large denominations.

2. *Sects/Fundamentalism tend to avoid state and society.* Young people are told to be separate from secular influence that might contaminate their life. Some fundamentalist denominations such as The General Association of Regular Baptists and The Independent Fundamental Churches of America, place personal purity as the mandate for the Christian. Other fundamental denominations such as the Baptist Bible Fellowship place soul-winning as the Christian's main responsibility, and personal holiness as the means whereby they gain spiritual power for witnessing. No matter what the emphasis, most fundamentalists feel separation is a vital aspect of living the Christian life. This priority comes out of a literal interpretation of Scripture.

Elizabeth Nottingham describes *withdrawing sects* as those who are similar to the monastic orders of Catholicism. She describes other sects as militants who are aggressive in their outreach. She goes on to maintain that Methodists and Southern Baptists were at one time sects but now they have made peace with the world. These groups no longer practice personal separation based on biblical command.[17]

3. *Sects/Fundamentalism is connected with lower socioeconomic classes.* Many of the large fundamentalist churches have a blue-collar clientele. At one time the Methodist church was associated with the poor and with time its clientele became richer; associated with that is the rise in liberalism among the churches.

Some liberal church ministers might criticize low-class churches, equating them with naivete or ignorance. However, ignorance is not their strength; sectarian vitality is found in obedience and action. Jesus indicated the rich man had as much difficulty entering into heaven as the camel passing through the eye of the needle (Mark 10:25). Other Scriptures criticize the rich (Matt 13:22, James 5:1-4) and commend the poor (James 2:1-4). Perhaps the rich have let money become a panacea by which they are isolated from the realities of life. At the same time, the poor are more aware of the harshness of life: lack of food, adequate shelter, financial security and recreational pleasure. The

---

[16] Troeltsch, *op. cit.* The following discussion is based on a summary of Vol. I, pp. 331–381, Vol. II, pp. 993–1013. This summary was made by David Moberg, *The Church or a Social Institution,* pp. 74–75. I have modified the summary for this text. I have made a full discussion of these points as they apply to Sunday Schools in *America's Fastest Growing Churches* (Nashville: Impact Books, 1972).

[17] Elizabeth K. Nottingham, *Religion and Society* (Garden City, N.Y.: Doubleday and Co., 1954), pp. 62–67.

teenager from the slum turns to Jesus Christ because his lack of money has isolated him from the pleasures of life, whereas the rich teenager from suburbia turns to Jesus Christ because, after having no financial needs in life, he seeks something else to satisfy.

Money produces self-sufficiency, and a man who has little need seldom turns to God. Perhaps the poor have more threats to life, so feel a constant need for the presence of Jesus Christ in their life.

4. *Sects/Fundamentalists have voluntary membership based upon a new birth for entrance.* In most mainline denominational churches the young person is confirmed or becomes a member at approximately 12 years of age, following a membership class, at which time the teenager is taught the doctrine of the church. However, sectarian/fundamentalist churches emphasize the conversion experience, which is the new birth. Young people are not exhorted to "join the church" or transfer their membership. The youth group is organized for evangelistic visitation, when non-Christian young people are presented with the claims of the gospel and are asked to become Christians. The ten churches in *America's Fastest Growing Churches* are growing through conversions rather than by proselyting members from other churches. One sign that a church is starting to move around the sociological cycle is that most of the new members transfer in from other churches rather than being converted in the church.

5. *Sects/Fundamentalists emphasize enthusiasm as a sincere expression of their dedication.* One of the basic differences between a fundamentalist and an evangelical is the emphasis placed on the emotional nature of Christianity. The evangelical stresses a rational approach to conversion; a young person must know the facts of the gospel and understand the implications for his life, to be saved. However, the fundamentalist teaches that a young person must have an experience for salvation. First, he must know the facts of the gospel; second, he must be moved emotionally (for instance, he feels love to God and hatred towards sin), to which he makes a response by his will.

Preaching at fundamentalist churches is aimed at persuasion, which centers on man's emotions. In some of the churches, the sermon is interrupted with shouts of "Amen," and a young person's zeal is considered an indication of his spirituality. Preaching in evangelical churches centers on communication, aimed at man's intellect.

The fundamentalists still emphasize the rededication service, where teenagers are asked to stand or come to the altar as an outward profession of an inner act of dedicating oneself to God. The evangelicals do not stress the rededication service; many of them feel that when teenagers make an emotional commitment at a youth rally and are not able to follow through during the week, they become discouraged and are potential dropouts. A minister in the Evangelical Free Church recently stated, "If a man is dedicated to God, it's a fact; he doesn't have to keep reminding God." The fundamentalist answers this rebuttal by stating, "God wants a man to be totally dedicated: intellect, emotion and will. If a man is moved emotionally, he will make an intellectual commitment to God."

6. *Sects/Fundamentalists emphasize the conversion experience.* The fundamentalist believes that a teenager who is born again will "feel" the difference. This is because at the act of salvation, he has a life-changing experience. Whereas, the evangelical stresses an academic conversion: i.e., when a teenager knows and accepts the facts of historic Christianity he is saved. The fundamentalist believes that many teenagers know the content of the gospel and have even believed (the word "believed" does not mean saving faith but mental agreement to facts concerning Jesus Christ), but that belief does not save. "The devils also believe and tremble" (James 2:19). One of the main reasons why teenagers drop out of church is that they know the facts of doctrine, but never experienced Jesus Christ in their heart.

First of all, a conversion experience is based on knowledge of the Word of God; a young person must know he is a sinner and that "the wages of sin is death" (Romans 6:23). This knowledge includes the basic facts of the gospel that a man must know to become a Christian. However, a teenager with this knowledge is not qualified for heaven. Emotions is the second step involved in a conversion experience. A young person's total being is affected; as results, he may hate sin and love God—both are emotions. Jesus declared that a man must love God with his whole heart (Matt. 22:37-39). The third step in an experience is to involve the will of man. A teenager must desire to be saved and act upon the knowledge he has, he must receive Jesus Christ (John 1:12). An emotional conversion does not mean an upheaval of feelings but an experience that embraces the total man. One indication that a church is slipping into liberalism is that it no longer stresses an experience of salvation, but rather emphasizes rational understanding of Christianity.

7. *Sects/Fundamentalists emphasize lay leadership at the pastoral level.* I have often been asked why Baptists grow so rapidly while the Presbyterians have slow growth. Perhaps one of the reasons is that every minister in a Presbyterian church must first graduate from a four-year college and spend three years in theological seminary. However, most Baptist groups feel that any man called of God can be a pastor of a congregation. The layman who works forty hours a week on a secular

job, can qualify himself to become a pastor of a church by constant study of the Scriptures, self-education through life's experiences, and a practical training through service in his local church. Many pastors of America's largest churches have never been beyond high school, yet are effective shepherds over the flocks where God has placed them.

Reverend Roscoe Brewer, youth minister, Kansas City Baptist Temple, has been responsible for preparing over twenty laymen for positions as full-time youth ministers. These laymen have had no formal training but have worked with Brewer as interns in youth ministry, and when he felt they were qualified, he recommended them to a full-time position.

Laymen bring spontaneous zeal to youth work that oftentimes is lacking in those who have theological education. Since teenagers are impetuous, they respond to the spontaneous enthusiasm of lay youth workers.

8. *Sects/Fundamentalists emphasize a mystical religious relationship to God.* Troeltsch indicated a mystical relationship to God is characterized by communicating with God apart from the five senses: i.e., sight, taste, hearing, smell and touch.There is a sixth sense by which the fundamentalist believes he communicates to God, "The Spirit itself bears witness with our spirit that we are the children of God" (Romans 8:16). There is nothing wrong with mysticism—all true Christians have Jesus Christ in their heart; conversion is, "asking Jesus to come into your life." Paul witnesses, "I am crucified with Christ: nevertheless I live; yet not I, but Christ liveth in me: and the life which I now live in the flesh I live by the faith of the Son of God, who loved me and gave himself for me" (Gal. 2:20). "Mystical" does not mean unreal, but refers to an unseen relationship with Christ. The basis for a mystical relationship is the objective revelation—the Word of God. Do not attempt to prove Christianity to teenagers by one's mystical relationship to God; you only reflect your walk with Christ thereby.

Some teenagers from fundamentalist churches claim to find the will of God by mystical processes: "I know it is the will of God for me to go steady with Jan," a boy stated recently. His conclusion was not based on the Word of God nor circumstances, it was simply what he felt. This mystical basis of finding the will of God is wrong, apart from the Word of God and circumstances. However, there is an inner assurance that comes to the teenager when he properly finds God's will for his life.

9. *Sects/Fundamentalists emphasize law more than grace.* Fundamentalists tend to live by a narrow code (the Law) and many times are accused of being legalists. This designation does not refer to salvation by law; fundamentalists always emphasize salvation through grace by

faith. By this is meant the complete sufficiency of the atonement of Jesus Christ applied to those who repent and call upon God. After a man is saved, fundamentalists emphasize separation from worldly practices and are accused of having a Christianity of *don'ts*. The New Testament teaches that a Christian is to live a disciplined life. One of the fruits of the Spirit is self-control. This self-discipline is not an end in itself but a means to spiritual power for evangelistic outreach. When the Christian teens refuse to smoke tobacco, partake of alcoholic beverages, or indulge in sexual appetite, it appears they are emphasizing legalism. But they are not trying to gain merit before God; they are simply obeying the teachings of Scripture in their Christian life.

10. *Sects/Fundamentalists believe in the personal bodily return of Jesus Christ, retribution for wickedness, and the establishment of the Millennial Kingdom.* The fundamentalists give strict allegiance to a literal interpretation of Scripture. Troeltsch noted that such interpretations forced him into a view that, "God will allow His elect to pass through tribulation and misery, but finally He will complete the work of redemption upon His return to earth and the establishment of the kingdom of God." Since judgment is coming, the fundamentalist believes that he must live a pure life and use every available means to reach every man before the unsaved go into judgment. Some might criticize the fundamentalist for having a "future-ethic" whereby the past is sacrificed on the altar of the future. Even though existentialism and teenagers' finding significance in the *now* has a place in ministry to youth, the impact of the future also has a bearing on the present. As a result, our youth programs should prepare young people for the future.

11. *Sects/Fundamentalists believe the work of redemption was completed in the atoning death of Jesus Christ.* Sociologists believe that the sectarian church placed much emphasis on the past and the accomplishments of the act of redemption. This, known as the "past-ethic," reduces hindsight in the young people's mentality: i.e., they must look to the past as a basis for present lifestyles. As a result, pragmatism and pervasive humanism are ruled out of a youth program.

12. *Sects/Fundamentalism believe in literal obedience to primitive church ideas.* The field of Christian education is the dividing line between evangelicals and fundamentalists. The evangelicals apply the methods of psychology, sociology and philosophy of education to youth work in the church. Principles of evangelical Christian education are formulated out of statistical studies among teenagers. Attempts are made to form the "normal" or "typical" youth work, then hold this as the norm or standard for all churches. The evangelical believes that methods change from generation to generation, although the message

is changeless. As a result, relevancy becomes a foundation stone for youth ministry. The evangelical adapts Christianity to the twentieth century; but in contrast, fundamentalists believe the *message and method* are implied in Scripture. Young people should obey the scriptural methods, such as house-to-house visitation, personal soul-winning, personal proclamation, private Bible study, public and private prayer, and separation from worldly amusements. These New Testament methods are found in the book of Acts.

Fundamentalists do not believe the church should become relevant to the sinner, but the sinner must become relevant (through repentance) to God's plan of salvation. Therefore, they do not embrace coffee houses, dialogue groups, Koinonia fellowships, the Jesus People, rock operas. The fundamentalists believe evangelicals who turn to relevant ministry are, in fact, turning away from Scripture.

13. *Sects/Fundamentalists teach constant renewal and revival.* Young people are urged to "dedicate" or "yield" themselves to God. The altar call is given at youth retreats, camp and youth rallies for young people to "get right with God." Their theological basis for constant renewal or revival is found in the doctrine of sin. When a young person receives Jesus Christ, the old man is not eradicated but a new man (the power of the Holy Spirit in the presence of Jesus Christ) is added to the teen's nature. The old and the new nature constantly strive for supremacy. Hence, the young person needs to be constantly reminded to place Jesus Christ on the throne of his life. When the Christian youth allows his sinful nature to control his life, he slips into sin. Therefore, he must repent or rededicate himself to God and return to the first principles of Christianity. The evangelical feels that rededication services are basically emotional in nature and temporary in results, hence they are looked down upon. Fundamentalists believe the evangelical has softened his attitude toward sin and separation from worldly amusements, therefore they no longer emphasize rededication.

14. *Sects/Fundamentalists expect to transform the world solely by the moral principles of the gospel.* The question of the social gospel is dividing the Christian world. Evangelicals are bringing social gospel into their ministry. However, they still emphasize personal regeneration as the core of their message. However, many evangelicals are in danger of losing their emphasis on personal evangelism because of social action, such as the war on poverty, feeding the poor, voter registration, and the drive for racial equality. This takes the form of evangelicals tutoring in poverty neighborhoods, helping in nursing homes, working in the Peace Corps, or directing athletic programs for the culturally deprived. The fundamentalist youth program is not antisocial action, but feels that the

greatest impact on the society is the changed individual. If Christian teens from a fundamentalist church work in an orphanage or old folks' home, they always associate (care) along with a direct ministry of preaching the Word or giving a testimony. The fundamentalist youth feels that a silent testimony is not enough.

15. *Sects/Fundamentalists differentiate between themselves and hypocrites or heretics.* Evangelicals have a greater tolerance toward those who deviate from their position than do the fundamentalists. Fundamentalists note a "hypocrite" as one who claims to live by the standard of Scripture but fails to achieve that standard either by his ignorance or deceived practices. A "heretic" is one who aspires to the beliefs of fundamentalism, yet has doctrinally deviated. Fundamentalist young people are taught that they must be pure in life and doctrine. Therefore, they must separate themselves from hypocrites and heretics.

At times fundamentalists are accused of being "fighting fundamentalists," but their motives are misunderstood. Some attack the late Bishop James Pike for his doctrinal deviation. For example, in one of his books he permitted premarital sex. Since the fundamentalists watch to protect Christian young people from being contaminated, they feel obligated to point out the heresy of Bishop Pike. Other fundamentalists carry crusades to fight Billy Graham or liberals as a personal vindication for their ministry or other subliminal motives. These fundamentalists might be motivated out of pseudo-charismatic qualities (messiah complex). The ministry must always be balanced, and young people should be separated from sin and its influence; yet one doubts if God calls a man to spend his main energies and time in attacking religious deviates. God calls us to win souls and build churches.

Evangelical—Institutional

The term *evangelical* is sometimes broadly applied to all Bible-believing Christians, including fundamentalists, evangelicals, neo-evangelicals, or conservatives. However, this is a wrong usage of the term; most fundamentalists do not want to be called evangelicals. The broad use of the term *evangelical* is usually used by mainline denominational spokesmen.

Evangelicals prefer to think of themselves as conservative in doctrine, yet *relevant* in methodology. One thing an evangelical knows for sure, he is not a fundamentalist. There are other names which might apply to evangelicals. The term *orthodox* or *conservative,* when applied, usually designates "that branch of Christendom which limits the ground of religious authority to the Bible." [18] As a result, the terms *orthodox* and *conservative* can be applied to Christians who are either evangelical or fundamentalist.

Christian Life defined eight trends of the evangelical that distinguish him from a fundamentalist:

> These include: a friendly attitude toward science; a willingness to re-examine beliefs concerning the work of the Holy Ghost; a more tolerant attitude toward varying attitudes on eschatology; a shift away from so-called dispensationalism: an increased emphasis on scholarship; a more definite recognition of social responsibility; a reopening of the subject of Biblical inspiration; and a growing willingness on the part of the evangelical to converse with the liberal and dialetical theologians. [19]

The sect/fundamentalist is characterized by a compelling concern to reach people by any and every means, persuading them to repent and turn to Jesus Christ. Crowds hungry for spiritual answers come to fundamentalist churches to hear the Word of God. Ministers give attention to the function of Christianity rather than to its form. Little thought is given to choir robes, printed programs, liturgy, or education of the minister (one indication that *Christian Life* shifted from serving a fundamentalist audience to an evangelical clientele is that they substituted the term *pastor* for the more sophisticated term *minister*). To the fundamentalists, evangelistic and educational function is more important than outward form. This truth might be illustrated by special music; it is more important for a soloist or choir to "speak to the heart" than to enunciate correctly or use a higher class of music (anthem). The following points reflect the institutional/evangelical interpretation of Christianity.

1. *The evangelical/institutional is committed to relevant Christianity.* The basic distinction between a fundamentalist and evangelical is his commitment to priorities. The fundamentalist believes that both message and method are found in the Word of God and that successful Christian action is an outgrowth of the application of biblical principles. The evangelical has a deep commitment to relevancy: i.e., that the gospel must relate to the needs of contemporary Christians as they live in a social setting of today. As a result, the evangelical is concerned about social action, that the gospel preached has an impact on the community. He cooperates with community projects such as drug abuse,

---

[18] Edward John Carnell, *The Case for Orthodox Theology* (Philadelphia: The Westminster Press, 1959), p. 13.
[19] "Is Evangelical Theology Changing?" *Christian Life*, March, 1966, pp. 16ff. There is little theological difference between the fundamentalist and the evangelical; they differ in methodology. The eight issues pointed out by *Christian Life* reflect a different approach to Christianity. Therefore, the field of Christian Education, a discipline of methodology, reveals where fundamentalists and evangelicals basically disagree.

temperance, and campaigns for civic decency. The evangelical points to the Old Testament prophets, indicating that preaching was socially-oriented, aimed at changing society. Therefore, this becomes his biblical mandate for political and social action.

Fundamental young people are told to be modest in their apparel and separate in their action. At the same time the evangelical leaders tell young people not to be "out of touch" with the times, that their testimony may be accepted by unsaved. Leaders among the evangelical churches feel that if their young people dress differently from contemporary society they can't make an impact upon the world, hence not be a testimony for Christ. As a result little is said about long hair, miniskirts or dancing among evangelicals, while these become points of contention among fundamentalists.

Relevancy has many other implications, such as the use of modern translations of Scripture, the use of contemporary music in youth rallies, the use of mod posters to advertise youth meetings, and emphasizing a number of community-related projects, so that the gospel is respected by the people of the community.

2. *The evangelical/institutional Christian appeals to efficiency and coordination as a basic premise for the ministry.* Organizational efficiency is a major foundation stone in the ministry of evangelicals. They point to the pattern of organization as being in Scripture and are concerned about wasted motion, wasted time, wasted energy. When they see a growing number of agencies in their churches, they organize a Board of Christian Education to coordinate their energy, rather than allow an omission or overemphasis in the church's outreach. The Youth Council is used to provide a single thrust for youth ministry. Whereas a church may have a contest among the Sunday School and youth program announced from the pulpit, the evangelicals feel they should be a unification of activity; therefore a board is organized on the biblical basis "In the multitude of counselors there is wisdom" (Prov. 11:14). Whereas the fundamentalist tends to place authority and leadership in the man, the evangelical tends to fear a man-controlled church or man-controlled youth group, and places authority in a committee.

3. *The evangelical/institutional Christian is motivated by rational appeals to the intellect.* One of the basic questions all Christians must answer is how to motivate the unsaved to salvation. The evangelical appeals to rational arguments to get a man converted: "Come now and let us reason together, saith the Lord," whereas the fundamentalist appeals to the emotions or the "felt needs." "How shall we escape if we neglect so great salvation?" These two positions are polarized to help clarify the position. Many young people are saved from raw heathenism

(he is not a member of a church family and has no religious background) and has learned that drinking, sex and "messing around" cannot satisfy the inner needs of his heart. When he comes to Jesus Christ, it is because his felt-needs have driven him to seek peace in Jesus Christ. This teenager's emotional experience becomes the basis of his salvation and the basis of his faith. "I know God exists because he saved me." He does not need a rational argument to prove the existence of God. The young person saved from sin has little difficulty with the theory of evolution or other attacks upon the inspiration of the Scriptures. He might say, "I know God created the world because He saved my soul from sin." This is another way by which the teenager indicates his experience proves the existence of God. He believes that God lives because his life has been changed. As a result the fundamentalists base their Christianity upon their experience (emotions). One of the weaknesses of fundamental Christianity is that when teenagers' feelings change, their basis of salvation can crumble. However, many remain in the church and are motivated to live for Jesus Christ throughout life. Many second-generation Christians (their children) become evangelical in their theological persuasion. These children are not raised in sin but are in Christian homes. They are not permitted to indulge themselves in the pleasures of this world. Therefore, many evangelical teens do not have a "felt need" for salvation. Since they do not repent from outward sins, there is little need to appeal to their emotions. Sunday School and youth programs become an educational experience, and their greatest need is to *know* Christianity. Many evangelical teens are "turned off" by the emotional appeals of Christianity, and when these young people become leaders in the church, they criticize the fundamentalists who continue their appeals to emotional Christianity. Therefore, the evangelical must have a faith that is reasonable, based upon an intellectual understanding of Christianity. The evangelical teen needs a clear articulation of his convictions. He speaks to his father: "If smoking is wrong, why can't you prove it to me?" Across the generation gap, another father is perplexed: "Why can't my daughter see that dancing is wrong?" The father feels deeply (emotions) that dancing is wrong, but the daughter wants reasons. The father feels that since Christ has saved him from sin, his daughter should not want to sin. However, the father never realizes that the daughter does not have his experience. Yet, the daughter, who reflects an evangelical point of view, loves Christ as much as the father.

However, a youth program cannot be built on either extreme; all teens need to have more than knowledge about Christianity on one extreme, and no program is complete that is based solely upon emotions.

4. *The evangelical/institutional youth program emphasizes positive*

44 SUCCESSFUL BIBLICAL YOUTH WORK

Christianity. Many fundamentalists are accused of being legalists, only emphasizing the *don'ts* of Christianity rather than emphasizing the positives. They accuse fundamentalists of motivating teens out of guilt feelings, which is the wrong basis for teaching separation from worldly amusements. The evangelical teaches that a young person should be separated from sin by first turning to God and, second, turning from sin (I Thess. 1:9). They teach that the positive turning to God automatically leads to the negative repenting from sin, whereas the fundamentalist emphasizes the opposite approach.

Many fundamentalists preach to teenagers to repent and stop dancing, attending movies, drinking alcoholic beverages. These sins are made an issue of salvation and a young person must repent from sin to be born again. The evangelical emphasizes a positive salvation: Christianity is accepting Jesus Christ. They teach that once a man is born again and has a new nature, the old sins will drop off as the new sap pushes the dead leaves off the tree each spring.

Both the fundamentalist and the evangelical claim to emphasize both positive and negative aspects of repentance; however, their emphasis becomes a point of contention. When the fundamentalist visits the evangelical church and notices short skirts, he feels the youth group has compromised and is hurting the Christian growth of the young people. A fundamentalist recently stated that a certain Christian camp that allowed a "Smokers' Point" where unsaved kids could go and smoke on camp grounds, but did not permit smoking around the buildings, was a camp that was growing liberal. At the same time the evangelical feels a positive ministry of teaching the Bible, witnessing to the lost, and involving young people in prayer will eventually produce a Christlike character in each teenager.

5. *The evangelical/institutional youth group ministers through proper organization.* Sociologists recognize that many religious movements in their primitive state grow because of dedication by their adherents. The movement is dynamic because of the powerful personality (charismatic leadership) behind the institution. As the youth group becomes involved in the total church, it must become institutionalized. Leadership changes with time, and authority passes from the dynamic leader to the controlling organization, i.e., the Board of Christian Education or the Youth Council. Since there are several members of the Council, each must be aware of the operation procedures; therefore, organizational charts and job descriptions must be clearly articulated and understood by all. Sometimes jobs performed by dynamic leaders go lax because no one will take their place. When a volunteer is found, he needs a careful job description to give him direc-

tion in his work. Since the job description was written by someone else, he lacks the zeal and enthusiasm to carry out his work, simply because he is working for someone else rather than himself. Sometimes the shift of leadership produces a shift in orientation; the worker no longer performs his job for the end results, he performs his job according to the organizational guides. As a result the organizational *form* becomes more important than the young people's *function*. After several changes of leadership, a youth group falls into disrepair and "institutional blight" affects the youth program. Usually the youth program is revived when a dynamic youth leader comes and gives definite direction to the youth outreach.

The sectarian/fundamentalist youth worker places high emphasis upon zeal and dedication, which is reflected in emotionalism. Many times he deemphasizes educational qualifications. (Some of the most successful youth directors in America have never been to college but are laymen who have risen through the ranks and become proficient at leading youth programs.)

6. *The evangelical/institutional youth work places more emphasis on the individual rather than the group.* The evangelical has a higher respect for man than does his fundamentalist counterpart. He feels man is the crowning achievement of creation and is the purpose of redemption. As a result, the evangelical builds his ministry on sensitivity for people and respect for individuals. Every teenager is created in the image of God and he has unique abilities. His "personhood" is slowly growing and each individual is more important than the total youth program. Therefore, the evangelical youth minister spends more time in counseling individuals, whereas the fundamentalist youth minister spends more time planning programs. The evangelical is seldom interested in a number-count of teenagers and is not interested in having the largest youth group in the community. He is more interested in the spiritual growth of his teenagers. At the same time the fundamentalist is most concerned about numbers, having a large youth group. Therefore, by that very nature, fundamentalists have more successful youth groups because they are more concerned about large attendance, which is one criterion for a successful youth group.

The fundamentalist youth minister places high emphasis on the youth group. He believes that a youth group with well-articulated standards and close Christian fellowship will build strong Christian teenagers. Hence, the group is more important, perhaps more strategic, than the parts. The fundamentalist youth director believes that if his group is growing in attendance and quality ministry, the Christian young person will also be growing. An army illustration best reflects the fundamentalist attitude towards his youth group. Just as the soldier loses his individuality in the army, so the Christian teenager loses his freedom when he becomes a member of God's army. One fundamentalist youth pastor recently asked, "Who ever heard of an army sergeant being interested in the needs of his privates? He trains them to be fighting men." As a result, the fundamentalist youth minister places heavy emphasis on the disciplined Christian life. When this militant attitude is lost, church growth and attendance begin to decline.

7. *The evangelical/institutional youth group has a broad basis for cooperation and fellowship.* Because the evangelical is committed to relevancy, he will cooperate with anyone who is getting results. The evangelical church is happy to cross theological lines to cooperate with liberals in a Billy Graham Evangelistic Crusade, because people are being won to Jesus Christ. At the same time, the evangelical desires to cooperate with the fundamentalist church because they have the same theological persuasion. The evangelical youth minister might phone the fundamentalist church to arrange a singspiration for teenagers, only to be refused politely. Evangelicals emphasize love, which is a reflection of tolerance for those not holding the same opinion. Fundamentalists reflect their love to the Lord through dogged allegiance to the tenets they feel are biblical.

8. The evangelical/institutional youth group is committed to meeting the needs of teenagers. The ministry in most evangelical churches is measured by its ability to meet the needs of young people. If the youth program is not well attended, the assumption is that their needs are not being met.

Dr. Lois LeBar, professor of Christian Education, Wheaton College, in her latest book, *Focus on People in Christian Education,*[20] builds an evangelical philosophy of ministry on the basis that needs are the starting point. The following cycle has become well known throughout the National Sunday School Association and other Christian Education conventions among evangelicals as a basis of ministry.

Dr. Howard Hendricks, professor of Christian Education, Dallas Theological Seminary, divides needs into four sections: individual, community, church, and world. Hendricks suggested a youth program should be built on meeting needs because when needs are being met, ministry is relevant and blessed of God. On the other hand, when men's needs are neglected, they stop attending church or youth group, whatever their primary organization.

The basic weakness of a need-centered ministry is found in a

[20] Lois LeBar, *Focus on People in Christian Education* (Westwood, N.J.: Fleming H. Revell Co., 1968).

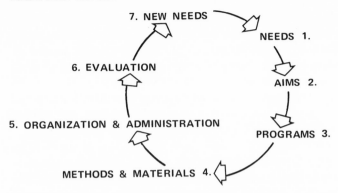

7. NEW NEEDS

NEEDS 1.

6. EVALUATION

AIMS 2.

5. ORGANIZATION & ADMINISTRATION

PROGRAMS 3.

METHODS & MATERIALS 4.

definition of the term *needs*. If ministry to teenagers is "meeting needs," all effort could be channeled into supplying food for the runaways or providing shelter for the dope addict. This ministry is then aimed at the "felt-need" level. These are the needs that become apparent to the consciousness of the teenager. When needs are interpreted as "felt-needs," then a youth ministry only alleviates the temporary problems of young people. These problems are usually physical and material, because these consume most of life's activities. Many churches that have given all of their energies in ministering to the felt-needs of young people stray from the biblical imperatives of the Word of God. At present, the YMCA (an organization that calls itself "Christian," that ministers to young people) now serves on the supposition that its task is to meet the needs of young people (felt needs). However, this organization was known at one time for its soul-winning ministry, but now has degenerated into primarily a humanitarian organization and has departed from the biblical imperatives of personal regeneration.

Ministry should begin with ultimate needs, which is the biblical imperative for youth work. The teenager's greatest need is spiritual—to be saved from sin, because he is a sinner. However, this *ultimate need* is only seen through the Word of God. The weakness in LeBar's chart is that she begins with *man's needs* rather than the Word of God. If a youth program begins with the Word of God (see chapter 9), then the ultimate need of salvation becomes predominant and guides all of the rest of the youth program.

The fundamentalists believe there are biblical truths that teens should learn; these lessons are not primarily practical (relevant), nor do they meet the felt needs of teenagers. However, these lessons must be learned because they come from the Word of God. Some biblical doctrine does not have immediate practical applications, but teenagers should give attention to learning biblical doctrine. As a result, fundamentalists give more attention to indoctrination than do evangelicals who give more attention to meeting needs. These are facts about God that should be taught simply because God is the source of Christianity. The major application of this issue is in the curriculum. The evangelical accepts relevancy as the foundation for building a curriculum for young people, while the fundamentalist feels a deep commitment to study of the Word of God and obedience to its principles are the basis for curriculum. He feels that the Word of God when properly learned will change the life of the teenager, making him relevant to God (which is repentance).

The basic foundation of denominational ministry is reflected in the religious life of the community. The youth work among denominations is tolerant of the outside world, no longer at war with society. One of the major aims is to make the teenager a better person in the society in which he lives. Of course the teenage society is saturated with perverse humanism and materialism. The young person is taught how to become a respectable teenager, rather than to be different according to God's standards. Inasmuch as rebellion is a part of the teenage community, much of the literature in denominational youth programs encourages youth rebellion against empty authoritarianism, American institutionalism, and economic capitalism, which they feel degrade the personhood of the individual.

The youth minister in a denominational church has a commitment to existential philosophical assumption. Therefore, he must help teenagers find self-identity; even his youth group must seek an identity in a changing world.

The seeds of relevancy found in an evangelical church blossom to full bloom in the denominational church. Young people at a United Methodist Camp are no different than the young people of the average American high school.

The fundamentalist places a high emphasis on the corporate community—the church. He believes that a strong church will produce strong Christians. Hence the whole is important, perhaps more strategic than the parts. The fundamentalist feels that if the church is growing in attendance and quality ministry, the individual Christian will also grow. He feels the illustration of an army best reflects the church. Just as the soldier is part of the whole and loses his individuality in the army, so the Christian is a member of God's army. Irenius said in the first century, "Christians, like soldiers and slaves, ask no questions." Therefore, the fundamentalist emphasizes yieldedness to God and active service through the church. When this militancy is lost, church attendance begins to decline. Hence, evangelicals have difficulty attracting a large crowd, while fundamentalists will have both a growing and a large attendance.

Denominational

The third category in the evolution of church growth is the "denominational" stage. Webster has defined it as "a religious organization uniting in a single legal and administrative body, a number of local congregations." However, the term "denomination" used in the sociological cycle carries a broader meaning than an organization of many small churches. A denomination represents a group of churches which allow central control to gradually centralize and decision-making power to slip from the members who founded the churches out of deep theological conviction, to clergymen who view their task through the eyes of professional competence. The term *denominational* can be applied to (1) a group of churches, (2) administered under a central organization, (3) that has been in existence long enough for the primary commitment of charter members at individual churches to slowly evolve to professional clergymen and (4) a state of institutional blight which settles throughout the social lifestyle of a movement. Institutional blight is the process of social decay where individuals, committees, and churches lose sight of the original goals of the founding fathers and succeeding generations unable to identify with the principles that formed the original catalyst, search for a new reason for existence. When the organization is unable to find a new *reason for existence,* the whole superstructure tends to drift with little aim. Voices within the denomination cry for a return to the original precepts, yet these prophets appear to have a hollow cry, because no one will heed them. One observer has characterized such denominations as having an *identity crisis.*

Even though the term *denomination* is used, the social process can refer to an individual church or a religious organization. The church first begins as a sect, then changes its nature and basic tenets. The church, desiring more efficiency, slowly builds an organization. The denominational stage of the cycle is the natural outgrowth of organizational efficiency of local churches. The denomination is an extension of local church institutional system at a "super-church" level. According to David Moberg, the denominational level of the cycle takes on added sociological characteristics. He defines these as:

> Formulism saps the group's vitality. Its leadership is dominated by established bureaucracy more concerned with perpetuating its own interests than with maintaining the distinctives that helped bring the group into existence. Ad-

ministration centers on boards and committees that tend to become self-perpetuating. Dominated by the small group, the organization may become like boss-ridden parties . . . the very small ones who, because of the position they hold, should be most ready and anxious to make the Christian ministry a real brotherhood, talk one thing and practice another.[21]

Deterioration

The final stage of deterioration in the cycle results from over-institutionalization of local churches, with the resultant disintegration of the denomination. Churches decline because the original purpose of the church changes. People lose interest because their spiritual needs are not satisfied; then attendance drops and income declines. Membership begins to fall off. Since there is no urgency in reaching the community, new candidates for the ministry are difficult to find. Churches go without pastors. Moberg describes the process of deterioration: "Diseases which show symptoms of this stage are: formalism, indifference, obsolescence, absolutism, red tape, patronage, and corruption." [22] The original spiritual vision of the founding group is gone. The impersonalization of people sets in. Schaller calls this "institutional blight." [23] The member feels detached from the church; the denominational headquarters are not responsive to their needs. The leaders at headquarters, removed from local church economy and individual responsibility, may feel they can and should lead the church into new programs of action, whether or not the individual members respond. In the past few years several denominational officials have attempted to lead a group of churches into programs of social action, because the denominational hierarchy feels the members at the grass-roots level are biased and/or ignorant. The officials of the United Presbyterian Church of America persisted in donating money to defend Angela Davis, charged with conspiracy in the death of a courtroom judge. According to an opinion poll, the church members voted against supporting Miss Davis, but the officials ignored their obligation to the clientele of the denomination. When denominational leaders no longer represent the membership, deterioration sets in when those paying the bills refuse to give and attend. Schaller observes:

> The inevitable decline of congregational economy and the accompanying socialization of the decision-making process within the hierarchy of the denomination is not necesssarily a deplorable trend. While it is true that

---

[21] Moberg, op. cit., p. 120.
[22] Ibid., p. 122.
[23] Lyle Schaller, Planning for Protestantism in Urban America (New York: Abingdon Press, 1965). Schaller gives an excellent summary of causes of church and denominational deterioration, especially analyzing the bankruptcy of many inner city churches.

power has a corruptive influence, it is also true that independence has encouraged irresponsibility.[24]

The long evolution toward centralization of church authority usually causes a church to operate more efficiently, resulting in a stronger denomination. The sect and institutional church become stronger through organized outreach. When churches shift to a centralized authority, they reach more people. But usually in the process, the members become less responsible for church direction, hence over a period of time the movement becomes weaker. The problem is time. Those wanting a larger, stronger church are willing to delegate leadership to the paid staff. When the professional gets results, the membership is generally satisfied. However, with the passing of time both the membership and leadership change, then the next generation of leaders alter the direction of the church, and the membership is either powerless to stop them or does not care. Schaller predicts, "It now appears that the future is almost certain to witness a further deteriorzation of congregational autonomy." [25]

CONCLUSION

The sociological cycle seems to indicate the fundamentalist sect begins with warm fervor to God and ends up a cold liberal denomination on the brink of deterioration. The naive observer will draw compartmentalized lines to categorize every youth group by use of the chart in chapter 3. The following guidelines will help the observer apply the principles to a youth group.

1. *The youth group may move through the cycle sociologically but not theologically.* A youth group may remain true to its original fundamental doctrinal statement, but can become cold, organized, and purposeless. Because a youth group is orthodox in doctrine, can we assume it is Christian in nature? What has happened? The group has moved through the cycle sociologically but not theologically.

2. *Groups reflect more than one phase of the cycle at a time.* Some denominational churches may embrace a modernistic theology but sociologically the youth group has the characteristics of a sect, then with the passing of time moves through the cycle. But, there are some large groups with denominational characteristics that have small sectarian traits. Moberg indicates, "The five stages (sociological cycle) in the church's lifecycle overlap." [26]

3. *The youth group may remain at one level over a long period*

24 *Ibid.*, p. 209.
25 *Ibid.*
26 Moberg, p. 122.

of time or reverse the sociological cycle. When the youth pastor becomes aware of the dynamics that make up this sociological cycle, he can control the future of the organization and slow up or reverse the tradition. Moberg indicates, "The process (sociological cycle) may be completed in the group within a generation or it may take hundreds of years, to enter the denominational stage. The process may be reversed; it is not inevitable." [27]

4. *Emphasis would be placed on young people rather than institutions*. When we observe the sociological cycle, we should not become pessimistic but realistic. The youth group is in trouble when we overemphasize youth chapels, gymnasiums, improving organization, or establishing efficient hierarchy. These improvements are not wrong, but when they become an *end* rather than the *means* to an end, deterioration sets in. We must carry out the aims of the New Testament.

5. *Work in churches that reflect your personal stage of sociological growth*. Youth leaders, like churches, travel through the sociological cycle. If in your religious experience, you are at the sect stage, you should attach yourself to a church that has sect characteristics. In like manner, you may lose your passion for "separation from alleged worldly practices" and become interested in the penetration of the gospel into the local high school through an institutional approach. Then, you should not work with a fundamentalist-type church but with an organization that has made its peace with the world. Later in life you may find your attitude towards church and society changing. You should then transfer your youth ministry to a church that reflects your sociological position rather than remain and fight.

However, the issue of theological truth is as basic to all decisions as to youth work. When a youth worker is advised to join a church that reflects his personal stage of sociological growth, this is not "soft-pedaling" conservative truth.

6. *Churches minister through their sociological limitations*. A fundamentalist church may have an excellent ministry spiritually nurturing its members, improving their character and giving them purpose in life. The young people may make an impact on the local high school through soul-winning. This young people's group may have little effect on the total high school as an institution in society. At the same time, an evangelical church may cooperate with high school "vocational day" and make an impact on the high school as an institution. Is Scripture sufficiently clear to say that the fundamentalist church is correct, and the evangelical church is incorrect?

---

[27] *Ibid.*, p. 123.

7. *Realize God can use youth groups in all levels of the sociological cycle.* Some may criticize the sect for its limitations, while others may criticize the evangelical for a broad influence. Who is to say God uses one type of youth group over another? There are advantages and disadvantages at each level of the cycle. God may use one type of youth group to reach one neighborhood, while another will be effective across town.

Conclusion

So we see that the church follows a cycle in relating to society. The sect/fundamentalism is born in revival fires and, as time passes, the group moves into a respected institution in the community, yet holding to its conservative convictions. Finally, the group becomes a highly organized denomination, where ultimately deterioration sets in.

3

AN ANALYSIS OF DIFFERENT TYPES OF YOUTH WORK

The youth groups usually reflect the beliefs and practices of the local church. This does not mean that all youth groups in fundamental churches are vibrant; in fact the opposite is true—some are dead. At the same time, some youth groups in liberal churches have all the characteristics of fundamentalism. Therefore, the question remains, "What are some of the distinguishing characteristics of youth groups that will identify them with the sociological cycle?" The chart "Analysis of Youth Work" will reflect the principles of the preceding chapter and integrate the sociological cycle of churches for the youth worker.

1. *The youth worker.* The fundamentalist position is rather clear. Paul Fosmark, youth minister of Fourth Baptist Church, Minneapolis, Minnesota, states, "The youth minister is the extension of the pastor's pulpit into the life of teenagers.'" [1]

He suggests that the work of the youth minister is to preach to young people, just as the main influence of the senior minister is to preach to adults. The way the senior minister ministers to his flock is the role the youth minister follows with his "youth flock." Donald Nelson indicates, "Liberal methodology has replaced the Biblical symbol of a man as the leader with a non-definitive category of a D.C.E.

---

[1] Paul Fosmark, *American Youth a Great Mission Field in Today's World,* "The Scriptural Office of the Minister of Youth," printed by Kansas City Baptist Temple, Kansas City, Missouri, 1969.

ANALYSIS OF YOUTH WORK

SECTS FUNDAMENTALIST	NEW ACCEPTED DENOMINATIONS EVANGELICALS	MAINLINE DENOM. LIBERALISM
1. Youth Worker The youth worker is the extension of pastor into the life of the youth.	Coach	Chaperone
2. Purpose Evangelism Soul-winning	Education Training Hour Approach	Worship Devotions (Celebration) Social Actions
3. Organization Centers around youth worker	Delegated responsibility Planning groups	Suggested by denomination
4. Ecclesiology Spiritual life is centered in the church as an institution. a. "In" group through new birth b. Separation from world c. Continual renewal	Church life prepares for life in the community. a. New Birth b. Relevancy c. Meaningful & articulated convictions	The church is the youth in the world. a. Dialogue to understand others b. Anti-legalism c. God gave all things to enjoy
5. Youth Expectation Disciplined life a. Asceticism and Pietism b. Doesn't mind being out of step with world	Integrated life a. Anti-compartmentalized life b. Christianity must be integrated with daily life.	Meaningful life
6. Approach to Youth Doctrine-centered	Need-Centered	Experience-Centered

and expects youth to follow a curriculum as an example. This is a departure from the Bible." [2]

Roy Zuck, former editor of Training Hour material of Scripture Press, Wheaton, Illinois, best typifies the position of the youth worker in the evangelical camp. He rejects the idea of the youth worker being "preacher," calling this approach an "Indian chief." Zuck suggests that the "coach" is biblical. He states:

> The ideal youth sponsor is the coach . . . the coach sponsor is one who helps or assists the young people in doing their own programming. Like the athletic coach on the football field, he helps the young people carry the ball themselves. As the coach seeks to inspire and motivate his team to do their best, so the sponsor seeks to encourage and motivate his young people to do their best in the program they plan. As the coach is on the sidelines more than he is on the field, so the sponsor is behind the scenes more than he is before the group. As the coach, the sponsor seeks to help his young folks build confidence in themselves. He coordinates their activities. He counsels them individually and in a group and seeks to help them improve. He is interested in each person individually. He receives no honor to himself; all the honor goes to the young people who are learning and growing as he helps them to do so.[3]

The denomination approach for the youth worker is more difficult to define. Perhaps Tani best reflects this position; we have characterized the young leader as a *chaperone*. That word has meaning, indicating the chaperone will associate with young people as an example for young people and he will give guidance as youth seek God's image.[4]

2. *The purpose of youth work.*—Paul Fosmark indicated, "We should preach the gospel to teens everytime we get them together." In a recent youth workers' convention Fosmark gave the following four points for successful youth activities:

(1) Much good singing
(2) Provide song books or song sheets for visitors
(3) Have a time for testimonies
(4) Have someone preach—win souls.[5]

Donald Nelson feels rather strongly that soul-winning evangelism is the key to successful youth work and writes:

> The training union concept is essentially liberal methodology in action in our

---

[2] Donald Nelson, *A Youth Program That Works* (Minneapolis, Minn.: The Fourth Baptist Church, 1961), p. 2.
[3] Roy B. Zuck and Fern Robertson, *How to be a Youth Sponsor* (Wheaton: Scripture Press Publications, Inc., 1960), pp. 13–14.
[4] Henry Tani, *Ventures in Youth Work* (Philadelphia: The Christian Education Press, 1957), p. 197.
[5] Fosmark, p. 52.

Baptist churches. We are attempting to utilize a methodology called for by the needs of liberal theology to arrive at goals and conclusions resident in Biblical theology. If one wants to know the reason as to the failure of the average Baptist church in our youth program that lies in a simple fact, i. e., we are using a methodology which is alien to our Biblical theology. These two are contrary the one to the other and incompatible. The liberal theologian's emphasis is upon education. The Biblical theologian's emphasis is upon evangelism.[6]

The main purpose of youth work in the evangelical movement seems to be education. A survey of Scripture Press Training Hour material reveals a wide variety of practical topics, each with a strong biblical basis. None of the topics will be uniquely soul-winning. However, curriculum writers emphasize that Christ is presented in every program and if young people are exposed to biblical truth through an educational experience, they will come to know Jesus Christ.

At a recent Sunday School convention in which 62 youth workers were present, I asked, "How many have as your primary purpose in the youth meeting, presenting the gospel to the unsaved?" Only cne person raised his hand. The reply from the group was, "We don't have unsaved at our meetings." The express purpose of a youth meeting is to provide a training experience and fellowship.

The main purpose of youth meetings in liberal youth meetings is worship. Most textbooks for mainline denominations suggested the main purpose of a youth program has been worship. The book that has been most used in past liberal settings to teach youth work would be *Ventures in Youth Work* by Henry N. Tani. He puts a devotional or worship emphasis in youth programs. Presently the courses in youth work are experience-centered and do not use a text. The contemporary term used for worship is *celebration*. Youth leaders from mainline denominations teach the teen to celebrate his faith, which is to worship.

3. *Organization for the youth program.*—The fundamentalism or sects approach to youth work depends upon a minimum of organization. Nelson describes this concept, "the youth pastor chooses his own leaders, trains them and develops a leadership team." [7] Rev. Mel Sabaka, youth minister of Canton (Ohio) Baptist Temple, does not have elections for youth offices—he appoints them, based upon the spiritual qualifications of young people. He feels a democratic election is only a popularity contest and will hurt the outgoing ministry of the church. For three years, the author took an informal poll of youth directors at the youth clinic at Kansas City Baptist Temple, trying to

---

[6] Nelson, p. 1.
[7] *Ibid.,* p. 4.

determine how many elected youth officers. Each year over two-thirds did not elect youth officers; many did not have youth officers.

The evangelical approach centers around delegated responsibility. Zuck has suggested that the entire youth group be divided into four planning teams; 25 percent of the young people are then responsible for one youth program a month. Fern Robertson, present Training Hour editor, Scripture Press Publications, states:

> One adult should be appointed as head sponsor or overseer of the entire group. He calls sponsor's meetings, delegates responsibility, attends quarterly planning meetings for setting up forthcoming programs, works with the youth-group officers in planning ahead for the year's activities, meets with the officers in regular business meetings, helps in the training of officers, and reports to the Board of Christian Education or the Christian Education director.[8]

The major denominations have had time to develop a superstructure of organization for the youth department. Each youth group receives the magazine, follows the organizational suggestions and implements the administration at the local church level. Denomination-wide "youth rallies" encourage youth to implement the total church program.

4. *Doctrine of ecclesiology.*—In fundamentalist groups, the spiritual life of the youth is centered in the church as an institution. These churches have a maximum number of youth meetings during the week. Young people are exhorted to be present for visitation. (During a recent week Canton Baptist Temple had 100 teenagers for Tuesday evening visitation). Many of these churches will require attendance at the weekly prayer meeting, a weekly activity night (Friday or Saturday), in addition to graded choir practice, and/or other activities. The fundamentalist youth might be at church three out of five nights per week—the motivation, "God's work comes first."

The fundamentalist youth groups have their "in" students, those who are born again, and the "out" students, those who do not live separated lives. Also, acceptance into youth group is based upon spirituality, enthusiasm, and constant renewal. Those who preach to young people emphasize "surrender, dedication, obedience and a continual walk with the Lord."

The evangelical finds himself with a different concept of the local church. The spiritual life of the teen is not centered in the local organi-

---

Roy G. Irving and Roy Zuck, ed., *Youth and the Church* (Chicago: Moody Press, 1968), p. 212. Fern Robertson gives a clear presentation of youth organization for Evangelical Church from the Scripture Press Training Hour perspective in this article.

zation. Church life emphasizes preparing a young person for life in the community.

Evangelicals emphasize the new birth as a prime requisite for salvation. However, the unsaved are not brought to their meetings to be converted, but rather accepted as individuals with the hope that they will be converted. The youth church meeting is not so much a place to bring the unsaved, but a place to come in and "prepare" them to go out and meet the world. Here youth examine their own Christian faith and test it against the teaching of today's society as well as against the beliefs of emerging cults. Youth will grow as they see the church structure and stewardship, dating, college preparation, and standards of right and wrong, witnessing, personality development and vocational choices.

It is difficult to categorize the denominational position of youth work. The statement that comes through is, "The church is the youth in the world." There is little emphasis on the organized church. The youth in the locker room or on the dance floor is the church witnessing to the world. Dialogue is important so that you may understand what others are saying. Reuel Howe's concept of "the meeting of meaning" of two lives reflects interpersonal relationships. Anti-legalism is another strong emphasis. The youth must find out "who he is" and resolve his identity-crisis. The concept of separation from worldly influence is gone. The youth in a denomination is taught, "God has given all things in life to enjoy." Since all things come from God—music, art, social relationships and education—everything is to be enjoyed. The modern youth enjoys his body and those of the opposite sex. He does not seem to have the guilt feelings of past generations.

5. *The expectations of youth.*—Nelson set forth a program that typifies most fundamentalists when he said, "The youth program of the Fourth Baptist Church works because it is a local church program . . . by an emphasis upon the Biblical teaching of separation, discipline and soul winning." [9] Young people are expected to live separated lives in accord with the group standards. The Church does not mind being out of step with society. It will support its young people and demand them to "come out from among them and be ye separate."

The evangelical church expects youth to live a well-integrated life. Roy Zuck has suggested some worthwhile objectives for youth work: [10]

    a. To lead youth to:
        (1). accept Christ as Saviour
        (2). commit their lives to Christ as Lord and Master

---

[9] Nelson, p. 6.
[10] Mimeographed notes, Scripture Press Publications, Inc.

    (3). be sensitive to the guidance and power of the Holy Spirit
    (4). become church members and loyal Christian disciples
    (5). participate in Christian ministries, world missions
    (6). witness for Christ, directing others to Him
    (7). be faithful stewards of their time, talents and money
    (8). use their leisure time constructively
  b. To help youth to:
    (1). genuinely worship the Lord
    (2). call in their knowledge and understanding of Bible truths
    (3). apply Christian principles to every area and relationship of life
    (4). develop habits of personal Bible study and devotion
    (5). recognize and respond to the will of God in all decisions

The denominational expectations of youth are more difficult to define. They emphasize a pluralistic culture and the need of the youth finding himself within a changing world. The church expects the youth to live a meaningful life in which he successfully answers the question, "Who am I?"

6. *Approach to youth.*—The fundamentalists give literal obedience to an inspired Scripture authority and to those ideals held by a primitive church. The fundamentalist not only believes doctrine is taught in Scripture, but methodology is also taught. The youth work must not only obey Bible doctrine, but obey scriptural methods such as soul winning, visitation, preaching, singing, and fellowship. As such, they believe in educational *indoctrination.* Many educators reject indoctrination in today's culture. Fundamentalists emphasize the input of educational "Bible facts," emphasizing Bible memorization and retention. But indoctrination must be accompanied by sensitivity to personal needs and an attempt to show how doctrine is practical for life.

The evangelicals place much emphasis on a need-centered approach to education. At the same time, the evangelical holds to the doctrine of inspiration of the Scripture. Doctrine does not change, but methodology must be adjusted for modern psychology, education and sociology. The liberal approach is centered in experience. Of course, lip service is given to the Word of God as the authority, however, the Word of God is interpreted through the experience and culture of today's society. The social-action gospel is prevalent in the mainline denomination (for youth work): i.e., they want young people of their church membership to become involved in their city projects, social work, and human relations.

Conclusion

Church youth work takes many forms in the United States. It is difficult to observe an average Sunday evening youth program and determine the theological persuasion of the participants. Some liberal churches have born-again Christians as youth sponsors, hence the youth meeting has fundamental characteristics. But eventually, liberal theology will influence the total program, even the youth meetings. This chapter gives the features that will characterize a fundamental-evangelical at liberal youth programs. Those youth workers who are familiar with this chapter will have an overview to all youth work and can better work in their immediate context.

Thought Questions

Section One

(Covers Chapter 1, "The Contemporary Youth Culture"; Chapter 2, "Trends in Church Youth Work"; Chapter 3, "An Analysis of Different Types of Youth Work.")

1. What are some of the causes for the unique characteristics of the contemporary American youth culture?

2. What is the first question of procedure the youth worker must ask?

3. Why is the youth culture experience-oriented?

4. How is pervasive humanism reflected in the adolescent society? Give illustrations and principles.

5. Are teens opposed to the traditional Protestant value system? How? When?

6. Describe contemporary teens' attitude toward religion. What is biblical about their religious desires? Where are they unscriptural?

7. What is the sociological cause for the drug traffic among teens?

8. Describe the evolving sex-ethic of contemporary teens.

9. What are the basic foundations for ministry with youth as suggested in Chapter 1?

10. What are the characteristics of a dying fundamentalist church? What can reverse the drift?

11. Summarize the fundamentalist church into one paragraph. What are the dominant traits of fundamentalism?

12. What is the basic difference between fundamentalism and evangelicalism? Where is this difference usually seen?

13. In what ways are fundamentalism and evangelicalism similar? Would an evangelical most likely seek fellowship with liberals or fundamentalists? Why?

14. What biblical principles do the evangelicals use to support their position?

15. What is the basic difference between evangelicals and liberals? Should they be placed in the same camp for fellowship?

16. Why are youth workers in fundamental churches more forceful and exert a greater leadership than at the other churches on the cycle?

17. The evangelicals are better organized than the fundamentalists. What accounts for this?

18. Why do fundamental churches have larger youth groups than those churches on other positions on the cycle?

19. What is the difference in problems experienced by the youth gorup with first-generation Christians, from the one with second-generation Christians?

20. Not every church will exactly fit the sociological cycle. What are some exceptions that can be expected in working with church youth groups?

SECTION TWO

KNOWING THE TEENAGER

Is there an average teenager?

Can young people be judged by statistics?

Have teenagers changed since we were kids?

What makes them tick?

What is the difference between adult and youth thinking?

Why do young people hang around in gangs?

What about teenage dating?

What do teenagers think about sex?

Are all teenagers the same?

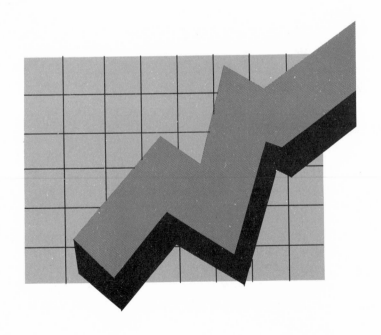

4

ADOLESCENCE—A DESCRIPTION

Adolescence has been called a variety of things from a disease to a miracle. People look back on the years from 12 to 18 as some of the happiest of their life—and also the most distressing. Adolescence is the age of revelation, awakening emotions and newly discovered capabilities. It is the age of revolution against adult control and adult direction. But adolescence is the age of anxiety and moodiness. Altogether it is the joy and pain of growing up.

Quick changes of mood color the whole adolescence period. Changing attitudes and behavior begin to show as the youngster approaches puberty. He suddenly becomes oversensitive about many things and hypercritical about his family, home and church. These are the years that are important to the junior and senior high school student. You can probably recall with ease what your last year of high school was like, but maybe you are rather hazy in the memories of your junior high school experience. A great many changes take place within the boy or girl between the junior high school and graduation from high school.

Who Is the Teenager?

Actually the teenager is three persons wrapped in one. You must unwrap the coverings to get at the core of the real person.

1. *The teenager's self-concept.* The teenager is the person he

65

thinks he is. The teenager's self-estimation determines the approach and attitude of the youth worker. What the teenager is may or may not correspond to real life. Even though what the teenager thinks himself to be may not be the real person, his attitude will have to be understood. This will help the youth worker to determine an approach in meeting his needs.

2. *Others' concept of the teenager.* The teenager as others see him becomes very important to the teenager. The opinions of his friends, teachers, parents and youth worker are very important in determining his personality and outlook on life. Their opinions may not be accurate but they will help the youth worker determine what the teenager really is. The teenager necessarily reacts to their evaluation of him as a person. What others thinks of us determines to a large extent the way we live.

3. *The real teenager.* The real teenager often is hidden and never brought to the surface. The real teenager is the person the youth worker is trying to reach. The true man on the inside may not be what the teenager thinks of as himself, and he may not correspond to what others think him to be. The many veneers of life must be peeled off to help the teenager understand himself as he really is. Socrates said, "Know thyself." A true self-appraisal is the first step to adjustment. Adjustment leads to happiness, confidence, and purpose in life. A false concept of one's self may lead to maladjustment and problems in life.

The youth worker must remind himself that God knows the individual as he really exists. Thus the worker depends on the leadership of the Holy Spirit and the principles of God's Word to know the teenager better.

Four Types of Teenagers [1]

One of the great extremes of human nature is the tendency to categorize human nature. Most new studies in physiology attempt to do this; but environment, social demands and personality are so complex that human nature resists any attempt at "pigeonholing" its makeup. The world has prejudged the teenager and comes up with broad categories. These categories may influence business or church leaders but should not influence the Christian youth leader. There are four broad categories of teenagers:

1. *The historical teenager.* This teenager has his existence in the minds of many adults. "The way it was when I was a boy" is often heard from adults today. Adults remember the past when they were

---

[1] Warren Wiersbe, "Teenagers Are Persons, Too." "*Christianity Today,* May 10, 1963, pp. 776, 777.

teenagers and try to understand teenagers today in light of their own actions. Even though adults think their image of the past is accurate, they are subject to error. With time one tends to glorify the past and remember only the good things that were done.

Teenagers do not change in their basic nature or development. The growth patterns, desires, drives and psychological makeup remain the same. But the expression of drives and growth changes. Many adults confuse outer expression with inner makeup.

The historical teenager is a "springboard" used by adults to attempt to understand modern youth. The historical teenager cannot help the adult understand youth because outer expression and inner makeup have been confused. The historical teenager is not a real teenager and exists only in the minds of adults recalling the past.

2. *The statistical teenager.* The statistical teenager is one that affects much of life today; however, this teenager does not exist. Many business firms receive substantial income for interviewing teenagers, conducting polls, and arriving at opinions on how the average teenager lives, thinks, and reacts. One firm may indicate "95 percent of today's teenagers drink hot tea with lemon." This statistic is then used to sell products and instigate fads, movements and commercial enterprises. The statistical teenager does not exist—he has his existence only on paper.

3. *The commercial teenager.* The modern media of communication present a vivid picture of teenagers. Motion pictures, television and radio present the teenager today on one hand as nearing perfection and also on the other extreme as a juvenile delinquent. The commercial teenage boy is very typical in his appearance. He looks like the latest TV commercial or an ad for a sports magazine. The commercial teenager does not have a real existence. He exists in the minds of the modern-media-oriented audience.

4. *The ideal teenager.* Much is written, portrayed and discussed concerning the ideal teenager. The ideal is supposed to be median between the extremes of terrible and wonderful. He is better than "average," he is ideal or desired. Much is said concerning the "ideal" teenager today. Scholars and psychologists try to understand him. Teenagers try to imitate him. However, the ideal teenager does not exist.

Who are teenagers? Are teenagers real? Yes. Teenagers are the youth who come to your church—the boy who leads singing in young people's meeting and the girl who joined the church last month. Teenagers are your children and your neighbor's children. They are the boy who cuts your grass and the girl who babysits with your children. Teenagers wear size nine shoes and cut-offs. They drink malts, eat pizza and go to football games. They worry over acne, cry over death, and doubt the existence of God. Boys stutter when they give a testimony and girls giggle in church. They date and neck or stay home and watch TV. Teenagers are the young people who come to your church.

The Average Teenager

Today's teenagers need to be understood and they need to be helped. You must have a clear picture of them before you can help in their developmental process. You must understand adolescent needs, characteristics, desires and interests.

Most people feel that teenagers are unstable. Instability may or may not be true of teenagers. However, how can we expect them to be stable in today's shaken world? The effects of two world wars, the daily talk of world destruction, and the unprecedented number of broken homes have all taken their toll on the lives of teenagers.

When we talk about instability of our teenagers, we need also to take a look at ourselves. Are we stable? We tend to think that we were more stable as teens than we actually were. Perhaps we are bewildered by the behavior of our teenagers because we have forgotten our own youthful behavior and/or misbehavior.

Teenagers must be accepted for what they are, rather than for what we expect them to be. Our expectations are usually called "normal" or "average." If we are not careful this "normal" or "average" becomes the standard set for all teenagers.

The average teenager will fall short of the normal or average standard at some point. Usually the church is very negative and condemnatory, and the teenager who falls short is frustrated (which includes all teenagers in at least one point). Church leaders sometimes cause more frustrations for teenagers than they imagine.

Also, when we set normal and average standards for teenagers, we judge half our teen audience as second-rate citizens. Fred does not sing well or does poorly in school and we feel he is not as good as Betty Jean who sings well and is an "A" student. If the church could only accept teenagers as people!

How Old Is Seventeen Years?

Take a look at Frank. He is 17 years old, only because he was born 17 years ago. Physically, he is big and strong—he will be offered a college scholarship for his ability as a football player. He has the body of a 19-year-old college sophomore. Mentally, Frank is not ready for college. He has the intellectual ability of a high school sophomore, a 15-year-old. Socially, Frank fits into the gang. He runs in the gang with the boys who are a year older in school. Socially, he is 18 years of age. Spiritually, Frank is 12 years old (meaning he has attained a spiritual level common to 12-year-old boys). How old is Frank? Where would you put Frank in Sunday School? With the 12-year-old boys, 15-year-old boys, 17-year-old boys, 18-year-old boys, or 19-year-old boys?

There is a danger in trying to classify every teenager. We cannot treat Frank as a 12-year-old or a 19-year-old boy. We must treat Frank as Frank. We must recognize individual differences. Every young person is at different levels of maturity in different areas of life—such as mental, physical, social and spiritual development. Therefore, teenagers cannot be classified and dropped into pigeonholes.

A few examples will serve to illustrate the point. Let us look at these youngsters and observe the way in which their physical, spiritual, social and personal development are interrelated.

1. *Debbie is a high school freshman.* Debbie has many friends and attends most high school activities. She is slightly smaller than the average girl and is regarded as "cute" by the boys. She is above average when it comes to sports, is well coordinated, and is physically strong for her age.

She has many boy friends and will not get serious with any, even though three or four would like to go steady. Debbie gets the best grades in her class with little effort. She enjoys school.

Debbie never misses church and, having musical ability, she sings solos, plays the piano for the evening service and participates in the youth choir. She is a born leader, and when she becomes a member of a group she usually "dominates" it. Every once in a while one of the teenagers will "block" Debbie's position of leadership. She becomes sensitive and will drop out of leadership for two or three weeks, but she will bound back as she receives social acceptance. Debbie will probably get a scholarship to college on graduation from high school.

2. *Earl is a junior in high school.* Earl recently came into the church. His best friend invited him to evangelistic meetings last fall. It was there he accepted Christ.

Earl lives with his father and younger brother and sister. His mother and father were divorced when he was in the seventh grade. He has been the "mother" in the house ever since. He can perform all the household responsibilities such as cooking meals, washing dishes, cleaning house and looking after little sister. He is primarily responsible for keeping clean clothes in the closet and washing the dishes three times a day. Even though Earl feels bad about not having a mother, he believes the home experience has made him more mature.

When Earl became a Christian he gave Christ his all. He never misses his time of devotions in the evening and is a regular in the Sunday evening youth activities. He is acquiring a good knowledge of the Bible. People note his dedication to spiritual things when he prays. When he graduates from high school he plans to enter a Bible college and go into the ministry.

Earl doesn't like to do homework and is only a "C" student. He is continually warned to do better if he wants to go to college. However, Earl believes he will have no difficulty in getting through college. He feels, "I can do anything I want to do—which includes getting a college education."

3. *Barbara is a senior in high school.* Barbara is considered very beautiful, though not sexy. She comes from a home where her father is in Christian work, though she is not known for her spiritual dedication.

Barbara has been only an average student throughout school, even though her teachers say she can do better. On her papers there are remarks such as "spots of brilliance" and "could be outstanding with some improvement." Barbara's parents would like for her to go to a Christian college, but she probably won't because she doesn't have the desire. She would like to get married and be a mother.

Barbara never misses church activities because it is expected of her that she attend. It's not that she is against church, she just doesn't show great desire and ambition in spiritual things. She has her Sunday School lesson done every Sunday and will take part in the youth activities program—if pushed. Barbara's father has said, "She could be an outstanding Christian worker—if she wanted to." Although she does not participate in worldly amusements, she sees nothing wrong in them for the unsaved.

Each of these teenagers is different with different needs. You will have to understand adolescents before you can work with adolescents. The next chapter will give some insight into understanding the nature and needs of the teen years.

Case Study [2]

Jerry is sixteen, but he isn't as well developed physically as most boys his age. He likes to work and is willing to work when asked— sometimes he even offers to do a particular job if he has done it before

---

[2] The case studies in this book are designed for group discussion. Use with the class if this book is used as a text, or reproduce and distribute to your youth group. Give the class time to read the characteristics of Jerry. Divide them into discussion groups and assign each group a question. Have each group report and discuss the answers in the large group.

and enjoyed it. He is always moving and active. He likes sports but doesn't play seriously.

Mentally, he has a ready wit. He used to be an above-average student. Now, he seems to be average or below. He knows he can do better and that everyone expects him to do much better—even his friends. He knows this but chooses to fool around and entertain people. If he were a girl, he might be called scatterbrained.

Socially, he fits in quite well because he is so outgoing and witty. He always has something to say. Often it is hard for him to settle down long enough even to listen to the speaker at young people's. He loves to tease and everyone knows he will, although many wish he would stop.

He is quite interested in his appearance. His clothes must be the latest style, although he doesn't take care of them. He is fussy about his hair—though the style is not extreme.

Jerry is a show-off with girls, but he doesn't date very often. The girls see him more as a pal or pest than as a fellow to date. He always has a good time with fellows and they all like him—perhaps because they don't feel any competition from him and they like his wit.

His best friend is a Christian but is very rebellious. When together, they talk and think cars, girls and pool.

His father is not a Christian and never attends church. The rest of the family have devotions together every morning. He does have personal devotions, but he isn't consistent in his own devotional life.

He has attended Sunday School regularly all his life. He became a Christian one night when he was 13, when he went forward during an evangelistic meeting. An adult led him to Christ. He can be quite a problem in Sunday School if the teacher isn't firm with him. He usually stays for the morning church service but rarely attends in the evening. He is always on time or early, especially for young people's, which he attends regularly. He does not take an active part unless asked, then he usually "goofs it up."

Our problem is how to help Jerry:

1. List Jerry's basic needs. How can these needs be met?

2. Can Jerry become a full-time vocational servant of Christ? What does he need to become a missionary? What would college do for Jerry?

3. Why is Jerry a show-off? Does Jerry need a "steady" girl? Why? Why doesn't Jerry do better in school? Why is Jerry a "wit"?

4. Do you think that Jerry's inner concept of himself is different

from his friends' concept of him? Perhaps neither Jerry nor his friends have the correct concept of this boy. Write out your idea of Jerry's concept of himself, others' concept of Jerry, and the real concept of Jerry.

5

AGE CHARACTERISTICS OF TEENAGERS

Teenagers are developing in several areas at one time. They are growing in their physical, mental, emotional, social and spiritual development at the same time. The intent of this chapter is to divide the teen life into four areas and examine each area separately. The four areas in order are: physical, mental, emotional and social. Spiritual development is related to all four and integrated into the total growth pattern.

Physical Development

Teenagers think of themselves primarily as physical, even though other factors enter into their life. For them, the body is the main factor they bring into adolescence. The body develops and changes, but still it is the same body. To this body are added the factors of mental, emotional and social development. All of these go to make up the personality of the teenager. The personality may be radically transformed during the teenage years. The development of the inner life is most important. However, the teenagers consider their bodies the most important factor in development—whether they are or not.

The physical changes which revolutionize the body during adolescence have a very significant effect on the other phases of life. In general, there are three stages of physical growth through which teens pass: early, middle and late.

During the early period, covering ages 12 through 14, young people experience the effects of puberty. Puberty is a time when the adolescent matures sexually—the earliest age at which a person is capable of procreating offspring. Young people experience a rapid and uneven rate of growth during puberty. A boy will find himself buying a size larger shoe every time he visits a shoe store and a girl will find herself three inches taller within seven months. As a result of these staggering rates of growth, this early teenage group experiences lack of coordination. The early group is characterized by the term *self-consciousness*.

The teenager is supersensitive about his appearance and his ways of life. He seldom realizes how he actually looks to others. It is how he thinks he looks and how he feels about this that counts. His awareness of himself comes suddenly. He has always had freckles but until now they have not bothered him. Realize that the teenager is beginning to see himself as he really is. A girl's feet have been long and narrow but only now do they become a problem. "Am I normal?" the teenager wonders. "What's happening to me?" Before adolescence the youngster takes all of these changes in stride but not so in the adolescence period. His acute sensitivity has made any changes in his body a small crisis.

Have real patience in working with teenagers who are growing into adolescence. Physiological changes sometimes trigger psychological problems. The early teenager's concern for his own physical appearance is so complete that it overshadows all else. He must learn to accept himself as he is. He must learn to accept his body as given by God.

Since fluctuations of mood and energy are characteristic of the teenage period of life, it does little good to lecture teenagers. The youth counselor who plays down the lethargy of the teenager and capitalizes on his bursts of energy will accomplish the most. The teen is extremely serious about himself and wants to be taken seriously. Fear of ridicule concerning his appearance can shut the teenager off to any and all outside help. The teenager desires his leader to have a sense of humor, but this sense of humor must never be turned upon the physique of the teen.

Teenagers must be prepared to travel this path to adulthood. Build a solid foundation for their growth. During the early stage of physical development, teens are experiencing the breakdown of many old habits; they are left wide open to acquiring new habits—we hope they are better habits. Make sure that teens are well prepared to meet this change in life. Furnish them with good literature and personal counsel so they may meet this rapid growth intelligently. Physical adjustment and maturity constitute the first and important step toward spiritual adjustment and maturity.

During the middle period, ages 15 through 18, the growth rate levels off and decreases. The body has almost assumed its adult proportion. The girl reaches her optimum size physically at age 17, while the boy reaches his physical peak at age 22. As a result the teen feels more confident and life is tackled with a greater degree of daring and independence.

As the teen proceeds through the early and middle stages, he is wide open to the pressures and expectations of his social group. The girl will want to dress like the other girls in her gang, rather than follow the suggestions of Mom. The character of teens is adversely affected when we ask them to stay ten years behind times in customs and dress. Let the teenager be up to date—if it's not immoral.

In the late stage, covering ages 19 through 24, the fellows catch up with the girls, never to lag behind again except in individual cases. This age group is characterized by physical maturity, the assumption of adult responsibilities, and the realization of adult proportions. The personality is becoming fully developed and the young person is off on new and exciting paths leading to adulthood.

During the late stage of growth, habits are fairly well formed; physical patterns are established and lives are evidencing the foundations and impressions gained through previous years.

Guiding Principles for Physical Development

1. *Create acceptance of physical makeup.* The body is given to the teenager from God. To a certain extent he is small, tall, fat, or an invalid because God has given him his body. The youth leader must lead the teenager not only to accept his body, but realize God gave it to him for a reason. The beautiful girl must not glory in her beauty nor must the fat teen with acne and unattractive features be bitter or disappointed. You, as the youth director, must never make fun of a boy who is awkward nor must you praise too highly the attractive girl. Adjustment and maturity come in acceptance of one's self.

2. *Develop scriptural attitudes toward the body.* The teenager must be taught that the "body is the temple of the Holy Ghost" (1 Cor. 6:19). His body is not to be abused, nor is it to be used in violation of scriptural principles. The Bible teaches that the body is not to be used as a vehicle for sinful purposes. Avoid any action that degenerates character or destroys morals.

The teenager considers his body important. He dresses it to extremes, develops it, magnifies sexual attributes and stuffs his stomach with hamburgers and pizza. The youth worker must get the youth to view his body as God does.

3. *The body is a vehicle for worship and service.* God desires the teenager to bring his body under control of the inner man. This is called discipline. When most of society teaches freedom, the Bible calls for self-control. "If any man will come after me, let him deny himself, and take up his cross daily, and follow me" (Luke 9:23). The body is to be controlled and used as an instrument to serve and glorify God. This is not a negative attitude. Paul said, "I keep under my body, and bring it into subjection" (1 Cor. 9:27). By this he meant the body should not be a hindrance to service, but should become a means of service. The teenager must see his body as a vehicle given to serve and glorify the God who gave it to him.

Mental Development

"I cannot understand teenagers," most people will argue. They can't understand teenagers or the way they think. What makes our teenagers think the way they think? Where do they get their wild styles? Have you ever noticed how interested they are in trivial things?

Often adults try to put teenagers into an "adult mold" and try to understand them. The teenager vehemently insists that he is an adult—when he isn't. The teenager doesn't think as an adult but as a teenager. First, let's look at the early teen—the junior high school student.

These young people love to daydream. Why? This mental preoccupation involves thought and will lay the basis for forming character and opinions as the years pass on.

Teenagers' interests change as quickly as their daydreams pass. One day Jim aspires to be a football star like his favorite champion; the next a doctor like his hero on TV. Mary will read the "true confession" magazine at the drugstore and aspire to be a movie star; next she desires to be a missionary in Mexico.

Daydreams can be healthy in building the aspirations of teenagers. Daydreams, at the same time, can be harmful. The teenager may set ideals for himself that are way out of proportion to his personality, physical build, and ability.

At this stage of life, present Christ—the most valid Hero of all. If teenagers pattern their lives after Christ, they will have a successful and fruitful development to Christian maturity. Can your teenagers see Christ in you? Shouldn't they?

How can they find out about Christ? What influences them daily? Literature is a constant part of their lives; make sure that they are supplied with *good* literature.

In the early teenage years their memories are keen, so supply them with memory work that will build good foundations. In order to stimulate good memory work, give them reasons why you are asking them to memorize. Teenagers won't memorize to obtain a prize—if they are typical teenagers. But they will memorize toward the end that their lives will be more like the Christ with whom they seek to identify.

Don't fill teenage heads with knowledge that is too deep or lofty. Treat and teach them as adults, but give them facts that are simple and concrete. We will build a solid spiritual life if we give them simple but understandable truths that meet their needs at their age level.

Teenagers love to laugh. But underneath the thin veneer of frivolity is a serious, searching mind.

Teenagers are cruel in their humor and *you* may become the butt of their joke. If they laugh at you to your face—good; if they laugh behind your back—beware. Even Christian teenagers test people through humor. Their first impressions of you will determine your effectiveness with them. Be able to laugh with them, even if their humor turns against you.

"Snap judgment" is characteristic of adolescence. Teenagers do not think through a problem, and their discrimination is not always best. They are capable of much serious thinking, but since they haven't had a lot of experience with thinking they may stop at first impressions. You must "stretch" the minds of your young people. When you lead a group discussion have your "gun loaded." Be prepared with information and facts. You may have to attack a young person who is not thinking deeply or logically. You may have to enlighten a young person who has stopped thinking.

Teenagers follow their gang leader, especially in mental suggestibility. He holds the key to the others' affection and respect. You should get next to the group leader and influence the gang through him. Not only can you influence the gang but this leader may enlighten you as to the needs of your youth group.

This natural leader may not be the elected leader of a high school class. Tim may be elected president but Randy may be the natural leader. Be prepared to get next to both. If you don't have time to spend with your young people, create time or let somebody else have your job.

The young junior high school students have just come through puberty. They are inquisitive about religious matters, but they are determined that you not know it. Inwardly they are searching for answers but outwardly they may be obstinate in rejecting yours. As they experiment with their new reasoning processes they are filled with doubts and uncertainties. One day they may seek and need your advice; the next day they will ignore you completely.

Unpredictable? Yes! At this confusing time of life, present to your boys and girls an image of stable and consistent spiritual maturity. Their ego receives a shock when they find they can't count on themselves. May they learn to count and depend on you.

Take a look in the high school department. Note one outstanding characteristic. These teenagers are extremely critical. Why? They have just come through puberty and their greatest developmental task is answering the question, "Who am I?" Before puberty, the young person thought of himself primarily as a physical body. The young person is seeking to find out "who he is," even though he can't verbalize his search. Adolescence could be called "a search for self."

As these teenagers are searching for a self, they are very idealistic. Pete thinks that he will make the New York Yankees, and Diane can only think of herself as a television personality. Teenagers expect the *best, ultimate,* or *optimum* of everybody and everything. Anybody who doesn't live up to their standards is criticized—even you. They criticize mother, father, sister and pastor. These teenagers haven't lived long enough to recognize their own limitations. They will criticize Dad for not producing, but they themselves can't produce by their own standards.

Teenagers constantly test others by their own standards. No matter how hard an adult will attempt to please the teenager, it is not good enough. At the same time youth are not always free in expressing their opinions unless they have a high opinion of you. If the kids sit around and sulk about the youth program, they probably criticize you behind your back. When they make you the target for criticism—face to face —be of good cheer; they love you. Open discussion can be a means of their spiritual growth.

When you plan your youth programs, keep the kids' criticism in mind. Allow opportunities for them to express their judgments. Let them know that you will not accept mediocrity, so why should they? Give opportunities for group evaluation. When they "blow their stacks" and criticize without a basis, call them up short. Analyze their faulty reasoning and show them where they are "off on a tangent." Cultivate an attitude in your youth group that "we all learn through our mistakes."

Critical thinking can lead to creative thinking. A group of girls can take some paste, newspaper, and poster board and create a sign that will cause Madison Avenue to be envious. Your teenagers may come up with a skit for Sunday evening that is more creative than those in the youth program book. Give opportunity for creativity in the high school department.

The important thing is that we guide them through this period of critical analysis. When the teen has learned to become "person-centered," thinking of others as well as self, he is on the road to maturity. So you should learn to understand the needs of teenagers at each level and seek to meet them accordingly.

Do you give advice to the teens? Beware! If you offer advice in other than an obvious way, remember they are very critical. They believe they are experts in most fields. Provide good Christian literature for them. Christian fiction, biographies, and devotional books will help.

Don't judge your teenagers by the standards you had when you were in adolescence. The Word of God is our eternal standard. Styles of clothes change and dating customs vary. We must seek to understand the subculture of the teenage life. They live in a pressure-cooker society. Still, teenagers are very susceptible to suggestion—especially if they think they decided it for themselves. As a youth leader, use diplomacy and tact, but above all be understanding and tolerant.

Adolescence is an impressionable stage of life. Use every opportunity to demonstrate a positive relationship of the Christian gospel. You may have to treat the teenagers as adults and yet understand that they are young and unsure of themselves. They need positive and consistent counsel, even though they will adamantly insist on independence. "We don't need your help," is the cry of teenagers and they reject our advice. But underneath, they appreciate guidance and example. They will accept, mimic and produce your life in theirs if you are worthy. Your best avenue to worthiness: produce Christ's life in yours.

The college student is beginning to worry about his life and how he is going to achieve. Wages, vocational goals, and personal abilities are foremost in his thinking. Young people need to face the seriousness of decision-making and then live with the results. Give them guidelines to direct their lives, make decisions, and face problems of adult life.

Constructive thinking is characteristic of late adolescents. They are becoming more consistent in guiding their own personality and career advancement. As they arrive at a better understanding of themselves, they narrow down their interests to specialized areas that fit more suitably with their personality. When Laura has to choose a college major, she is forced to consider her own desires in life and abilities to carry out those desires. John has to choose a profession, so he gives it serious consideration. Christian teenagers should be diligent in choosing "the path of life." As a youth director, provide them with biographical studies of men of God who have achieved their own goals in life. These biographies help them know *how* to go about achieving their own goals. Provide them with good reasons for scriptural study and Bible memorization. These teenagers demand to know what the Bible will help them "achieve" in life. Emphasize "how-to" programs.

These late adolescents have a budding cultural life. Their tastes and appreciation are growing and developing. Show them the beauty of a personality when Christ has control of the life, again demonstrating the practical results of a Christ-centered life.

In the field of humor, it is still important that you be able to take a joke—one aimed at you as well as at others. The humor of teenagers at this stage of life has become more subtle—more personal. They like to match wits with one another and enjoy laughing at themselves when the joke is on them. You must be willing and able to join in too. Because the youth in the upper teens has increasing ability to think along constructive lines, allow opportunities for him to use his abilities and ideas. Be ready to advise and counsel when needed. The youth should be permitted and encouraged to plan and promote a special program. Their specialized interest and vitality can do much for your youth program.

Discipline problems are greatly lessened in the later teens. Rational thinking can be the appeal for good conduct. Serious discussion about behavior can yield much fruit. They will measure your influence by the life you live before them. They can spot a "phony" more quickly than the younger teen. If you don't really desire to spend time with them—don't. They will sense your true attitude and then your words will really have no effect.

"What am I going to be?" Often the first major choice with far-reaching implications the teenager must make is between a college preparation course and a general high school program. What he is going to be after he graduates from high school is usually begun by his high school course program.

The high schools of today are increasingly pushing the teenager to decide his vocational future. The vocational choice is one of the major developmental tasks the adolescent must make—before he is equipped or ready to make such a decision.

The factors surrounding a sound vocational choice are complex. The adolescent does not know enough about work to choose a vocation that will continue to be satisfying to him after high school. Families sometimes pressure a teenager into a field for which he has little aptitude or interest. Sometimes the choice of a job boils down to the social status a youth wants or what is available in the want ad section. A girl who has hopes for an early marriage has the problem of preparing for a vocation. Should she prepare for a job or should she look for a man? She must do something for security reasons. Increasingly among teenagers is the problem of young girls who find themselves married and with children but discovering in actuality they would probably prefer a career. There are many other factors to be considered. Will the job offer hours and wages that are acceptable? What about security? Does the young person want to work with people or things? Does he want to be dependent or independent? Does he want to work for himself or for others? Can he take orders? What kind of job or profession will make him happy? The amount of vocational guidance given to teenagers in school is gradually increasing. Much more effective guidance needs to be given by the churches.

A common opinion today is that any teenager can do anything after he graduates from high school. The world is lying at the doorstep of every graduate—only to be conquered. Any teenager can go from the log cabin to the White House. This may be the common reaction and outlook on job opportunities today—but this is not the scriptural attitude.

The Scriptures teach that there is a gift (a capacity for service) given by God to every young person. The teaching of spiritual gifts (Ephesians 4, I Corinthians 12, Romans 12) is a needed subject for teenagers today. The Bible teaches that every person is given a capacity for service both in and out of the church. Therefore, every young person should find the will of God for his life and the call of God for His service.

Some feel that only young people entering full-time service receive a call from God and have a place in the will of God. This is not true. Every young person has a call of God and a capacity of service given by God—whether this is to be a homemaker, a public school teacher, or a nurse.

Guiding Principles for Mental Development

The youth leader will want to apply the following principles in guiding the mental development of teenagers to full maturity in Jesus Christ.

1. *Never laugh at their problems.* The youth leader will have to accept the mental struggles of youth. If you tend to belittle the teenager and laugh at his problems you can never minister to him. Also, beware of easy "cure-all" answers to problems. The youth needs empathy and understanding when he is struggling with a problem.

2. *Recognize religious and spiritual doubts.* Some youth workers are disturbed when their youth have doubts. They should be concerned for teenagers who have no doubts. Growth comes through stress and

pressure. Mental growth results from mental stresses. The youth faces opinions that contradict childhood beliefs. As the youth struggles to synthesize all information coming to him into a consistent belief—he will have doubts. This is when the youth leader is needed. The youth must be guided through doubts to spiritual reality.

3. *Provide leadership built on an intelligent interpretation of the Bible.* Youth demand answers to the doubts that face them. The Word of God has the answer to the mental problems of young people. Their answers are not found in rationalism, logic or science. However, the Bible when correctly interpreted will be viewed rationally, logically and scientifically. The Bible will then speak to the problems of youth in an intelligent manner. When the Bible is thus approached by a literal, inductive interpretation, the results will be embraced by the teen looking for intelligent answers to intellectual problems.

4. *Never be ashamed to admit, "I don't know."* Too many church leaders have an answer to every problem. Some of these answers are like the modern cake mix—"ready mixed." Problems are complex. Times are demanding. Personalities are multiphased and conditions are multilateral. Therefore, beware of superficial answers, and be careful of trying to answer when you don't know. As one wise man said, "Be careful of speaking to the edge of your knowledge; you might fall off."

5. *Provide information before asking for convictions.* Many teens have convictions that are "second-generation." They believe their parents' convictions without having any personal understanding. We don't want to produce hypocrites. Empty convictions are useless. At the other extreme are teens who rebel against their parents and believe the first alternative presented. You, as a youth leader, should not be guilty of fostering such ideas. One weakness of adolescents is that they believe the first opinion presented and stubbornly hold to that opinion in light of contrary facts. This is probably because of self-esteem and rebellion against adult control of their thinking. Therefore, make sure the beliefs of your teenagers are well grounded on facts.

6. *Teach youth the difference between criticism and evaluation.* Show them the difference between destructive and constructive criticism. Constructive criticism is evaluation. We want teens to think for themselves. This thinking involves an analysis of weakness in present projects and a possibility for improvement. Why? How? Where? These should always be in the teens' minds. The youth are critical. They want progress and advancement. They are not bound by tradition and they can view objectively. Therefore they will be critical. Their criticism may be rebellion against adult authority. They may criticize Pop, Mom and you.

However, the young person should be taught to change his criticism into love.

7. *Reach and teach youth through their interests.* The teen is interested in life—cars, dates, eating, sports and vacations. Young people are interested in themselves. Their personalities are awakening and their bodies are developing. The high schooler is interested in *achievement*. All youth can be reached through their interests. You will have to be interested in their interests if you are to reach and teach youth.

Emotional Development

"Change, excitement and color" characterize the emotions of the junior high school student. They go from mountain peak to valley as quickly as they will later change gears on a car. Their physical and mental development affect their emotional stability.

The emotions of these early teens may be controlled by appealing to "shame" or "gang pressure." Don't use these techniques only; build strong inner discipline. The inner forces may not be sufficiently present in the teen, so build their "self-acceptance." Understand the youth but don't ever count them out.

The high school student *enjoys* his emotions. He looks for opportunities to experiment with them and stimulate them. Recognize emotions—crying, laughter, peace, hate, arguments, bereavement, frustrations. However, don't let emotions just be feelings. Emotions can be a "mirror" to reflect the personality within. Use emotions as a launching pad for teaching.

In the college-age student, emotions have reached a point of "controlled rationality." The late teens understand themselves. Also, the older youth is not so chaotic in expressing emotions. Time is needed for him to come out of the valley of despair and climb the hill of peace. College-age young people delight to conform to adult emotional patterns. May they see a needed example in you.

Check List for Emotional Growth [1]

1. Do I often feel guilty about the things I have done?
2. Am I troubled over the lack of self-confidence?
3. Can I take disappointment in stride?
4. Do surprises sometimes cause me to panic?
5. Can I laugh at myself?
6. Do I have a tendency to feel gloomy and depressed?
7. Is my sleep frequently disturbed? Do I have difficulty getting to sleep?

---

[1] Lois LeBar, Unpublished classnotes. Used by permission.

8. Do I often feel nervous and tense inwardly?

9. Are my problems usually inside myself rather than outside?

10. Do I often seem to say and do the wrong thing?

11. Do I feel crushed by failure?

12. Do I often push myself to do more than I can do comfortably?

13. Does it bother me because I can't live up to my high standards?

14. Do I have trouble getting realistic goals for myself?

15. Do I find it hard to make decisions and abide by them?

16. Am I usually able to discern the will of God in large and small matters?

17. Do I keep putting off the things that I don't like to do?

18. Does it seem as if I am often getting a bad break?

19. Do I feel tired and weary a great deal?

20. Do I feel insecure about the future?

21. Do I steer clear of situations in which risks are involved?

22. Am I able to accept the responsibilities that come my way?

23. Am I more attracted than threatened by new experiences and new ideas?

24. Am I able to put myself heartily into what I do?

25. Do I enjoy being alone as well as being with other people?

26. Do I feel an integral part when in a group?

27. Do I express myself freely and naturally in a group?

28. Are my feelings sensitive and easily hurt?

29. Do I resent people in authority and people with status?

30. Do I tend to blame others when things go wrong?

31. Do I tend to dislike people who disagree with me?

32. Do I respect the many differences that I find in people?

33. Is it difficult to find people who really understand me?

34. Do I limit my friends to just a few?

35. Do I resent people who have to correct or criticize me?

36. Do I find it difficult to refuse anyone a request, though it may be unreasonable?

37. Does it disturb me that I like and dislike a person at the same time?

38. Do I have personal relationships that are satisfying and lasting?

39. Do I enjoy being both conventional and unconventional?

40. Do I get satisfaction from simple, everyday pleasures?

Sex is no joke to the adolescent, even though he may joke about it. Physically he has reached sexual maturity; emotionally he has not reached the maturity of judgment concerning sex control and understanding. Spiritually he is groping for values in life—adult values. As the sex organs mature, there is increased capacity for sexual arousal. Lead the teenager to accept himself for what he is.

Sex is not dirty or low; it is the most wonderful gift that God can give to any teenager but it must be kept within the limitations that God has decreed.

Morality and self-control constitute the greatest problem with the deepest implications for the adolescent. The problem is confused by multiplicity of standards of conduct. The home has one standard; the school has one standard, and the church has a different standard. The teenager must see the standard of the Word of God for every area of his sex life.

Sex is exploited in much of the literature and many of the television programs which the teenager sees. The larger culture in which he lives appears to talk one way and to act another in its central behavior. The teenage crowd has its own ideas as to what is acceptable concerning sex.

The natural rebelliousness of teenagers will often result in revolt against the more rigid moral ideals set down for youth by the adults of society. Youth leaders must understand this rebellion by teenagers, but never forget that the youth is an insecure person searching for the answer to the sex problem. Lead the teenager to the standards of the Word of God.

The adolescent's quest for values is not limited to sex alone. There is a great desire on the part of the teenager to find an adequate pattern of behavior, ranging all the way from etiquette to a broad concept of integrality. The teenager wants to be at peace with himself, and to be accepted by his age mates—yet he is idealistic enough to want to be acceptable to society.

"I wish you would tell me what to do" is a frequent plea of the adolescent to the youth leader. He needs controls and limitations, for in restrictions there is security. He needs to feel grownup and mature. This will cause him to resist and defy controls, but given no restrictions he is likely to lose his sense of values. Without the youth worker to help draw the line of desirable behavior, he may have a feeling that no one cares what he does. He may react to this feeling by unrestrained behavior. You are not narrow-minded to limit teenagers to the Word of God. The nature of adolescence and common sense dictate that the teenager must be given a standard of behavior that is authoritative and directive.

Guiding Principles for Emotional Development

1. *Judge emotional response at its age level.* At each phase of life's

development we have different expressions of emotion. You can't judge the 13-year-old and the college senior in the same way. The young teen has extremes in emotional feeling and has not learned to control himself. He can move from joy to depression more quickly than the older teen. His emotions are fleeting. The older a teen becomes, the more he can control his emotions by rational means. Each emotion and each teen will have to be judged in light of his own age characteristics.

2. *Don't expect youth to respond as you do.* Devotion and convictions are shown in different ways. The quiet boy will express religious love through a quiet, controlled personality. The girl with an outgoing personality will "bubble" with life as she testifies of Christ. Both may have the same deep emotional love, yet show it in different manners. Both may be different from you, so don't expect teens to respond emotionally as you do.

3. *Present an image of emotional consistency.* We are constituted toward extremes in our emotional life. We enjoy extreme laughter when happy and extreme crying satisfies us when we are sad. We must be emotionally qualified to help teenagers.

(a) We must be unchangeable. This is emotional stability. The adolescent is very unstable and demands stability in his leader.

(b) We must be emotionally balanced. Here we are to provide the "image" to the teenager that will cause him to have confidence in us.

4. *Give scriptural values to sex life.* Since sex has become the catalyst of modern society, you can't ignore the subject. If you never treat the problem of morality and sex, the teenager will conclude the Bible is out-of-date and your ministry does not meet his needs. At the same time you can go into an expanded program of sex education. Too much knowledge, too early in life, will cause problems. Curiosity, desire to experiment and frustration are the result of an over-expanded program of sex education.

The necessary facts of sex should be explained in the light of the Word of God. Sexual distinction, functions and enjoyment are from God. They are a gift of God, to be used in accordance with the will of God and ultimately for the glory of God.

Social Development

Teenagers love to be in a gang. Giving, receiving, sharing—all are part of the thrill and risk of growing up. Social development is the most important, yet least understood, developmental task of the adolescents.

In the junior high school, teenagers enjoy physical activity and games in which they can make a name for themselves. Spectator sports are not very appealing here. The teenager wants to be at the center of things and share in the action. As a youth worker, you must be willing to participate in these activities with them or else you will have very little influence.

In planning for their recreation, use group games. Try not to single out one teenager to represent the team. If he fails he is ostracized by the group. A gang of junior high school students would rather participate than have someone participate for them.

You will have to prove that you are worthy of their respect. Their powers of judgment and reason are beginning to take form. They consider themselves to be authorities on many matters. Therefore, you must be their "proven authority" or you will merit little respect and confidence. Of course their desires are very idealistic. In the Abraham Lincoln tradition, a boy sees himself in the White House and a girl marries a bank president. Present Christ to these junior high school students as the only perfect One who will meet their standards. Some might say we must lower our standards. No! Who are we to destroy the dreams of youth?

In the middle teenage years, sports activities are used to gain individual attention and excellence. Spectator sports are gaining in popularity but organized sports are still high in the interest of this age group. Use these interests to establish rapport with your young people. Attend their high school group sports events when possible. You can demonstrate your interest and concern for them—not only by attending the games in which they are involved, but also by commenting on the high school team both to individuals and the group. If they know you give time to their interests, they will be willing to give time to your interests—the work of Christ.

The average high schooler is about as large physically as the average adult. But in their social development, high schoolers are growing kids. They are not at home in the presence of many adults; for this reason they distrust themselves socially. This distrust makes them critical and cynical. You must prove yourself in their sight before they will accept your leadership. Give them a solid example to believe in—someone they can trust. Teenagers are searching desperately for worthy beliefs and social standards. Don't fail them now.

The high schooler is probably aware of his own social shortcomings. Perhaps he has risked himself in a social situation and experienced defeat. You can best provide teenagers with helpful answers now. Show them the relevance of Jesus Christ in their everyday social needs. Most teenagers want a good reputation with their particular group—not necessarily with the adult world. Show them why and how Christ fits into their lives, giving them the only reputation that is everlastingly satisfying.

Make sure the church is providing social outlets for the desires and needs of your teenagers. If the church will not meet the social needs of the teenagers, they will go elsewhere.

In late adolescence, social ideals are becoming more realistic and practical. The post high schooler wants to know what can be done to solve his real life problems and how he can build a future.

High schoolers are beginning to recognize and accept social authority. Be sure you live up to your position as youth *counselor*. Also, the teen leaders must develop and present Christian standards based on God's Word. Here we will find willingness on the part of teenagers to seek help and counsel of church leaders. They will accept guidance from respected leaders. This is an opportunity that depends on you; don't miss it.

In this later period of development, the young people are interested more in the quieter skill games. Use games where mental alertness is needed. Be ready to provide suggestions for some good clean games to satisfy their needs.

Self-criticism has become more realistic. You'll discover that the young people at this age are earnestly trying to improve themselves objectively. As the teen is able to see himself in a more honest light, his attitude will mature. He will need encouragement at this point. Most of all, teenagers should be shown the ultimate goal of their self-improvement: the glory of God.

Drive for Social Acceptance

Teenagers have a great need to belong. They want to belong to— my crowd, my gang, or my girl. Out of this need grows slavishness to the group. This need shows up in the fads of the day—the way the boys and girls dress, the way they wear their hair, the slang expressions, the places they go and their hangouts. The gang usually sets the pace and the rest must follow. "But, Mother, all the kids have one" is a frequent plea.

1. *The clique.* The need to belong finds expression in several relationships. There are small intimate *groups* or *cliques*. To be a part of a popular clique in school carries high prestige. Cliques are usually made up of pupils from the same socio-economic background. Members of the clique agree on whom to include or to exclude from membership. This group usually constitutes the greatest source of suggestibility to the teens. Cliques are relatively stable and furnish "belongness" to the youth who joins.

2. *The gang.* The gang is a large amalgamation of youth. The membership is usually fluid. This group is usually informal, and membership relatively accessible. Teens who join a gang usually come from

different socio-economic backgrounds. The gang usually congregates at a favored hangout which offers food, soft drinks and a place for social relaxation. Here the members can show off before an appreciative audience. The gang furnishes a place to meet new people and the teenager feels he belongs.

Teenagers enjoy a crowd. Assemblies where everyone sings and claps are enjoyed. To be with the gang at church, youth meeting, youth rallies and parties is considered fun. High school pep rallies are exciting and a mob at a football game is thrilling. Many times young people will look to see whether there is a crowd before they venture to pay the admission price or to enter the young people's group at church.

Teenage Dating

1. *One foot in the Junior Department.* As boys and girls approach adolescence, there is an increasing interest in each other. As they mature physically, interest for the opposite sex deepens and becomes all-important. There is an intense need to be attractive to the other sex. Standards of attractiveness, particularly in early adolescence, are modeled after the most popular boy or girl in the church. You can do some directive counseling to show them the scriptural standard of love, courtship and marriage.

The boy who has been blissfully unaware of dirty hands and ears now spends hours combing his hair, taking baths, and experimenting with sweet-smelling toilet articles. The girl who had to be reminded of her nails and to comb her hair becomes engrossed in primping before a mirror, manicuring her nails and arranging her clothes. The teenager who has not made a mature adjustment to the social demands of culture often makes real progress now because of the strong need of acceptance by the other sex.

2. *The first steady.* The first attempts at socialization are made through informal mixing. There is security in numbers. Next comes dating in groups, and then pairing off. Going steady has become a custom for many of the high school population as a form of guaranteed dating. Nobody wants to be left out.

Social adjustment in the early teens does not run smoothly because girls mature a little earlier than boys. They want the boys' interest before the boys are ready to give it to them. Sometimes a girl who fails to attract boys at this age becomes afraid that boys don't like her. She may react by chasing the boys or using too much make-up and overdressing in the attempt to make herself more attractive. This type of girl needs your direction. Sympathy from one who understands will help her to understand herself.

3. *In love with love.* The teenager has mixed feelings about affection. He wants to demonstrate what he feels inside when he is with people he likes. But his oversensitivity makes him uneasy about gestures of affection. The church has not given good direction to young people and teenagers as to how to show affection. There are pure and positive standards held by the church based on the teachings of the Word of God for the young people. But we have not helped them. At the same time the youngster is bound by the fear of being rebuffed or rejected by the opposite sex. These feelings make him hide his true approach to the opposite sex. Sometimes it is great enough to keep the youngsters from participating in any and all social activities.

Most adolescents overcome their early uneasiness about dating and they *fall in love with love.* There are many jokes today about "puppy love." But the statement that is truly typical of the adolescent is they are "in love with love" rather than being in love with a member of the opposite sex. Normally the boy-girl relationship wears itself out in a few weeks and partners switch to new steadies who will last for a few more weeks. A few may go steady throughout their entire high school years, but rarely does a boy or girl plan to marry his high school steady.

4. *Maturity in mating.* Dating, going steady, being part of the gang are all steps of becoming an adult among adults. Learning to get along with the same sex and the other sex, to look upon girls as women and boys as men, to become ready for marriage, family life, and church life—all are parts of becoming a member of the adult society. Adolescence is the opportune time for young people to establish a proper relationship with the opposite sex. If this task is not accomplished successfully during these years it may never come naturally again. Close boy-girl relations and a sense of belonging to a group helps the teenager's self-confidence and diminishes his insecurity. You must recognize that good relationships are essential to adjustment.

Group pressure becomes a vital factor in adjustment at this period of life. The teenager's friends are eager to give him tips on the things to do and the things to say. Comparing notes, they profit from each other's mistakes and successes. Conventional behavior of his age group has become so much the standard for the teenager that mothers no longer say, "When I was a girl I did it this way." Rather, it is, "What are the other girls or boys doing?"

Some parents may forbid going steady; others may even forbid dating, with the result that the boy or girl is driven further away from parents' suggestion and direction.

The church is a natural place for young people to find companionship. It often provides the greatest opportunity for boys and girls to widen their circle of acquaintance. Young people who date Christian young people eventually will marry Christian young people. The adolescent who dates outside the church will marry outside the church. Help keep adolescent friendships on a wholesome level. Skating, swimming, picnics, hobby groups, and other clubs are all possibilities for the church to explore in providing for boys and girls to have fun together.

Guiding Principles for Social Development

1. *Provide leadership that is indirect, tactful, yet firm.* Teenagers are rebellious. They are idealistic and everything is black or white. They set ideals and standards for adulthood which they expect to attain. They have not had the experience as adults to discover that they cannot attain.

The teenagers respond to proven and respected authority. Often they rebel against domineering authority, because it causes an inner conflict. They want to be like the other teenagers, yet they want to be adults. They will recognize authority that has proven itself. Therefore, when you display authority over them, you should be firm, never letting them get away with mischief. At the same time, you should be tactful and direct. Be careful of laying down the law unless you have the resources to carry through.

2. *Give qualified approbation to all young people.* Teenagers are very sensitive. They need great assurance in life. Many of them portray the apex of self-assurance, yet inside are fraught with self-distrust. They want approval from adults and they demand it from their peers. Therefore, you must give qualified approval and acceptance to all teenagers. Find something in which all can be successful. Set goals that are attainable—not adult goals. Provide some personal satisfaction that will motivate them in worthy ambitions in life.

3. *Present Christ as the ideal.* In junior high school, teenagers are looking to people. It is said that they are great hero worshipers. There-fore, hold up the person of Christ as the ideal. In high school they are beginning to think about work. They will do anything that will add to their reputation and they will refrain from anything that will detract from their reputation. Present the work of Christ as ideal. In the college-age class they are beginning to think in terms of other people. Purposeful functions crowd in on their lives. Therefore, interest them in the service of Christ as the ideal.

4. *Provide information, interpretation and example to help de-velop scriptural social attitudes.* Teenagers display the extremes of life.

They desire to be alone; they desire to be with others. They want to know people and they need a knowledge of social graces, self-control and poise. They need a wholesome attitude of social life that is evidenced in maturity. This life must be governed by rationality and a sense of social graces. Guide them in the formation of scriptural attitudes on social life.

Young people must be given direction in social graces. To know the right thing to do and how to do it creates self-confidence and adjustment. An unhappy backwash sometimes results from a teenager's great need to conform. He behaves as though he could not risk involvement with anyone who is different. A "different" boy or girl may be one who is highly intellectual, who thinks differently from the group and is not afraid to say so. He may dress differently, have ideals too high or too low for the group.

5. *Gulfs created by different social and economic backgrounds must be especially noticed.* The youth worker should note individuals who do not conform to the church group and attempt to help them adjust both to themselves and to the young people around them. Be on guard for danger signals—social isolationists. The youth worker can help such boys and girls satisfy their social needs by encouraging them to join groups that will welcome them and to form friendships with other teenagers who have similar interests.

Conclusion

Teenagers are rebellious against adult authority. They are trying to live as responsible adults without the facilities to do so. They have the physical maturity of an adult, yet the self-adjustment and security are not there.

The conflict of adolescents with parents frequently blocks easy communications in the problems which bother teenagers. Still the teenager needs adult direction and understanding. The youth director then becomes a crucial person in the adolescent's world, offering one of his first and most vital adult relationships. The way the youth worker responds can help or hinder the youth's development or progress toward maturity. He is a key figure for teenage identification and imitation. The youth is sensitive to the youth worker's behavior and how he treats him and his schoolmates. He learns from adults—not only by what they say, but by how they live.

The teenager wants to be treated as a mature person, whether he is or not. He responds to the attitude of trust and respect. He doesn't want to be told, but wants to find out. It is the obligation of the youth worker and the church to provide him with this opportunity.

Being able to talk it through will help the adolescent more than anything else. This is not an easy period. The teenager is shy and reserved about things close to him. Sometimes the teenager actually has to learn how to express his innermost feelings and to put into words what is bothering him. The young person's sensitiveness about his emotions may hamper the youth worker in gaining the teenager's confidence. You must feel free and easy with him and draw him out. Sympathy and understanding are qualities which you must cultivate.

This, then, is the teenage period. He is neither child nor adult. He is far from understanding his own behavior and from being able to predict his own conduct. He cannot determine his own relationship with God. The teenager is experiencing a great period of insecurity. He has desires and drives that he does not yet understand. He is only beginning to understand himself. The teenager wants to be accepted, understood, loved and exalted, but he is afraid of getting too close to others.

The teenager has strong ideals and a sense of right. He is trying to find a coherent system of values that will reconcile his desires with his beliefs. The teenager is confronted with making serious plans about the future. These decisions demand that he assume responsibility and maturity that he does not yet have. The teenager has little desire to take this responsibility; he prefers to be told and sometimes to be led by the hand.

You must draw the teenager out. He must be guided in the path of maturity. The teenager demands his freedom and independence but he runs away from it when faced with its actuality. By the time of graduation from high school, the teenager has come close to biological maturity. He may continue to grow intellectually and physically until he is in his early twenties, but most adolescents have accomplished their growth by the time they are eighteen.

CASE STUDY [1]

Jack is a senior in high school, reared in a nominally Christian home. He attends Sunday School and church almost every Sunday and is active in the young people's group.

Jack must work part-time after school or on weekends for his spending money because his parents are not well off. Jack gets paid above average for a high schooler on part-time employment.

Jack's job is at a drive-in theater owned by his boy friend's father. He is to keep the grounds clean, cut the grass, and do needed painting. On Saturday nights he directs the traffic.

---

[1] This case study is designed for group discussion.

Jack enjoys his job, but he is so tired Sunday mornings that he sleeps late and occasionally misses Sunday School, although he is always at church. Everyone knows that he is working at the drive-in and missing most church activities.

Jack's boss knows that Jack is a churchgoer and appreciates the fact that he is a good, honest, hard-working fellow. Jack has witnessed to him and has opportunities to witness to others with whom he works.

Jack doesn't really believe that a Christian should go to shows. He justifies his job because it's a good chance to earn some money. On the other hand, Jack knows that he is missing out spiritually, since he has to miss the young people's meetings and occasionally Sunday School. But Jack rationalizes that other fellows have to work and miss church activities too.

Working for a drive-in has begun to bother Jack. He is wondering if it is good for a Christian to work in this environment. However, he has not made up his mind whether it is right or wrong.

Recently the policy of the management of the drive-in has changed. They have begun showing "adults only" films to stimulate business. Besides what he sees on the screen, Jack observes a lot of heavy necking going on in the cars. Jack has observed some of the "faithful church members" attending the "adults only" films. When they are around, he tries to stay out of sight. If it's all right for them to attend, then he feels it's all right for him to work for the drive-in.

In six months Jack plans to go to a Christian college. When he filled out an application blank, he signed a statement that he would abide by the rules of the college. Jack hasn't seen the college handbook, but it's common knowledge that students of the college aren't allowed to attend the commercial movies.

Jack feels he needs the money to go through college. His parents can't help him too much financially. If he works right up to the time he leaves for college, he will have enough money to see him through the first year. The high school counselor advised him to make the money, so he wouldn't have to work part-time the first year in college, for he would have a tough time in college with studies.

Jack's parents have indicated they would not help him financially if he quits his job. However, they probably will help him because they are very proud of his initiative and drive. Jack and his parents have not discussed his dilemma.

1. Should Jack continue working till he leaves for college? Why? If he works part-time in high school, couldn't he work part-time in college? He'll have to work part-time during his second year in college.

2. Will Jack's faith be strengthened or weakened by his con-

tinuing to work? Is Jack an effective witness to the other employees by remaining on the job? Could he be more effective by taking a stand?

3. What should Jack do about the church members he sees attending the "adults only" shows? Would Jack be a hypocrite by working in a commercial movie now, and not attending later at college?

4. How can Jack obey his parents, yet be a testimony to them? How can Jack help them understand his problem?

Thought Questions

Section Two

(Covers Chapter 4, "Adolescence—A Description," and Chapter 5, "Age Characteristics of Teenagers.")

1. How does the teenager get his spiritual life? Is it sought, caught, taught, inherited, or implanted from above?

2. List what you consider to be the most important physical needs in teenagers. How can you meet these needs?

3. What should be your attitude toward changes in the teenager's body?

4. Do you have any teenager in your group who is shy and awkward? What can you do to help him?

5. Trace the development of imagination through the three stages of life—early, middle, and late. How can you use the teenager's imagination to the glory of God?

6. Why is adolescence the age of doubt? Is there any physical basis for this? What is the chief cause for doubt? How would you deal with spiritual doubt?

7. List what you consider to be the basic intellectual needs of adolescents. How can you meet these needs?

8. Is adolescent daydreaming a danger or an asset? Why?

9. In general, is the adolescent's memory any different from the pre-adolescent's? Should teenagers be given memory work from the Scripture? What is the purpose of Scripture memorization?

10. What part does reading play in the growing mental independence of young people? When is the reading interest strongest? What kind of books would you suggest for your youth?

11. What can you do to give your youth vocational guidance?

12. What do you consider to be the greatest emotional needs of teenagers? How can you meet their emotional needs?

13. Is the sex drive from the body or nature of the teenager? What rules would you follow in sex education for teenagers?

14. What are some good and bad points of the emotional type of

revival meeting? To what extent are the methods of a highly emotional youth meeting justified?

15. How can a clique work to strengthen a church youth group?

16. Is the "gang period" an opportunity or a problem to the Sunday School organization?

17. How can you encourage healthy dating habits among your youth?

18. Do adolescent social attitudes make it imperative that adult guidance be largely directive or indirective?

19. How much responsibility has the church for the social life of its young people?

20. Are teenagers more children than adults? Should we treat them as overgrown children or immature adults?

SECTION THREE

IDENTITY CRISIS AND THE TEENAGER

How does the teen become a person?

What makes teenagers think differently during puberty?

Why do teens ask "Who am I?"

What is meant by "teens are becoming a person?"

When teens develop "self-identity" is this egotism?

Is self-identity a biblical doctrine?

How do teens develop a negative self?

6

ADOLESCENCE: A TIME OF IDENTITY CRISIS

The question today's youth most consistently asks is, "Who am I?" They are a searching generation. They are not willing to accept traditional answers and roles just because "that's the way it's always been done." They want meaningful answers, answers which can stand the test of careful scrutiny, answers to build their lives and futures on. They want to understand themselves and their world; they want to understand their role in their world. They are asking questions about themselves. This internal examination leads to a search for self, also labeled an "identity crisis." To affect today's youth, church leaders need to know the basics of identity crisis and self-identity. It is the purpose of this section to provide some of the basics church leaders need to know to properly cope with the questions of the "searching generation."

Puberty and Identity Crisis

Psychologists are finding that youth goes through an "identity crisis" as he passes through puberty. The word "puberty" comes from the Latin word *pubertas* (to grow hair), one sign of physical maturity. Puberty is the doorway to the mystical land of adolescent experience. Puberty is a physical renaissance. A flood of sensory phenomena descends upon the youth when he becomes aware of many facts and stimuli coming to him from the outside world of which he has been unaware previously. The child living in the sheltered protection of the home has never realized the inconsistencies of his parents. Suddenly, with an awakening of the reasoning power and the emergence of objectivity, the adolescent becomes critical of his parents. The young male teenager quarrels with his mother over being late for dinner. The teenage girl disagrees with her father over allowance or a new dress. However, later in the teens the girl tends to attack the mother more than she does the father and will usually disagree with her mother more than the boy will disagree with his father. Perhaps the mother is becoming the model for the teenage girl's growing identity, causing more difficulty as the girl attempts to escape "Mother's apron strings."

The word "adolescent" is derived from a Latin verb *adolescere* which means "to grow into maturity" or "to grow up." For the purpose of this book, the following definitions will be used: (1) Sociologically. Adolescence is a transition period from a dependent childhood to an independent, "self-sufficient" adulthood. (2) Sexually. Adolescence is the time immediately following the emergence of the youth's ability to reproduce himself biologically. (3) Emotionally. Adolescence is that age of self-awareness, when the youth realizes he has an inner nature and searches for an identification of that nature by asking the question "Who am I?" (4) Chronologically. Adolescence is the time span from approximately 12 to 19 years of age. (5) Culturally. Adolescence involves entrance into a subculture where the youth will usually identify with and accept value systems of others in his subculture (clique or gang) rather than identifying with and accepting the values of the family. (6) Physically. The beginning of adolescence is marked by "pubescence" (a period of time of physiological development during which the reproductive functions mature). The exact time of puberty when the reproductive organs reach maturity varies greatly and seems to be related to socio-economic as well as geographic factors.[1] The emergence of puberty in the average teen arrived approximately 19 months earlier in 1966 than it did in 1947. This means that the average youth of today is entering puberty almost two years prior to those of Second World War vintage. The physical changes of puberty take place in a time span of approximately two years that usually begins around the middle of the sixth grade for girls and the seventh grade for boys. Muuss has said, "At perhaps no other period in human life, except birth, does a transition of such importance take place. And though physiological changes take place at all age levels, the *rate* of

---

[1] Ruth Benedict, *Pattern of Culture* (New York: The New American Library, 1950). H. Remplein, *Der aufbau des seelenlebens bei mensch und tier* (Nuenchen: Bayrischer Schulbuchverlag, 1950). V. V. Greulich, "Physical Changes in Adolescence," in *Adolescence, Yearbook of the National Society for the Study of Education*, p. 43.

change during this period is immeasurably greater than in the years that precede and follow it." [2]

Many modern-day scholars believe that the elongated period of time called adolescence is the invention of a technically advanced society. The prolonged time of puberty is not a physiological necessity but a social invention.

In many societies the transition from being a child to an adult is smooth, and society does not recognize the period of change. In some societies there are puberty rites to transfer a person from childhood to adolescence or from childhood to adulthood. Some of the primitive societies recognize that after puberty the young man or woman obtains adult recognition and has adult privileges.

Characteristics of Puberty in Girls

1. Skeleton growth
2. Breast development
3. Straight pigmented pubic hair
4. Maximum annual growth increments
5. Kinky pigmented pubic hair
6. Menstruation
7. Appearance of axillary hair

Characteristics of Puberty in Boys

1. Skeleton growth
2. Enlargement of testes
3. Straight pigmented pubic hair
4. Early voice changes
5. Ejaculation
6. Kinky pigmented pubic hair
7. Maximum annual growth increment
8. Appearance of downy facial hair
9. Appearance of axillary hair
10. Late voice change
11. Coarse pigmented facial hair
12. Chest hair

Any of the above characteristics (one or a combination of the above) could be used as an indication of the beginning of puberty. Obviously, puberty is not one of the above events, since in no case will all of them occur simultaneously. Neither do any of the above appear instantaneously. Consequently there is a lot of overlapping in the designation of puberty. When one speaks of teenagers today reaching puberty 19 months earlier than 1947, he is talking about a statistical figure, measured primarily when girls begin to menstruate and reach

---

[2] Rolf E. Muuss, *Theories of Adolescence* (New York: Random House, 1962), p. 6.

the characteristic age of puberty. If puberty is synonymous with the attainment of reproductive maturity, there is one qualification. Most girls have a period of one or more years of sterility between the first menstruation and the ability to conceive and reproduce.[3]

Adolescence is a time of life when the individual is undergoing actual physical change. As a result, he is concerned with his inner self-image. The outer physical changes trigger inner turmoil.

Major choices—such as occupation, friends, as well as marriage—face the adolescent. The adolescent asks himself if he has the ability to perform in life. When such major decisions face the adolescent, the self-image is more likely to support his choice if he has a strong self-identity or betray him if his self-identity is weak or rejecting.

Self-identification begins to grow because adolescence is a period of unusual change. During puberty a boy may grow several inches or gain up to 20 percent in weight in a matter of a few months. When the adolescent looks in the mirror, he sees pimples and becomes emotionally perplexed. The flat-chested girl desires a figure and is embarrassed when people call attention to her lack of feminine characteristics. Sexual drives increase in intensity. New desires surge through the young person.

Perhaps one of the reasons self-identification is currently awakening during adolescence is because the teenager is enjoying youth at a time when adults live in a society that worships "youth." The youth-oriented culture has made possible the advantages, freedom, and training not available to previous youth. The adult expectations that are projected on teens tend to have a reciprocal effect. The young, wanting to live up to expectations, still rebel in order to form their own life patterns.

Self-identification grows because the adolescent begins following a different pattern of thinking. Memories are keen in the early teen years. With the onset of puberty, the ability of the pre-teen to memorize is curtailed. Not that they memorize less, but the ability to memorize is not as productive as before. Memory is best in the pre-teen years because concrete or material concepts are used as thought patterns. After puberty, the teenager begins to think in abstracts and rationalize by different patterns. As the teenager begins to use the ability to think by using concepts, he begins to rationalize as well as apply logical reason.

What Is Identity Crisis?

The apparent pioneer of self-identification psychology, especially in relationship to a theory of adolescence, is Edward Spranger, professor emeritus at the University of Berlin. He called his theory *geisteswissen-*

---

[3] Muuss, *Theories of Adolescence*, p. 8.

schaftlichen (cultural science) psychology. Spranger believed that the first pattern of adolescent development is experienced as a form of rebirth in which the individual sees himself as another person when he reaches maturity. The second pattern is a slow, continuous growth process and a gradual acquisition of cultural values and ideals held in society, without a basic personality change. Spranger's third pattern is a growth process in which the individual actively participates. The youth consciously improves and forms himself, overcoming disturbances and crises by his own energetic and goal-directed efforts.[4]

According to Spranger there are three areas in which a structural change of the organization of the psyche can be observed. These are: (1) discovery of the ego or self,[5] (2) gradual formation of a life plan and (3) the selection and integration of a personal value system.

Spranger does not say that the child has no ego, rather that adolescence is a time when the ego is discovered and united. Prior to puberty the ego was present but divided. Now, the juvenile begins to reflect upon himself by directing his attention internally and analyzing himself. He discovers the internal ego and experiences it as separated from the external world. This results not only in loneliness but also in a need to experiment with one's own undifferentiated ego in order to establish ego unity. This brings about three effects:

1. A challenging of all previously unquestioned ideas and relationships. Thus there is rebellion against tradition, mores, family, school, and other social institutions.

2. An increased need for social recognition and interpersonal relationships.

3. A need to experiment with different aspects of one's own ego, trying out and testing one's own personality.

Many of the books treating youth work and/or adolescent development from a Christian perspective have not attempted to integrate identity crisis into a biblical perspective. Unwillingness to deal with the topic may reflect the "ostrich with its head in the sand" attitude of some Christians. On the other hand, Christians may not be aware of the problem. Of 406 teenagers surveyed for *The Sunday School Times,* approximately half of the responders indicated they had not had a problem with identity crisis, giving responses such as, "I have never asked myself, 'Who am I?' "

The emerging focus of literature about adolescence today is upon

---

[4] A concise discussion of Spranger is found in Ralph Muuss, *Theories of Adolescence* (New York: Random House, 1962), pp. 46–47.
[5] The term *self* should not be confused with pride or egotism. Pride is a higher estimation of oneself than is actually true. Self-identity deals with accepting oneself as you are and recognizing the potential you can become.

self-knowledge or the self-image. Two authors, Schlien and Rosenberg, have pointed out this trend in recent writings. Schlien, writing in *Religious Education Journal* in 1962, summarized all the work done prior to that time and depicted carefully the signs of development in interest in the self-image concept. Schlien stated in his opening sentence,

> In the past dozen years, the field of psychology has undergone a fascinating change in focus. The concept of the self is once again prominent.[6]

To substantiate his statement, Schlien examines Carl Rogers and Helgard, who have made valuable contributions to personality theory:

> Carl Rogers, "The self has come back into psychology." Helgard made a plea for the "study of the self as indispensable to a complete understanding of defense mechanisms of the Freudian ego." [7]

Morris Rosenberg, writing four years later, underscored Schlien's conviction by stating:

> In recent years, the fields of psychiatry, psychology and sociology have all experienced an upsurge of interest in the nature of the self-image . . . all have found the idea of the self-image relevant to their concerns.[8]

Unfortunately, cultural lags exist which usually delay the introduction of relevant material into the fields of education and religion. Such a gap does exist regarding the identity crisis. In a doctoral dissertation done at the University of Arizona, Martha Schroeder concluded that in sixty books referring to high school counseling:

> A. Only thirteen of sixty attempted to discuss self-concept.
> B. Methods and techniques of implementation of self-concept in the counseling process were conspicuous by their absence.
> C. The major purpose served by the review was to confirm the confusion and need to eliminate the semantic ambiguity which characterized these discussions of self-concept theory.[9]

Four Reasons Why Self-Identity Is Imperative

The first reason for the importance of self-identity is the youth's special capacity to recognize and develop a self-consciousness which can think, evaluate, choose, love, hate, and live in this unique human

---

[6] John M. Schlien, "The Self-Concept in Relation to Behavior: Theoretical and Empirical Research," *Religious Education*, Vol. 57 (July-Aug. 1962), p. S-111.
[7] *Ibid.*, p. S-111.
[8] Morris Rosenberg, *Society and the Adolescent Self-Image* (New Jersey: Princeton University Press, 1965), p. 3. This is perhaps the best documented study on identity crisis. Rosenberg surveyed 5,024 high school students before coming to his conclusions.
[9] Martha A. Schroeder, "The 'Self-Concept' Theory and Its Functional Significance for Counseling in the Secondary School Setting," *Dissertation Abstracts* (Michigan: University Microfilms, Inc., 1964), p. 203.

manner. The self-identity is like a person who stands above the human body, observing the actions that go on within, yet remaining a part of that which is within. The development of a self-identity into a constructive and healthy reality looms as the greatest task facing the teenager. Schlien states flatly the position of the self-theorist on the matter.

> To put it very simply, self-theorists do not believe that the organism is wholly subject to the conditions of and conditioning by the environment. They believe that the organism (human) has a special capacity (which makes it human, and without which it is less than human) to develop a SELF, which is self-conscious and self-evaluating, and which, therefore, chooses, acts upon its environment and has much responsibility because it has volition.[10]

To act meaningfully an adolescent must develop an adequate self-image, to guide in the construction of an adult personality.

The second reason for the development of self-identity is the number of problems facing the adolescent today. Rosenberg defined these briefly as follows:

A. Problem decisions, reasons for awareness of self-identity
B. Physical change, a reason for awareness of self-identity
C. Adolescence, a period of unusual status ambiguity [11]

These problems overwhelm the youth and demand answers, forcing the youth to identify himself. Too often Christians think the major question facing teens is finding the will of God or making correct choices. The identity question is deeper. The teen who knows himself has a clear picture of what he is. He is the teen who can make the correct choices. He can find God's will and implement it for his life. Some teens who do not have ego strength—that is to say, they do not have self-identity—may be manipulated to make correct choices in the present; but when they are removed from parental influence, they will probably not be able to stand against outside pressure. The Christian teen who knows himself, his strengths, weaknesses, values, and aims in life, is the one who can properly guide his life.

The third reason for identifying self is the demand of finding a satisfying vocational path in life. The question of a lifework needs solutions quickly. In the immediate future the youth will be brought face to face with life's great choices. In the next few years he must make critical decisions that will irrevocably shape his life. Among these are vocational choices, educational choices, marital choice, and other

---

[10] Schlien, p. S-111.
[11] Rosenberg, pp. 3–4.

choices of a philosophical and spiritual nature that become an indelible part of the realistic self-image of the now pliable youth. Rosenberg says:

> There are several reasons for this heightened awareness of the self-image during this period of adolescence (15-18). For one thing, it is a time of major decision; for example, the individual must give serious thought to his occupational choice. The individual must urgently think about what he is like if he is not to make a disastrous choice . . . He must also think about marriage. When an individual is found with a serious and urgent decision and when a major basis for this decision is his view of what he is like, then the self-image is likely to move to the forefront of attention.[12]

It is not difficult to see the vital role of the self-image if satisfactory choices are to be made in these critical years of development.

To an adult—parent, teacher or youth leader—"growing up" may mean nothing more than heavier, taller, bigger, increased appetite, outgrown clothes, another year, another grade of school! To the teenager, growing up is much more than this. He finds himself in a continuous search for himself. "Too often this search is fruitless," declares Schneider.[13] Self-knowledge will guide the search for self, as indicated by the Kuder Preference Test instruction booklet.

> Try to get as much information about your interests, abilities, and the jobs you want to consider. The more you know about yourself, the more opportunity you have to make wise plans for your future.[14]

Self-identity is not the same as maturity or independence. The teen is searching; many times he does not know the object of his quest, but there is an inner disequilibrium that drives his search for self-fulfillment. An adequate self-knowledge will guide the teen to maturity. Also, the teen must in time cut himself off from parental control and form an autonomous responsibility for his life. This independence is achieved after self-identity is found. Many youths are geographically independent from their parents, but emotionally they are still tied to "Mother's apron string" because they never found themselves. People without self-identity are usually the extension of their parents' personalities. Therefore, independence and maturity are the goal of self-identity as stated by Schneider.

> This is, in a real sense, the crowning achievement of adolescent striving. Without self-identity, the adolescent does not know how to work toward

---

[12] *Ibid.*
[13] Schneider, *Search for Identity,* p. 144.
[14] Frederick Kuder, *Kuder Preference Test* (Chicago: Science Research Assoc., Inc., 1950).

independence. Without self-identity he finds it difficult to grow up and to continue moving toward the goal of adult responsibility.[15]

Eternal consequences are a fourth reason making it imperative to help teens find self-identity. Many teens, and adults, are social derelicts; and their lives are useless to themselves, to society, and to God. Each person has a unique contribution to make in life, but many do not have the inner strength to give to others or to God. As a parasite, the person without identity lives off those around him. He is like a vacuum, and the law of nature teaches that the surrounding elements fill a vacuum. Schneider described these teens,

> Adolescents often manifest lack of self-identity which is one of the reasons why they are at times uncertain, confused, and extremely vacillating in their opinion, behavior or goals. We see this clearly exemplified in the high school senior who cannot decide whether he should go on to college, go into the army, or get a job; and in the college student who cannot decide on a definite curriculum. We see it also in young adults, who, having left college, flounder from one position to another. We see it exemplified in the extremely large number of boys and girls who, after a period of one or several years, leave the convent or seminary because of a 'lack of vocation,' often bitterly disappointed, disillusioned, and more confused than they were before. There are countless instances of such vocational disorientation that has its roots in the failure to achieve self-identity.[16]

The teen can control his life. God has not left the young person to aimless determinism, bumping into obstacles throughout life. God intends the young person to use the mental facilities, will power and energies at his disposal to direct his life. Obstacles should not determine his life, but the inner person who sees the obstacles should guide the outer life.

> All experience is evaluated as friendly or dangerous, interesting or boring, possible or impossible, etc., depending NOT upon the nature of the experience so much as upon the SELF-CONCEPT OF THE EXPERIMENTER.[17]

But identity diffusion negatively affects behavior patterns, therefore it is imperative to build an adequate self identity. Youth who do not find themselves lapse into what Erik Erikson calls *role diffusion*. They do not become themselves, but as the vacuum attracts the surrounding environment, these teens play-act the lives of those around. A boy chews on a toothpick and plays the role of "tough guy." Another might attempt to play several roles, portraying the person who is nearest and

---

[15] Schneider, *Search for Identity*, p. 144.
[16] *Ibid.*, p. 140.
[17] Schlien, "Self-Concept," p. S-115.

exerting the greatest influence at present. Then other teens develop deeper psychological problems of role diffusion. As a teen once yelled, "I'd rather be someone bad—to be no one is hell!" Erikson notes,

> The danger of this stage is role confusion. Where this is based on strong precarious doubts as to one's identity, delinquent and outright psychotic episodes are not uncommon.[18]

And again in the same context, after describing the cruel intolerance and discrimination in adolescent groups, Erikson adds:

> It is imperative to understand (which does not mean condone or participate in) such intolerance as a defense against a sense of identity confusion.[19]

Diffusion of self-image is another of the problems in the developmental tasks before youth. Perhaps all teens go through this stage of role diffusion before they find themselves. Erikson aptly describes the adolescent in suspended ambivalence between past and future,

> . . . There is a "natural" period of uprootedness in human life: adolescence. Like a trapeze artist, the young person in the middle of vigorous motion must let go of his safe hold on childhood and reach out for a firm grasp on adulthood, depending for a breathless interval on a relatedness between the past and the future, and on the reliability of those he must let go of, and those who will "receive" him.[20]

Examining Self-Identity

The definition of self-identity becomes vital if we are adequately to help teens find themselves. Self-identity must find its own self-identity in "Who or what am I?"

Some credit William James as the modern originator of the concept and importance of identity.[21] James equated *I* with *ego,* and in this reflection he called it *me;* together he called it *self.* A man's *self* is the sum total of all that he can call "his." This self is considered as being constructed from three constituents: a "material," a "social" and a "spiritual" self.[22] Carl Rogers defined the self-concept as a person's view of himself. The *self-structure* is a person viewed from an external frame of reference.[23] The ubiquitous observer stands within and views the many facets of personality, the many roles played in life, and the changing moods and, as the observer, perceives the internal person. He

[18] Erik H. Erikson, *Childhood and Society,* 2nd ed. (New York: W. W. Norton Company, Inc., 1964), p. 262.
[19] Erikson, *Childhood and Society,* p. 262.
[20] Erik H. Erikson, *Insight and Responsibility* (New York: W. W. Norton Co., Inc., 1964), p. 90.
[21] David J. De LeVita, *The Concept of Identity* (Paris: Mouton and Co., 1965), p. 29.
[22] *Ibid.*
[23] Schlien, "Self-Concept," p. S-111.

also controls the total person. The knowledge one has about his self is powerful, whether the knowledge is correct or not, for a person lives out the personality styles he perceives he possesses. Some live up to their perceived view of self-expectation, others fail. Some are aware of their perceptual self; at other times it is subliminal but self still controls behavior. Self-perception not only controls actions but also controls the emerging self-identity and reinforces the idea of the emergence of the ego.

> The emergence of the ego plus the development of the self-concept and the self-ideal are closely correlated in adolescence with the development of the self-identity.[24]

Morris Rosenberg defined the self-image as a "self-picture" or a mental "self-portrait," [25] as though the person visits the art gallery and views his portrait. Yet, just as no painted portrait is a perfect photographic reproduction, so the self-image is not identical to the real self. Self-image is the present attitude toward the self which one wants to become, what one knows he is not, what acts or attitudes one values, and what one wants to be perceived by others. Those who like what they see in the mirror of developing self-image are generally healthy persons. Those who reject what they see or those who have a hazy, imperceptible view are generally those who need help. Perhaps a change in their self-perception is all that is needed, but like the old witch in "Snow White" who demanded from the mirror to be called beautiful, they recognize themselves as not the "fairest of all." A change of self-perception takes time, exposure, and sometimes professional therapy. Many years are usually wasted in developing a distorted self-perception, and much energy is needed to change that image. The change begins with a shift in attitude, as writes Rosenberg:

> We conceive of the self-image as an attitude toward an object. (The term attitude is broadly used to include facts, opinions, and values with regard to the self, as well as favorable orientation toward the self.)[26]

The person who has established a clear and correct self-identity is usually a mentally healthy person. He has a proper grasp on the external world of reality, has identified life's goals and is pursuing them, and is accepting others, because he is accepting himself.

> Self-identity is a quality of personal experience and of existence that is linked to the growth of the self-concept and the self-ideal, and means a

---

[24] Schneider, *Search for Identity*, p. 139. Compare De LeVita, p. 29.
[25] Rosenberg, *Adolescent Self Image*, p. xiii.
[26] *Ibid.*, p. 5.

clear awareness of one's role and status in life, one's goals and purposes, and one's relationships to reality, to society, and to a Supreme Being. The person with self-identity knows the answer to such questions as "What am I?" "What am I supposed to be or become?" and "Where am I going?" The person lacking self-identity, on the other hand, is confused and uncertain as to what he is supposed to be and where he is going.[27]

The present self-image is only one of a number of self-images which might be considered. James also mentioned the ideal self or what the individual would like to be or "stakes" himself on becoming.[28]

The various writers are saying, then, that there are several self-images, each of which must be identified and accepted for what it is worth. Rosenberg does a rather complete job of compiling all of the ideas of different self-images. These are as follows:

1. Present self-image—what he really is
2. His committed self-image—the type of person he has staked himself on becoming
3. The fantasy self-image—the type of person he would like to be if unencumbered by reality
4. The ego ideal—the type of person he feels he should be
5. The future or possible self—the type of person he feels he will become
6. The idealized self-image—the type of person he most enjoys thinking of himself as
7. The presenting self—the picture the individual attempts to project
8. The accorded self—what other people hold of the individual
9. The inferred self—what the scientific investigator is able to learn about the individual [29]

Conclusion

The self is one of the important factors governing adolescent behavior. The teen is developing a "self-image" and the adolescent years will be important in determining his personality that will remain with him throughout life. The following chapters will examine the impact self has in every area of life.

---

[27] Schneider, *Search for Identity*, pp. 139–40.
[28] LaVita, The Concept of Identity, p. 29ff.
[29] *Ibid.*, p. 274.

7

HOW SELF-IDENTITY IS FORMED

Self-identity is formed in relationships. The teen develops his personality in meaningful interactions. This chapter will trace the personal growth of self-identity; first in relationship to spiritual development, second in relationship to social adjustment, and finally in relationships to psychological growth.

Spiritual Development of Self-Identity

The thought of being "nobody" is intolerable; and the adolescent prefers being a "bad somebody" to a "nobody." However, when a teen is searching for identity, or seeking for a "self," this does not mean he is becoming selfish. He simply wants to become a person. The selfish person desires to become something he isn't. He grasps after glory or recognition. God "resists the proud and gives grace to the humble" (I Peter 5:5). *Pride* tops the scriptural list of God's most-hated sins (Proverbs 6:16-19). Anyone who is totally wrapped up in self-glorification certainly has a distorted self-image. The opposite extreme to self-glorification is total rejection of one's self. Reverse pride is denying what you are—to belittle oneself. This is as detrimental to the personality as egotism. A person should accept himself for what he is; this is self-respect and is not sinful. Jesus allowed for self-respect when He said, "Love thy neighbor as thyself" (Luke 10:27). Rejection of self with also lead a teen not to respect others. To belittle oneself

111

falsely will not lead to an esteem of others. A person can love others only in direct proportion to a proper respect for himself. This is why self-identity is important for teens. Dr. Cecil Osborne says,

> . . . A proper self-love is the starting point for loving another person. If we do not love ourselves properly, we can never truly love anyone else; for we tend to project on our own disguised self-contempt. . . Self-love does not imply narcissism, egocentricity, selfishness, or a warped self-interest. It does imply: I too, am a person loved by God. . .[1]

The Bible asserts that men are what they think of themselves, "For as he thinketh in his heart, so is he" (Prov. 23:7). If a person's self-concept is distorted to either extreme, his actions will be either narcissistic or hostile toward self and others. If he believes himself to be a defeated, inferior, and inadequate person, then soon his actions will reveal these characteristics.

> Whatever you feel yourself to be at the center of your emotional nature, that is what you really are existentially and your actions will be in harmony with your self-concept.[2]

Obviously neither extreme can lead to a healthy personality. Teens should reject the extreme attitudes of "I am everything" (egotism) and "I am nothing" (self-rejection).

Teens find their self-identity as they receive love and learn to give it in a depth-relationship. Teens begin to grow into a healthy personality when they realize they are worthy of love and another person wants their love in return. A loving mother can lead a child into a mature self. When the child reaches adolescence, his self-image continues to grow as he matures in love-relationship. Erich Fromm described love in his book, *The Art of Loving*.

> I am loved. I am loved because I am my mother's child. I am loved because I am beautiful, admirable. I am loved because my mother needs me. . . . I am loved for what I am, or perhaps more accurately, I am loved because I am . . .[3]

Happy is the teenager who is the recipient of such loving acceptance. Love bartered across the bargaining counter of behavior or gotten in the backseat of a car will not give the adolescent a sense of being loved as a person. As the teen becomes conscious of God's eternal love for him, he gains self-awareness and self-respect. No single additional

---

[1] Cecil G. Osborne, *The Art of Understanding Yourself* (Grand Rapids, Michigan: Zondervan Publishing House, 1967), p. 197.
[2] Erich Fromm, *The Art of Loving* (New York: Harper & Row, 1956), p. 36.
[3] *Ibid.*, p. 34.

factor can contribute as much to one's sense of self-esteem as to be loved unconditionally. (God loves without conditions, Romans 5:8.)

The teen learns self-identity as he realizes there are limits and laws in life. The teen who wants to be absolutely free, doesn't understand life or the universe in which he lives. God has placed us in society that has laws and put us on a planet that is controlled by laws. The teen is loved enough to have fences set about him which keep him from hurting himself and others. To be under authority is synonymous with acceptance. No parental or societal jurisdiction is exercised over those that do not belong to them.

God has set boundaries in the areas of sex and interpersonal relationships; He has further instituted the home, the church, and society, which also have boundaries separating acceptable from unacceptable behavior. God's love is demonstrated not only through the bounds He sets, but also by punishing violations of them.

God has given the conscience as a radar to spot the danger zones of behavior. Parents play a major role in the conditioning and giving of a set of values to that conscience. Commenting on the restricting power of the conscience, Blaine states,

> Adolescence is the period when the underlying core of the conscience laid down in the early years is most needed. This is a time of necessary rebellion —when superimposed values seem false and artificial. The individual self becomes all-important and the search for what comes truly from within, and therefore seems real as a consuming task. It involves experimenting with new ideas, new ways of behaviour, and different ways of dressing, and the trying out of new goals and ambitions; but always as the limiter of action there remains the basic core of conscience provided by childhood training from the parents which prevents completely self-defeating and self-destructive behaviour . . .[4]

Restrictions, discipline, and guidance give the teenager a clear picture who he should be. A child who is pampered and never disciplined will expect the same treatment later in his teens and on into adulthood. He does not understand himself nor society.

> The young child is able to absorb into his self-regulating apparatus the prohibitions and restrictions of his parents and to make them a part of his permanent and irrevocable inner self. The parents' ability to influence their children's future is never again so great.[5]

The authority of the parents is but a prelude to the lifelong sub-

---

[4] B. Blaine, Jr., *Youth and the Hazards of Affluence* (New York: Harper & Row, 1967).
[5] *Ibid.*

mission to the authority of school, society, the law, and to God. Adjustment to the control by parents leads to adjustment to society.

While the teen finds himself by accepting controls, he must learn to deal with freedom. Often the young person desires freedom of the open road or open waterways. As a result, he feels that the lack of restraint signifies real freedom. The cultural heritage in the United States places a premium on freedom. The freedom of choice also brings with it the responsibility to accept the resulting consequences. In God's system, man is left free to choose but God has graciously given "means of grace" to bring each person to salvation. But in the final analysis, man can accept or reject. True freedom is being committed to the Lord Jesus Christ. One need not be a slave to sin (Rom. 6:18-22), but can be free to be a servant of the Lord of the universe. Rousseau observed, "Man is born free, and everywhere he is in chains." Teens are free, but they reject that liberty. They are plagued by conformity in their dress, music they listen to, places they go, possession of the "right" things, etc. They are slaves to the teen culture yet they reject their parents' society. The teen who has a strong identity can break away from slavish conformity to teen mores. He can control his own life. The Christian teenager is free to make his conformity God-ward rather than man-ward.

As the teen reads the Scripture, he identifies with those who have served God. The convictions of Daniel, the boldness of Elijah, the faith of Abraham, and the patience of Job all speak to him. When he views the experiences of men and women in the Bible, those experiences demand some interpretation. The Bible is not filled with empty moralisms or rusty cliches, rather it deals realistically with life's problems. When the teen identifies with Bible personalities, he is doing more than learning factual information. He is building up an intellectual and emotional attitude (self-image) which will help him make right decisions.

A minister once claimed, "Ninety percent of the Bible deals with life situations, not theological standards—therefore, the Bible is related to life." The emphasis of this minister's remarks is correct. However, to say that only 10 percent of the Bible deals with theological standards is erroneous. Theological standards undergird the entire Scripture and reflect themselves in the everyday life situations of the Bible. Theological standards, both negative and positive, are the mortar that molds one's self-image. When the Bible teaches, "Thou shalt not take the name of the Lord thy God in vain, thou shalt not steal, thou shalt not murder, thou shalt not commit adultery," it is molding the teen's "negative self." The negative self in relation with the conscience determines the action of each individual just as much as the positive self.

A Christian teen has been taught in Sunday School the Ten Commandments. He goes in the supermarket. Deep within his subconscious is a negative self that says, "I am not a thief." ("Thou shalt not steal.") Therefore, when the clerk is in the back room filling an order and the only other customer is not watching, the young person does not walk out the front door without paying. Stealing is not in harmony with his negative self.

After the adolescent considers God's love and has found himself under authority, he reads God's Word and realizes he is free. Next the teen must consider God's claim upon his life. If man is truly created in the image of God but is separated from God because of his sin, then he must re-establish a relationship with God. Here the teen finds true identity. The adolescent must see himself as a unique person in four areas. First, he is created in God's image and likeness. God was pre-eminent in creation. Man is made in God's image and is preeminent above the world. Second, man is superior to all creatures of this world. God put man in dominion over all that has been created. Third, man, like his Master, is a rational being. He can think, reason, and express emotion. Fourth, man is spirit. This is not a psychological existence, but a created reality. Man has an immaterial spirit that will live forever. The teen must come to see himself as an individual, uniquely himself, and see that there is something within him that separates him from all other people. That something which God as creator gave to him is his soul.

The adolescent will need to consider who and what God is. He must also determine what spiritual gift God, through His Spirit, has given to him. "In each of us the Spirit is manifested in one particular way, for some useful purpose" (I Cor. 12:7 NEB). To know himself, the individual must know God's gift for him as a unique person. Through this recognition of his relationship with God, the adolescent will form part of his self-image.

Social Development of Self-Identity

Personal relationships are just about the most important aspects of life to a teenager. As a person relates to others, he learns self-identity. The individual learns a set of expectancies from parents, peers, significant individuals, and society in general as he relates to these each day. The teen learns that he is good or bad, that he is accepted among peers or rejected, that he is a good student or a poor one, or that he is a part of society or an outcast. These relationships help to determine a teen's positive or negative feedback from society, resulting in a positive or negative self-esteem. Those who have received positive reinforcement throughout life usually have a good, strong self-image. Negative re-inforcement results in self-rejection.

The self-image, whether good or bad, strong or weak, tends to reinforce itself. In a study by Mussen and Porter (1959), a person was found to put his self-image into behavior. "Self-concepts are translated into action, and contribute further support to the adequate social functioning." [6] When the individual is able to function adequately in society, the reward is positive. Therefore, as the teen relates to society around him, his self-image takes shape.

People with low ego strength usually like to put on a front or mask. Why do people wear masks? Basically, they fear discovery will lead to rejection but experience has shown just the opposite. When a person frankly admits a weakness, he places himself in a category with most other members of the human race. He is usually accepted if he takes off his mask. Taking off a mask is different from striving for acceptance. Striving for acceptance by reading personality books or studying etiquette, will not solve the problem for the mask-wearer.

Rosenberg found that teens with weak ego strength tend to rate themselves lower than others in the possession of desirable characteristics, except the item "having a good sense of humor." Those who have weak ego strength think it can be hidden, but Rosenberg suggests, "They are, however, probably less successful in deceiving others than they think." [7]

The work of Sigmund Freud indicates that the individual who loves himself *more* will thereby love others less. Freud believed that a person had a certain "capacity" of libido (energy). If the person expressed this on himself, he had little left for others. Erich Fromm disagreed, "The individual's attitude towards humanity, toward human nature, is one of central axioms of his life theory. If he trusts and respects human nature, then he will trust and respect himself, since he is himself a member of the human race. If he hates and despises others, then he will have a fundamental concept for himself." [8]

Rosenberg's studies of teens indicated that Fromm's relationship of people (if he trusts others, he will trust himself) was correct, but the order was reversed. Rosenberg felt that mistrust, hostility, or rejection of others began in a person's attitude toward himself. Those with weak ego strength were skeptical or rejecting in their relationship with other people. A high school boy with weak ego strength was asked about his

[6] B. McCandless, *Children-Behavior and Development* (New York: Holt, Rinehart and Winston, 1967), p. 265.
[7] Morris Rosenberg, *Society and the Adolescent Self Image* (New Jersey: Princeton University Press, 1965), Chapter IV, p. 1.
[8] Erich Fromm, *Man for Himself* (New York: Rinehart, 1947), Chapter IV, p. 1.

concept of the human race, "Everyone is a hypocrite; you can't trust anyone." A girl had this opinion, "Everyone wants to get out of life for themselves everything they can; they cut a lot of corners." [9]

Those with weak ego strength tend to keep to themselves. They put up a high wall between themselves and their friends. It is all right to throw bits of information or to lean over the wall and talk, but nobody gets in. They don't have the strength of personality to let people "look around" inside their personality. Eighty-four percent of the high school students were asked how long this feeling of loneliness or isolation had occurred, they usually said "back to childhood." They gave answers such as, "I never talk about personal things to anyone." [10]

The teen's identification with other persons is one of the basic means whereby he discovers his self-identity. Identification in personality development is not one person attaching himself to a second, as one might attach two pieces of cloth or two sheets of paper. A teen identifies with a prized person and emulates his basic traits. Identification is carried out in many ways. Some of these factors are:

1. The biological inheritance naturally leads to identification. The boy most naturally will identify with a man, and the young girl will have an "ideal self" with whom she identifies—a certain woman whom she admires.

2. The pressures of society upon children cause them to identify with their own sex. From the moment mother puts pink upon the baby girl, and the young father sticks a catcher's mitt in the crib of the baby boy, society begins to pressure a child to identify with its own sex. The distinct clothes, the different bicycles, and the separate bathrooms pressure the child to identify with his own sex.

3. The degree of love shown a child by the person with whom he identifies influences the degree of identification. The four-year-old boy who attempts to identify with his father is more likely to do so if his father shows love and acceptance to the boy. A nine-year-old boy may idealize a ballplayer. Yet, when the ballplayer brushes aside his request for an autograph, the junior boy no longer wishes to identify with his hero. Identification is greater where there is love and a warm relationship.

4. Identification is greater if a child's needs are met by the person with whom he is identifying. Identification will be greater between a young high school girl and a "Miss America" candidate if the potential Miss America has the attributes the high school girl needs. For instance, the candidate for Miss America is disciplined, dedicated, and

---

[9] Rosenberg, p. 182.
[10] *Ibid.*, pp. 182–83.

excels in playing the piano. The high school girl has a desire to play, yet cannot force herself to the routine of practice. When the high school girl sees her "heroine" do what she cannot do, a need is met.

5. Identification is greater when there is a degree of acquaintance between the individuals involved. The unknown movie star will not have as much influence on a young high school girl as the homeroom teacher in high school who is in her late twenties, wears stylish clothes, and drives a Mustang.

6. Identification is much easier when the ideal has a clear role in the perception of the teenager. The older person who is confused in his Christian life will not have a positive influence on the teenager who is seeking to identify. When the "hero" has a strong concept of "who am I," it is easier for the adolescent to identify with him.

7. The attitude of the "ideal" to the teen will affect the relationship. The teenager is more likely to identify with someone who treats him as a person rather than someone who treats him as a child. Attitudes of respect, sharing, and love will make for a positive identification, whereas attitudes of belittlement or toleration tear down the identification process.

8. The natural abilities of the child to be like his "hero" determine the case of identification. When the young boy attempts to identify with a ballplayer, identification is easier if the young boy is athletically inclined. The beautiful model will not have much influence for a homely girl, because she "lacks" natural ability to be a model.

9. Identification is greater when the temperament of the teen is similar to that of the identified person. Studies are not sufficient to show whether young people identify with those who are like them in temperament or they become like those with whom they identify. However, it is conclusive that when teens identify with those of like temperament, the identification process has the greatest influence.

Identification may have a host of meanings. However, what happens in molding the teen's life is most important. It may mean some of the following:

1. The teen and his model have the same behavior.

2. The model has influenced the teen, who reciprocates by mimicking.

3. The teen may mimic the attitudes, not the behavior of the model.

4. The level of the unconscious personality may be affected. The teen's "self" may be constructed to become like that of the model.

5. Only a part of life may be affected. The teen may attempt to

become like the model in one specific behavior, rejecting other aspects of the model's life.

6. Identification may be a superficial product. The teen's behavior is related to the model's outward behavior, but the internal persons are not similar.

7. Identification may become a process. As the teen learns one action of behavior from the model, this leads to a second or to an accelerating series of acts.

Identification is as simple as a small boy assuming his father's walk, posture, and the tilt of his head. It simply means that the adolescent's behavior is similar to his model's.

Negative identification is similar to the negative self. It results in self-identification but in a dissimilarity of behavior to the model. When a teenager has negative feelings (that is, he dislikes the model), he has negative identification. He makes either a conscious or unconscious attempt to become opposite to the model.

A high school boy works out on the basketball court, endlessly practicing a hook and a one-hand set, just as his hero. Does the high school boy practicing basketball become his real self when he plays the game as his hero? The high school girl sits in front of her dressing table to coax the mirror into reflecting the smile, the blush, and the nod of her favorite heroine. When the smile, nod, and blush are displayed in public, is this the true girl?

Many people claim to be "weak-willed" when their problem is a weak ego. A person who has a poor self-image cannot see himself in the role of a strong, forceful, or directive individual. He sees himself as one who is carried along by the tide of society. Perhaps this person considers passivity (surrender to the Lord) a virtue. What he considers virtue may be nothing more than a projection of his own weak self-image.

Can the weak-willed person build a strong will later in life? Can the indecisive businessman become more decisive? Yes! The person who changes his self-view can become more decisive in handling decisions.

Marie Alice had a problem with her pastor who expected high standards of himself and the young people. He had the keen desire that young people should live clean lives. On occasions he spoke against smoking, drinking and dancing. But the pastor did not stop there. He had many discussions with young people, giving reasons why they should abstain from these practices.

Marie Alice was a borderline case. She had great potential and at times showed deep spiritual desire. Marie Alice had an overt desire to be popular among the boys. The pastor observed this and counseled her regarding her weakness. "It's not that I'm rebellious against the Lord," indicated Marie Alice. "I just have a difficult time yielding this area of my life." Marie Alice went on to say, "I sincerely enjoy musical expression through dance." On previous occasions, Marie Alice talked to her pastor about dancing, and she knew why she should not dance. "I'm a weak-willed girl and just can't seem to control myself," she insisted. "I just can't say no." What will turn Marie Alice from a weak-willed adolescent to a self-determining young lady of convictions? Can Marie Alice stand up against the pressure of the crowd? Perhaps Marie Alice has convinced herself that she is weak-willed when she is not. She can stand up against the arguments of her pastor. The image that Marie Alice has of herself determines her actions. The self-values (desire to be liked, desire to express herself) were the motives that formed her self-image.

For Marie Alice to change, she must first understand her self-image, then understand the pressures that molded her self-image. However, self-understanding does not come easy. Marie Alice can look in the mirror, read psychology books, or even read the Bible. These may have little influence on her life, unless it is taken in perspective. Marie Alice must build a meaningful relationship with friends and adults who can truthfully "tell her what they think of her." When friends are honest, Marie Alice will understand the positive and negative aspects of her personality. When friends and adults are frank with her, she knows she is being accepted with both her positive and negative qualities. The fact of being accepted is more basic than knowledge about her strengths or weaknesses. Acceptance by others builds self-identity, and ultimately the person who knows himself can have a strong will.

A person with weak ego strength is more likely to take criticism as an inner-personal threat. In Rosenberg's study the adolescents with weak ego strength indicated, "Criticism or scolding hurts me terribly." The same adolescent was deeply disturbed "when anyone laughs at him or blames him for something he had done wrong." [11] At the same time, some adolescents with weak ego strength have built in a defensive reaction. They indicated that it did not matter to them what others thought. Two-thirds of those adolescents who had weak egos confessed that criticism "bothered them very much." In another case where those with low ego strength were observed, the observer indicated these people's reactions to criticism was "touchy and easily hurt." [12]

On the other hand, teens with weak ego strength were hypersensi-

---

[11] *Ibid.*, p. 169.
[12] *Ibid.*, p. 170.

tive to "dishing out" criticism, ridicule, and chastisement. Rosenberg gave the example of one girl with weak ego strength who indicated, "I don't want to hurt other people because I've been hurt, and I don't feel that I'd like to hurt others." [13] Perhaps this is because the person with weak ego strength lacks confidence in his own judgment. If he criticizes others, they may in turn criticize him. Fearing the retaliation, those with weak ego strength stay clear of confrontation. As a result these people place much value on "harmony" and getting along with people. "It's the Christian thing to do," stated a high school boy who would rather let people run over him than face an issue. Many people mistake meekness for a psychological adjustment to weak ego strength. The person with a strong ego does not mind facing the issue (truth), for truth is more important than feelings.

In Rosenberg's study those with weak ego strength found it awkward or difficult to meet new people or strike up a conversation with strangers. On the other hand three-quarters of those high schoolers with strong ego strength said, "I find it easy to make talk when I meet new people." [14] Those with weak ego strength tended to avoid meeting strangers and many times avoid their own friends. Social contacts seemed to threaten them. Two-thirds of the high school students with weak ego strength interviewed by Rosenberg said, "I prefer to pass by school friends, or people I know but have not seen for a long time, unless they speak to me first." [15] One boy with weak ego strength answered Rosenberg's questions stating:

> When you are small it is much easier making friends because you don't feel you are going to embarrass yourself meeting new people . . . but when you get older it is not so easy. You begin to think what a fool you can make of yourself in the eyes of a person you don't know. I kind of become shy and withdrawn.[16]

The teen's opinion of himself is going to be significantly influenced by (1) his self-image, and (2) what he imagines others think of him. Thus Rosenberg has found, "It is not surprising to find those people who consider themselves unworthy, are more inclined to feel that others share this opinion of them." [17] At first glance one may say that teens who have low opinions of themselves should "think positively" because other people have high opinions of them. However, Rosenberg's study has not indicated this. The teen with low ego strength may be quite

---

[13] *Ibid.*, p. 170.
[14] *Ibid.*, p. 171.
[15] *Ibid.*, p. 173.
[16] *Ibid.*, p. 174.
[17] *Ibid.*, p. 176.

correct in assuming that others do not value him highly.[18] Thus, if an adolescent feels he is not well accepted, he probably is not well accepted. He communicates this nonverbal attitude to others. People believe his message that he is unacceptable, and they reject him.

Self-punishment becomes an important factor in understanding young people. The teen with low ego strength who rejects himself is rejected by others. Thus we can conclude that the path for good relationships with other people is first a good relationship with yourself; accept yourself.

Some teens might assume that the way to become more friendly, is to force themselves into sociable contacts, thus learning interpersonal success. However, Rosenberg's findings point to the contrary. "The person with weak ego strength often makes special efforts to gain sociable qualities. His misfortune lies in the fact that those people are often most popular who do not strive for popularity." [19]

Role performance, or the roles played by teens in their subculture, is still another factor which helps shape self-image. More attention is given to role performance today in understanding adolescence. Role performance is simply defined as "That behavior of an individual which is performed in the fulfillment of a role, that is in accordance with the norm." [20] The president of the student body does not always do as he wishes; he performs according to the demands and standards of his office. He performs the role of the class president. The basketball star, the cheerleader, the valedictorian, and the girl going steady with Fred, all perform roles in accordance with the expectations of their position.

When a sophomore is playing the role of second-string tackle, is he really himself or is he wearing a mask? He may "butter up" the coach in an attempt to get the starting role, or he may go all-out in practice to get into the starting lineup. In life the sophomore is sarcastic and "mouths off" to adults. He is also lazy and indifferent about most things except football. Which is the real sophomore—the boy diligently playing the role, or the sarcastic student?

As you study the adolescent subculture, you become aware of the many roles that encumber each teenager. The average teenager plays more than one role at a time. Mark may be president of the youth group at church, secretary of his homeroom class, and vice-president of the journalism club. These are formal roles, whereas his informal role may be going steady with Joan. Mark also is studying for the ministry, and

---

[18] *Ibid.*, p. 176.
[19] *Ibid.*, p. 178.
[20] Robert Welch, *Identification and Its Familial Determinants* (Indianapolis: The Bobbs-Merrill Co., 1962), p. 17.

is the preacher's son. He is expected to be a better Christian than every-one else.

Formal roles are those which are forced upon a teenager by rec-ognized positions in our society. Formal roles might be class officers, club officers, positions on athletic teams, or other recognized positions with "power" and requisite standards. The informal roles of teenagers are more difficult to define and describe. However, the informal role has clear standards, but they are usually never articulated. For instance, the girl who has been jilted has a specific role to play in the high school subculture. She is not to look hurt and offended and is now free to flirt with all of the boys. When she sees her former "steady," she either smiles or nods her head while underneath she may feel embarrassment, or contempt for the former friend. The formal role is more understood by the adult society than is the teenage informal role. The "in" adoles-cents understand its requirements, while adults stand off and shake their heads. As the teen plays his different roles, he learns to see himself in light of the roles he plays or does not play.

Psychological Development of Self-Identity

Self-image is determined largely by what is thought of us, both by God and society. However, the person will help determine what he does with the information coming to him from the outside. It is the self which accepts or rejects the information fed to him. The self is a unique creature. The self is the only creature that can continuously help to create itself. There are many natural endowments given at birth. The plant and animal world are determined by the creator. However, man alone continuously assists in the fulfillment of his nature. The poet Wordsworth describes the process, "So build we up the being that we are."

Since the self-image is key to understanding human personality and human behavior, growth in self-image produces growth in the teen's personality and his behavior. Norman Vincent Peale has said much about the power of positive thinking. This may have some merit, but there is also much error. Put a young boy on a bicycle and tell him to "think positively" and give him a push down the street. He may end up in an accident. It takes more than correct thinking. Yet, the boy who has been diligently practicing and has conquered his fear may, through the power of positive thinking, actually ride a bicycle for the first time. The power of positive thinking *cannot* work when it is inconsistent with the circumstances. Yet, a person through positive thinking may bring about growth in his self-image, and his self may apply the rules of life and ultimately change life.

24

SUCCESSFUL BIBLICAL YOUTH WORK

The ability to discover oneself may mean the difference between success and failure in life. What may be success to one man is failure to another, so each man must know his capacities and abilities and from these formulate his own goal.

Each of us carries a mental blueprint of our lives. We are our own creative architect. The blueprint was in the drawing process in a non-verbal way throughout our pre-adolescent years. With the arrival of adolescence the job of draftsman is taken over more and more by the teen. A person's self-image has been built up over the years from his own beliefs about himself. Maxwell Maltz has observed concerning self-image, "We do not question the validity, but proceed to act upon it just as if it were true." [21] Whether one's image of himself is true or false, he acts upon it as if it were without error. A musician may teach piano for thirty years, feeling he is a good musician because his self-image has told him this. However, the same person may have had more natural gifts to become a teacher in the public school.

Most people "act out" the sort of person they conceive themselves to be. The man who conceives himself to be "not very gifted" may end up in a 9:00 a.m. to 5:00 p.m. job and he happy that he is employed. If this person had the will power, or even the opportunity, he might have become a stockholder and board member in the company. The high school student who sees himself as "dumb" in English but smart in arithmetic will usually "act out" his image of himself. In class he may have a mental block to literature and as a result receive a "D". Because he sees himself as exceptional with numbers, he may score well in calculus or physics. No doubt the report card will bear out his self-image.

One psychologist speaking of self-image indicated that self had three principle elements: (1) the imagination of one's appearance to the other person, (2) the imagination of one's judgment of that appearance to the other person, and (3) some sort of self-feeling, such as pride or mortification at one's appearance.[22]

Each person has more than one ego. The following points indicate the type of ego that each person has.

1. *Ego ideal.* Each person has a conception of himself as he wants to be. The beginning public school teacher sees himself as principal of the school, whereas the high school graduate sees herself married to a rich banker, living in the prestigious section of town. As the mayor of a midwestern town remarked, "There are 2,000 presidents born in this town every year." He was speaking of the aspirations of the younger generation, illustrating the ego ideal which is inborn in all. Each of us

---

[21] Maxwell Maltz, *Psycho-Cybernetics* (New York: Prentice, Hall, Inc., 1960), p. 2.
[22] Charles Horton Coolie, *Human Nature and the Social Order* (New York: Charles Scribners Sons, 1912), p. 152.

should honestly face the question, "What do I want in life? What is my ideal? Do I want a loving-relationship with another person more than anything else? Do I want exaltation and the applause of men more than anything else? Do I want security, ease, and freedom from fear more than anything else?"

2. *Ego as others see us.* The poet Robert Burns said, "O . . . to see ourselves as others see us." This might strengthen some personalities, yet shatter others. Some people imagine themselves as well liked by their friends, when really behind their backs they are laughed at. One pastor who thought he was successful was unaware of the fact that the board had called a secret meeting to discuss how to get a resignation without hurting the pastor's feelings.

3. *The self-image.* The self-image is how a person sees himself in his honest moments. When he lies on his bed at night and sleep escapes him, he sees himself as he really is. This self-image can be divided into seven categories.

a. *Content.* When a person thinks of himself, what is the content of the self-picture? Does he see himself as intelligent or a loving human being? Some may think of themselves as being interested in sports, while others feel they have good human relations. An artist? A businessman? An athlete? Or an unhappy person? All these form the content of one's self-image.

b. *Direction.* Direction means consideration of your self-image as favorable or unfavorable. Does one have a favorable attitude toward his self-image? Some see themselves in the "best light," while others have an unfavorable attitude. A 19-year-old boy said, "I never do anything right."

c. *Intensity.* A person may feel very strongly about either a favorable or unfavorable attitude toward himself. The high school boy who has a strong, favorable attitude toward himself may be called an egotist. One such egotist was overheard, "I may not be the best in the world, but you won't find anyone better." In the same way a person may be intense in his self-hatred. He may hate himself enough to commit suicide, yet not have the courage to do so.

Also, there may be weak feelings toward one's self image. A teenager may have a positive or poor image of himself but the intensity of his feelings about himself are weak.

d. *Importance.* This involves a consideration of how important the individual is in his own thinking. A person may have a weak or strong opinion of himself, yet thoughts about his self may not take up much of his thinking. His self-image is not important to

him. On the other hand, some teenagers are so important to themselves, they are egotistical; they think of nothing else.

e. *Stability.* Some people have a consistent, firm attitude concerning
themselves. " I know I'll make good in business someday," expressed a teenager. This was a stable self-image he held throughout life. Even through several setbacks, he saw himself being
successful in business and eventually one day succeeded. Stability
of self-image deals with the intensity, importance, and direction
given the self-image. Am I strong in my feeling of self-esteem?
Do I consider myself as an important subject? Do I have a favorable attitude toward myself? If the answer is a stable yes, then
the person has a stable self-image.

f. *Consistency.* Consistency deals with the content of our self-image.
Do I usually see myself in the same role? If the teenager vacillates
from truck driver to college professor to airline pilot, he is inconsistent. However, if his self-image remains in the area, say of
sports, then he is consistent in his self-attitude. Consistency deals
with continuity of self-image. Stability deals with intensity, direction, and importance.

g. *Clarity.* Some people have a clear, sharp picture of themselves.
Others have a vague, hazy, and sometimes blurred self-image. It
is as though they were viewing their lives through a rain-spattered
glass.

One cannot generalize about people and call them introverts and
extroverts as has been done in the past. These seven categories indicate
the personality can have many dimensions. Thus, if one can learn what
the individual sees when he looks at himself, he may determine better
how this individual will function in life.

4. *Negative ego.* Most people not only know who they are, but
many know who they are not, as well as who they do not want to be.
The Christian housewife knows she is not a prostitute and is horrified
at the thought of sexual intercourse with anyone but her husband. The
bookkeeper knows he is not lazy and would not become like those who
take multiple coffee breaks or "lags" in work assignments. The negative
self is like the stabilizer of an airplane, giving a straight course through
turbulent winds.

There seems to be a type of vicious circle in determining one's real
ego or self-esteem. What one is or what he sees himself as, determines
what he does. And what he does determines how he sees himself, which
in turn determines his basis for self-esteem.

With no attempt there can be no failure: with no failure, no humiliation.

So our self-feeling in this world depends entirely on what we *back* ourselves to be or do.[23]

Rosenberg makes a distinction between *self-estimate* and *self-value*. Self-estimate is how the individual actually rates himself with regard to a particular personality characteristic. The term "self-value" indicates how much the individual cares about the quality of his personality. Rosenberg indicates that the term "self-esteem" refers to the individual's overall self-acceptance or self-rejection. Therefore, self-estimate and self-value are part of the bricks and mortar of self-esteem.

Since self-values are of such importance to the individual, they raise the broader question: what social and psychological factors influence the selection of self-values?

The motivation in selection of self-values is wide and variant. For example, a teenage girl identifies with her mother and values those qualities in her mother that are outstanding or emphasized by the mother. However, if the teenage girl is rebellious to her mother, she may mimic or identify with those qualities that the mother lacks or disdains.

There is one motivation for selection of self-values that cannot be disputed. People select self-values which maintain or enhance their self-esteem. A person selects a system of self-values which builds his self-estimates. If a girl thinks she is good at sports, she may decide that athletic qualities are important to her. If a boy thinks he is poor at music, he may decide that he does not care about artistic expression. In Rosenberg's study of 5,024 high school students, 80 percent of those who considered themselves good academic students said they cared a great deal about academic quality. At the same time, only 12 percent of those students who considered themselves rather poor in academics said they cared a great deal about attaining good grades. Rosenberg concluded, "In the long run, we would expect most people to value those things in which they are good, and to try to become good at those things they value." [24] However, there is always the person who strives in the face of disappointment and physical impossiblity to be good at the thing he knows inwardly he cannot attain. This "martyr" needs help to understand his own self-image.

Rosenberg makes another observation, "If each person can choose his own values, we are led to an interesting paradox of social life, namely, that almost everyone can consider himself superior to almost everyone else, so long as he can use his own system of values." [25] A boy

---

[23] William James, cited in Rosenberg, *Society and the Adolescent Self Image*, pp. 309–10.
[24] Rosenberg, *Society and the Adolescent Self Image* p. 250.
[25] *Ibid.*, p. 251.

who is a good football player considers himself to be better than the other boys on the youth committee at church. The three other boys consider themselves superior to other committee members. One is on the honor roll at school, another has excelled in the school orchestra, and the last considers himself physically handsome. Each boy may acknowledge the superiority of the others in qualities which he considers unimportant. This feeling of superiority is not necessarily wrong; sometimes it may build strong ego strength and add worth to life. But, in other students it may build pride and poor relationships with other people.

Many teenagers get into trouble because their self-values are not equal to their ability. A high school junior envisions himself making the first string basketball team while he does not have the coordination. Joan, a high school senior with limited ability, plans to enter music in college and ultimately make her living through music. How do people arrive at wrong self-values for life?

1. Self-values are acquired long before the opportunity to test them adequately. A child from a musical family may learn to value and desire musical skill, but only later in life does he become aware that he has insufficient talent for his desire. He must change his self-image and self-values. However, Rosenberg points out a problem, "Self-values, particularly if established early and reinforced by 'significant others' may be quite difficult to change even if, at a later time, it is the individual's interest to do so." [26] Few people change their life's occupation after age 40, even though they are unhappy in their present occupation. Their self-image has molded them into a niche, and to change their occupation would be to reject themselves.

2. Self-values relate to goals as means relate to ends. The young student in college sees himself as a physicist (goal), yet he has no value or desire to algebra (means); but this boy has grown up in a home where his father was a teacher of mathematics in junior high school. The aspirations of the father were implanted into the self-image of the son. The boy cannot give up his self-image of becoming a physicist because that would be denying himself. Yet, there is no love for algebra.

In the same way a girl has a self-image of being a wife (goal). The church she attends tells her to give little if any importance to physical or social attractiveness (means). Since physical and social attractiveness are relevant means for attaining the goal of marriage, they are important to her and cannot be easily dismissed from her mind. She does not want to give up her goal of being married; therefore, she has conflict with her church over the "avenue" to marriage.

---

[26] *Ibid.*, p. 301.

3. Self-values are derived from the community norms and may not be in keeping with the self-image of the individual. Fred is a college freshman who sees himself as a good Christian. He is from a Christian home and at an early age learned what is right and wrong, what is important and unimportant. Now, as a Christian away from home and attending a secular college, he finds himself in conflict with the university morals. He finds that he desires the approval of his classmates. He wants to excel in terms of their values, not his own. He can enhance his own self-esteem by abandoning their values which are not appropriate to his self-image. However, he is likely to call down upon himself the disapproval and contempt of the university crowd. Rejection by the university crowd probably would diminish his self-esteem and bring worse conflict. Self-values cannot be changed just to suit the convenience of the personality. Self-values are a part of the personal philosophy or orientation to life.

To change one's life, one must change his self-image. But how does one change his self-image? There must be some motivation for deciding that the old picture of oneself is in error and that one needs a new picture. There are many factors that cause a person to decide the present self-image is inadequate. First, his experience may show that he is not happy or cannot produce by the present self-image. The college professor sees himself as an excellent instructor in English literature. Yet, not a single sophomore signs up for his elective, and his required course is taken only because students cannot get into other sections. The dean calls the college instructor in and tells him perhaps teaching is not his gift. Experience shows the college professor that he must change his self-image. Perhaps he is better at research.

A second reason for changing one's self-image is "new knowledge" about oneself. Jerry, a high school sophomore, had a self-image of himself as "second-rate academically." After taking an IQ test, Jerry was told that he had an IQ of 130. For the past four years Jerry had been telling himself that he was not able to do high school work. Therefore, he was going to take a vocational course. After hearing that he "had it," Jerry began to apply himself and was soon scoring above average.

Third, one's self-image changes because of new relationships. Through a meaningful relationship one learn a new worth of himself. Rebecca had been a high school junior classified as a "loner." She was chubby, yet cute. Because she had few close friends, her life was wrapped up in reading novels, homework, and serving as a nurse's aid. Frank noticed her and dated her once . . . twice . . . three times. Rebecca's life changed because of the new relationship. When Frank told her that she was "cute," she tried to become the girl that he wanted her to be.

In life, many act and feel, not according to what things really are like, but according to what their imagination tells them they are like. Twelve-year-old David finishes a piano recital, and his ability is average. However, parents, friends, and buddies tell him that he is great. In actuality, he made several mistakes, and his nervousness put the audience on edge. Yet, the compliments of friends and parents convinced David that he was good. Next time he played at a recital, his nervousness was gone because he thought he was good, and he performed without error —just as he had done in practice.

Eleven-year-old Mike stands up before the Christmas pageant to recite Luke 2:1-20. He supposes that his buddies in the back row are sitting there laughing at him. In actuality they envied him for they wanted the part. But he imagined his buddies in rollicking laughter. Therefore, his emotional and nervous reactions were the same as if he had faced hoots and cat-calls.

It follows that if one's ideas and mental images concerning himself are distorted or unrealistic, then one's environment will likewise be inappropriate. Therefore, what should be done?

1. *Be sure you are right then go ahead.* My father used to tell me, "Son, people won't always like you nor will you always do the *perfect* thing." Dad knew that I was human, even though he wanted me to do the best. Then he would tell me, "Be sure you are right, then go ahead." If a person sees himself doing the right thing, he will have confidence and self-esteem.

2. *Most people will give us the break that we give them.* The average person on the street is not a cruel, vindictive villain looking for opportunities to kick us in the face or knife us in the back. Most persons will give us the opportunity that we give them. Still, one cannot generalize about human nature. There is always the hot-tempered, loud-mouthed person who will criticize everything. A high school algebra teacher who fit this description was called by his students "wall-to-wall mouth."

3. *Picture yourself mastering each situation.* Most of us tend to do this. This can be called "mental role-playing." One simply imagines himself in various situations, then acts out in his mind what he will do and say whenever the situation comes up in real life. This will give one poise when the situation finally arrives. Also, a person will realize that his actions and feelings are the result of his own self-image. This gives a person the level called confidence that psychology has always maintained is needed to change his personality and life.

4. *Self-knowledge makes you less vulnerable to hypothetical fear.* Too many are dependent upon other people's applause and support. These people become hurt by tiny pinprick criticism or so-called "omis-

sions" by their friends. Those who are most easily offended and those who rely heavily on other people are those who have the lowest self-esteem. However, teenagers who have strong self-esteem can take the "slams" because they have a true or strong picture of themselves. If a person feels undeserving, doubts his own ability, or has a poor opinion of himself, he will usually crumble at the slightest criticism.

Dr. Maxwell Maltz gives the following advice to patients, "Relax away emotional hurts." He explains his cure as follows:

> I once had a patient ask me: "If the forming of scar tissue is a natural and automatic thing, why doesn't scar tissue form when a plastic surgeon makes an incision?
>
> The answer is that if you cut your face and it "heals naturally," the scar tissue will form because there is a certain amount of tension in the wound and just underneath the wound which pulls the surface of the skin back, creating a "gap" so to speak, which is filled in by scar tissue. When a plastic surgeon operates, he not only pulls the skin together closely with sutures, he also cuts out a small amount of flesh underneath, so there is no tension present. The incision heals smoothly; even then, there isn't a distorting scar.
>
> It is interesting to note that the same thing happens in the case of an emotional wound. If there is no tension present, there is no disfiguring emotional scar left.
>
> Have you ever noticed how easy it is to "get your feelings hurt or "take offense" when you are suffering tensions brought out by frustrations, fear and/or depression?
>
> This simple everyday experience illustrates very well the principle that we are injured or hurt emotionally, not so much by other people or what they say or don't say, but by *our own attitude* and *our own response*.[27]

There is a difference in the self-values of boys and girls. In the process of boys identifying with boys and girls identifying with girls, there is a good bit of similarity, but there are also important differences. In Rosenberg's test, girls consistently gave importance to such self-values as: interpersonal harmony, friendliness, sociability, pleasantness, ability to get along well with people, and virtue. The list of self-values of boys included: physical courage, toughness, athletic ability, interpersonal control, dominance in their relationship with others, ability to get people to do what you want, freedom from naivete, and versatility (boys are likely to care about being good at many different kinds of things).[28]

Even though boys have certain self-values that are different from

---

[27] Maltz, p. 143.
[28] Rosenberg, p. 301.

girls, both boys and girls have some similar characteristics. Both groups tend to consider it important to be intelligent, to be sociable and well-liked, to be dependable and reliable, to have "interpersonal courage" (i.e., to stand up for your rights), to be independent and self-reliant, and to be mature (i.e., not to behave childishly).[29]

---

[29] *Ibid.*, p. 254.

8

A BIBLICAL PERSPECTIVE OF IDENTITY

The Biblical concept of self in the Christian is one of the most important issues in helping a teen, or any other person, discover and establish his self-identity. Every Christian—every person who has received Jesus Christ into his life—is a new and different person (II Cor. 5:17). God has added to his life. God has created, or actually re-created, the person into a new being with a new nature. When Jesus Christ spoke of this process, He called it a birth from above, a spiritual birth or rebirth produced by God the Spirit (John 3:3ff.).The old manner of life for the Christian has been left behind, and a new one has taken its place. Therefore, the Christian has, or should have, a new lifestyle and a new mind-set i.e., a new way of thinking and looking at things. Therefore, the Christian is a new and different being or self.

The Christian is also an individual who is loved totally and unconditionally by God. There is nothing that can ever separate the Christian from this love, according to Romans 8:31-39. Nothing he does in this life ("neither death nor life," v. 38), nor anything that is alive will ever separate him from God's love. Because God's love for him is assured, because he does not have to earn love, the Christian can have a deeper security than others. God loves the Christian as he is, whatever his true self may be. This is not to say, however, that God does not expect the Christian to become more Christ-like. He does expect that. The Chris-

133

tian can rest secure in the knowledge of God's love, while discovering his true self.

When God re-created the Christian, He added a new dimension, a new potential, to the Christian's self. This new dimension is Jesus Christ's power in the Christian (Phil. 4:13). The Christian is now able to conquer whatever situation he encounters (Rom. 8:37). The Christian has the strength to face and overcome his circumstances and surroundings because Jesus Christ is producing in him the power to do so. Therefore, the Christian can have a greater confidence than his contemporaries—as self-confidence in Christ.

God has provided for the Christian all that is necessary to be a total person. The Christian can be a person with real love, not only for his friends, but for his enemies as well; he can express the very love of God (Rom. 5:5). He can have that deep, inner joy that remains through trying circumstances because it is the joy of Jesus Christ Himself (John 15:11). The Christian can also have an unshakable peace of mind, totally incomprehensible to those around him, which remains even when things go wrong; it is Jesus Christ's peace (John 14:27). The same applies for the rest of the fruit of the Spirit (Gal. 5:22-23): patience, kindness, faithfulness, gentleness, and self-control. These are qualities of life that the Holy Spirit produces in the Christian's life. These qualities characterized the life of Jesus Christ Himself. God has provided these so that the Christian can be a complete, Christlike being.

The pertinent question at this point is how these characteristics, how this potential can be integrated into the self and realized in daily life. The key is the Holy Spirit, who produced the new life in the Christian (John 3:5,6), and He is the one who energizes the new nature of the Christian (Gal. 5:16,25; 3:3-5). The Holy Spirit is also the One who helps the Christian realize more fully the love of God (Rom. 5:5). The Holy Spirit is the one who produces the power and dynamic of the new life (Eph. 3:16). He is also the One who produces the qualities of the Christ-like life (Gal. 5:22). This is why the Christian is commanded to allow himself to be continually filled by the Holy Spirit (Eph. 5:18). The word "fill" means the person is so full of what fills him (Holy Spirit) that he is completely under its control. In this case, He provides both the direction and power for the person's actions. Three conditions are necessary for the filling of the Holy Spirit. The Christian must confess sin that is in his life because sin hinders the work of the Holy Spirit (Eph. 4:30; I Thess. 5:19), as well as the Christian's fellowship with God (I John 1:5-9). The Christian must also yield his life to God, turning it over completely to God's control

(Rom. 6:11-13; 12:1; Eph. 5:18). Finally, the Christian is filled by the Holy Spirit and lives his life under the Spirit's control by faith (Gal. 5:25 cf. Col. 2:6; Gal. 2:20). This last aspect is most vital and is the key to the consistent Spirit-filled Christian life (Rom. 14:23; Heb. 11: 6; Gal. 5:5, 6). Faith in this respect is an utter and total dependence on the Holy Spirit's power, as well as the certainty that this power is in operation in his life, in every situation the Christian faces.

The Spirit-filled life is not only vital in the realization and integration of everything God has intended for the Christian as a new and total person, it is also absolutely necessary for the Christian in order to discover what his new self-identity should be and become, as God intended it (I Cor. 2:12). The Holy Spirit assists the Christian in seeing who he is, who he has been made and what he has been given by God, and who he can and should become as a person. The Holy Spirit enables a person to recognize his actual self and empowers him to realize his potential self (John 16:13; II Cor. 3:18). This knowledge helps close the gap between these two "selves" and assists to harmonize the various aspects of self-image. In fact, not only does the presence of the Holy Spirit mean the Christian's potential self can be more effectively realized, his potential self has been increased since he has become a new person.

The Spirit-filled life is not a cure-all for identity crisis, but it is an absolute necessity for the proper solution of it. If the Christian teen is living the Spirit-filled life, he will be able to more readily discover and more effectively establish his self-identity. This is true because he is following God's direction and using God's power; it is also true because he is allowing the Author of the Bible to use the Bible to help him understand and achieve self-identity. This last statement cannot be overemphasized. It is in the Bible that the Christian, under the Holy Spirit's guidance and teaching (John 16:13-15), finds the facts and materials from which he needs to establish a Christian self-identity.

Thought Questions

Section Three

(Covers Chapter 6, "Adolescence: A Time of Identity Crisis," Chapter 7, "How Self-Identity is formed in Teens," and Chapter 8, "A Biblical View of Identity.")

1. What happens to youth during puberty?
2. What effect does physical development have on the emerging self-identity?
3. What is self-identity?

4. Why is the "identity crisis" a relatively new area of study?

5. How is maturity and a strong self-identity similar?

6. The teen has more than one self-identity; what are some of the others?

7. How does spiritual growth help the teen to develop a strong self-identity?

8. Does family discipline or permissiveness develop a healthy ego?

9. Why do some teens wear a mask?

10. What role does having early-teen heroes play in developing a healthy ego?

11. What hero makes the greatest impression on youth?

12. What importance does criticism have on ego development?

13. Why do teens play roles? What are some of the roles played by teens?

14. Explain the difference between an ideal-ego and a negative-ego.

15. How do self values form the ego?

16. Why is a "loner" a potential problem teen?

17. What will proper self-identity knowledge do for a teen?

18. When does emphasis on the ego become pride (hence becoming sinful)?

19. What can a Christian do to have a healthy ego? How can the child of God gain a proper self-identity?

20. What relationship does the new birth have to identity crisis?

SECTION FOUR

THE PURPOSE OF MINISTRY TO YOUTH

What are commonly expressed aims in church youth work?

Should every youth meeting be an evangelistic meeting?

When should youth worship the Lord?

Does a coffee-house ministry reflect the main aim of youth work in a church?

Why do some youth workers put more stress on the rededication service than do evangelicals?

When does a youth group begin to die?

9

THE AIMS OF CHURCH YOUTH WORK

This is the most important chapter in this volume, because aims determine all that is done or not accomplished in youth work. If a youth pastor has "relevancy" as an aim, then his program will be reflected with coffee houses, rock music or street demonstrations. "Relevancy" raises the question, "How much of the contemporary society should be adapted into a youth ministry?" Or, the opposite viewpoint poses a question, "How much can the youth ministry resemble the New Testament?"

This chapter has a simple thesis: *The aims of youth work are no different than the aims of a local church.* The youth are part of a local church, but that does not mean their aims are *partial* rather than *wholistic.* Many traditional youth programs have had partial church aims, i.e. they have adapted some but not all the aims found in Scripture. For many years youth work has centered around the Training Union or the training hour. The catalyst of ministry to youth has been a training approach that centered on Sunday afternoon programs. Most Christian educators agree that this approach now accomplished limited results. At one time Christian Endeavor dominated church ministry to youth. The catalyst of Christian Endeavor was a worship approach. The Christian Endeavor approach, like the Training Union approach, only had partial aims rather than incorporating all the aims of Scripture.

This chapter maintains "wholistic aims" are needed in youth work. When a youth pastor plans his program, he should attempt to fulfill every biblical command.

This chapter makes a distinction between aims of youth work (aims guide our activity) and the goals of youth work (a goal is the ultimate purpose toward which the process is moving). Some educators claim there is no distinction between aims and goals. However, the careful student will discover that, just as there is a distinction between the two, so there is a distinction between aims and goals, as well as a correlation. A valid aim points in some direction, it is directed to a goal. For the most part, aims are active and goals are passive. Aims are likened unto the bow and arrow held in the hands of the archer; he must give proper direction—his aim must be correct. The goals are likened unto the target, it gives perspective to the process called archery. The archer aims; when the arrow misses the target, it reveals the aim was wrong.

A youth worker needs clear aims to give purpose and direction to his energies. Vieth said, "Aims . . . are the outcome of one's philosophy of Christian Education." [1] The correct philosophy of youth work grows out of the Word of God and is not a creation by man. Biblical youth work obeys the commands of the Word of God; therefore, the aim of youth work is to carry out the aim of the New Testament.

Eavey states that, "An aim is attention brought to focus to make possible expenditure of energy for achieving a predetermined purpose." [2] Many youth workers are not clear in their aim, as a result they "spin their wheels" and accomplish little for God. Hard work or sincerity will not accomplish eternal results if the youth pastor is not guided by biblical aims. Correct aims are important. The clearer the aims, the more can be accomplished by the youth worker in the lives of young people. Therefore, this chapter is an attempt to give clear New Testament aims for youth work. Fallaw notes, "Aims are immediate steps taken one after the other in class sessions toward goals which keep the teacher and pupil moving on the way to achievement of the final goal." [3] Therefore, there are many aims for youth work. But each aim should interrelate to give direction to the process. In a Sunday School class the youth worker has several aims: he wants to communicate biblical content and to get teens to respond to the gospel; also he wants teens to

---

[1] Paul H. Vieth, *Objectives in Religious Education* (New York: Harper & Bros., 1930), p. 45.
[2] C. B. Eavey, *Introduction to Evangelical Christian Education*, ed. by J. Edward Hakes (Chicago: Moody Press, 1968), p. 55.
[3] Wesner Fallaw, *Church Education for Tomorrow* (Philadelphia: Westminster Press), p. 146.

have Christian fellowship. These are several aims, leading to a definite goal—the maturity of the young person.

One broad goal of all Christian activity is "to glorify God." This is the predominant theme of the Psalms and should control all that is done by the Christian teenager. The shorter catechism asks, *Q.* "What is the chief end of man?" *A.* "Man's chief end is to glorify God and to enjoy Him forever." [4] Christian teens should glorify God; however, it is sometimes difficult to know *how* to glorify God. The best way to glorify God, is to carry out the aims of the New Testament. When we fulfil the biblical aims, we give our attention to the biblical goal which is to glorify God (the end result). Eavey gives a definition of goal: "A goal is the ultimate purpose or destination towards which the educational process is moving. Aims assist in achieving the goal(s). Goals are the objectives which one seeks to attain." [5]

The aim of all youth work is the aim of Calvary: to bring lost people into right relationship to God. The ultimate goal is that God is glorified. There isn't a better way to glorify God than through salvation of the lost. Steps to be taken in accomplishing this goal come from many directions, and lead to one goal—the glory of God (see chart for comparison of aims and goals).

The Aims of Youth Work

The aims of the church are the aims of youth work. There is no place in Scripture where God spells out a different set of aims for young people than for all Christians. Also, there is no place in Scripture where God spells out a different set of aims for the youth program from the aims of the local church.

The Great Commission contains the aims for the local church. This is the last command Jesus gave before returning to heaven and has been characterized as the strategy for the church.

"Go therefore and make disciples of all nations, baptising them in the name of the Father and the Son and the Holy Spirit, teaching them to observe all that I commanded you; and lo, I am with you always even to the end of the age" (Matt. 28:19,20 The New American Standard Bible).

The Great Commission has three aspects but is one command: (1) evangelism, (2) baptism and (3) teaching. Christian young people cannot choose what aspect of the Great Commission they will obey. Since it is one command, to disobey part makes one disobedient. If a youth worker only emphasizes teaching and neglects evangelism, he is

[4] *The Shorter Catechism,* ratified by the General Assembly of the Presbyterian Church in the United States. (Richmond: John Knox Press, n.d.), p. 3.
[5] Eavey, *An Introduction to Evangelical Christian Education,* p. 56.

not carrying out the Great Commission. God's strategy is evangelism, baptism and education. Youth programs that do not include baptism are not biblical youth programs, although what they may be accomplishing may be good.

The first aspect of the Great Commission is found in the word "teach" (verse 19), which is translated *disciple*. We are commanded to go disciple (evangelize) all nations. Implied in the word "disciple" is reaching the lost, communicating the gospel to them and leading them to Jesus Christ. When we are discipling (evangelizing), we are causing teenagers to follow Jesus Christ. Hence, true New Testament evangelism gets people to follow Jesus Christ and His commands. Therefore, youth work involves more than presenting the gospel to the unsaved or sharing salvation with them. We should attempt to persuade them to become Christians, causing the unsaved to follow Jesus Christ. The youth worker should get his young people to follow Jesus Christ, and when they do, the youth worker has a successful youth ministry. There is no success in the Lord's work without successes. Therefore, we want more than large crowds of youth to follow Christ. We want youth to become His disciples.

The following outline gives the full implications of a biblical youth program. Your youth program will be successful if you apply all the aims of the New Testament.

I. EVANGELISM

(Disciple, Matthew 28:19)

Overall Aim: To make disciples of as many people in the world as possible.

1. *By showing compassion on the needs of man.* The first aim in youth work is a heart of compassion for teens. When Jesus saw the multitudes, He was moved with compassion (Matt. 9:36). This is love translated into action. You reflect compassion by getting up at 2:00 a.m. to counsel with a teenager who has run away from home or by giving up a favorite television program to go soul-winning. The first biblical criterion for effective youth work is love for teens.

2. *By having a vision of what God can do for the lost.* The second step in evangelism is vision. You must have a vision of what God can do in the life of your young people and through your youth group. First, vision involves faith, you believe God can change their life, therefore you work to that end. You believe God can bring revival to the youth of your city, therefore you plan evangelistic programs. Before you can have a great youth group, you must have vision. Second, vision involves

foresight, and this lies in the youth director. As a man of God, you must have the ability to: (1) See first, (2) see most, and (3) see farthest into the future. Just as the Old Testament prophet was called a seer, you must be the eyes of God and see the world as God sees it. "Jesus went about all the cities and villages, teaching in their synagogues, and preaching the gospel of the kingdom, and healing every sickness and every disease among the people. But when he saw the multitudes, he was moved with compassion on them, because they fainted, and were scattered abroad, as sheep having no shepherd" (Matt. 9:35,36). If you want to build a great youth work, you must have a great vision of what God can do through your teenagers.

The third aspect of vision is insight into young people. You must see the degradation of sin and the damnation of sin. The degradation of sin ruins their lives now and the damnation of sin will send them to hell in the future.

The final aspect of vision concerns seeing God. You must have a correct vision into the nature and person of God. God wants to work through you; He loves teens and He can transform their lives. You must have a correct view of Scripture to have a correct vision of God. Since the Bible is the foundation of correct doctrine, you cannot build a biblical youth work without building on the Bible.

3. *By bringing the lost under the hearing of the gospel.* You cannot assume that young people want to come to a youth meeting or desire to come to church. It is your duty to reach them. Reaching is defined: "Motivating a young person to give an honest hearing to the gospel." You have not evangelized the young people in your community until you have reached them for Christ. This is simply using every acceptable means to (1) make contact with lost young people, (2) motivate them to come under the sound of the gospel, and (3) having an attractive program to present the gospel. Most fundamental churches neglect to reach teenagers. The apostle Paul defines reaching as: "And unto the Jews I became as a Jew, that I might gain Jews; to them that are under the law, as under the law, that I might gain them that are under the law . . . to the weak became I as weak, that I might gain the weak: I am made all things to all men, that I might by all means save some" (I Cor. 9:20-22).

Reaching is using every acceptable means to communicate the gospel to young people: radio, newspapers, visitation, activities, retreats, evangelistic services, mailings, telephone, bumper stickers, tracts, testimonies, etc. However, a youth leader cannot do *everything* to reach young people. A rock concert to get young people in church would not fit the criterion of reaching, because we have not motivated them to give an honest hearing to the gospel. Reaching must be controlled by a New Testament aim and accomplish a New Testament goal.

A youth program cannot use every technique and gimmick, even if it works. One fundamental church had a contest whereby a church-worker rode a minibike down the aisle of the church sanctuary, indicating that the teen who brought the most visitors could win the minibike. Even if the youth director attempts to get the visitors saved, is this an acceptable method? A pastor recently said, "I will do anything to get people saved!" Anything? Would he lie, coaxing people to church by promising something he couldn't deliver?

Obviously, every technique is not acceptable to the youth worker who attempts to live by the standard of Scripture. Principles and techniques must be controlled by biblical aims and accomplish biblical goals. If not, they are rejected as being unbiblical.

4. *By sharing one's Christian experiences with the lost.* Young people love to share their testimonies with others. The New Testament calls this witnessing. "Ye shall be witnesses unto me" (Acts 1:8). The witness is one who shares his experience. A person who sees an accident and is called into the court as a witness, is not expected to give his opinion of who caused the accident. He testifies what he has seen or experienced. His opinion or interpretation of the accident is not allowed. Just so, teenagers should witness to others what Jesus Christ has done for them. (1) They should witness what they have seen of Christ, (2) what they have heard of Christ, and (3) what they have experienced. The changed life is the best testimony for Jesus Christ. When Peter and John were called before the council concerning their preaching, they gave the following witness: "For we cannot but speak the things which we have seen and heard" (Acts 4:20). This was a witness and not a sermon to the council. In the same trial, the healed man who had been lame from birth stood with Peter and John. He shared with the council what had happened to his life: "And beholding the man which was healed standing with them, they could say nothing against it" (Acts 4:14). His testimony was an effective tool of evangelism.

Give your young people many opportunities to share their testimony when winning souls or when just "rapping" with other teenagers.

5. *By communicating the gospel to all men.* Teenagers love to share, but they need to go farther than giving their subjective experiences. They need to give the factual content of the gospel. The gospel gets lost teenagers saved. This is preaching, whether the gospel is given to one or to a multitude. Many youth groups employ the colloquy, or buzz groups in the programs; however, God has promised to bless old-fashioned preaching. Preaching gets teenagers saved. Dr. Lewis S.

Chafer, past president of Dallas Theological Seminary, often said, "You haven't preached the gospel until you have given people something to believe." Jokes and deathbed illustrations make teenagers laugh or weep, but the content of the gospel (biblical facts) saves the soul.

Preaching is simply a clear and complete presentation of the content of the gospel to lost people. It is more than teaching. Teaching gives the facts of the gospel, preaching gives biblical content with persuasion and compassion to convince the audience to become Christians. Many American churches talk about evangelism, proclaiming the gospel to the lost. New Testament churches talk about soul-winning, proclaiming the gospel with persuasion.

The gospel is twofold. First, it is *propositional* truth, the fact that Jesus died for sins. He was buried and He rose again the third day. All people should hear this message because Christ died for all. However, the second aspect of the gospel is *personal* truth, Jesus Christ is the gospel. A lost teenager may understand the propositional truth of the gospel, i.e. the fact that Jesus died, was buried and rose again, yet not be converted. Salvation is more than understanding. The lost teenager must receive a person—Jesus Christ. Jesus Christ saves the teenager from sin. Christ must live in the heart of the teenager for him to become a Christian (John 1:12).

Some youth groups are satisfied to have a small intimate coffee-house ministry, because this fulfills their aims. Other youth groups have a dynamic evangelistic outreach aimed at evangelizing every teen in the city. The youth of Canton Baptist Temple (Ohio) attempted to win every teen in the city to Jesus Christ. They rented a booth at the county fair, went into the parks on Sunday afternoon to witness to every teen and then went door to door. Mr. Mel Sabaka, youth director, believes every person is lost and every person should be saved, therefore, he has a super-aggressive program.

6. *By persuading the lost to receive the gospel.* Persuasion is a conscious attempt to motivate lost people to accept Jesus Christ and repent of their sins. The youth pastor urges teenagers to repent and believe. Some people dislike the invitation at the end of a gospel message, where young people are invited to come forward and receive Jesus Christ. An invitation may put teenagers on the spot, but it is biblical persuasion, inviting them to be saved. The lack of persuasion in today's preaching reveals a weakness in the church. Paul indicated, "Brethren, my heart's desire and prayer to God for Israel is, that they might be saved" (Rom. 10:1). In this same desire to persuade Israel, Paul said, "I have great heaviness and continual sorrow in my heart. For I could

wish that myself were accursed from Christ for my brethren" (Rom. 9:2,3).

The youth director does more than share the facts of the gospel with teens, he uses all the motivational devices at his command to get the youth to accept Jesus Christ. When the youth director preaches to youth, he uses humor, illustrations and "pithy sayings" to get youth to make a positive decision for Jesus Christ. However, emotional persuasion must be based on an intellectual communication of Bible content.

In my previous book *The Ten Largest Sunday Schools,* the pastors were successful in building the largest churches in America because of their priority given to evangelism, persuading the lost to receive Jesus Christ. This was reflected in the invitation (altar call) at the end of sermons. The primary purpose of a church is evangelism, reaching a town for Christ. One of the best contemporary examples of evangelism is the Thomas Road Baptist Church where the pastor, Jerry Falwell, characterizes his strategy of "Saturation Evangelism." He uses telephone, television, radio, public newspapers, a church newspaper, house-to-house visitation, Sunday School buses, posters, direct mailing, camping evangelism, alcoholic ministry, prison evangelism and many other outlets to saturate a community. Since the youth program should reflect church aims, the primary purpose of a youth group is to evangelize the youth of its community.

II. BAPTISM

(Church, Matthew 28:19)

Overall Aim: To identify each Christian with a local church.

The second major thrust of the Great Commission is to baptize the new convert immediately after salvation. Baptism is an outer symbol of inner reality. The convert is identified with Christ in His death, burial and resurrection. When the new Christian is placed under water, he is identified with Christ in His death and burial; when he is taken out of the water, his is identified with the resurrected life of Christ (Rom. 6:4,5). In the New Testament, when the believer was baptized, he also was added to the church (Acts 2:41,52). Just as baptism marks our being placed in Jesus Christ, so baptism marks our being placed in the body of Christ—the local church. Therefore, when Christ commanded the disciples to go and "baptize," He was commanding to go and "church" people, i.e. get them identified with a local church.

The key to successful, growing Christians is the continuous ministry of a local church. The lack of emphasis on local church evangelism is hurting God's cause on earth. Too much emphasis is placed on high school youth clubs, radio evangelism, coffee houses, and interchurch camping. These organizations may have a place in God's plan, but were never intended to take precedence over the local church. We live in a day when it is fashionable to attack the local church for its hypocrisy, lethargy, failure or lack of relevancy. Interdenominational agencies have risen to public attention because it is believed the church has failed. But the church, with all of its failures, is still the institution founded by Christ. The local church still has priority in God's plan of evangelism, education and edification.

The American economy emphasizes the independence of the individual. Teens are told to "do your own thing." The high school has made each teenager the "locus" of all decisions, meaning the youth is told he has the right to choose what is best for him within his own perspective. This influence has led to license on the part of many Christians. Many young people feel the church has no rightful claims upon their life. When Christian teenagers are not under the authority of the church, they are easily led off into doctrinal tangents, live unproductive lives and are slothful in service. True, the Christian teen has freedom in Jesus Christ, but this liberty is exercised within the framework of the local church. The church is never pictured in the Scripture as a social club; it is an organized army, equipped for battle, ready to charge the enemy. A good soldier is known for his discipline; he follows orders and is personally armed for battle. Christian young people should be under the discipline of the Word of God, which means also under church discipline. The local church has the following aims for all believers. These aims should be applied to the teenage congregation:

1. *By getting each believer under the discipline of the Scriptures.* The word "discipline" has a positive and negative connotation. Positive discipline is simply the constructive commands of the Word of God, preached and taught (I Cor. 14:3). In this way the Scripture edifies, exhorts, and comforts the believer. The Word of God sets doctrine straight and gives the teenagers a basis on which to live. Negative discipline corrects false doctrine and false living. When the youth pastor points out the sin of teenagers in his preaching, he is exercising negative discipline. He may counsel with a young person concerning attendance at a questionable amusement; this also is negative discipline. Discipline is not found in consensus of the deacons or in a congregational meeting. A disciple is disciplined and his standards are found in the Word of God.

The main reason a youth worker wants to get teenagers to attend church every Sunday or to come to a youth meeting, is to get them under the teaching of the Word of God. Some might criticize that youth pastors only want to count "nickels and noses." Some youth directors emphasize attendance to swell their ego or to win a contest. These are wrong reasons to stress church attendance. Teenagers should be in the house of God so they may hear the Word of God and grow thereby (I Pet. 2:2).

One weakness of the Jesus People is their opposition to the local church, which is a manifestation of their antiestablishment viewpoint. Most of them reflect the freedom cult of America and do as they please. Since the local church was instituted by Christ (Matt. 16:18), every teenage believer ought to be identified with a New Testament church which has oversight over his spiritual welfare.

2. *By using the total abilities of each Christian for God's purpose.* The second purpose for attempting to get teens in a church is to help involve them in Christian service. Every Christian ought to be involved in service, since every Christian has a gift. Paul indicated, "Every man hath his proper gift of God" (I Cor. 7:7). A gift is an ability to serve Jesus Christ and accomplish spiritual results. God gave these abilities to be used for His glory. Like the parable of the talents, if we don't use our abilities, God removes our opportunities. Therefore, the aim of churching people is to utilize their ability in service to God. If every young believer becomes involved, first the local church grows, and then the individual teen grows. The aim of a youth group is to have every young person spiritually trained and every young person active in service. Since God has given everything to the believer, the Christian teenager should be taught to give to God in return. The primary emphasis in the New Testament is the local church and Christian teenagers should feel their loyalty to the local church. First, it is their obligation to attend the primary services: Sunday School, morning and evening church and prayer meeting. This is a biblical stewardship of their time. Since the Christian is concerned about reaching the youth community, he should attend the primary youth meeting. Christian young people do not have the right to choose whether or not they will miss church services; they should attend services unless providentially hindered.

Christian teenagers should be taught to give their money to God; as a matter of fact, they should be taught as young children when they first begin attending Sunday School. Giving is the stewardship of their treasury.

The stewardship of talents is where every Christian young person serves Jesus Christ with the gifts that are his. Many times his service is through the youth program, other times through the larger church program.

3. *By encouraging fellowship among Christians so they may*

strengthen one another. Christians are urged to have fellowship for the purpose of edifying one another and supporting one another in their faith (I John 1:3-4). When youth share their testimonies, both the defeats and victories, they encourage others and are thereby encouraged. Many youth groups place small-group fellowship or Koinonia group dialogue as the main purpose for their existence. Although fellowship is biblical, it is not the main purpose for a youth group. Groups who minimize evangelism or the power of the gospel can never have biblical fellowship. The gospel makes teenagers one in Jesus Christ and He becomes a center on which they can have fellowship.

4. *By producing corporate worship and motivating Christians to private worship.* Worship is not an optional choice for teenagers, it is their obligation. They should worship both privately and publicly. Jesus noted, "But the hour cometh, and now is, when the true worshippers shall worship the Father in spirit and in truth: for the Father seeketh such to worship him" (John 4:23). Worship must be in spirit (enthusiasm or with one's total being) and in truth (accurate according to God's standards). "True worship" implies false worship. Jesus knew people would worship in the wrong way. You should be sure your teens worship according to the Scriptures. Since God wants worship from man, it is the teenager's duty to worship God. (See chapter on worship.) Worship is not man-centered, it is God-centered. Worship is not concerned with the needs of teenagers, it is the teenagers' concern with magnifying God. The accepted phrase *worth-ship* defines worship, for it is giving God the worth due to Him.

5. *By becoming the focus for an organized outreach into the community.* The unstable teen needs the stability of a local church. The church is a community of believers who exercise watch-care over the spiritual development of the teen. The human (sinful) nature does not like discipline so we have some teens who find it difficult to follow the leadership of the youth pastor. "The church is a group of baptized believers in whom Christ dwells, under the discipline of the Word of God, organized for evangelism, education, fellowship, worship and the administration of the ordinances." The church should have an organized evangelistic program. Paul reflects an organized outreach: "Have taught you publickly, and from house to house" (Acts 20:20). This organized spread of the gospel resulted in "All they which dwelt in Asia heard the Word of the Lord Jesus, both Jews and Greeks" (Acts 19:10).

An organized evangelistic program is complete in *kind* and *coverage.* All kinds of organized outreach should be included in a youth program: personal evangelism, mass evangelism, mailing evangelism, rest home and hospital evangelism, beach evangelism, and radio-TV evangelism. Also, complete evangelistic coverage includes: house-to-house visitation, rural evangelism, summer trips to Appalachia (home missions) and outreach to foreign mission fields.

A church is indwelt by Christ in a unique way (Rev. 1:13, 2:1), different from an interdenominational gathering, different than when two Christians gather for fellowship (Matt. 18:20). Christ is the light of the world (John 8:12), who shines out of a gathering of Christians into the darkness of this age. The youth group is an extension of the church and should reflect the light of the gospel into the youth community. Since God does all things decently and in order (I Cor. 14:40), the evangelistic outreach of the youth group should be systematic and comprehensive. When evangelism is haphazard (left up to the inclination of each believer) there is omission and overlapping in reaching the community. Some needy sections are overlooked and the popular "in" cause gets all the evangelistic attention.

6. *By administering the church's ordinances.* Both the Lord's table (I Cor. 11:23-26) and baptism (Matt. 28:19) are commanded. These are church ordinances and are administered by the church. Individuals and interdenominational agencies do not have the authority to administer these ordinances. If teens have not taken advantage of these symbols they are not obeying the commands of Scripture. Therefore, a well-rounded program to youth will include the correct use of the ordinances.

III. EDUCATION

(Matthew 28:20)

Overall Aim: To teach each Christian to obey the Scriptures.

The third aspect of the Great Commission is teaching or education. The church is given the responsibility of carrying out the example of Jesus the Teacher. He spent time with His disciples. The Sermon on the Mount begins with this observation, "His disciples came unto him: and He taught them" (Matt. 5:1,2). After He taught the disciples and the multitudes, we find this explanation. "He taught as one having authority, and not as the scribes" (Matt. 7:29). The content of Christian education is suggested in the Great Commission: "Teaching them to observe all things whatsoever I have commanded you" (Matt. 28:20).

A youth group is first aimed at evangelism, reaching the young people in the community for Jesus Christ. After the unsaved become Christians, they must be taught the Word of God. Also, you have attending your youth group young people who have grown up in a Christian home; these too must be taught the Word of God. Therefore, a youth program must have a strong teaching ministry. Even though teaching goes on in the Sunday School the youth pastor should use other meetings to teach his young people the Word of God. Remember, the priority of a youth program is evangelism, the focus is the church: education is a means to an end, never the goal of youth effort.

1. *By communicating the content of the Word of God.* The first educational aim of youth work is that every pupil should know the core doctrines contained in the Bible so that he will be protected from the contamination of sin, will be built up in the Christian life, will understand God's will for his life and become a productive Christian, winning others to Jesus Christ (Titus 1:9,27). The thrust of Christian education is Bible indoctrination, "teaching them to observe all things whatsoever I have commanded you" (Matt. 28:20). The word *doctrine* is simply the noun form of the verb *to teach.* Therefore, when we are teaching the Word of God, we are indoctrinating young people with the Scriptures. Jesus spoke concerning the subject matter of teaching, "Whatsoever I have said unto you" (John 14:26). As a result, Christian education is transmissive in nature. Some complain against indoctrination, indicating it lacks compassion for the student and is not experience-oriented. Indoctrination is usually interpreted to mean "rote learning" or simply "parroting" facts without understanding. However, the Scriptures indicate biblical teaching leads to understanding and that pupils should have experience with the Word of God (see Section VI on teaching). A biblical program of teaching young people aims at a complete, comprehensive, consistent attempt to communicate all of the Bible, meeting the students' needs.

2. *By training each Christian to use his skills to carry out God's plan for his life.* If teaching content is the first step of education, then training in skills is the second. Training puts content into operation that has been communicated in proposition form. Some make the Training Union program the catalyst of their youth ministry. To do so is to neglect the balanced ministry as seen in the Great Commission. However, other youth works have swung away from the unworkable Training Union, and have left out training altogether. This extreme also is wrong. Training puts into operation what is taught through theory. Jesus indicated in the Great Commission, "teaching them to observe" (Matt. 28:20). The aim of a church is to train young people to be able to adequately carry out their responsibility of evangelism, worship and service, in and out of the church.

The aim of training is good churchmanship where teenagers are good productive members of the house of God. "That thou mayest know how thou oughtest to behave thyself in the house of God, which is the church of the living God" (I Tim. 3:15).

3. *By including Christian values and attitudes to all believers.* The first aim of education has to do with content and the second aim has to do with skills. The third aim has to do with the attitudes of life, the area that has been ignored by many educators until recently. Teens' attitudes will reflect the quality of their Christian life. The church should aim to communicate Christian values and attitudes in accordance with the standards of the Scriptures. First, a teen's attitude is based on his knowledge of Scripture and, second, his knowledge is usually based on the completeness of the church youth program. First, build positive biblical attitudes as reflected in the fruit of the Spirit (Gal. 5:22,23), and reinforce negative attitudes so they will abstain from all appearance of evil (I Thess. 5:22).

4. *By motivating Christians to live a godly life as called for in the Scriptures.* Teaching biblical content without understanding will not produce growth in Christian teenagers. First, "The god of this world hath blinded the minds of them which believe not" (II Cor. 4:4). The unsaved cannot understand spiritual things (I Cor. 2:14); after salvation some of this inability remains. Therefore, biblical teaching takes away blindness and causes teenagers to grow in Christ. The youth director can only impart limited (natural) insight into the Word of God. The Holy Spirit is the one teacher who takes away spiritual blindness and causes teenagers to understand (supernatural) the Scriptures. "But the Comforter, which is the Holy Ghost, whom the Father will send in my name, he shall teach you all things, and bring all things to your remembrance, whatsoever I have said unto you" (John 14:26).

You want to give your young people more than Bible content; you want them to be fully matured in Jesus Christ. Paul spoke to his young babes in Christ that he wanted to give them his soul, "We were willing to have imparted unto you, not the gospel of God only, but also our own souls, because ye were dear unto us" (I Thess. 2:8). This is the ultimate aim of a youth pastor so that every young person would be as spiritually mature as he. Paul expressed it this way, "Be ye followers of me, even as I also am of Christ" (I Cor. 11:1).

5. *By supporting the aims and sanctity of the family.* The youth program cannot neglect the home, Christian or not. Your teens are exhorted, "Obey your parents in the Lord: for this is right" (Eph. 6:1). Therefore, your program is an extension of the influence of a good Christian home. The center of all that is taught in youth program is to respect the authority of parents and recognize the dignity of the family. "Honor thy father and mother; which is the first commandment with

Biblical Aims

Based on the Great Commission (Matt. 28:18-20)

A. To make disciples of as many persons in the world as possible (Matt. 28:18):
1. By showing compassion on the needs of man.
2. By having a vision of what God can do for the lost.
3. By bringing the lost under the hearing of the gospel.
4. By sharing one's Christian experience with the lost.
5. By communicating the gospel to all men.
6. By persuading the lost to accept the gospel.

B. To identify each Christian with a local church (Matt. 28:19):
1. By getting each Christian under the discipline of the Scriptures.
2. By using the total abilities of each Christian for God's purpose.
3. By encouraging fellowship among Christians so they may strengthen one another.
4. By producing corporate worship and motivating Christians to private worship.
5. By becoming the focus for an organized outreach into the community.
6. By administering the church ordinances.

C. To teach each Christian to be obedient to the Scriptures. (Matt. 28:20):
1. By communicating the content of the Word of God.
2. By training each Christian to use his skills to carry out God's plan for his life.
3. By inculcating Christian values and attitudes to all believers.
4. By motivating Christians to live a godly life as called for in the Scriptures.
5. By supporting the aims and sanctity of the family.

METHODS

PRINCIPLES

TECHNIQUES

Biblical Goals

Goals for a Christian

That Christians be mature (well rounded), equipped to carry out the aims of Scripture.

Goals for a Church

That biblical churches be planted to evangelize its community.

Goals for the World

That all persons in the world be evangelized.

Goals for eternity

That God be glorified in all ways.

promise" (Eph. 6:2). Many homes have failed the teen, but that does not give you the right to disobey God and deny the sanctity God requires for the home. You will have to respect parental wishes concerning late hours and dress standards. You will have to build into your youth a respect for their parents, even if they don't want to, because it is commanded by God.

Conclusion

Aims give direction to the youth worker, the goals are the outcome you desire. Aims give purpose to the youth worker planning a program; he uses goals after the program is finished to judge his results.

Techniques are the "way we operate" to accomplish youth work. The youth worker is not left to create technique on his own. Otherwise he might use drugs to get kids to "feel" Christianity or he might use a persuasive speaker (but lost) to convince youth to get saved. The results do not justify a technique. A technique must flow out of biblical aims and meet the demands of biblical goals. A Sunday School contest may be a gimmick that makes attendance grow, and kids attend because of its novelty, but they do not give an honest hearing to the gospel. Actually, the kids feel the gimmick cheapens God. Therefore, it is not a biblical technique, even though attendance swells.

The youth worker who attempts to follow the Great Commission will have clear aims for his ministry. First, God expects successful evangelism, that he win young people to the Lord. Next, converts must be baptized, which involves identifying him with the local church. Finally, teenagers should be taught the Word of God, be trained for Christian service, understand the meaning of Scriptures and assume the values and attitudes of the New Testament.

10

MATURITY—THE GOAL FOR CHURCH YOUTH

God wants each teen to grow: "Desire the sincere milk of the word, that ye may grow thereby" (I Peter 2:2). Growth is the process of life: children grow, plants grow, animals grow,—each grows in its own way. But growth is not the goal—maturity is the goal. Growth is the means, maturity is the end result. The goal of every believer is to become mature. This goal is described, "For the equipping of the saints for the work of service, to the building up of the body of Christ; until we all attain to the unity of the faith, and of the knowledge of the Son of God, to a mature man, to the measure of the stature which belongs to the fulness of Christ" (Eph. 4:12,13, New American Standard Bible).

I. MATURITY

Biblical Goal: That Christians be mature (well rounded), equipped to carry out the aims of Scripture.

The word "perfection" in the King James version of Scripture carries the meaning of maturity. In the verse "For the perfecting of the saints" (Eph. 4:12), the word used comes from the root word "perfective" meaning "to mend the nets." When a fisherman mends the nets they are made complete or whole. Maturity is seen as the man who is complete or whole in every area of life.

Ephesians 4:11-16 is the key passage on the teaching of maturity. In verse 14 we are told not to be like unstable children, "That we henceforth be no more children, tossed to and fro, and carried about with every wind of doctrine." A mark of maturity is stability, and teens who are not mature are unstable. The passage applies to doctrinal maturity but can be related to every area of life. Be mature. Be stable, like full-grown adults.

The passage teaches that maturity is equal to the "perfect man, unto the measure of the stature of the fulness of Christ" (Eph. 4:13). Maturity is the goal of spiritual development that comes at the end of the growth process. We do not find the Scriptures calling a babe in Christ mature. We are to "Grow up into him in all things, which is the head" (Eph. 4:15). The standard of maturity is likeness to Christ.

When is a person mature? Can a 13-year-old boy be mature? Does one become mature at 21? How old do you have to be to become mature? There are two definitions of maturity. First, we see maturity as a sliding scale, while second, we view maturity as a static concept.

1. *Maturity—sliding scale concept.* In a class a teacher will sometimes grade on the curve if the whole class scores low; some will automatically pass and some will automatically fail. The curve is relative. Applying this to the grading of maturity, maturity is a relative thing. A 12-year-old boy is considered mature when he displays all the qualities of 12-year-oldness. When a boy displays the physical looks of a 12-year-old boy, the social attitudes and actions, and the satisfactory psychological adjustment for a 12-year-old boy, we say he is mature for age 12.

Those 12-year-old boys who display a level of life equal to age 10 are said to be immature. We say those boys who are developed beyond their age are advanced beyond maturity.

Those who hold a sliding scale concept of maturity feel that a boy can be mature all his life. As he maintains an average rate of development, he remains mature. A boy can be a mature 5-year-old, a mature 10-year-old and ultimately a mature 20-year-old.

Those who think maturity is relative feel that an adult can be 40 and be immature. A 40-year-old woman who does not display 40-year-old characteristics is immature. Hence, maturity is not only relative, but it is not permanent. A person must continue to grow, to continue to be mature. The 40-year-old woman may be immature at 40, but may have been a mature 20-year-old. She stopped developing with advancing age and stopped maturing. In one sense, we are always approaching maturity but never mature, always growing but never fully developed.

2. *Maturity—adulthood (or static concept).* The second concept states that maturity is synonymous with adulthood. When a child is half-grown, he is half-mature. When a teenager is almost grown, he is

almost mature. Maturity is viewed as an unchanging goal toward which all growth is aimed. The goal of physical, mental, social, emotional and spiritual growth is maturity. Once we reach that elusive age we become mature and hold this the rest of our lives.

Those who feel that maturity is the unchanging goal of development say most people reach this aim in the late teens or early twenties. Some never reach maturity and go through life as immature adults.

The goal of every believer is to be mature—to be complete. The goal by which we measure our youth program is the maturity of youth —are they complete in Jesus Christ?

There are steps to maturity. The youth worker should evaluate his overall program to make sure he is including the steps that lead to maturity.

Adjustment Leads to Maturity

First, the teen must be correctly adjusted to God; this is called the filling of the Holy Spirit (Eph. 5:18), whereby the young person is walking in the spirit (Gal. 5:25). This adjustment comes through yielding oneself to God and actively attempting to carry out the commands of the New Testament. Next, adjustment involves a teenager's proper relationship to every area of life—social, physical, mental, emotional, and spiritual. Adjustment is the process of living every day. Adjustment is solving problems, getting along with people, and being honest with oneself. Adjustment is one of the most important necessities in life. Young people are constantly adjusting. They must adjust to the will of God, to their jobs, to their school schedule, to "steadies" or to parents. When they are adjusted, they are growing to maturity—the goal of youth work.

One of the characteristics of a living organism is its ability to maintain itself in a state of adjustment or equilibrium. The basic definition of adjustment is to "fit." A youth must learn to fit into every situation of life. As we apply the term "adjustment" to youth, and speak of good or bad adjustment, we refer to this fitting of a person to the situation in which he finds himself. A farm boy may adjust to a city high school, or to a university campus. A couple just married may adjust or fit into marriage relationship. Adjustment is good or bad as it enables or fails to enable a youth to fit into a total situation with a minimum of conflict. The goal of youth work is that every teen be well-adjusted.

1. *Needs.* Equilibrium is the same as satisfaction. The teen has a basic need of satisfaction. When the need (drive) is met he grows properly. Just as water seeks its own level, so the human seeks satisfaction in all areas of life (physical, mental, social and psychological). Just as

there are natural needs, there are supernatural needs. Man has a need in his heart for God, but he refuses and will not seek God. When a teen seeks God, his drives are met, hence he is satisfied. Many Christians are ascetic by nature and rebel against the concept that they should seek satisfaction. However, there is an element of truth in the teaching that all humans should have satisfaction. The Scriptures teach that spiritual satisfaction is a valid goal. "Thou wilt show me the path of life: in thy presence is fulness of joy; at thy right hand there are pleasures forevermore" (Psalm 16:11). Perhaps the reason most Christians are ascetic is that they feel satisfaction is selfish and they should "die to self." The Scriptures do not teach self-mortification, but that we have been put to death with Jesus Christ and now we are to act on this historical fact by "reckoning" and "yielding" (Rom. 6:11,13). Our death to self is a once-and-for-all act in the death of Christ. Now the teenager should live for Christ. Living involves a basic state of satisfaction.

God's will is that all Christians live happy, satisfying lives. When a person is basically satisfied he is most productive in growth and service. Yet there are some Christians who feel that misery, strife and tension develop inner character. They would desire the teenager to suffer unhappiness and go "through the valley of the shadow of death." These people have a martyr complex and don't have a proper understanding of growth. It is not how deep and dark the valley, but what we learn in the valley causes growth and character. A teenager who spends all of youth in adverse circumstances, with pressures and trials, is not guaranteed a strong character and maturity. The lessons of slums and broken homes teach us that well-adjusted, mature people are not the automatic product of such environments. If anything, these environments breed continual misery and unhappiness, generation after generation. Not environment but the lessons from environment produce adjustment and maturity.

God would have all teenagers to live satisfied happy lives, even in the midst of trial. We are to be satisfied with the Lord at all times. A Christian has the right to a happy life and this happy life is expressed in one term—*satisfaction*. There is only one way to satisfaction and this is through adjustment. A Christian is constantly making adjustment. His life must be adjusted to the will of God. This involves an adjustment in his thinking (mental), his relationship with others (social), his acceptance of his gifts and place in life (psychological), and his walk with God (spiritual).

2. *Drives*. Drives in the human being are an attempt to restore equilibrium. When the body or soul gets out of balance, the person

attempts to restore the equilibrium. Such psychologically produced equilibriums we call drives, and these drives might be said to be the basis for activity. When a drive is sustained in the youth and there is a prolonged period of unsatisfaction, the result is tension. Adjustment once again brings on satisfaction as tension is alleviated.

3. *Adjustment.* Sometimes, when youth are blocked in the activities that may lead to a release of tension, they will substitute for the normal response, another response that will suffice. For example, the teen who is unsuccessful at school and cannot satisfy his need for social approval by academic success may seek satisfaction by playing up his achievements in other fields of endeavor—by bragging about his love conquests, or ability at sports, or even an unnatural claim of spirituality. The youth may withdraw to daydreaming, and by living in a make-believe, imaginary world, may satisfy his needs by imaginary successes.

4. *Adjustment cycle.* It is characteristic of an organism to remain in a quiescent state when its drives are satisfied. But the ordinary teenager rarely, if ever, arrives at such a state of perfect balance. Even the well-balanced youth who may have a good home, adequate food and clothes, who is happily settled in school and has a fine group of friends, who is healthy and enjoys school, who may appear to have everything

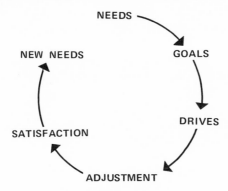

he wants, may need more. He may need more money, more clothes, a more pretentious home, better grades, more popularity and security for life, more love, more power, or more than a hundred things to satisfy his needs—the needs that society has created for him.

The youth leader can point out several alternatives for the teenager in attempting to lead him to a proper adjustment for his situation: (a) why he needs more, (b) satisfaction with present circumstances, (c) proper motivation of desires, (d) how to wait till desires can be provided, (e) ways in which to acquire more, (f) that desires are out of line with necessities.

Maturity is being satisfied with having attained the goal. Yet at the same time maturity is never satisfied because new goals are set up. There are then new drives and a dissatisfaction until the new goal cycle is attained.

The goal of our ministry, then, is to help teenagers set up proper personal attainable goals, establish avenues of gaining these goals, and recognize the state of satisfaction in accomplishment. By doing this, we help the teen to maturity.

This cycle must be repeated over and over, and is known as adjustment. Adjustment must be in every area of life—physical, mental, social, emotional and spiritual.

Why Teens Are Not Mature

In the average teenage Sunday School class, two 15-year-old boys may sit together. Both come from the same type of background and neighborhood, and both have the same kind of experiences at high school. Yet one boy may live a very happy, satisfied Christian life, while the other is bound up by fear, tension, and misery. God wants all Christians to live a happy life. What causes one to be well adjusted and satisfied and the next to be unproductive and miserable?

There are many reasons that a Christian teenager may not live a satisfied Christian life. Most of the causes have to do with the youth's outlook on life. Money, social standing and popularity do not give basic satisfaction. Some teenagers from poor socio-economic backgrounds are well adjusted and satisfied because of a proper outlook on life. Others who have material prosperity, popularity and family security are living unhappy and unproductive lives because of an unbalanced adjustment and improper outlook on life.

Teenagers do not live happy, prosperous lives—for many reasons. Most of the reasons deal with the inner life of the youth and not the outer circumstances. If teenagers have properly adjusted to their inner drives, abilities and goals, to outer circumstances, demands, and incentives, they can be happy. Therefore, we shall deal with the inner forces that prevent adjustment in teenagers.

1. *Personal goals that are unattainable.* Teenagers face frustration because of unrealistic aims. The 12-year-old boy saves for a new car and the 13-year-old girl falls in love with a college sophomore. When the unattainable goals are self-imposed, a youth counselor can show the futility of attainment and guide the youth to seek that which is within his reach, yet still a challenge.

2. *Personal goals that have no challenge.* The teen does not receive satisfaction in reaching a goal that is too easy. Many times we insult the intelligence of our youth because the goal is not a challenge. Two boys are near the top of their class academically. Jack has an excellent IQ and Bill is an average student. If Jack were to get the highest grade in class without trying, there would be little satisfaction because there was little challenge. If the average student, Bill, got the top honors it would mean more to him. The greater the challenge the greater the satisfaction. "To do the easier when the harder is possible constitutes the greatest tragedy in life."

The wise youth leader will make sure the goals chosen by his teenagers have a challenge. If exercise produces growth in the physical body, then a goal that causes the youth to reach will produce maturity in the spiritual life. "A man's reach should extend his grasp, or what's a heaven for?" (Browning). The youth leader must be careful not to let the young person choose a goal too far away. Repeated failure will kill incentive. Allowing a teenager to continue his attempt to sing solos at a youth meeting when he has no voice will kill further desire to serve the Lord.

3. *Personal goals that are too long-range.* All teenagers should have a long-range goal in life. This involves what they will be, what kind of life they will live, what type of person they will marry. However, to have a long-range goal with no step-by-step plan is frustrating. The teenager is fooling himself when he has a long-range goal to be an architect, yet makes no plans for preparation in high school courses. This teen is always desiring and never arriving. He can't have satisfaction and adjustment. Teenagers should have vision—and not illusions. The mature, well-adjusted teen can think in terms of a goal and the means to that goal.

4. *Personal goals that are only short-range.* "Tomorrow" or "next time" is the password to immaturity. Many youth can think only in terms of short-range goals. These young people are usually happy and satisfied, yet don't have a blueprint for their lives. Short-term goals are usually tangents. Young people who choose these day-to-day goals may find themselves steering away from a course of productivity and service in their lives.

Life is like a golf game. As long as we go straight off the tee, down the fairway to the green, everything is fine. When a teenager gets lost in the woods, he loses all sense of direction. A wise counselor will always direct the teenager to an ultimate pattern of life in keeping with the will of God.

5. *Personal goals set by someone else.* Many teenagers find them-

selves walking down a path in life that brings no happiness. This path may be the choice of mother or homeroom teacher. Some boys are forced to go to college because father never had the chance. Girls find themselves pushed into early sophistication by domineering mothers. Most teenagers find happiness when they can live their own lives. Of course adolescent freedom is within the limits of God's standards.

When the youth leader deals with teenagers who have their goals set by someone else, the problem is compounded. Both the teen and the other person needs help. If the problem is compounded by the parent, the youth leader must respect parental authority, yet lead the youth to self-determined goals in life.

6. *Personal goals too high for inner ability.* All too often, teenagers will choose a goal that is possible but not probable. A boy with an extremely low IQ may choose to go to college. A girl who does not have grace or natural beauty will choose a modeling career. How to deal with these young people constitutes a problem. Is it wrong to encourage them to do what they cannot do? To dissuade them may be cutting the vine from the branch. There are several reasons why goals are too high for inner ability: (a) teenagers don't have the background, (b) teenagers lack social graces, (c) a particular girl may lack mental ability, (d) they may lack the experience, (e) they may lack money.

The youth worker will need to understand the nature and needs of young people, then help them form worthy goals in life. When young people choose goals below or beyond their capacity they shortchange themselves. Attainment of a worthy goal can bring satisfaction and lead to growth and maturity.

Path to Maturity

The Bible teaches adjustment or satisfaction. This is seen through several scriptural qualities. These qualities are available for all believers, and applicable to teenagers. Since these qualities are expanded in many other sources, the following explanation is not comprehensive, but shows the relationship between the scriptural qualities of life and adjustment which leads to maturity. Spiritual maturity is being rightly related to the will of God and the Word of God.

1. *Goal of adjustment—peace.* Peace in the Bible is seen in at least two ways:

a. Peace with God—the work of Christ on the cross, into which the believer enters at conversion. This truth is seen in Ephesians 2:14-17; Romans 5:1. The teenager must enter into the "peace with God" relationship before he can enter into the "peace of God" relationship.

b. Peace of God—the inward tranquility or satisfaction of the believer who commits his anxieties to God. The person who would experience *peace of God* must first experience *peace with God*. At this point the youth worker should realize he cannot lead the teenager to true peace of soul until the question of salvation is settled.

The peace of God is promised to the believer as a result of those who deal with anxieties. "Be careful for nothing; but in everything by prayer and supplication with thanksgiving let your requests be made known unto God. And the peace of God . . . shall keep your hearts and minds through Christ Jesus" (Phil. 4:6,7). Youth counselors should attempt to lead teenagers into the peace of God. Note the realm of peace is "through Christ Jesus." The means of peace is through the release of prayer, and the results of peace come after anxieties are satisfied. Therefore, the peace of God and steps to maturity are the same thing.

Note that the peace of God has no equal in worldly adjustment. Christ promised peace that the world could not give. "Peace I leave with you, my peace I give unto you: not as the world giveth" (John 14:27). Beware of trying to bring satisfaction into the youth's life apart from spiritual adjustment. Spiritual maturity is being rightly related to the will of God and the Word of God. If the teenager is divorced from the ministry of the Lord and the Word of God, there can be no peace. "These things I have spoken unto you, that in me ye might have peace. In the world ye shall have tribulation" (John 16:33). Here Christ indicates the person will have inner anxieties, frustrations and misery apart from the Word of God. Some counselors have counseled young people on several occasions apart from spiritual truth and dynamics. These youth leaders have felt inclined to deal with mental doubts only in philosophical terms, or petting in parked cars only in biological reactions. On these occasions, they failed the teen seeking help by not throwing the light of the Word of God on the problem. Christ has promised that peace comes through Him. The youth worker should keep the goal of maturity always before him. The youth need inner peace and satisfaction, which leads to maturity.

2. *Goal of adjustment—satisfaction.* A Christian is commanded to find satisfaction in his Master. "Delight thyself also in the *Lord;* and he shall give thee the desires of thine heart" (Psalm 37:4). The drive to have satisfaction or delight must be filled in every life. The teenager demands satisfaction. This drive for satisfaction was placed in his psychological and biological makeup. Don't blame the youth for these urges; they are following the compelling urges of the inner man. The question is, "How do they satisfy their urges?" Perhaps some respon-

sibility falls on the shoulders of youth leaders for not providing the biblical means of bringing satisfaction to the teen.

When the teenage student is rightly adjusted to the will of God, the result is satisfaction. "Not doing thine own ways, nor finding thine own pleasure, not speaking thine own words: then shalt thou delight thyself in the *Lord"* (Isa. 58:13,14). The teenager should live Jesus Christ at the center of their lives. Therefore adjustment is seen as rightly related to God's words, not our words; rightly related to God's pleasures, not our pleasures. Adjustment and satisfaction lead to maturity when the teenager delights in the realm of God's provision for his life.

3. *Goal of adjustment—joy.* The Christian teen should live a life of joy, happiness and satisfaction. Joy comes only as a result of the Christians being in right adjustment to God—the source of joy. "The joy of the *Lord* is your strength" (Neh. 8:10). Joy is the positive reaction of fulfilled desires and drives. "Thou wilt show me the path of life: in thy presence is fulness of joy; at thy right hand there are pleasures for evermore" (Psalm 16:11). The Christian is commanded to have joy and express it to others. "Rejoice in the Lord alway: and again I say, Rejoice" (Phil. 4:4).

The youth leader must understand the source and secret of joy if he is going to help teenagers. Young people demand and need happiness. This does not mean we are to give in to their selfish demands or treat them as children. True obedience brings joy. Perhaps a youth leader can help a teen find joy and satisfaction in obeying the commands of God's Word.

The aims of Christian education of young people are ultimately the aims of the church. These aims are clear and give direction to the youth leader. These goals are sometimes difficult to verbalize or implement in a life. But goals should nevertheless remain the constant guidepost. Between the immediate ministry and the ultimate goal are years of heartache and pain. The youth leader may get lost from one youth meeting to the next unless there are clear ultimate goals. The following check list was suggested by Dr. Lois LeBar to evaluate maturity.

CHRISTIAN MATURITY

Outlook on Life

1. Is all of life integrated around Christ, who is revealed through Scripture by the Spirit?

---

[1] Dr. Lois LeBar, Unpublished material. Printed by permission.

2. Is concentration on Christ rather than on work or people so that we can live above circumstances?

3. Are we able to see life as a whole and the relationship of parts to the whole?

4. Is all of life sanctified, even to the smallest detail and most humdrum routine?

5. Do we take every circumstance that the Lord sends as an opportunity for learning?

6. Do we see problems as challenges because we have faith in what God can do in us and in others?

7. Do we discern God's part and ours—what can and should be changed, and what cannot be changed?

8. Are we free to be natural and spontaneous, disliking masks and walls that separate and deceive?

9. Are we free from attitudes that poison the spirit—doubt, guilt, self-pity, resentment?

10. Can we face and accept reality as it is—openly, honestly, heartily?

11. Are we progressively developing depth of insight and experience?

Relation to Work

12. Do we spend our limited time and energy on and get excited over the things that count most?

13. Have we strong drives from pure motives, yet are not so serious but that we can laugh at ourselves?

14. Have we spiritual courage to work for convictions, though risks are involved?

15. Do we suspend judgment until all the facts are in, then make wise decisions and abide by them?

16. Have we an experimental, creative spirit that is open to new ideas in an exploratory, evaluative way?

17. Do we consistently work for high standards, yet remain flexible in our thinking?

18. Do we work consistently without yielding to moods or waiting for prods?

19. Are we known as dependable people who can carry projects to completion?

20. Have we sufficient discipline to control deep longings over a period of time and postpone present satisfactions for future good?

21. Can we take disappointment in stride and keep from depressed moods?

22. Do we derive intrinsic satisfaction from everyday work and simple pleasures, with a continually fresh appreciation for what life brings?

Relation to People

23. Have we a healthy respect for the individual rights and contributions of other people?

24. Can we identify with the needs of others, going out to them, forgetting self?

25. Are we ready to take the role of humble follower or status leader, according to the need?

26. Can we be comfortably related to people above and below us in authority?

27. Do we enjoy being both conventional when conformity is important and unconventional in making a unique contribution?

28. Are we ready to admit graciously our own failures as well as commend others?

CONCLUSION

Maturity is a measure of quality. It is not *how much* one does that determines maturity; it is *what* one does with the opportunities at hand that determines maturity. Maturity is not how old the teen looks but is measured by his outlook. He is as mature as the way he sees his life. Maturity is not measured by observation of physical features; maturity is measured by our view on life and other people. The goal of our youth work is that the teen become mature.

Blessed are the unsatisfied when they have a goal. Many of our teenagers are unsatisfied and their lives are filled with frustration. Christianity does not have a goal for teenagers—it is a goal. Young lives should be productive for Christ, satisfying to teens, profitable to the church and counting for eternity. They could be, if youth leaders understood the biblical goal of maturity and then translated it into challenges for teens.

Thought Questions

Section Four

(Covers chapter 9, "The Aims of Church Youth Work"; Chapter 10, "Maturity—The Goal for Church Youth".)

1. What are wholistic aims for church youth work?

2. What is the difference between aims and goals? How does this difference apply to church youth work?

3. Why should the aims of youth work and the aims of a local church be the same?

4. Many do not agree by their practice, that the aim of youth work is evangelism. Why does this aim give success to a youth program?

5. Does the aim of evangelism for youth work mean that any means can be used to evangelize youth? Why?

6. Define "reaching." How can you get youth to give an honest hearing to the gospel?

7. Youth like to share their faith. What more is needed in biblical evangelism? Why?

8. Why should we emphasize both the *personal* and *propositional* nature of the gospel?

9. Give the definition of a church. Does the church you attend fit this definition? Why do youth need to attend an organized church?

10. Is education an important goal for youth work? Why?

11. What is maturity? At what age does the teen become mature? Can he lose his maturity?

12. What is the relationship between drives and satisfaction? What happens when the teen never gets satisfaction?

13. Why is adjustment important for the teen? What is the relationship between adjustment and maturity?

14. Why do teenagers drop out of the church? (Answer from your own observation.)

15. What problems with historical overtones does your church have with young people?

16. If a person is a mature Christian, but not familiar with the Bible, should he be a youth leader? Why?

17. How old should a person be before becoming a youth leader? What are the disadvantages of "older folk" becoming youth leaders? Should a person in the mid-twenties be used to direct youth?

18. Should youth leaders "buddy" with the kids, or should he command their respect with a more mature standard of living?

19. Should the pastor or a layman be the youth sponsor in a church? Why? Would you change your answer if the pastor were gifted for youth work and the layman had limited abilities?

20. What is the main standard for success in working with young people?

SECTION FIVE

THE CHURCH PROGRAM FOR YOUTH

Who should give leadership to a youth program, the youth council or the youth director?

What is the biblical position of the youth director?

Can good youth programs be produced from program books?

Should a youth group elect a girl as president?

How can a youth director get teenagers to take responsibility?

How much organization is needed in a youth group?

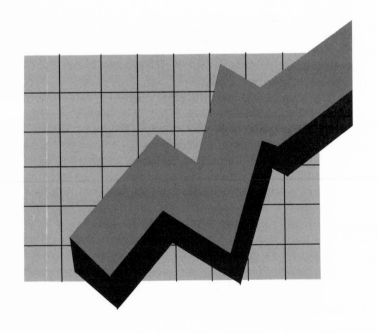

11

FUNDAMENTAL CHURCHES—LED BY A YOUTH DIRECTOR [1]

The fundamentalist believes that both message and method are found in the Word of God, whereas the evangelical is committed to the message of the Word of God but believes methods can be found in contemporary society. As a result the evangelical will base the methods for his ministry on the latest research in education, the latest techniques, or what is "relevant." (See Chapter 10.) The fundamentalist believes that methodology is found in the Word of God and the youth leader applies that methodology to carry out his ministry to teenagers. However, when the pages of the New Testament are examined, the position of minister of youth or youth pastor is not found. The following offices are found, "And he gave some, apostles; and some, prophets; and some, evangelists; and some, pastors and teachers" (Eph. 4:11). Note that the position "youth pastor" is not found in the Scripture. On this list, the apostles were not permanent gifts to the church. They founded the church, their ministry was accompanied by accredited signs and they were inspired by the Holy Spirit to give us the Scriptures. But this office is not in existence today. The role of an evangelist was to spread the Word of God into all places and establish local churches. The office of an evangelist is similar to the foreign missionary today. A prophet was one who spoke the Word of God; he preached (I Cor. 14:3). The

---

[1] See chapter on "Trends in Church Youth Work." To understand the underlying philosophy this chapter deals with leadership of youth groups in fundamental churches.

pastor and teacher were the same office; they shepherded the flock of God (a local church). Later the office of deacon (I Tim. 3) is mentioned in Scripture. A deacon assisted the pastor in ministering to the flock. God wisely did not dictate in the Scriptures the specific office of youth pastor or minister of youth.

Our country has developed a unique youth-oriented society with an overemphasis on the needs of young people. To meet this need, churches have created the role of youth director, mostly since World War II. The question remains, "Where does a youth director fit into the scriptural delegation of authority?" God called a pastor to shepherd the flock. There was one shepherd for the seven churches in the book of Revelation (2:1,8,12,18; 3:1,7,14). On other occasions there was more than one minister (Acts 20:17), as when Paul sent to Ephesus and called the elders (plural) of the church from Ephesus. The office of elder is synonymous with a pastor. We do not suggest that one of these elders was the youth pastor [2] of Ephesus.

The senior minister, therefore, must exercise personal leadership for every ministry in the church or delegate his leadership to someone who can help him. Usually, a pastor gives leadership to the youth ministry in a small church and as the congregation expands, he shares his ministry with someone else. But in the final analysis, he is the shepherd of the flock; he is responsible for the youth ministry. When the pastor can no longer exercise a direct ministry to young people, he delegates the job to someone else. Therefore, *the youth pastor's office is an extension of the senior pastor's ministry into the life of the youth of the church.* The youth group remains an integral part of the total church and is under the direct shepherding of the senior pastor. Even though the youth pastor is in a subordinate position, he uses his gifts, initiative, faith, and ability for spiritual results. The senior pastor shares his ministry with the youth pastor.

Sometimes the church becomes too large for the senior pastor to effectively preach, teach, and counsel with every area of his church. There are too many teenagers for him to oversee. Here he must get assistance from other co-workers and delegate to them that responsibility. At other times, the pastor's abilities are not adapted to young people. Perhaps he doesn't understand their subculture nor does he enjoy ministering to them. At this time he should secure someone who can meet the needs of young people and minister the Word of God to

---

[2] The title youth pastor is synonymous with youth minister, youth director or youth co-ordinator. It applies to the person who gives most of his time and energies to working with youth in a local church. There are many applications of this principle to the position Minister of Christian Education, also called Director of Christian Education.

them. In either case, the youth pastor becomes the extension of the pastor's ministry into the life of the young people.

Since the youth worker is an extension of pastoral ministry to the life of the church, the question naturally arises, "What is pastoral ministry?" There are five duties of the pastor indicated in the New Testament, each one portrayed by a different word. Even though these duties are the role of the senior minister, they are delegated to the youth pastor and he should carry out these ministries among the youth of the church.

1. *Elder (Prebuterors).* The elder's main responsibility was administering the local congregation. Historically, the elder was a part of the deliberative assembly in Israel. Peter writes, "Likewise, ye younger, submit yourselves unto the elder" (I Peter 5:5). His administrative or leadership duties are seen in the exhortation, "Let the elders that rule well be counted worthy of double honor" (I Tim. 5:17). His leadership role is also seen in the qualification for an elder. He had to administer his own house before he could supervise the church, "For if a man know not how to rule his own house, how shall he take care of the church of God?" (I Tim. 3:5). Therefore the youth minister should exercise leadership direction for the youth group. Whereas many evangelical youth groups operate with a youth committee or a Board of Christian Education, many fundamental youth groups place leadership in the youth director who in turn is responsible to the pastor. The senior minister is not a law unto himself. He is responsible to the congregation and ultimately to God. Some might criticize the fundamentalist position saying the youth minister becomes a dictator. Even the Scripture speaks about ultimate authority of the elder, "Neither as being lords over God's heritage, but being ensamples to the flock" (1 Peter 5:3). Therefore the youth minister is not to lord it over the young people but to be the true example as a shepherd of God. In a recent youth clinic at Kansas City Baptist Temple, the author asked the question, "How many youth pastors use a youth council or elected high school officers to give leadership to their youth group?" Out of 150 present, 128 indicated they did not have a council or elected high school officers; they were responsible for carrying out the aims of the youth group.

2. *Bishop (Episcopes).* The senior pastor is a superintendent or overseer of the church. Paul's instruction to Titus (Titus 1:5) indicated an elder and bishop were the same office. The word "bishop" means to oversee, and the flock were to submit themselves to his guidance: "Obey them that have the rule over you, and submit yourselves, for they watch for your souls as they that must give an account, that they may do it

with joy and not with grief: for that is unprofitable for you" (Heb. 13:17). Since the youth director is an extension of the senior pastor's ministry, he must oversee the youth flock just as the senior minister gives direction to the total flock. Sometimes the youth director must announce rules for the spiritual growth of young people—i.e., there will be no radios at camp—so young people may give themselves to the study of the Word of God and not be attracted by outside influences. By the same principle, the youth director may make the rule that no hot pants are allowed at youth activities. He is simply exercising his delegated duties as bishop of the youth flock.

The youth director will have difficulty carrying out the role of bishop and overseeing his youth flock because of the emphasis on freedom in our youth society. Just because discipline is difficult does not mean it is impossible. Those who argue for a relevance-oriented youth ministry will not approve of the youth director who exercises discipline.

3. *Shepherd (Poimen).* A shepherd's main responsibility is to feed the flock and see that each sheep grows healthy. The youth minister is a shepherd and he should "Feed the flock of God which is among you, taking the oversight thereof" (I Peter 5:2). Paul told the elders from Ephesus that they were to "Take heed therefore unto yourselves, and to all the flock, over the which the Holy Ghost hath made you overseers, to feed the church of God" (Acts 20:28). Here we see a combination of three duties for the pastor: the elder administers the flock, providing for its direction; the bishop takes oversight over its internal affairs; and the shepherd feeds his flock by providing food.

The youth pastor should feed the young flock, teaching and preaching the Word of God to young people. This is one of the main reasons for the growth of the master teacher plan of teaching in the high school Sunday School department. Rather than dividing according to ages, the entire youth department gathers to hear the youth pastor teach the Word of God. There are many advantages for the master teacher plan in the high school department. (1) The youth pastor should teach Sunday School because he is the one charged with the responsibility of feeding the flock. (2) The youth pastor, because of his training, should know the Word of God better than the adults who work with him (most youth classes in traditional churches have laymen as teachers). (3) The youth pastor should be able to relate the Word of God better to the young people because he knows their needs and background. (4) The youth pastor is trained in communication and should be able to teach the Word of God to young people, even though the room is large and there are more present. (5) Each young person in attendance can know more of the total number of youth in the church rather than just a small Sunday School class. (6) The young people can sit with their friends that they invite to come to Sunday School. (7) The invitation to accept Jesus Christ is usually more effective after a strong presentation of the Word of God. (8) The master teacher class can continue growing and will not level off in attendance. There is no implied danger level (lack of space, or class-size limitation) in class growth. (9) Visiting teenagers will more quickly visit a large crowd (a crowd draws teens), therefore more unsaved will visit the master teacher class than the small self-contained classrooms.

Many criticize the master teacher plan, feeling that it is merely an accommodation allowing for large numbers of young people to come to Sunday School. However, the master teacher plan recognizes the biblical principle that God works through the gifted man (the youth pastor), and that the Holy Spirit can teach best (John 14:26) through the equipped man of God who is called to minister to his flock.

4. *Preacher (Kerux)*. The fourth major role of the senior pastor is a preacher, one who exhorts the congregation. Paul indicated "whereunto I am appointed a preacher." He also told his young son in the faith, "Preach the Word" (II Tim. 4:2). The purpose of preaching (or prophesying) in the Scripture was threefold: "But he that prophesieth speaketh unto men to edification, and exhortation, and comfort" (I Cor. 14:3). Some feel that young people do not need or want preaching, simply because they do not like it. As you enter the average church congregation, you see the teenagers sitting in the back rows passing notes, or looking otherwise disinterested. Many have fallen into the snare of believing teenagers feel "preaching is irrelevant." However, the Word of God gives a high priority to preaching, because through the preaching of the Word of God, believers grow, false doctrine is corrected, sins are pointed out and the unsaved are brought to Jesus Christ. Since young people need preaching, the youth pastor should preach to young people. Paul Fosmark, Minister of Youth, Fourth Baptist Church, Minneapolis, Minnesota, said, "Preach to young people when you have an activity. Do not give devotionals." He indicated preaching was more than sharing the gospel; preaching was aimed at getting a decision in the heart of young people.

5. *Teacher (Didaskalos)*. The last role of the senior pastor is teaching the Word of God. This is perhaps his most influential role, because here he is following the example of Jesus Christ. The book of Acts was addressed to Theophilus, indicating that it was a continuation of "all that Jesus began both to do and teach" (Acts 1:1). Before Christ ascended into heaven, He commanded His disciples, "Teaching them to observe all things whatsoever I have commanded you" (Matt.

28:20). The youth minister should teach by private counseling, teach by example, and teach when young people are gathered in groups. He should teach in Sunday School, on retreats, in youth camp, in counseling sessions, in Vacation Bible School, and in Bible studies.

The youth group is an integral part of the local church and comes under the authority of, and is in need of, the direct superintendence of the pastor. The youth pastor is the extension of the pastor's ministry into the life of the young people, carrying out the duties that the pastor has to the whole flock. The pastor's role to the total flock, is the example of the youth pastor's role to his flock.

Observations

Both the pastor and youth pastor recognize that they are servants of God, called of God and in the final analysis are responsible to God. Neither are to lord it over the flock of God. At all times the youth pastor is responsible to the senior pastor, but both must recognize that their personalities need to adjust to one another.

Since the youth work and the total church ministry intermesh in so many places, communication is essential. Both the pastor and youth pastor must remain men of good will and mutual trust. At all times the youth pastor supports his pastor. The pastor must display professional ethics and support those who work for him. The pastor must recognize that his authority to lead the church was not gained through personal desire or native ability. His authority is given by God. Therefore, he does not "lord it over" the youth pastor. The senior pastor exercises biblical leadership over the youth pastor, who in turn exercises biblical discipleship. The senior pastor never attempts to make the youth pastor a scapegoat or embarrass him in his work, because the youth pastor has his authority over teens and they must look to his leadership. The senior pastor does not destroy the leadership and example of his youth pastor, he enhances it.

The youth pastor can solve many problems by remembering that he is a subordinate. He does not work for a committee, neither does he work for the deacons. He is responsible to the shepherd of the flock. Therefore, the youth pastor always works "through channels." He always supports the pastor and the main church services have priority in the youth program. Remember, the senior pastor is *their* pastor; you are the youth pastor. Do not pull their loyalty from the pastor or cause disloyalty.

12

EVANGELICAL CHURCHES—ADMINISTERED THROUGH A YOUTH EXECUTIVE [1]

Whereas the fundamental youth director assumes more authority for directing his group, the youth director in the evangelical church has a different structural church organization, hence his youth group is administered differently. Usually the church is more organized and less dependent upon the pastor for outreach, stability and direction. Laymen have a greater voice in the internal affairs of the church and there are more committees through which the affairs of the church are handled. Here, laymen have a greater voice in their church. These laymen are usually deeply concerned for the spiritual welfare of their teens and voice this concern through the Board of Christian Education or the youth executive.[2]

The youth director must exercise greater cooperation with parents, the church board and other agencies in the church. As stated in chapter 10, he is the coach, a phrase coined by Dr. Roy Zuck of Scripture Press. The coach gives direction, but his influence is behind the scenes; he counsels, plans and meets with groups of interested adults (committees). The coach attempts to get all people of the church involved in the youth program because he believes the church belongs to all its members, adults and teens alike.

---

[1] See chapter on "Trends in Church Youth Work" to understand the underlying philosophy. This chapter deals with operating principles for evangelical churches.
[2] This chapter appears in the original release of this volume.

The evangelical youth group usually meets *before* or *after* Sunday evening church service, although some churches have their youth fellowship meet one evening during the week. No matter when your youth group meets, the principles in this chapter are designed to help you plan, organize and evaluate the youth program.

The youth fellowship is not another Sunday School class, nor is it a worship program designed for teenagers. The program is different and unique. The youth fellowship differs from Sunday School in its objective and adult guidance. Whereas the evangelical considers Sunday School primarily teaching in nature, he considers the youth fellowship to have a training purpose. However, elements of both teaching and training are found in both. The place of adult supervision differs in each program. In the youth Sunday School class the adult teacher takes an active role of group direction, whereas in the youth fellowship the youth director is like the director of a play. (The director guides in the rehearsal, planning of props, and total impact. The youth, like the actor, must be the one who plays the role and meets the audience. Both actor and director are responsible for success or failure of the play).

The Organization of the Youth Society

While many people today laugh at organization and make fun of committees, those youth groups that are organized get things done. The automobile is an important symbol to teenagers and may also symbolize the youth fellowship. The automobile takes you from where you are to where you want to go. There are many body styles, brands and varying amounts of horsepower under the hood. Each car is built with a different emphasis, usually designed for a certain type of person. But each automobile is built with a basic purpose—transportation. To the teenager, a smooth-running automobile that supplies transportation is "cool." So also the youth fellowship that is well organized and smooth-running will attract teenagers and get the job done.

Grading the Youth Society

The youth fellowship group will probably be divided into three groups. The age group should be organized on the basis of needs and interests of the various people within the group. If you recognize the age grouping of the public school system within your community, you will probably be "in step" with your youth groups. Many communities divide their youth (all youth 12 through 24 years of age) into three groups:

Junior high school department, ages 12 through 14, or those enrolled in the seventh, eighth and ninth grades. (Some districts are moving to middle school which accommodates sixth and seventh grade only.)

High school department, ages 15 through 17, or those enrolled in high school.

College and career youth, ages 18 through 24.

In some churches there are fewer youth in one department than in another. The question comes, "Should we combine age levels?" Some churches put the junior high school and high school age levels together. The tendency to combine age groups is greatest when the groups are small. Church leaders feel a large group can be more effective. This is not always true. Unless unusual circumstances prevail, don't combine age groups. Young people like to be graded up. That is to say, junior high school students like to be with the high school group. The high school students like to be with college young people. However, most young people dislike being graded down.

What about putting two age groups together for a larger attendance? Check your aim for a large group. Are you *number*-conscious or *person*-conscious? Large groups tend to inflate the ego of the leaders. The youth like a large group but would rather sacrifice numbers to be with those of their own age group.

Some churches have a limitation in available facilities, making it necessary to combine the young people's age levels. Once again, this is not completely satisfactory. Use homes in the immediate neighborhood rather than combining age levels at the church. Where there are as many as four or five junior high school students or college and career youth, it would be better to grade them in a separate group than to combine the age levels. The age levels can be combined at special times for special programs, but for the weekly meetings this is not wise.

Some churches have combined age groups, such as junior high and high school students, and young people from both groups attend. Usually the young people who attend such a meeting are those who are extremely faithful or their parents require them to attend. These young people would attend no matter what age combinations were used. However, these young people will rarely, if ever, bring their friends from school. Also, the church is not ministering to their specific interests and needs. While they may be attending now, they are potential dropouts.

Types of Organization

The organization of the youth fellowship should reflect the number of youth in attendance. Three types of organization are suggested: The Youth Council—suggested for churches with multiple youth groups. Youth Executive—suggested for average-size youth groups. The youth executive would administer the youth fellowship program. The church should have a Board of Christian Education to administer the total youth program and give guidance, coordination and counsel to the youth executive. Youth Department—used in churches that have an average-size youth group. The officers for the youth department function for all youth agencies. For example, the secretary would keep records for the youth Sunday School class, youth fellowship, youth recreation program, etc.

Determine the type of organization that best serves the youth group. Then adopt and adapt the program for the aims and ends of your youth group.

1. *The Youth Council.* The youth council is made up of three or four young people from each youth department in the youth division. (These young people should either be elected or serve on the youth council by reason of their office in their own youth group. For example, the president of the junior high section would serve by reason of his office.) Also, the youth council would be made up of the youth sponsors, the youth pastor and/or director of religious education, the pastor, and some members of the Board of Christian Education. The youth council would be responsible to the Board of Christian Education.

Some churches have suggested that the adults who serve on the youth council attend and share in the discussion but not vote. Many allow them to vote. The youth council should meet every three months and have the following responsibilities:

a. Election of a youth to serve on the Board of Christian Education;

b. Survey the total youth program to see if all of the needs of youth are being met and avoid duplication of activities;

c. Plan for youth advancement from one department and/or age group to another;

d. Plan division-wide activities for all youth of the church ages 12 through 24.

The youth council would not be a policy-making body but would give direction, coordination, and counsel to each organization.

2. *The Youth Executive.* If the youth group is not large enough to have young people to organize fully into more than one department for each age group, then don't add a youth council. Adding organization for the sake of organization will breed a sterile youth program. A small executive committee elected by the young people can run the youth program. The supervisory role that would have fallen to the youth council would be assumed by the Board of Christian Education.

The young people should have the right to elect a representative to the Board of Christian Education. The Board of Christian Education would be responsible for the appointment of a youth sponsor. (If you are from a church large enough to have a youth council, then the council would select the youth sponsor.)

The size of the youth group will determine the size of your executive committee. Some churches have a president, vice president, secretary, treasurer, publicity chairman, and at least four chairmen in the area of program planning. Other churches with fewer youth have fewer officers. They usually divide the responsibility among their president, vice-president and secretary-treasurer.

3. *The Youth Department.* Some churches elect one executive committee for all youth agencies. The president would assume the leadership of all the youth agencies, i.e., the youth Sunday School class, the youth fellowship and other activities. This program has worked for some groups, but it has its weaknesses. A minimum of young people are involved in leadership, and one of the aims of the youth program is to train the young people in leadership ability.

Setting Up the Organization

The meetings of the youth executive [3] should be informal sessions, emphasizing planning and sharing. *Fellowship* is the key word. Even though informality is the rule of the day, carry on the business in an orderly manner. The youth president should preside and be alert to the spirit of the group. In many cases the informal attitude of this group will permit the president to summarize what he feels to be the will of the majority.

The youth executive committee becomes the spark plug of the total youth program because it takes the initiative in getting things done. If possible, distribute the responsibility for the youth program as widely as possible. Only when a young person takes some responsibility for the youth program will he feel any loyalty to it. The executive committee's chief responsibilities are to plan, direct, and evaluate—in short, to be an executive group.

At times the executive committee will set up short-term committees with specific jobs assigned to them. Don't set up committees just because the youth program always had a committee, or some other youth group had that committee. Make sure committees have a real and immediate job. Standing committees with indefinite responsibilities make for poor machinery. When teenagers lose interest, the machinery rusts.

---

[3] The term "youth executive" is used in this section, but should be applied to all youth organizations. The youth council will be composed of several youth groups, each having a youth executive committee. The officers of the youth department would also be an executive committee.

An automobile with rusty machinery doesn't attract or operate. So, instead of putting every teenager on a committee at the beginning of the year, wait until there is a specific job, then select a committee. But don't wait without working. The old adage is still true, "Use 'em or lose 'em." Teenagers won't attend unless they're involved, so let's involve each teenager in the youth society.

The executive committee becomes the key unit in the youth organization. The youth officers who make up the executive committee should be elected by the vote of the majority. Young people with leadership ability (creativity, ideas, natural gifts, willingness to work) are not always the most popular members. Youth groups tend to elect the most popular—not the most qualified. However, those who are elected should have the respect of the other teens in the church.

The executive committee should meet every month. Select a convenient date and see that it is circled on the calendars of the young people. Don't forget to have the secretary remind the kids periodically of this meeting. Work through the officers to direct the growth of the young people's group.

Beginning the New Year

Let's assume it's the beginning of a new year—September. The youth executives have been elected. Now what does the sponsor do? First, meet with the president and begin finding out his plans for the coming year. Does he understand his role as president? Are his personal goals for the group high enough? Is he afraid of the job? Is he going to be a dictator? He may be a meek leader who needs encouragement. Help the youth president have confidence by thorough planning for the first executive meeting of the new year.

Let the new president know of the plans and aims for the coming year. Let him know of the experiences for the past year. What are some new ideas? Be in touch with all of the youth and let the president know how the gang thinks.

At the first executive meeting, perhaps an opinion poll should be taken of all the new leaders. What do they want to do for the year? What do they feel are the "needs" of the youth group? What other questions do they have? As an opinion poll is taken, many areas of interest may be found among the youth that might form a basis for program activity.

After the interest or spiritual needs of the group have been determined, begin to set aims or goals for the coming year. Remember, the goals cannot be built solely around the immediate interest of the group. These young Christians need many experiences and much information to help them grow in their Christian life.Young people have needs that they are unaware of. Expand the thinking of the executive committee; add your suggestions as to needs and goals for the coming year. A planned youth calendar may cover necessary activities. Don't let the executive committee ignore some units of study because "no one checked it out."

The executive committee should give careful preview to the entire year. Units of study can be decided (one month or three months). Certainly some of the subject matter and programs will be decided. Members of the Board of Christian Education who are concerned with planning the entire church program can help coordinate the youth program with the church as a whole. Perhaps they know of certain emphases in the youth department of the Sunday School or other aspects of the church life that will help young people.

In the first executive meeting of the year plan for the emphasis of the year. Some points for year planning are:

1. *Make the year aims attainable.*

2. *Make the year aims understandable to the youth.*

3. *Phrase the year aims in a scriptural context.* (Use a verse from the Bible if possible.)

At the first executive meeting of the year plans should be made and work projected that will be as close as possible to God's plan. In order to fulfil the purposes of the youth fellowship, we must have the direction of God's Holy Spirit. Plans should not be made independently. Therefore, the officers must spend time in prayer, self-examination, confession and rededication. Begin the meeting by having a period of devotions, carefully planned beforehand. Do not ask John, at the last minute as he enters the room, to lead in prayer and read the Scriptures. This can't be called worship. The devotions which are meaningful to John will become meaningful to the executive committee.

The executive committee should have a spirit of fellowship and nothing develops fellowship better than shared work. Also, shared food develops fellowship. A supper together or light refreshments at the end of the session will deepen the fellowship and provide needed relaxation after hard work.

Monthly Activities of the Executive Committee

In addition to the discussion of programs, the executive committee should be concerned with other aspects of the monthly meetings. The interests and responsibilities for the total youth program should be given attention. The following list suggests some of the duties common to most executive committees.

1. *Finances.* Is the youth fellowship on a sound financial basis? Do the teenagers have to carry the ball financially? If your church has a unified budget, how much is allotted to the youth activities? The executive committee is responsible for making its own budget and adapting it for the coming year. Each teenager should be expected to contribute to the support of the youth program. Perhaps the entire financial burden cannot be on the shoulders of the young people, but young people who take no financial responsibility for their affairs will take little spiritual responsibility.

2. *Membership.* The membership committee usually interprets its responsibility as "getting more." Securing additional members is not the only responsibility for this committee. Careful plans should be made to interpret the meaning of membership to all young people. The youth fellowship where "everyone comes" doesn't have as loyal a membership as those who have some form of requirements.

3. *Absentees.* Don't take attendance for granted. Also, don't assume the absentees will be back. Plans should be made to follow up those who are not in attendance.

4. *Special occasions.* Has the executive looked forward to the special occasions coming up in the next several months? See if the planning calendar is up to date. Begin by making necessary plans now.

5. *Business.* The necessary business for the youth fellowship should be planned and carried out by the executive. Most of the business can be expedited by the youth executive. Don't spend a lot of time in the youth fellowship on business and housekeeping problems. The youth fellowship should give guidelines to the executive and let them carry out details.

6. *Program calendar.* Make a youth fellowship calendar for each month or quarter; then post it on the bulletin board so all young people may know of coming events. This way the youth can save dates and develop a sense of expectancy about the program. The calendar should list dates, time, programs and other special information.

Program Planning

There are two ways to divide the young people into program committees for the youth group. In either type of arrangement, the young people are divided and placed on one of the program planning committees. The secret of involvement should be captured. Each youth should be on a committee which in turn becomes responsible for a regularly scheduled program.

1. *Program planning committee—monthly responsibility.* The youth group would be divided into four groups (four to ten youth on each

committee). Each committee would be responsible for a program each month. The programs would represent more variety and all the youth would be used.

2. *Program planning committee—topic responsibility.* The youth group would be divided into groups with each young person assigned to a program committee according to his interest or talent. The program committee might include the following subcommittees:

a. Christian life committee
b. Christian witness committee
c. Christian outreach committee
d. Christian churchmanship committee
e. Christian fellowship committee

Whether the monthly responsibility or topic responsibility approach is used, the youth will need certain guidelines. Some youth executives assign a date on the calendar to a program planning committee and let them determine the topic. Even though this is often done, the youth program will probably suffer. Program planning committees will probably "drift" from week to week, taking the easiest way out. There will be no coordination of plans to help meet immediate needs.

The executive committee should assign the topics for each program and let the program committee work out the presentation. Plan the programs for a quarter in advance. First, clarify the aims. What are the objectives for the next quarter? What are they trying to do through the Bible studies they plan and the activities in which they engage? Second, suggest the activities. Study, worship, service, and recreation should supplement one another. Third, delegate responsibilities. The individual program planning committee needs to know what, when and where. Teenagers will serve leaders who make it clear where they are going.

Scheduling activities is not merely a matter of putting down topics and units. Help the executive committee review the resources that are available. Program plan books are available at Christian bookstores. Denominational youth magazines have suggestions for activities. Young people are creative in program planning. What visual aids and resource help are available in the church library? Don't forget the pastor and director of youth; they are resource individuals. Look outside the church; there may be resource persons in the community. A local Christian college may have a library, Christian education curriculum room, or teachers who can help give guidance to your youth group. Beyond this, other churches and youth directors may give some help.

No "ready-mix" program out of a youth plan book will completely satisfy the needs of the group. If literature is used without modification and adaption to the needs of your local youth group, the results will be somewhat disappointing. Be creative. Use the literature as a "spring-board" to launch into a creative program. However, every coin has two sides. Some youth groups would be vastly improved if they used the literature "as is." Groups who do not use a correlated curriculum usually flounder or go "off on a tangent." Using printed youth material "as is" may not be effective for a group, but it is probably more effective than using no literature at all.

In program planning be creative! Dig up ideas, follow leads, and think out the program. This may be a bit difficult for some, but it pro-duces growth. Take young people to seminars and Christian education workshops where they may learn how to plan, organize, and be creative.

Some groups need an "interest finder." You may ask, "What is an interest finder?" An interest finder is simply a check list (one of your own devising) to discover what topics are of keenest interest to the youth group. Ask the youth to check twenty questions which they would like most to discuss in the next quarter. Analyze the results in the executive meeting and use these findings to determine the individual programs for the Sunday evening meetings.

The following questions are suggested to help formulate the "interest finder":

1. *My faith*

a. How can I know that there is a God?

b. How can I know that I am saved?

c. Why should I pray? For what should I pray? What are ways of praying?

d. How can I help others find Christ as Saviour?

2. *My Bible*

a. How can I know the Bible is the Word of God?

b. How did we get our Bible?

c. How can God speak to me out of the Bible?

d. How can my Bible help me solve the problems of daily living?

e. Does the Bible have mistakes?

f. What are some practical methods of Bible study?

3. *My church*

a. Why are there different denominations? Which church is right?

b. What are the qualifications of a good church? How can we improve our church?

c. What meaning does church membership have for a young person?

d. What is the meaning of baptism and the Lord's table?

e. Why should I go to church? How can I get more out of it?

4. *My home*

a. What makes a home Christian?

b. What responsibilities does a teenager have in a Christian home?

c. What things can a family do together?

d. How much freedom from parental authority have I a right to expect?

e. What help can I expect from the church in choosing my wife (husband)?

f. What preparation can I make now for establishing my own Christian home?

5. *Foreign missions*

a. Are the heathen really lost?

b. Why send missionaries to other countries when there are so many unsaved in America?

c. Is Christianity right and all of the other religions of the world wrong? Why?

d. What is the relationship of the teenager to foreign missions?

6. *My life's work*

a. How can I find my spiritual gifts (abilities)?

b. How does God lead a person to find his life's vocation?

c. What are the opportunities for vocational Christian service?

d. What are the Christian standards for success in life's work?

e. What is the Christian's relationship to military service?

7. *Personal conduct*

a. What is the Christian standard about petting?

b. What is the Christian standard about social drinking?

c. What is the Christian standard about smoking?

d. What is the Christian standard about gambling? (Should one match pennies?)

e. What should be the Christian attitude about swearing?

f. What is cheating?

g. How do teenagers overcome temptation?

h. How can I stand up for my convictions when it means going against the pressure of the crowd?

i. How can a teen overcome evil thoughts?

8. *Companionship*

a. How should a Christian choose his intimate friends?

b. What does a Christian boy look for in an ideal girl? What does a Christian girl look for in an ideal boy?

    c. What constitutes going steady? How old should you be to go steady? What can you do on a Christian date?

When an interest finder is used in planning programs, needs may be met centering on the interests of the young people. List the topics which the youth group thinks are most needed, use a planning calendar to assign a topic to each week.

If an interest finder is used, describe the programs that will be coming out in the next few months in the printed periodical. The youth quarterly may talk of needs and problems that deal with topics youth want discussed. These youth planning books are usually well written and readily available. The youth counselor should be present when the topics are chosen and assigned to program committees. Try to make sure that the topic assigned has resource materials available. What may seem like an excellent topic, "The Christian's View of E.S.P. (extra-sensory perception)," may be a fizzle when presented because there is no adequate material available to guide the group.

If the group uses the program planning committee—topic responsibility approach—the suggested methods will work with some modification. The interest inventory will still be used to find the needs and problems of the youth group. After program topics are decided upon, they will be channeled to committees dealing with the assigned subject. The committee could be directed to material in the curriculum plan book.

Some of the committees and their area of responsibilities might be as follows:

1. *Christian life committee.* This committee is concerned with helping youth grow in a vital Christian faith and life. Areas in which this committee has responsibilities:

    a. Christian beliefs
    b. Personal commitment and dedication
    c. Personal growth and maturity
       Bible study
       Prayer
       Worship
       Standards of the Christian life
    d. Individual behavior (Christian moral standards)
    e. The Christian heritage (church history)

2. *Christian witness committee.* This committee is concerned with helping young people make Christ known to others by all they say and do. Suggested areas of concern:

    a. Personal evangelism
    b. Stewardship (time, talents, and treasures)
    c. Christian vocation (finding God's will for our life)

d. Young people and foreign missions

e. Young people and home missions

f. The local church and missions

3. *Christian outreach committee.*

4. *Christian churchmanship committee.* This committee is concerned with helping young people understand the needs of the church, to formulate Christian convictions, to meet these needs through their personal training and to take their place as children of God in the house of God.

a. Service to the local church

b. Service to the community

c. Training in specialized skills needed to be an adequate and useful church member

d. Training in leadership ability and skills

5. *Christian fellowship committee.* This committee is concerned with helping young people experience in all of their relationships the bond of Christian fellowship which comes from faith in the Lord Jesus Christ.

a. The local church as a special place of fellowship

b. The teenager-parent home life

c. Boy-girl relationship

d. Recreation, leisure time

The executive should keep ahead of the group with good plans, programs, discussions, and projects. Keep program moving at all times. Plan well, present plans with enthusiasm, and enjoy carrying them out. Then the youth will grow as Christians and serve with happiness.

One of the secrets of program planning with young people is activity—don't let it go stale. As a teenager on the program committee once said, "Keep it steamed up all the time." This was his way of expressing the need for action and movement. Make young people proud to invite outsiders; soon the outsiders will be insiders. The youth sponsor will have to inspire them from the background—keep pushing without making it obvious.

The Role of Sponsor in Program Planning

What is the role as youth sponsor in program planning? Some youth sponsors jump in and plan the program. They choose the songs, write the script, plan the advertising, arrange the Scriptures, and organize the announcements. The young people are just pawns on the chess board to be "manipulated" by the youth director.

"Think of all the experience they are getting," says this youth director. "I may do a lot of the planning and foot work, but in the final analysis the young people put on the program." This is the usual justification of the directive youth director, and to a certain degree he is right. However, the youth are not given a chance to be creative and to express the gifts that God has given to them.

"Anything you can do, the young people can do." Such a statement may sound trite, but it contains dynamic truth. The young people can plan programs, organize advertising, and arrange for the Scripture reading. They can do anything you can do. Therefore, your question might be, "What is the role of the youth sponsor in helping teenagers plan programs?"

1. *Help the group decide clearly what its purpose is.* The youth director should meet with the program planning committee. Let one of the high school students be the chairman of the committee and preside over the business. The youth director should probably be an ex officio member, without vote. Help guide the young people through suggestions and contributions. Always point out the goal and purpose of the program.

At times the youth sponsor may have to challenge the immature thinking of one boy who wants to steer the path of the committee away from its original goal. Other times the youth leader may have to lift the goal of the program. Some teenagers only want to be entertained when they could have a more valid goal—education.

2. *Help the group become aware of its own dynamics.* Sometimes teenagers are so task-centered that they are only interested in finishing a job. The youth sponsor should point out to them their own dynamics. Note the teenagers who have made the contributions and point out what lessons they have learned about one another in the program planning committee. Show the group how they have taken responsibility and how this has helped them to grow in their spiritual life. Also, observe some of the difficulties they had in solving problems. This insight may help the group solve problems more easily in the future.

3. *Help the group become aware of latent talents, skills, and other resources within its own membership.* Sometimes the youth sponsor may have to pull quiet members into group discussion. Polly may have excellent contributions to make but is a little hesitant. A good youth sponsor may know more about the young people than those on the planning committee. Point out Polly who is a good soloist and Maggie who plays the piano. Perhaps the group should know that Jerry speaks well in public and Dave plays the trombone. These can be used in the next group program.

4. *Help the group develop methods of evaluation.* There are two ways to improve a program. One, make the suggestions for improve-

ment. Two, lift the group's level of self-criticism so the teenagers themselves may improve the program. Do this by helping the group become aware of how other teens are feeling. Also, making them aware of the opinions of other church members will improve their evaluation. If teenagers criticize their program, they will improve it. If *you* criticize their program, they may become rebellious.

5. *Help the committee accept new ideas.* Sally may be quiet and yet be a deep-thinking girl. When she offers a suggestion, Jerry is quick to be hostile. Sally won't defend her idea because of her shyness. The other teenagers won't come to Sally's defense because of natural teenage inhibitions. The youth director may have to call Jerry up short and take an objective look at Sally's idea. Sally's contribution may become a symbol of defeat for her. Instead, it can be accepted, analyzed, or become a "springboard" to another thought. Take advantage of a moment of frustration and embarrassment to lead the group of teenagers to new motivation and insight.

6. *Help the committee create new jobs and tasks as needed.* A committee has been called a group of people who "keep minutes and waste hours." Teenage committees tend to perform what can be done by individuals. Point this out. If Jim is to be the song leader, let him pick out the songs. When eight people in a committee try to pick out the songs, twenty-five minutes may be used. Let Jim choose the songs. However, Jim should know the theme of the meeting and how many songs are to be chosen. When a person is given a task to do, make sure he has guidelines.

Conclusion

A youth group is like a platoon of men or a group of musicians. The youth director is not the dictator; the evangelical believes the youth director must first minister to each person in the group and then he may work through the group. Just as the conductor must work with the individual musician and the sergeant works with his soldier, so the youth director is concerned with individuals. He believes that strong individuals make a strong group. The evangelical is willing to sacrifice group excellence for individual growth. His ultimate aim is the symphony or the battle, therefore time is invested in training and practice.

13

FACTORS OF A SUCCESSFUL YOUTH PROGRAM

There is much speculation over what makes a successful youth group. Most church groups claim to have a program for youth that is relatively successful. One organization even named itself *Success with Youth,* reflecting the desire of most people to reach and teach youth, or at least to reverse the decline of youth in the typical church. Since most want a successful youth program, the question should be asked, What is *success* in a youth ministry? Michael Rustin attempted to solve that problem and determine what caused some youth programs to prosper and why others fail.[1]

Successful senior high youth programs were evaluated of five evangelical denominations in the Minneapolis-St. Paul area. Each denomination furnished information on their five most successful high school youth programs, and only one typical or average program. Three categories were formed: first, the five most successful churches (1-5) were analyzed; second, the lowest-ranked churches or the least successful group (21-25) was surveyed; and, third the typical youth group was questioned. In this chapter these three groups will be presented (1-5) successful, (21-25) least successful and typical or average.

[1] E. Michael Rustin, unpublished thesis "Factors Associated with Success for the Senior High School Program of Selected Evangelical Churches." Deerfield, Ill.: Trinity Evangelical Divinity School, 1967.

Rustin accepted two criteria for success.[2] First, a youth program must be growing in numbers (increase in enrollment and/or attendance). Second, the youth must be involved in the total program of the church. Rustin appealed to another researcher for reinforcement of his standard of success.

> One test which may be applied to a youth program is the proportion of participation on behalf of the young people. Do they participate? . . . Another test would be to determine the proportion of young people in the community who are drawn into activity and through the youth program are brought into membership with the church. Is the youth program a mission agency to win other young people for Christ? [3]

The following analysis is included to reflect a "standard of success." Many workshops for youth leaders are based on how-to-do-it; this chapter is based on how-they-did-it.

The Church

Churches with successful youth programs tended to have larger Sunday morning attendance (384 average, compared to 204 for typical churches), larger Sunday Schools, and much larger church membership than the typical churches.

This finding reverses the old wives' tale, that a large church must be superficial. Most people believe that when more teens attend, there is more anonymity, less dedication and softening of standards, hence a less effective church. The opposite is true: the larger the group of teens, more attention must be given to standards, meeting individual needs and a greater degree of devotion.[4]

The degree of conservatism in the churches was based on separation from the world and separation from false teachings. Fundamentalism related most highly (in 70 percent of the programs), and with overall success (in 60 percent of the churches). The two denominations considered to be the most conservative of the five denominations, were ranked as having the most successful youth groups in their churches.

----

[2] This author agrees with Rustin and Peters that attendance and involvement are important factors of success. Rustin says these are the only factors that can be measured; however, this author would add two other standards for successful youth work, (3) the changed lives of teens and (4) correspondence with the aims of the New Testament. Some might not feel these two added standards are objective, but the author disagrees. The standard of a changed life is objective. Several statistical studies have measured the values and attitudes of teens. The belief is that changed values and attitudes (outward expression of teens) reflect a change in the inner personality. The last, aims of the New Testament also are objective (see chapter 8, AIMS OF YOUTH WORK).

[3] Clarence Peters, "Developments of the Youth Programs of the Lutheran Churches in America," unpublished Th.D. dissertation, Concordia Seminary, St. Louis, 1951, p. 385.

[4] Elmer Towns *The Ten Largest Sunday Schools* (Grand Rapids: Baker Book House, 1970). I found that larger churches were more fundamental and had higher standards of separation, rather than the reverse.

The Church and Its Community

The economic status of each community was rated as wealthy, well-to-do, comfortable, poor, or very poor. All of the most successful youth programs were in the comfortable category, as were four of five programs in the least successful group. Three of five typical churches were also in the comfortable, which means that economic background did not determine if a church was successful or not. No church in the survey was in the wealthy or very poor category.

The Church and Its Senior High Youth Program

More converts were registered in the most successful high school programs than from the other groups. In fact, 80 percent of the least successful churches and typical churches reported no converts. Since their aim was not evangelism they were not winning the lost. One-third of the converts in the successful churches were gained through evangelistic services; 25 percent came from activities and others through the soul-winning of the pastor, Sunday morning services and other events. The 21-25 group recorded converts only through the pastor, while the typical group listed converts only through youth and worship services.

In the most successful churches, 22 percent of the youth converts had initial contact with the church through other youth in the church, 21 percent through the Sunday School, 21 percent through activities, and 28 percent through evangelistic meetings. They reported no converts as a result of initial contact at camps, retreats, clubs or youth groups. Churches in the 21-25 group had no initial contacts through any of these agencies, while the only converts (two) in the typical youth group were through initial contact with the youth group.

More high school young people visited the most successful churches, averaging 15.6 visitors per month. The 21-25 group averaged 11.0 visitors and the typical group 4.0 visitors. (Since the typical churches were smaller than the most successful, this could account for part of the variation; however, churches in the 21-25 group were larger than the most successful churches.) Therefore, the youth group that has the most unsaved at a meeting is the youth group that will win the most to Christ.

Evangelistic meetings were held in all of the most successful churches while only 40 percent of the 21-25 group and 60 percent of the typical group held such meetings. The most successful churches had more senior high visitors at their evangelistic services; 40 percent of the 1-5 successful youth groups had seven or more visitors of senior high age, while the least successful churches, 21-25 averaged 2.5 visitors and the typical youth group averaged 3.0 visitors.

The most successful churches supported their youth groups most highly. Average contribution from the successful 1-5 churches was $747.60 per year, the 21-25 group $130, and the typical $42. This bears out the principle that it takes money to operate a successful youth group. Cause or effect was not noted: i.e., money was the cause of their growth, or they got money because they were successful. In either case, the church that wants to successfully reach its youth must be prepared to invest finances.

Church Facilities

More facilities were available in the successful churches than in the typical churches. One of five most successful had a youth center, compared to two of five in the 21-25 group, and none from the typical group. Two out of the five most successful youth groups had gymnasiums. Four of five of the least successful churches had these facilities, but none of the typical churches. Three of five of the successful churches had rooms for youth, compared to two of five typical churches.

Therefore, a church must provide space for youth to keep from being unsuccessful, but space itself is not the criterion for a successful youth program. The successful youth program comes from a dynamic ministry, not the simple provision of buildings.

Church Library

Church libraries were found in all of the least successful youth groups and the typical, whereas only one of five of the most successful had libraries. This was a startling conclusion since most would expect a library in successful churches. Perhaps the answer lies in the type of program. Successful churches have an activity program that is not oriented to research. Perhaps kids in these churches had other access to books.

However, the one library from the most successful group had more Christian education books than did the other: 85.7 for the 1-5 group, 61.0 in the 21-25 group, 20.7 in the typical group. The most successful churches had more books for senior highs than the typical. Averages were 28.7 for the 1-5 group, 33.3 for 21-25, and 9.3 for the typical group. Books were checked out most frequently by senior highs in the most successful churches. Averages for one month were: 1-5 group, 4.3; 21-25 group, none; typical group, .7.

Organization of the Church

The Committee giving guidance to church education in the successful churches met more often than those of the typical churches. All of the most successful met more than 11 times a year; 80 percent of churches in the 21-25 group and 33 percent of the typical churches met over 11 times.

The successful churches tended to coordinate the Sunday School with the youth group more than the typical churches. The successful churches all coordinated the youth program with the Sunday School. In the least successful group, four of five coordinated; and typical youth groups, only two of five attempted coordination.

Whether or not churches had a Christian Education Board showed no apparent relation to the success of its youth group.

Church Staff

More full-time paid staff were found in the successful churches (excluding maintenance, secretarial, musicians) while the typical churches had more part-time staff members. In the successful group, two of five had full-time assistants, and two of five had full-time youth pastors, while the other two groups had neither of these. This just supports the principle that personnel are needed to operate a youth group.

Paid youth workers from the most successful churches devoted more time to senior high youth. Average number of hours per week was 27.6 for direct ministry to youth in the 1-5 group, 9.8 hours for the 21-25 group, and 5.4 hours for the typical group. It is interesting to note that three of five of the typical spent less than seven hours per week with their senior high youth. No wonder a paid worker who spends so little time has a typical youth group.

The average amount of time devoted by paid workers for each youth involved in at least one activity of the church was greater in the most successful churches. The average per week was more than double in the most successful churches (½ hour) compared to .2 hours per week for the 21-25 group.

Paid workers in the more successful churches participated more in school events. Workers averaged 4.6 visits to the high school where their youth attended in the most successful group, 4.0 visits in the 21-25 group, and 2.2 visits in the typical group.

Senior high youth were invited into the homes of paid workers more often in the successful group. Average number of visits to the youth pastor's home that were not part of planned activity was one every two weeks in the successful churches compared to one per month in the typical churches.

Outreach

Unconverted youth were most likely to be found in the most successful groups. Four of five of the most successful, three of five in the 21-25 group, and none of the typical churches had unconverted youth in their groups.

The most successful also had more visitors. There were 7.4 visitors per week in the successful group, compared to 1.6 in the least successful group, and .4 in the typical group.

The greatest growth in the previous year was observed in the senior high youth programs of the most successful churches, increasing in four of the five groups. One of four of the 21-25 group increased, and half of the typical group decreased.

Youth Group Sponsors

The youth sponsors are laymen who assist the youth director carrying out the program. They counsel, lead singing, handle discipline problems, prepare food, administer records or take care of physical equipment.

More youth group sponsors were found in the most successful churches, averaging 3.4 sponsors per youth group; the least successful group averaged 2.8 sponsors and the typical group 1.8 sponsors.

A ratio of one sponsor to 15.6 youth was reported in the most successful, 18.7 in the 21-25 group, and 18.4 in the typical group. Four of five of the most successful, one of five in the 21-25 group, and no typical churches had a ratio of less than one sponsor to each ten youth.

More than half the sponsors in the successful churches had college degrees, compared to 20 percent of sponsors in the typical group. All of the youth workers in the most successful churches had training in personal evangelism, while 40 percent of the other groups lacked such training.

The youth sponsors in the successful churches spent more total hours per week with young people, all more than eleven hours per week, averaging 51.6 hours per week. In the 21-25 group, one of five averaged more than eleven hours, with an over-all average of 9.8 hours. None of the churches in the typical group averaged more than eleven hours, with overall average hours of 4.5.

Average time spent by each youth sponsor per week was highest in the most successful churches: most successful youth groups spent, 11.4; other sponsors in the other two groups spent 3.9 hours. Most successful churches devoted an average of .7 hours per week per youth, while the average for the others was .2.

Total time spent by youth sponsors and paid workers was highest in the most successful churches, with four of five averaging more than twenty hours per week, overall average of 79.2 hours. The 21-25 group averaged 20.6 hours, two of five with more than twenty hours. Average hours of the typical group was 6.4 per week; none averaged more than twenty hours.

Youth Meetings

All of the most successful churches had regular meetings, compared to four of five in the 21-25 group and three of four in the typical youth groups. One of five of the most successful met one week night, one of four from the typical group met after the Sunday evening service, and all others met before the Sunday evening service. Youth group meetings were less likely to be discontinued for the summer in the most successful groups.

Social Life

The most successful youth group tended to have activities more frequently. Two of five from the most successful group, one of five in the 21-25 group and none of the typical group had activities more than once a month. More outsiders attended the socials at the most successful churches: 1-5 group, 6.8 visitors; 21-25 group, 5.4 and typical group, 3.2.

Camp and Retreats

The most successful churches more often had camps of their own, and were less likely to send their youth to more than one camp. Two of five of the most successful had their own camps, while none of the others maintained their own.

More retreats were held by the most successful churches, which averaged ten per year; the 21-25 group averaged .8 and the typical .4. This proves that when a church ministers to a group of teens, it is likely to have success.

Conclusion

These statistics are included for two reasons: first to show what are the factors of success in a youth program, and second, the fundamentalist and/or conservative churches are more successful in youth work than are other churches.

All the conclusions of Rustin are not included in this chapter. Only those pertinent factors were chosen; the careful scholars can find the others in his thesis. We are grateful to Dr. Rustin for showing to us that youth work can be successful.

Thought Questions

Section Five

(Covers Chapter 11, "Fundamental Churches—led by a Youth Director"; Chapter 12, "Evangelical Churches—Administered Through a Youth Executive"; Chapter 13, "Factors of a Successful Youth Program.")

1. Why was the office of youth director not mentioned in Scripture? Who is responsible for the growth of Christian teens in a church?

2. Why does the pastor delegate his responsibility to the youth to a youth director?

3. What office does *elder* imply for the youth director?

4. On what biblical basis does the youth director make rules for his youth program?

5. Why is the master-teacher approach to Sunday School considered biblical?

6. Examine the master-teacher class and list the weaknesses. Are the weaknesses of sufficient weight that the master-teacher class should not be used?

7. What is the basic difference between the evangelical and fundamental approach to the office of youth director?

8. List the strengths of youth director in the evangelical church. Will he have a better-administered program?

9. What are the strengths of the youth director in a fundamental church? What positive contributions will he make to his youth group?

10. What are the logical ages to divide the youth? Why?

11. When would a youth council be used to administer a youth program? Why?

12. The youth department is employed with a small church; list the advantages and disadvantages.

13. When qualified youth are not elected to the youth executive, but the election becomes a popularity poll, what can the youth director do?

14. List the duties of the youth executive. What is its primary job?

15. How can the youth sponsor guide the youth executive?

16. Suggest some ways that a youth executive can get ideas for programs.

17. List several myths about youth work that Rustin's research dispels.

18. The most successful youth groups are located in the more conservative churches. Why? Suggest some reasons that come to your mind.

19. What are the two criteria to determine *success* in youth programs. Why do you agree/disagree with these criteria?

20. What one aspect makes a youth group more successful than any other?

SECTION SIX

TEACHING TEENAGERS

Do teens learn differently from children?

How can we cause young people to want to learn?

How can we get teens to study the Sunday School quarterly?

When are young people ready to learn?

How can we get teens to explore the Bible?

Should an invitation be given after every lesson?

What is the best method of teaching teens?

Why are the new social groupings effective teaching techniques for teens?

14

WHAT GOES ON IN SUNDAY SCHOOL CLASSES

This chapter examines four teachers at work, teaching teens.* Rather than tell you how to teach, four case studies are included to show you what might happen in a classroom. All of the following illustrations have strengths and weaknesses. There is no best way to teach. The situation, lesson aims, students, teacher and time determine what techniques and approaches will be used. These case studies will give you the "feel" of teaching young people.

MRS. STRAUSS'S CLASS

You arrive at church late one September Sunday morning after Sunday School has begun. You see an old-fashioned building with its tall steeple; white paint is peeling off the sides. Unkempt landscape and rickety stairs give a "worn" look. The Sunday School superintendent greets you warmly, informing you that Mrs. Strauss is expecting you and offers to take you to her room. The eleventh graders meet in the church basement. You open the door and see Mrs. Strauss sitting among a group of teenagers. This is the typical sit-in-a-semicircle-with-the-Bible-on-your-lap. Mrs. Strauss rises, greets you, and expresses pleasure at your visit. In turn, she introduces you to each of the young

---

*Use the following case studies for class discussion. Divide the students into small groups and have them analyze the strengths and weaknesses of each situation.

people who sit and look at you curiously. You find a seat at one side of the circle, and she returns to her place in the center.

As Mrs. Strauss resumes her teaching, you look around the room. The room is small, high-ceilinged, and apparently old. The round-back, spoke chairs are obviously of the last generation. There are signs that Mrs. Strauss has spent time and effort to change the appearance of the room. Bright curtains hang at the windows, which are above eye-level. Along a wall there are three low bookcases holding several volumes of books. In one corner is an easel with a blackboard; the other corner has a small square table with secretarial records and extra quarterlies.

The young people in the room present a wide variety of dress and appearance. One boy wears a metal brace on his left leg, but a seat on the end gives him room to stretch his leg and avoid an uncomfortable position. Most of the boys are well dressed with sport jackets, ties, and polished shoes. Since the room is cold, most of the girls have their coats on.

As the young people sit in a circle, half of them have a Bible and a quarterly in their laps. At present the quarterly is on top of the Bible and the young people listen to another student read. Mrs. Strauss uses the chalkboard to outline the lesson and asks questions. Then she asks, "Are there any questions?" As Mrs. Strauss attempts to talk about Bible study, you note that she tries to make the lesson "real." You notice that the young people's talk has more of a conversational than a recitation tone. How casual Mrs. Strauss is, you think, until you realize that she is carefully drawing each young person into the discussion, and with comments and questions is aiding him to become involved.

Mrs. Strauss spends some time discussing what happens between faith and public confession of salvation. Leading them from one Bible verse to another, she continually asks questions. The young people seem to enjoy it.

Before going on to a third verse, Mrs. Strauss helps the group visualize in their minds an illustration of faith in action. She listens to the suggestion of a fellow who tells what a boy might do as a clerk in a supermarket.

"What do you suppose he should do with a six-pack of beer?" Mrs. Strauss asks, as they apply the question to everyday life. The young people seem to be intrigued with this bit of mystery. Mrs. Strauss encourages the young people to describe their reaction to shoppers and their ideas as to Christian testimony and witnessing to friends at the store. She asks what other young people would do if they had to sell beer when working in a supermarket; she gets a variety of responses.

Mrs. Strauss lets the kids speak their minds, challenging one another. She calls on individuals who seem to want to say something but have no initiative to take the floor. You observe how the interest increases as extra details are filled in, each young person wanting to add his bit.

"This is a good lesson," one girl comments. "I like this lesson, and tomorrow I will find out if Hank sells beer." You wonder who Hank is. Mrs. Strauss chimes in, "I wish Hank came more regularly to Sunday School; I feel that such discussions would help him in his Christian life." You begin to get the picture; Mrs. Strauss is interested in Hank, even though he is not here.

At this time Mrs. Strauss nods to Frank. Immediately he takes over the discussion, talking about the young people's meeting.

What shall we plan for the weekend? Several of the young people speak together, "Let's start with a hootenanny." "Good," says Frank, and he rises and goes to the chalkboard. Here he starts writing the suggestions that come from the members of the class.

Observations

In Mrs. Strauss's class the youth were learning many facts and relating them to life. Is there any evidence of cooperation in the learning procedure? Who had the total responsibility for learning? Who is in the center of the room? Is this right? What do you see in Mrs. Strauss's class that you like? Do you identify with her? What are the reactions of the youth to Mrs. Strauss?

GORDON LUFF

Gordon Luff uses the master teacher plan for his large junior high Sunday School class. Over 300 early teens gather each Sunday morning in one large open-session teaching situation. As you walk into the church gymnasium, you note that the athletic environment has been minimized and the room is decorated to appeal to junior high school students. There are several tables on either side of the door with a junior high school student sitting behind each table. On each table is a section of the alphabet and junior high schoolers "check in" for attendance and other records. A few feet away is another table with a large sign "Visitors' Registration." Two ladies sit behind the sign and register all new newcomers.

Several youth counselors congregate around the door greeting the teenagers as they come, keeping a special watch for newcomers. The newcomer is greeted, taken to the registration table, then introduced to other teenagers. On the back edge of the basketball court, where the scorer's table is usually located, a large platform with a contemporary backdrop is the focus of attention. The chairs are arranged in a large semicircle amphitheater facing the platform. The amplification system and speakers on either side of the platform help each teen to hear what's going on.

Most of the teens are standing in small clusters in the hallway and at the back of the chairs talking with one another. Other teens are seated. Sunday School class doesn't start for ten minutes. On the platform a college boy plays the electronic piano and his friend plays the bass guitar. The background music sets the mood for the singing later on.

On the left side of the platform are twelve large posters. Each brightly colored poster symbolizes a team of junior high schoolers: the Road Runners . . . The Purple Pelicans . . . The Straight Shooters. Later, during the lesson, the youth are divided into their teams for discussion of the lesson with the youth counselor. These teams form the basis for follow-up. The counselors are responsible to contact absentees from their teams, as well as endeavor to reach unsaved teens and get them in Sunday School. The teams also become the basis for meeting personal needs through counseling.

Gordon Luff believes a super-aggressive program will attract and keep teenagers in Sunday School. All types of young people attend his class. Stereotyped hippies with long hair and mod clothes walk in and usually sit together. Also, the "greaser"—those with dungarees, sweat shirts and motorcycle boots—sit together. Some have plastered-down hair. Most of these ride the Sunday School bus and keep to themselves. Other varieties of teens are seen: those from middle-class homes, others in expensive dresses, boys with conventional haircuts; all seem to feel accepted and come back week after week. Even though there is not a genuine mixture of the teens, the program seems to attract them back each week and has become the basis of feeding them the Word of God.

One of the youth counselors leads an aggressive song service, the electronic piano and bass guitar accompany when a rhythmic gospel chorus is sung, all of the kids begin to clap their hands to the beat. After gospel choruses, the tempo is slowed and hymns are sung. Most of the kids join in singing. Next, two teenage kids, one boy and one girl, give testimony of how they found Christ as Saviour. Notified of this assignment a week in advance, they are well prepared; each speaks clearly into the microphone. Teenage ushers pass the plates as the offering is taken.

When it's time for announcements, Gordon Luff comes to center stage and announces the roller skating activity, visitation, the attendance contest, and the proposed trip to Disney World during the summer. He especially emphasizes visitation: "All Christians should be soul-winners." He explains the variety of appeals. "The carnal kid is not motivated by spiritual reasons; therefore, we have a contest and give a mini-trail bike," states Luff. He goes on to state that the spiritual kids respond to the love of Christ and attend because of the commands of Scripture.

Luff teaches the Sunday School lesson to all 300 junior high kids, using verse-by-verse exposition of Scripture. Since he knows the Scripture better than anyone else in the department and can communicate with the teens in their own vocabulary, he is the natural choice for a teacher. Also, Gordon has mastered the techniques of teaching and keeps the attention of the class. Most of the youth would rather hear Gordon teach because he is more interesting than the others who teach. Also, he keeps the lesson centered on early teen problems. However, about every fourth or fifth week he allows one of his counselors to teach, both to develop their ability and to give variety to teaching the Word of God.

Therefore, since Luff is best equipped to minister to the teenagers, he is considered the *master teacher.* There are twelve young adults who act as counselors in the youth Sunday School department. They act as secretaries, helping take attendance as the kids come in; other counselors meet and talk with the kids before class. Here many of the youth problems are uncovered and appointments are made to counsel with them later. If there is any response at the end of the lesson, the counselors deal with those kids who come with spiritual needs or who seek salvation. The primary responsibility of counselors is to go visiting with the teenagers on Thursday evening.

Before Gordon Luff took over the Junior High Department, only sixty pupils came each week. At that time the pupils studied out of the quarterly, answering questions asked by the teacher. They were reprimanded for not having their quarterlies filled out. Since it was a large church with many absentees, Luff determined to construct a program that would attract all the youth of the church to Sunday School.

When Luff took over the department, only the kids from Christian homes came to Sunday School. They met in six small cubicles for class. The teachers were conscientious and well prepared, but could not adapt the lesson to the lives of teens. The worship period was a short preaching session.

Now the lesson is Bible exposition with practical applications, but Luff usually ends the lesson with an invitation to accept Christ. The youth stand as an invitation hymn is sung. Those who are lost are invited to walk forward and receive Christ. Youth counselors deal with those who come forward, carefully explaining salvation or dealing with problems. Luff does not give an invitation each week. He explains, "Sometimes we do not have the unsaved present. Also, if there are only a few non-Christians, the counselors know who they are and go talk to them about Christ." He goes on to explain that a visitation program is planned each Thursday; the kids and counselors go out to witness to the unsaved, inviting them to Sunday School. The Christian kids grow when they see they influence a person to accept Jesus Christ.

Observations

In Gordon Luff's class, the emphasis is on the group, keeping them interested in the Word of God and getting them to respond. The master teacher was used because he could get more results than the other teachers. Do you feel he communicated more Bible content than the others? Did the students learn more? Did the youth enjoy their experience?

JIM PHELPS'S CLASS

You arrive a few minutes before 10:00 in a substantial, typical city neighborhood at First Church. The grounds are well kept, the large trees on the church lot give you a feeling of stability. As you walk through the halls of the educational building, everything seems to be orderly and the buzz of the Sunday School classrooms tell you, "business as usual." The Sunday School superintendent meets you in the hall and asks you to wait for the youth to leave their Sunday School departments and go to their individual classrooms. You and the Sunday School superintendent stand at the head of the stairs and watch the proceedings. Some teachers walk along with their students; others are stationed in the halls at various intervals. You look forward to viewing seventh graders. This is a bright, exciting age—just out of the junior department. The junior high department meets together for opening exercise, then they divide into small classes. The classes are divided by age and school grade. Jim Phelps's class comes out of the department and heads toward the classroom. The boys are in an orderly row. They enter the room and file to their seats.

When the Sunday School superintendent learns that you want to visit Jim Phelps's class he looks pleased, and states that he would like to tell you something about the Sunday School and its families.

The majority of the youth in Jim's class come from families ambitious for their children and greatly interested in their spiritual welfare. Many of the parents plan to send their youth to Christian liberal arts colleges or Bible colleges. Most of them expect that their boys will go into the ministry or will be in professional schools, such as law and medicine. In addition to this, most of the parents are concerned that their young people receive adequate preparation for college in the public schools.

The Sunday School has a reputation for the demands it makes on its young people. The Sunday School superintendent feels that these demands are reasonable. She says, "We believe in learning in this Sunday School, and we believe in standards too. Standards are for learning, and standards are for conduct." As you go into Jim's classroom, you take a seat in the back. The square-backed chairs are arranged in four rows. The first two rows are empty, the third and fourth rows are made up of fellows. At first Jim Phelps walks the aisles slowly, checking each student's quarterly to see that the work is done properly. As he checks the report item by item, he admonishes those who have been late, haven't brought their Bibles, or have not filled out their quarterlies. Seventeen pupils appear awake, intelligent, and ready to learn. Four boys seem somewhat older than the others and stand out for their size.

The walls of the room are painted green. There is a map of Palestine on one wall, a set of books on shelves, and several closed cupboards. In the front of the room hangs a portrait of Abraham Lincoln, far above the eye level of the students. A vase of plastic flowers stands in the corner on the table. After the inspection period Jim Phelps opens his spiral-back book of lesson plans. The back of the book is kept for review. He goes rapidly around the class, reviewing the material that has been covered in past lessons, calling on the students to give responses, usually as quickly as possible. He catches one of the larger boys looking in the quarterly for an answer. "Ralph, you know I want you to memorize this material. Don't look up the answer in the quarterly." Students who answer the questions promptly receive smiles and nods of approval.

Jim Phelps goes to the chalkboard and begins to write the plan of the lesson for the day. Ralph looks unhappy—he has been humiliated in front of the class. Jim Phelps turns again to reprimand the same two boys for whispering. If he has to mention it once more, he says, he will speak to their fathers. He passes out mimeographed questions to to be looked up in the Bible. The room is very quiet . . . you begin to get uncomfortable as you sit in silence for fear some movement of yours will disturb the young people. Jim Phelps either sits at the desk and keeps an eye on the students or walks up and down the aisle to see that everyone is working. He pauses to read over the shoulder of a student to see if he can help. Everyone is working.

After the assignment time is over, Jim announces, "Now, class, let's go over our work." Each youth is asked to read his passage aloud. Others are reminded to keep the place. Some read fluently, others stumble through their passages. Jim frequently stops a youth in the middle of a paragraph and asks the next reader to go on. In this way he finds several who are not keeping the place. He says nothing but looks displeased.

Now Mr. Phelps explains the lesson. The Scriptures are important and he gives a careful analysis of each verse. Applications are made to everyday life. Sins are pointed out, and young boys have no doubt about what they are not to do. The room becomes hushed. There are no questions. The boys stare at their shoes or out the window. One boy digs in his pockets and is obviously occupied with something other than Sunday School.

Observations

Perhaps you found yourself approving and disapproving of methods used by Jim Phelps. This is natural. Were your likes and dislikes based on your personal prejudice, or were you trying to consider what you saw in light of what is best for the youth? What does Ralph think of Mr. Phelps? Will this help others in the class? What will they think if they miss their assignment? Will Jim Phelps or Mrs. Strauss communicate more material?

MISS CULVER'S CLASS

The educational building of First Community Church looks quite modern to you as you approach it. So do the houses for blocks around in the new subdivision. You arrive just prior to the beginning of Sunday School, along with the children. As you pass through the halls, you note that most of the teachers are in their classes or departments talking with students or working out last-minute details before the bell rings. As you go into the youth department, the departmental superintendent expresses pleasure at your having interest in observing the ninth-grade class. The open session seats around sixty teenagers. In the background Christian music is playing. You note in one classroom, off to the left side of the large auditorium, three pupils are talking with a teacher. In the center of the auditorium before Sunday School starts two teachers are talking with a group of five teenagers. You look over the schedule that has been handed to you:

First Community Church
Junior High Department
Introduction

Leader ....Harry Anderson, Grade 8
Song Service ....Mary Frank, Grade 9

Special Music
Ensemble—Gordon Stevens High School

Announcements ....Jim Peters,
Youth Fellowship President

Debate: "Resolved: Christians Should Not Date
Non-Christians"

Song ....Mary Reese, Grade 9

Class Dismissed

After the opening session you are dismissed to a large well-lighted classroom. You note the freedom of the students as they come into the classroom. Three big bulletin boards illustrate current projects of the class. The corner bookshelves hold many books on a variety of subjects, including both Christian fiction and reference materials. Shelves on the opposite side of the room contain materials you assume are used for handwork, research, and teaching aids. There are four large tables in the room, and you note that the boys and girls begin rearranging their chairs around the tables to suit themselves. Others go for supplies to the cupboards lining one wall. You are surprised to see a large half-made scale map of Palestine on one of the tables.

When the bell rings, the young people begin coming to attention by facing the teacher, Miss Culver. The offering basket goes around the room, and one of the junior highs finishes the secretarial work and goes out to report to the departmental secretary. You count 21 students and notice that most of them are neatly and attractively dressed. A boy goes to the front of the room, leads in prayer, and reads the Scripture for the day. He is Harry Anderson, class chairman, elected for a three-week period, you later learn. Harry asks for a report from two committee chairmen, one dealing with plans for a class Thanksgiving party, the other dealing with plans for a Gospel youth team. One girl interrupts and asks about a problem concerning the uncompleted map on the table. A boy indicates that it would be a waste of time for the whole class to discuss this committee's problem. Sue agrees and indicates it is not necessary for the whole class to become involved. Miss Culver explains that this will be covered later in the lesson and that students who have assignments should begin thinking in terms of their reports for the day. Harry asks for a report on the research projects given to the different teenagers. One girl tells about a phone conversation with a professor in a nearby Christian college. You are impressed with her easy manner in speaking to the class.

The class is turned over to Miss Culver, who talks briefly about last Sunday's lesson. Some of the youth make comments on what was covered last Sunday. A list of the most pressing things to be done in Sunday School class today is placed on the board. Next to the list are written the names of committees and students responsible for each activity.

One girl indicates her Bible resources committee is having trouble finding the names of all the places in the Bible as well as locating them on the map. Miss Culver indicates that she thought they would have trouble in this area and gives them a resource book; the committee goes immediately to a table and begins to look for the answers.

The construction committee goes to the table and begins working on the map of Palestine, painting in the different sections of the country, as well as filling in the names of places supplied by the Bible resource committee.

You ask if they plan to show a relationship between the Bible and everyday life. "Not in this group," a boy answers. "This map is our job. It was our idea, too. Therefore, we get to make it. The group over in the corner is trying to fit the Bible to life. We felt we had to work on practical applications, so we formed a committee."

You go to Miss Culver with your question about practical application. She laughs. "The young people in this church are so conscientious about living out the Bible that they suggested something should be done. So they wanted a committee to make it practical. I knew this was not the way to do it; however, I wanted them to find out this frustration for themselves."

"Well, how do you make the Bible live in their everyday life?" I asked. She went on to say, "After we have done our work in committees, we discuss it in the whole class. In this discussion we point out scriptural principles that I believe will form their values and ultimately change their lives."

You walk over to the committee working on practical application. "How do you like it?" you ask one of the boys. "Well," he says cautiously, "the committee is all right, I guess, but I got on this committee because no one else would serve. I can paint ships, water, and people better than any kid in this class—maybe better than anyone in the whole church. Miss Culver says we should all serve on one committee and not do what we do best. Maybe next time I'll get on the committee I like."

You move on to another group which is working in a far corner of the room. "We're writing a play to present our map to the rest of the Junior High School Department." You ask if they have learned much about life in Bible times. "Oh, quite a lot, I think; as we act out life in Bible times, it will become more meaningful to us. We had to do a lot of reading and find a lot of pictures on just how life was."

You walk by the group doing the research. "How are you coming?" "Things seem to be going great," answers Sue. This is the group that complained earlier of difficulties. But the book Miss Culver gave them seems to be answering a lot of their questions. They seem to be working smoothly now. Apparently they have talked over their difficulties and have gained a new sense of direction.

Miss Culver moves from group to group, stopping here to watch a particular activity, pausing there to make a comment or ask a question.

Toward the end of the class period the whole group is called together. The map committee shows their progress and receives suggestions from other members of the class. The chairman of the research committee announces that his group finished their report for the whole class, and the map can now be finished. The committee on the play indicates some of their problems. The don't want to be childish; they want to be professional in presenting the project to the class.

Observations

In Miss Culver's class the youth were learning many things about the relationship of the various fields of study and their school experiences and life. Do you think they learned as many facts as in Mrs. Strauss's class? Did their learning have meaning for them? Should youth enjoy their Sunday School experiences?

EVALUATION

You have made some classroom observations. Mrs. Strauss, Gordon Luff, Jim Phelps, and Miss Culver were viewed in the teaching position. In order that classroom observation may result in more meaningful learning, it is imperative we have in mind certain basic concepts that determine the effectiveness of learning. Remember, teaching is the guiding of learning activities. As has been stated before, learning is not the accumulation of facts; neither is teaching the impartation of facts only.

The effectiveness of teaching depends upon the organization of experiences for learning. Principles of teaching are necessary, but many times these principles cannot be determined because they are intimately related and merged into one another. As a result, when we observe teaching, we are looking at one process. However, the effectiveness of teaching depends upon six principles of teaching: background, focus, interaction, individual differences, learning materials, and judging results. The following outline is intended to separate the factors of teaching and give you a framework to observe and evaluate Mrs. Strauss, Gordon Luff, Jim Phelps, and Miss Culver.

1. *Background.* Here we consider the context in which learning goes on. Remember the background does not prepare you to teach, but the background actually is part of the teaching process. In Mrs. Strauss's class the context of learning was the textbook approach—Bible and quarterly. The questions she used, in appearance at least, opened avenues for appreciation and exploration, but this wide context was dealt with exactly like a textbook. The whole assumption for learning was a verbal stimulus-response basis. The lessons possessed the quality of concreteness. There were only limited opportunities for exploration, discussion, and thought.

Gordon Luff also approaches the lesson for a verbal stimulus-response learning process. He is attempting to overcome the past adverse teaching conditions and needs the enthusiasm and good will of his students. Therefore, he builds his class on motivation, attempting to solve problems. Questions are handled in small groups; the large group is limited to inspiration and communication of Bible knowledge.

In Jim Phelps's class the entire background lacked a dynamic appeal and had the general character of a lesson to be learned under compulsion. The Sunday School time was spent mainly on mastering material of content with little or no use of any type of teaching aids. Students' needs were not considered, nor were the students motivated to exploration and desire for spiritual life. The content of the lesson will be forgotten as soon as the student leaves the class; however, the objectionable features, such as Ralph's humiliation, will be remembered.

The background of learning in Miss Culver's class, while still verbal, differs both in content and dynamics from that of the other teachers. The new material is intrinsically interesting and vital to the students. Students seem to enjoy their learning experiences and we might call it "meaningful learning." The world of the Bible was brought concretely and impressively into relationship with Sunday School learning.

2. *Focus.* Under this heading we consider the direction or focalization of the learning process. What demands the attention of the teacher and student in the classroom? In Mrs. Strauss's class, focus was established by the announced passage or page in the quarterly, or the topic.

Learning is thought of as an information-getting process. Reflection, analysis, and reasoning were done, but all effort was still subject-centered.

The focus of Gordon Luff is salvation. He ends his lesson with a gospel invitation. The Christians are exhorted to attend visitation and win the lost to Christ. Luff feels the Word of God will cause a Christian to grow as well as bring conviction on the unsaved.

In Jim Phelps's class the focus of attention was designated by filling out quarterlies, assignments and questions. The pupils' purpose was to cover the material, and Jim Phelps's purpose was to find out whether the material had been covered. The students will read aloud in class and memorize, but the material will do little to change their lives. In Mrs. Strauss's class learning not only involves facts to be acquired but activities to be experienced and problems to be solved. Memorization was not the focus, but rather understanding was needed to make progress in the lesson. The lesson was centered around experiences rather than facts.

3. *Interaction.* Here we consider the social interaction between the teacher and pupil; between pupil and pupil; and between pupil and others. The teacher is not the only source of teaching. Youth will perhaps learn more from other youth than through the teacher. No Sunday School class is an island; each teacher must depend on other personalities to help in the teaching process. Note that Mrs. Strauss is at the center of the room. She is the dictator, even though a good one. The students' social pattern was characterized by submission as a result of their imposed self-discipline. The teacher did most of the talking, although she asked several thought questions. Even though there was a good bit of give and take between teacher and pupil, the teacher was still in control. The room seating and physical equipment did not contribute to class freedom. There was some limited delegation of authority.

Interaction is planned for the small group in Gordon Luff's class. Here questions are raised both by the counselors (teachers) and the pupil. The counselors realize it is their duty to contact students before class as well as during the week. The main session is a strong presentation of the Word of God with no interaction planned. Psychologists call this S-R (stimulus-response); the teacher stimulates and the pupils respond. Accordingly, the greater the stimulus, the greater the response. The pupils respond to the strong leadership of Gordon Luff, whereas they are turned off by Jim Phelps.

The pupils have very little respect for Jim Phelps, and he displays his lack of respect for the students in his class. The atmosphere is one of military subjection rather than an educational atmosphere of creativity and mental excitement. Negative discipline prevailed. Jim Phelps has an attitude of keeping kids out of trouble, rather than submerging them into the lesson so that they have no time for deviate behavior. There was little attempt to show a relationship between the topics and sub-topics, even though there was lip service to making the lesson applicable to life.

Note that Miss Culver was not in the center of the room. She did not stand as a dictator giving out orders but rather as a fellow seeker after the truth. There was student interest because there was purpose. The social interaction was characterized by cooperation. Discipline was not negative but rather was generated by participation in a common learning task—map-making, play-writing, research, etc., in which all had a responsibility. Every student in the room had some relationship to an overall class project. At times the coordination broke down, but there were channels for functional unity. There was a spirit of cooperation, group morale, and esprit de corps.

4. *Individual differences.* All students are different. They have different educational backgrounds, psychological make-ups, social maturity, and spiritual levels of achievement. Motivation is different; so is the I.Q. Therefore, we can't expect all students to learn the same thing, nor can they learn at the same rate. Each student is an individual and he must be treated as such. In Sunday School class we grade as close to age as possible, hoping to localize some of these differences, but still a teacher instructs individuals, not classes.

Mrs. Strauss appeared to be interested in students, but notice the room was organized into a homogeneous group. The entire class was expected to attain the same educational goal, even though individuals were recognized and dealt with through questions and answers. There was little or no social relationship in the classroom between individual teens or groups of young people. The students were judged on their verbal responses in class, even though Mrs. Strauss expressed interest in Hank.

Gordon Luff has slanted his class to mass appeal, realizing that a strong group will reach the individual and ultimately pave the way to minister to the individual. Luff feels the fringe teens will attend an attractive program. He says, "The average teen will not attend if put on the spot; here they can have security in anonymity, and from their attendance can be led into participation in class activities."

Jim Phelps treated all of his students alike. There were uniform lesson experiences on a uniform schedule. Note the definite time schedule to which all had to adhere. As in the army, the individual has to "give" himself for the majority. Individual differences were expressed in nods of approval to those who read well and frowns for those who could not.

In Miss Culver's class individual effort as well as group effort was seen. The choice of work (writing a play, making a map, doing research) showed a great variety of interest and yet was related to a common class project. Note that one boy served on a committee that was not to his liking, even though he chose to do so. The individual was motivated to activity, insights, and understanding, rather than to the accumulation of facts.

5. *Learning material.* Here we see the building blocks of education. The content is important but also the sequence of content. Knowledge, skills, and attitudes all make up the learning material. There was an attempt on the part of Mrs. Strauss to structure learning by introductions, previews, questions, and arrangement of material. The basic assumption was to review the old in preparation for study of the new. The main center of interest was the molding of subject matter into a logical pattern. The sequence of material to be learned came through sequence of subject matter rather than through the pupils' interest.

Since the quarterly method had not worked and the kids had a mental block to class manuals, Luff uses a verse-by-verse exposition of the Bible. The other material used to attract attention are: contemporary music, attractive banners and backdrop, testimonies and participation songs. Bible facts, applied to life, are Luff's building blocks for learning experiences.

Jim Phelps's basic assumption was the accumulation of knowledge and facts. The order of the learning material was determined by the Sunday School quarterly. Routine reading (aloud and quiet) predominated in the class. Jim Phelps might say that teaching is presenting a block of facts held together by requirements. Note the opposite in Miss Culver's class. The lessons to be learned in this class were more than facts. Students learned how to state a purpose and to carry it out. As they planned their projects together, they learned how a Christian community should work together. The contributing of ideas to a committee and the collecting of information will help the pupil as he serves on other church committees, working in a creative manner for the glory of God. These small committees will have to seek consensus and make decisions. Learning to make decisions together is a needed lesson to be learned in the church. The concept of doing one's share of the work reflects the believer's relationship to the body of Christ.

6. *Judging results.* Evaluation has to do with the way a teacher determines the success or failure of his teaching. In public school a teacher may give a test to evaluate his teaching and the pupils' learning. This evaluation is reflected in the report card. In the Sunday School class evaluation is less tangible. Mrs. Strauss will probably evaluate the class

on the basis of direct results. The change in the life will be judged more by the accumulation of facts in the mind than by inward changes of the life. Good students don't drink beer; they attend Sunday School, answer questions, and fill out the quarterly.

Gordon Luff was getting the success he desired, a large attendance and youth coming forward to accept Christ. However, we might ask if he is satisfied with the group of kids who sit together, the greasers and the hippies. Also, we know that youth make professions of faith, but are they continuing in the church and are their lives being changed?

Jim Phelps's students were judged on how they responded in class. Those who answered questions promptly received smiles and nods of approval. Those who weren't paying attention were embarrassed. The good student is quiet and responsive; the bad student is not.

In Miss Culver's class she is willing to let the students fail. She let them form a committee on practical application, knowing this is not the way to apply the Bible to life. She said, "I wanted them to find out this frustration for themselves." Evaluation of the Sunday School class's teaching will be based on the total learning process.

Two objectives were evident in this class:

(a) The understanding by Miss Culver of the pupil as a learner and,

(b) The understanding by the student of himself as a growing child of God. The all-round development of the student becomes the aim and the point of judging such a lesson.

Note where "you" were in each room. You were the observer and actually took a field trip to the Youth Sunday School class. In Mrs. Strauss's class you sat to one side of the circle. She was the center and if she so chose, she could turn the lesson over to you. The lesson was in her command. In Jim Phelps's class you were ignored. He had little time for visitors, and you were not a part of the class; as a matter of fact, you were uncomfortable. Jim Phelps, like Mrs. Strauss, was in charge. However, she used human techniques to reach the students. When you attended Miss Culver's class, you had freedom. Note you walked about, carried on conversations with students and with groups. Yet you didn't interrupt the lesson—you were a part of the lesson. Miss Culver was not in command, but she seemed to be in control. Learning seemed to be centered in each student, rather than in the teacher.

Which teacher do you think will be the most effective? Who will communicate the most Bible content? Who will change lives? Which teacher will the pupils enjoy, and for whom will they work hardest? Which teacher will have immediate results? Long-lasting results? Which teacher can the Holy Spirit work through best?

CONCLUSION

As you observed these classrooms, you may have found yourself approving or disapproving the various activities and procedures you saw. Your reaction was only natural. What you like and dislike is based upon your training thus far. You have built up an "ideal teacher" in your mind. You judge and evaluate all teaching by this ideal teacher. Remember, some of the things you dislike in some teachers may be effective in terms of teaching; the things you dislike may produce learning. Also, some things that you like in teachers may not be effective.

These "concomitant" learnings are sometimes more influential in molding the students' lives than stated aims. You as the teacher will have to determine what you want to produce in the students. Then upon your foundation you are set to begin teaching. You will be able to accept or reject methods on the basis of whether or not they contribute to the results they want. The next chapters in this section will be concerned with the nature of learning, structuring the Bible lesson, and the methods of teaching.

15

LEARNING AND THE YOUNG PERSON

Sunday morning and it's time for the Sunday School lesson. You have studied well, and your lesson plan is written. You've spent time looking for illustrations and have some practical ones from the fields of sports and current events. You have spent time in prayer. During the lesson you express yourself well and students seem to be attentive. You cover the material well and use several teaching aids. However, something is wrong. You discover they aren't learning. The true test of teaching is a change in the students. Are teenagers learning anything from your teaching? If students aren't learning, then you aren't teaching.

When you attempt to teach the Bible to young people, unless learning takes place, your effort is wasted. There is no teaching without learning. In this chapter we would like to analyze how the teenager learns. For the most part, the teenager learns as all other people. The principles and laws of learning are the same; however, the application of these principles to the young person is different. The young person lives in a society all his own and has drives, needs, ambitions all his own. As you understand how the laws of learning apply to the teenager, you can better become a teacher of teenagers, guiding them into learning experiences.

DEFINITION OF LEARNING

Learning is progress in the use of abilities that comes through ex-

220

perience drawn from the curriculum, reflecting a continuous pattern in the life.

Learning Is a Change

Unless the young person's life is changed, he has not learned. He may repeat a Bible verse by rote or answer the question from the Sunday School quarterly, but if there is not an inner change with an outer manifestation, there has been no learning.

This change comes in several ways:

1. *Improvement.* Learning may reflect itself in better motor co-ordination or better mental facility. The change may be the teenager's improved ability to solve the problem he is facing. The change may be new insights into life or a new interpretation of his role in life.

2. *Experience.* The teenager must show progress in his learning of abilities as reflected in his experience. Experience is not just an emotional feeling. Too often religious experience is interpreted to mean feeling— love, hate, joy or repentance. The term "experience" can be defined in four steps:

(a) Experience begins with a stimulus from the outside: something that attracts attention and demands a response. You, as the Bible teacher, come from without and must produce a spiritual response in the lives of your pupils.

(b) The teenager must have a sensation. Sensation simply is the bridge from the outer world to the inner man. The material and experience being presented in class must come through one of the senses—sight, smell, hearing, taste and touch. The senses are the windows of the soul, the media of communication by which you as a teacher may stimulate the pupil to learn. One law of teaching indicates that the greater the stimulation, the greater the sensation, and ultimately the greater the response.

(c) After a sensation there must be perception. Perception is the teenager's understanding of the experience and material as well as his interpretation of the meaning. Perception is the youth's insight into relationships. He sees the relationship of the stimulus to his inner understanding. Differing backgrounds in young people will produce different perceptions. True perception by the youth brings on response.

(d) A response comes when the teenager acts on the stimulus. The response should achieve the aims of the lesson. It should be the desired outcome of teaching. Many times we have little response because we plan indefinitely. We do not know how we want the teens to respond to the Word of God.

3. *True Learning.* A teenager may sit in your Bible class. He may show progress in the use of his ability as reflected in his experience and yet not have a true learning experience prompted by the spiritual and educational aims of your class. True learning must satisfy the goals of the lesson and come from the demands of the material. A teenager may sit in class and count the bricks on the wall. He can recite the number of bricks or any other thing he might count, but he has not learned, for this experience was not prompted by the aims of the class. The aims of the Bible class must be accomplished to produce a valid learning situation.

Learning Is a Continuous Experience

True learning must produce a continuous experience in life. The teenager may commit to memory facts, verses, and outlines, yet forget them in six weeks. Has he really learned? Have the facts become a part of him? If true learning has taken place, the lessons become a part of him and become continuous in his experience. He may forget some of the facts, but they have added to his sum total of knowledge and will influence him in experience, decisions and activities of the future. True learning has a permanent effect upon the individual.

THE LAWS OF LEARNING

When teaching teenagers, you cannot expect to break the laws of learning and accomplish good teaching. You must understand the laws of learning, work with the laws of learning, and apply the laws of learning if you are going to accomplish any results in the life of the teenager. The laws of learning are more important than the application of any teaching technique in the classroom situation. Therefore, it behooves the teacher of teens to understand the nature of teenagers and the laws of learning as they apply to teaching teens.

The Law of Motivation

Learning is most effective when the teenager is properly motivated. The youth who wants to learn is the youth who will learn. Motivation is 90 percent of teaching. The teacher of teens may have a poor presentation and a withdrawing personality, yet if this teacher motivates the teen to want to learn, he has overcome the most difficult task of teaching. The teacher who motivates well teaches well.

Motivating the teenager to work is difficult and calls for diligence by the teacher. To motivate the teenager to work, the teacher must work.

There are a few practical applications that can be used in motivating teenagers. Some of the following may be applied to youth work with success:

1. *Testimony*. When someone indicates a reason that he has had success, this stimulates the teenagers to seek the same route. A testimony can be given by the teacher or the teens themselves. Use of the testimony motivates young people.

2. *Band wagon*. The band wagon principle gives the idea, "Everyone is doing it, why aren't you?" The business world uses the band wagon principle many times to oppose the principles of the church. The church and the Bible class teacher may use this to motivate the teenager. "Everyone is studying the Sunday School lesson, why aren't you?" The band wagon principle brings the pressure of teenage society to bear on the youth.

3. *Illustrations of achievement*. Teenagers are motivated to action when they hear about other teenagers who have had successful avenues of action. Tell often of teens who live for Christ, teens who serve Christ, teens who have successful, satisfying lives.

4. *The whip*. The whip is motivation through reproof. As a teacher, you may reveal the faults or basic lack in a young person. By pointing out the failures of the teen, he is motivated to work better, study harder, or strive longer. Be careful of over-use of the whip. Constant reproof of the teen makes him a hardened skeptic. However, the teenager who has a desire for excellence can be motivated to greater heights by a true evaluation of his lacks and faults.

5. *Commendation*. Commendation is a method of motivating teenagers by appealing to their success. Praise motivates the youth. The general law of teaching shows that the dull student is motivated by praise, while the bright student is motivated by rebuke and challenge.

No matter how weak or inefficient the teenager, give him some praise. Churches tend to over-use rebuke in motivating teenagers. We are exhorted in God's Word to judge nothing before the time. After this exhortation God has given us the promise, "Then shall every man have praise of God" (I Cor. 4:5). If God will find some good in every person who enters heaven, how can we who are his servants find less?

6. *Statistics*. The use of statistics reveals to teenagers the true nature of the situation. Statistics are a great method of motivating individuals. When the teenager is told that 90 percent of young people wear this fashion, or 75 percent attend this event, this motivates them. Marks in school are statistics that motivate. A passing grade on a driver's license test moves them to learn. Statistics may be college entrance, selective service rank, or seniority at the place of employment. Statistics give reasons for actions and impetus to follow through. Statistics force

reality into the teenager's subjective thinking by putting the situation in its true perspective.

One of the greatest faults of the church is the faulty use of statistics. We quote facts and numbers without seeking to validate their truthfulness. In using statistics, make sure that they are valid. Then be careful to quote statistics in light of their qualified application. When statistics are rightly used, reasons become concrete rather than theoretical.

7. *Peer pressure.* The teacher may motivate by bringing pressure on the teenager through other young people. One of the greatest pressures on teens is the need of conformity. Teenagers receive their suggestions from the gang or clique. The youth leader who can move his entire group and thereby bring along the individual is the successful youth leader.

As a youth teacher you may motivate through negative means, which may include embarrassment, threats, and punishment. Note that this may bring results for a while but soon loses its effectiveness. At the same time you as a teacher may motivate through positive means which involve rewards, recognition and commendation.

After all is said and done, the most effective method to motivate teenagers is through prayer. Prayer moves God to move men. Pray. Pray much. Pray much for your teenagers. Pray much for your teenagers to want to do God's will.

The Law of Activity

Learning is most effective when the teenager has interaction with that which is to be learned. Picture the average teenager in the Sunday School. The teacher is talking. The student is sitting with both hands in his pockets. He is staring at the floor. His feet shuffle back and forth. If he had a question, he does not have the freedom to ask. The teacher believes that talking is teaching and listening is learning.

In the area of activity the teacher must produce an atmosphere that is conducive to learning. The teenager will learn according to his involvement with the subject. Only as he becomes involved with the Word of God can he learn. The Bible must be examined, not explained! The Word of God must be discovered, not declared! Revelation is not only propositional; it is personal.

At the same time you must realize that vigorous teaching does not produce vigorous learning. The law of activity indicates that the teenager must be active rather than passive. "We learn to do by doing." Activity with the Word of God motivates to further learning.

The Law of Readiness

Learning is most effective when the teenager has been prepared to learn. When the young person comes into the Bible class "cold" and unprepared, he cannot realize the greatest contribution of the class. He needs a background for active participation and class discussion. This background comes as the teen opens, studies, memorizes, searches, and explores the Word of God for himself.

The law of readiness has been called the law of assignment. We give assignments or homework to teenagers for many reasons:

1. *To prepare students for class*
2. *To teach the teenager*
3. *To apply the lesson to everyday life*
4. *To structure the experience for learning*
5. *To cause teenagers to see their own lack and hence to stimulate in them a spirit of inquiry*
6. *To cause students to see the relationships between facts, experiences, and life*
7. *To review what has been taught in former lessons*

Getting teenagers to do assignments and Sunday School lessons is one of the most difficult tasks of the teacher. The teacher who would get the teen to prepare lessons must himself be prepared. He must study far enough in advance so that he can give some preview of what is to come. He must study far enough in advance so that he can guide the teenager in reading, research, and answering questions. Ask the teenager to do extra work. Ask him to do interviews concerning the Sunday School lesson. The teenager can gather opinions from other people concerning the questions of the lesson. Creative thought can be used.

The teacher may have a negative attitude toward the assignments. He may not understand their value and he may not want to get involved in extra work in making assignments or in listening to students' results. Also, he may not want to be exposed to the possibility of students demonstrating that they know more than the teacher. You as the teacher should believe in the value of assignments. Give assignments because you want the teenager to become more interested and satisfied in his experience of studying the Bible. Be prepared to give assignments. Know what you are going to do and what you are going to ask. Many Sunday School publications have plans for daily Bible reading, questions for discussion, and directions for research. Use them. Put some life into the assignment. Avoid routine and dullness. Make assignments vital and interesting. You as the teacher must grasp the occasion for some interesting bit of conversation on the assignment. Indirect, spontaneous assignments by the teacher will arouse more response than any dull, monotonous statement that something should be done for next Sunday. Think through the assignment:

1. *Are the questions clear and specific?*
2. *Are they easy enough for this class?*
3. *Are they challenging enough to arouse interest and curiosity?*
4. *Do they make sense and seem worthwhile to the student?*
5. *Are they too long? Too short?*
6. *Are they related to the aim of the lesson so that they can support the general discussion?*

Expect results. Get across the attitude that you expect the student to come through with the assignment. Most teenagers will respond to the youth leader who expects something from them. There needs to be a serious note of responsibility. The teacher and the teenager must have the attitude of working together with God for his glory. The teacher has his part, and the teenager has his part. As partners in the experience of studying the Word of God, offer help to the teenager. After the class session pause to give a few moments to discuss the assignment with certain teenagers. Give them encouragement. Visit them. Help them in any way in which you can.

Take a few minutes occasionally during the class period to go through the assignment. Checking up on the assignment is the most important occasion in the Bible lesson. This is the time when the results of the assignment are shared with the class. Never neglect to call upon them for the assignment when it is due. The student who is not called on when he has his assignment ready will usually become discouraged and stop studying the Word of God.

The Law of Apperception

Learning is most effective when the truth to be taught is learned through truth already known. When working with teenagers, take nothing for granted. Many teenagers will give you the impression that they know it all. They do not. They put on a mask to cover up the inability to perform as adults, when they desire to be accepted as adults. The teacher who takes nothing for granted but builds upon the foundation is the one who gets results. However, when the teacher has built a lesson in previous weeks, he can build on that which is already taught. But first, review to be certain of the foundation. Remember, the basic assumption in teaching is not *how much* but *how well* we teach.

All teaching must advance in some direction. Teenagers who sit in the class are either growing in faith or becoming skeptics. There is no neutral ground in the classroom. A good teacher constantly builds on past knowledge—but most important, he builds.

Knowledge does not pass from the teacher to student as bread is passed from one basket to another. Learning is a process of graded steps and the teacher must give diligence to see that the teenager takes each step in its own logical sequence. Make sure that the learning steps are broken down into small steps so that the teen can scale them by himself. To do this the teacher must find out what the teenager already knows. Here is where the use of the question is vitally important. Make the most of the youth's knowledge and interest. Ask him questions. Encourage him to ask questions. Relate every lesson to the former lesson. Make sure by a good review that he understands before you proceed to the next point.

The good teacher proceeds from the known to the unknown. A bridge is important between the two. This bridge in the last analysis is a relationship. And learning is seeing relationships. Some relationships that can be seen are the parallels of two Bible verses, the parallel of a problem and answer in the Word of God, the parallel of a scriptural principle to everyday life. In the final analysis Christianity is a relationship.

16

METHODS OF TEACHING YOUNG PEOPLE

The aim of the first section in this chapter is to show you what must be taken into consideration when choosing a method of teaching youth. Other sections deal with a brief description of methods of teaching teenagers. Teaching may be in a Bible class, Sunday School class, Sunday evening Christian Endeavor, or other Christian youth work.

BASIS FOR CHOOSING TEACHING METHODS

Age of Your Class

The age of your group is one of the most important concerns to you. Have you considered the three basic age groups: 12-14 years, early; 15-17 years, middle; and 18-24 years, late. Each group has its own needs.

1. *Early.* In the early age group (12-14 years), you will find a tendency toward being together and doing things together rather than individual activity. So you must then plan your teaching to meet the needs of youth as a group. But this group will have a tendency to do things in two separate groups, boys against girls.

2. *Middle.* In the middle group (15-17 years) you will find them becoming interested in doing things together as a gang. Here you will find mostly mixed groups, perhaps not as couples but as a mixed gang. You will find individuals in this age group becoming interested in those

of the opposite sex but still they will do things as a gang if they are planned in an informal way. You will find that this age group is most critical and that their thinking is greatly gòverned by the latest fashions and what they read. Cliques will become more of a problem, so you must plan your lesson to work away from these cliques and toward a Christian goal. You will find that much prayer will be needed to analyze this age group and to know how to meet their needs.

3. *Late.* The late group (18-24), consisting largely of couples and college students, has a need completely different from that of the others. You will now need to plan programs along a more intellectual line with a logical aim behind everything that is said and done.

Needs of Your Class

What are the needs of your group? Have you stopped long enough to consider just what would best meet the immediate needs of your group or class? If not, stop now and do so before your organization grows less interesting or you lose another young person. Are they being taught how to be future leaders, Sunday School teachers, presidents of groups or church leaders? Perhaps a study in leadership and qualifications of deacons or Sunday School superintendent would be good material for your class's next study series.

Have you tried sitting down and making a mental or written list of the needs of your group? Keeping these needs in mind would produce a better method of presentation. Needs determine the method of approach.

You will find that the needs of your group will vary with environment. Economic, social and educational background—each of these things must be taken into consideration before choosing a method of presentation.

Needs of Your Students

After noting the age of your group and the needs of your group as a whole, consider the needs of the individuals within that group. Each of these individuals differs completely from all the others. The make-up is different. This extends to life in every area—physically, mentally, morally, socially, and emotionally.

Have you noted any peculiar characteristic of an individual as he appears in a group? Have you visited his home? If you haven't, do so. When you are planning a lesson, remember you are ministering to needs of individuals within a group. You must consider the individual needs of every student. Have you geared your teaching to meet some need in Jim's life—the blond fellow who is popular in your group? Is your teaching geared to meet his need, which may be a dating question?

Enthusiasm of Your Students

What about the enthusiasm in your group as you prepare to lecture? Are some of the students asleep or talking so that you do not get their attention? Maybe you should try some other method of presentation. Have you ever thought of discussing this with your pupils to determine which type of presentation they like best? Unless your method is interesting, you will soon lose their attention and perhaps the student. Let your pupil and his needs be your guide in the methods you choose. Here again you will find age groups' needs and individuals' needs entering into the picture as you plan what method to use.

Facilities at Hand

1. *Equipment.* Having the proper equipment—chalk, board, maps, pictures, reading materials and audiovisual equipment—is vital. The facilities at hand will largely determine what methods will be used.

2. *Time.* Do you have adequate time to present the material through the method you have chosen? Something that is not finished during one class or meeting period will not hold interest when finished at a later time. You as a leader are responsible for planning or seeing that you have the time to present your method. Remember, going overtime is not the answer to a program that has too much content. Interest is lost when the bell rings.

3. *Place.* Do you have sufficient room for your presentation? Is the seating capacity sufficient to allow room for your pupils? If they are crowded together, interest will be harder to hold. Is the room adequately ventilated, lighted and heated? All these things must be taken into consideration if you are to be an effective teacher.

The Aim of Your Class

What is the purpose in your class for next Sunday? Is it just to fill up time, to entertain, to hold interest, or is it geared to meet a need in the lives of the members of your class? Every meeting, small or large, should have a goal. The purpose you have in mind should always be to meet the need of your group. The method and purpose should fit together perfectly.

The Spiritual Level of Your Class

If you consider your group a relatively immature one, then you have an idea as to some of the needs of the group. You may now plan a class and use methods of presenting the need for a dedicated life to Christ. Do not try to teach an immature group as you would a mature group, because you will not be meeting their immediate needs.

Then again, if your class is a spiritually mature group and is living for Christ, you have the opportunity of leading them into a deeper spiritual knowledge of God. You may also use this type of class for planned expression, projects, or creative expression. This group will probably have resource individuals. Planned responsibility may be used to help the youth get experience that they may use as they become the future leaders of the church. Use methods that will apply to your group in the light of whether they are carnal or spiritual Christians.

THE LECTURE METHOD IN TEACHING TEENS

Illustrations [1]

1. *Mr. Herman's class.* Mr. Herman has just taken over the teenage Sunday School class. He had been warned that they were not interested in the Bible. Therefore, he determined to get "ready" for them. The apparent solution, Mr. Herman reasoned, was to show them he meant business on the very first day and not to let up on this policy or discipline. After all, the Bible says, "Discipline yourselves." At the first sign of resistance, he barked at the ringleader to sit still, obey God, and listen to the lesson. Later he reported to the parents some out-of-school behavior he had discovered in one of the boys of his group.

Mr. Herman rigidly assigned the Sunday School lesson and made precise requirements of the young people who came. The amount of material to be covered necessitated a daily detailed time schedule. "This is one Sunday School class that's going to get results."

In the same way Mr. Herman had disciplined himself to cover the lesson. If his students strayed from the subject matter, he called them back to the topic with the remark, "We have much to cover, there is no time to lose." He chided them repeatedly to "redeem the time." Mr. Herman tried pop quizzes as a method to motivate his students to better study. In private talks with the young people he urged them to try harder to meet the curriculum demands of the lesson. Mr. Herman not only demanded a great deal of his students, he expected a lot of himself. He spent long hours preparing lessons, phoning absentees, and visiting sick pupils. The young people of the church were aware that he was a very conscientious teacher and that he was not hostile to them personally. It was not that Mr. Herman was not interested in the young people as human beings, he was.

---

[1] Elmer L. Towns, "How to Lecture Youth." Reprinted by permission from LEADER, © 1965, David C. Cook Publishing Co., Elgin, Ill.

As the teaching year progressed, tensions mounted among the young people in Mr. Herman's class. Some students quit coming. Others whose parents attended Sunday School continued to come but showed apathy or rebellion. The conscientious students responded. Several young people dropped out of church altogether.

2. *Mr. Belford's class.* Mr. Belford's youth class meets in a large old church. Trees and shrubbery, a bit tall and overgrown, give the church an air of stability and belonging to the neighborhood.

If you arrive in Mr. Belford's room early, you will note a number of students in small groups talking informally or working on a variety of projects. One group of students is working on a debate to be presented next Sunday. Another group is going over the opening exercise worship service to be presented that day. Still a third group is discussing a research project assigned by Mr. Belford. After the class begins, you note a warm spirit of cooperation in the class. There are some Christian magazines as well as a few biographies available. A class of nine youngsters is seated around a table with open Bibles, quarterlies, and pencils ready. Mr. Belford has studied well, has his lesson plan written out, knows what methods he is going to use. Some would say that he lectures to the students. He prefers to call it a "conversational discussion" method of teaching. Mr. Belford introduces the subject by relating it to a problem in life. Next he asks for student reactions. "Maybe we could start off with a few quick reactions. What impresses you about it? Who wants to start?" Several students start to talk and Mr. Belford nods to a girl across the table, "Mary, you start."

There is a spirit of permissiveness. When Hank, a shy sophomore, responded, he did not feel that he needed to make a speech. Most of the young people feel that they can interrupt Mr. Belford at any time in the lesson to make a point or ask a question. One teenager said, "Class is like a bull session on the Bible."

Since the students are sitting around the table, Mr. Belford also sits. The table makes it easier to write. Often Mr. Belford refers to the quarterly, and the students fill out the questions there. There is no attendance problem in his class.

Mr. Belford's classes are considered difficult but exciting. The youth feel that he cares about both his subject and them. Often a student will suggest a question that stumps Mr. Belford. In these cases he works with the student to find a solution to the problem. Mr. Belford feels that he can do a good job in making the Bible live for his students and he is confident that his classes are contributing to the development of their maturity by challenging them to think for themselves and stimulate their interest in the Word of God.

Evaluation

Mr. Herman's lecturing is not wrong; it's the way he goes about it that's wrong. Both Mr. Herman and Mr. Belford lecture, but they have different attitudes toward the lecture. Today many authorities criticize the lecture, yet the lecture is still the predominant method used in Sunday School. You will probably continue to use the lecture. I know I will. Let us do all we can to improve its use. First, we should give a definition. The lecture method might be better called "oral presentation by the teacher." Lecture is the procedure that includes all oral presentation by the teacher, whether it be by way of remarks made to clarify issues, to elaborate upon pupils' answers to questions, to supplement data already at hand, or whether it be by way of an extended formal exposition, or to indicate how something is to be done.

Oral presentation is used to a great extent at all levels of instruction. Lecture cannot be avoided, even at the teen level. It is impossible to eliminate oral presentation even from the methods of instruction that allow for greater pupil participation. Lecture must, then, be done effectively and intelligently with understanding of the laws of the teaching-learning process. If you have a sense of responsibility for the quality of your work, you will wish to master the technique of effective oral presentation.

Advantages of the Lecture

1. *The lecture makes possible the effect of the spoken word.* Spoken words are more effective means of communication, on the whole, than printed material. Inflection, emphasis, and explanation make the oral presentation an energetic and dynamic method of transferring knowledge. Teenagers are at the age when they can begin to think in concepts and are motivated through the lecture. The spoken word has a dynamic quality which draws men, causing them to follow the direction of its emphasis.

2. *The lecture makes possible the effect of the teacher's personality.* Through lecture the total impact of the teacher's personality becomes greater. Sometimes communication is affected by the way we express ourselves more than the content of our expression. At this point attractive Christian character does much to communicate. Teenagers will be motivated by what you are, as well as by what you say. The teacher should be fully organized and properly prepared to interpret the material to the teenager. The lecture affords opportunity for the imparting of information so that the teacher can be certain of the correctness of the statement. Good organization insures good teaching.

3. *The lecture saves time, space and energy.* When a teacher uses

the lecture, more ground can be covered in a short period of time than by use of any other method. Some classes, particularly teenagers, are large. The lecture can be prepared and presented to a large group better than other types of teaching methods. Then too, it is easier to lecture than to teach by the discussion or question method or any other method. Since not all teachers are well trained in the more difficult methods of teaching and many churches find it difficult to enlist and train many teachers, the lecture is more popular. However, just because it is popular and easy does not mean it is always the most effective method. Care must be used in choosing the right method of teaching teenagers.

4. *The lecture makes possible more effective use of supplementary material.* Most other methods of teaching revolve around the lecture, such as discussion, question, drama, forum, panel and debate. Often written material presents only one view. The textbook or Sunday School quarterly presents one side of the picture, but the teacher through lecture can give a wider experience and interpretation to the text. Lecture can present a broader picture.

5. *The lecture provides a method of giving the pupil proper perspective.* Immature minds experience difficulty in making proper evaluations. Teenagers are growing into adults; however, they are still immature in their understanding. The lecture can cause them to see relationships, give them reasons, and discriminate between what is important and what is not important. Through the lecture the teacher can use motivation and/or indoctrination.

The lecture must be made interesting with up-to-date illustrations from real life. There must be a striving after pupil participation because teenagers are growing rapidly, and interest is the key word. Teenagers may be restless and awkward and unable to find a comfortable position in their chairs.

Lectures must be well supported with good authority and allow the teenagers to think for themselves. Teenagers begin to question the validity and authority of presented ideas in school, home and church. This is the age when they want to reason everything out and they are asking "why."

When lecturing to teenagers make sure that new concepts are always introduced. They enjoy the thrill of adventuring with their minds. Leave some time for review of each past lecture, but don't bore them with review. Teenagers are experiencing an increase in their memory span and too much review becomes boring. They accept the challenge of new concepts. Teenagers like to think.

Lectures must take on the practical nature related to the actual problems in their lives. This satisfies their desire for pragmatic knowledge. What they hear must work in everyday life. Lectures must not be too dogmatic or try to force ideas upon teenagers. They must present a reason "why." The lecture must be logical and orderly. Arguments must be clear because teenagers have a new sense of independence and self-sufficiency. They have a great desire to think for themselves.

When to Use the Lecture with Teenagers

1. *For large classes.* When the class is large and pupil participation must be limited, use the lecture. However, always speak to individuals, never to the group, no matter how large the group becomes.

2. *Limited background.* When pupils' background and introduction to the subject are limited, use the lecture. Do not use pupil participation and ask the teen for an opinion he has not yet formed. You will seriously hamper the effective use of pupils' participation if they have a limited background.

3. *Introduction of new material.* When introducing new or unfamiliar subjects, use the lecture. Here it is easier to give a summary, survey, and introduction into the entire subject. The confidence of the speaker's voice will give assurance to the teenager as he listens. The entire attitude and expression of the teacher is building up to the climax. Such expectancy on the part of the students will gain and keep attention. This is especially good when introducing new or unfamiliar material to the teenager.

4. *Limited seating facilities.* When the classroom seating arrangements are limited and are not conducive to informal discussion, use the lecture. There may be other circumstances presented by the physical facilities of the room that require the lecture. Use common sense in choosing your teaching method.

5. *Restricted time.* When time becomes restricted, the lecture can be easily altered. It is easy for a teacher to expand or to detract from the material when lecturing. When students are participating it is sometimes hard to restrict their contributions. When you are discussing printed material, it is sometimes difficult to skip over material. However, when the lecture is being used, material can be deleted and the lecture can be easily summed up.

6. *To motivate, provoke, and stimulate.* Use the lecture when the entire personality of the teacher is geared to provoking and stimulating thinking and imagination on the part of the public. Every method of motivation should be used to cause the student to think. When a teacher imparts vision, he is imparting some of himself. The lecture can best be used to impart vision. The lecture must challenge, motivate, and show the value of things, because a teenager's mental abilities are at the most

productive stage. The lecture can incorporate the vast amount of knowledge and background of the teacher and make it pertinent to the teenager. The many years of judgment and experience can be brought to bear on the immediate situation, and hence motivate, stimulate and provoke the student to thinking.

When Not to Use the Lecture

1. *When experience is a necessary factor in learning.* Practice perfects theory and theory perfects practice. There must be demonstration and opportunity to learn in every situation. For example, one learns to teach by teaching. The teenager learns to pray by praying and he learns to explore the Bible by exploring.

2. *When the class is small.* Small classes are well suited for other methods of teaching. Small groups do well in exploration, silent thinking, discussions, and/or questions. Use other methods with smaller classes. However, do not rule out the lecture method in small groups.

3. *When students are eager to participate.* You must not stifle their desire to learn by enforcing silence. When pupils want to participate, you must not force them to sit and listen to a lecture. Involvement equals learning.

THE DISCUSSION METHOD IN TEACHING TEENAGERS

Teenagers love to talk. Therefore, use the discussion method often when working with teenagers. Discussion enlists the active cooperation of the whole class. The teen will actively participate in class if he knows that he has the opportunity to discuss, may be called upon to give an opinion, or is listening to a fellow teen give an opinion.

Advantages of Discussion

1. *Discussion broadens the thoughts in the class by presenting all sides of a vital question.* Sometimes the teacher may be narrow-minded or ill-prepared. Through discussions, students who have background and viewpoints can add their opinions. Opinions added by other teenagers, with reasons, arguments and conviction cause the student to think. Discussion produces thought.

2. *Discussion teaches tolerance and cultivates respect for the judgment of other teenagers.* Most young people reach the teens with attitude of "know it all." It is difficult for them to realize that parents, teachers, and friends know as much as they do. In discussion, arguments from an opposing point of view are entered with reasons and stimulation. Teenagers learn to give and take in a discussion.

3. *Discussion gives pupil and teacher practice in thinking clearly,*

honestly, and persistently. Churches must do more than indoctrinate. Churches must produce young people who think for themselves. Mature faith is not blind faith but rational faith. Discussion can stimulate teenagers to think clearly and persistently and hence arrive at mature faith for themselves.

The Teacher's Attitude Toward Discussion

1. *Discussion demands more ability, resources, and preparation on the part of the teacher than any other method.* Hence, discussion brings out the very best in some teachers; however, some teachers are lacking in their own resources and should be careful about leading a discussion.

2. *Discussions are limited to provocative problems in which there are different viewpoints within the group.* It is difficult to have a discussion over a point in which all are of common consent. Also it is difficult to discuss a Bible passage in which there are no conflicting interpretations. The nature and aim of the class will determine whether you should indoctrinate and lecture, or discuss and stimulate thinking. If you are going to lead a discussion, you must know the limitations, capacities and interests of each member of the group. Do not press a teenager beyond his own resources. Do not call for an opinion from a teenager when he has not had a basis on which to form an opinion.

3. *Discussion requires thorough preparation in advance on the part of every member of the class.* When leading a discussion, you must do more preparation than when leading a lecture. In lecturing, you present the material that you have on hand. In a discussion any subject may be brought up and you should have some background. If the class and the teacher do not have a thorough preparation for discussion, then it merely becomes "a pooling of prejudices and ignorance." Good discussion demands resources from materials, opinions, facts, and arguments. In the local church, most often, resources reside in an individual. Make sure the key individual is present for a good discussion.

How to Lead a Discussion

The teacher must open by developing, within his group, a "problem-attitude of mind" through the skillful presentation of questions. Next, the problem must be defined by different members of the group stating the matter as they see it. Then all the possible ways of acting under the circumstances should be considered. Once more the leader should skillfully ask questions which will shed light on the material. Each proposal must be weighed pro and con and, if necessary, assigned to committees or individuals for further study and then reported to the next class. Alternatives should be listed on a chalkboard, and continual summarizing should be made throughout the discussion to bring out the exact status of the problem. In the summary, the teacher should clinch the argument in a few words and give impetus for the discussion to follow. After the thoughts have developed into a coherent pattern, he should define it in a conclusion. Once the best solution is decided on, the last step is to plan a definite program to utilize the decision in future study or activity.

Dangers and Weaknesses of Discussion

Discussion demands more ability, resources and preparation on the part of the teacher than many other methods. Also, it is limited to provocative problems in which there are differing viewpoints within the group, but common interests. Discussion requires that the leader know the limitations, capacities and interests of each member of the group.

Discussion requires thorough preparation in advance on the part of every member of the class, lest it be merely a pooling of prejudices and ignorance. Also, discussion necessitates making sources of material relating to the problem available to the student. Finally, discussion requires time for the participants to learn the procedure itself.

THE QUESTION—ANSWER METHOD [2]

Bill Blake came home from Sunday School discouraged. He taught the youth class. Things weren't going well and he was ready to quit. The eleven students weren't responsive and Bill felt he was morally obligated to resign.

His wife knew that he studied well and was desirous that the boys grow spiritually. She was shocked to hear Bill talking of quitting and asked him why.

"I just can't seem to get through to the kids. I don't know what they are thinking in class. They don't seem to be with me, nor care about the lesson."

"Perhaps your answer is not to resign, but change your method of teaching. Why don't you try using a lot more questions in your teaching?"

"Use questions with them? Not me! When I'm in class and telling them what to do, I'm all right, but when I ask questions they clam up."

Bill's wife had been a schoolteacher. She replied, "Maybe I can give you some help on how to use questions. Try coming to class with a series of thirty questions on the Bible passage you're trying to teach. Continually ask questions of the teenager. If one question doesn't get a response, go on to the next question. Surely if you use the question method of approach, you can reach them and know where they are."

[2] Elmer L. Towns, "How to Use the Question and Answer with Teenagers." Reprinted by permission from LEADER, © 1965, David C. Cook Publishing Co., Elgin, Ill.

"I don't think so. When the students begin to discuss, they run away with the class. Instead of wanting to talk about the Bible lesson, they just want to talk about their own interests and problems."

"Maybe through the question you can find out what they are interested in and help them."

"If I allow them to ask questions, they may put me on the spot and find out I don't know much about the Bible. I'm afraid I'll have to leave this questioning to someone else. I'm just a teacher; I tell them what to do."

Do you feel like Bill? Do you feel as though you don't know how to use the question and answer method of teaching? Are you afraid to use the question in the classroom?

Questions and answers appeal to the nature of teenagers.

Teen age is the stress and strain period of life. Young people like to ask the question "Why?" The question and answer method of teaching appeals to their nature. Use it—it stimulates their natural tendency to inquire into the unknown.

Joan, a seventeen-year-old girl, may sit in class with a nice smile. Her face shows attention to the lesson and her Bible is open in her lap. However, her mind may be confused. She doesn't understand why Christ would spit on the ground and apply clay to a blind man's eyes to heal him. Use the question with young people to test their understanding of the facts and their ability to have insight into the Word of God. If a teenager is confused on step three, he will never reach step four.

The teenage mind is like the medieval castle. The teacher must storm the walls. Use the question to arouse curiosity and stimulate their interest in class. "If Jesus were God, how could He die?—He is eternal life." "What is death?"

Teenagers enjoy the thrill of adventuring with their minds. They are experiencing an increase in their memory span and they accept the challenge of new concepts. Ask questions to cause them to think.

Some youth workers are disturbed when their young people have questions. They should be concerned when teenagers have no questions. Growth comes through stress and pressure. Mental growth results in mental stresses. The youth faces opinions that contradict childhood belief. As the teenager struggles to synthesize all information coming to him into a consistent belief, he will have questions. Fight fire with fire. Question his questions.

By properly directed questions you can ascertain what your pupils have already learned. Also, you can correct misconceptions and help teens to see the relationship of the Word of God to their lives. Questions aid young people to organize their thinking and lead them to fruitful expression of their ideas.

Mr. Henry, a salesman, taught the high school class. Many times he was too busy to prepare properly but relied on his "gift of gab." Because he went to college and was on the debating team, he could think on his feet. It was seldom that a high schooler stumped him in class.

Sometimes when questions did stump Mr. Henry he would bombard the students with questions, hoping that the smarter pupils would give him the correct answer. He also did this when he didn't prepare well enough. If you teach like Mr. Henry, be careful, or you may get yourself trapped between third and home plate.

Mr. Henry also liked to throw out difficult questions. Many of these questions were raised in the philosophy class at university. These questions were perplexing and many times caused students to question their faith. Mr. Henry delighted in using this kind of question because he said, "It arouses the student's curiosity and stimulates his ability to think in new realms." However, Mr. Henry raised some questions that he didn't answer. Remember, teacher, questions cannot impart facts in Bible knowledge. If your questions drive students to find answers in the Word of God, you will produce educated enthusiasts. If not, you will produce hardened skeptics.

A good question should be brief, clear, direct, challenging and original. Ask the question of the whole class before selecting one pupil to answer. If you mention a pupil's name first, the rest of the class goes to sleep mentally. Give the pupil time to answer. Just because the classroom is silent, it doesn't mean that learning is not going on. If the pupil has difficulty, rephrase the question and make it a little easier. Don't embarrass the teen.

Accept any answer or any part of an answer that has value. Use any suggestions and never make the teen feel silly, whether he asks the question or answers the question. Be courteous. Question and answer is a give and take proposition. Avoid calling on or accepting too many answers from the same student. Teachers often go to two extremes. Marion is continually called on in class because she always has the right answer or John is picked on because he seems to be uninterested and unwilling to participate in class. Learning equals involvement; therefore, involve all students through the question.

Throughout the history of teaching, the question and answer method of education has been recognized for its value. Socrates made the question famous as a form of teaching, although the method of questioning was used long before his day. The question lay at the very heart of the teaching methods of Jesus Christ, as the gospel record discloses more than a hundred questions asked by Him. Today, among the multiplicity of methods, much teaching is done by means of the question, either as the chief method or as a component part of other methods of teaching.

Teenagers love questions. To them life is a question mark.

PANEL DISCUSSION

Teenagers seek authority and direction. Even though they like to discuss and take part, they also seek and need mature direction. This can be brought to them through the use of a panel discussion.

A panel discussion is an informal discussion by four to eight persons with different points of view, or backgrounds of knowledge and experience, before an audience. It may involve about fifty minutes of panel discussion with a half hour allotted to audience participation. Summation by the chairman ties the ideas together.

A panel encourages interaction, provides perspective through information and additional knowledge, and stimulates the audience to join in the problem-solving process.

How to Use a Panel

1. *Participants.* The members of the panel should be specialists in the area to be discussed and experienced in the art of discussion. The chairman is the key to successful panel discussion. He must regulate, focus, guide, clarify, point up key factors, and summarize the total contribution made.

2. *Preparation.* The room should be so arranged that the participants can see and talk with one another, yet be easily seen and heard by all members of the audience. The number of participants should be limited to five or six; more would make a balanced, integrated discussion difficult. Three or four are preferable. If an audience participation period follows, no more than an hour should be given to the panel. Agreement should be reached on the following points:

   (a) Scope of the discussion

   (b) Division of the problem into discussable topics

   (c) A specific time limit for each phase

   (d) The assignment of any special individual responsibilities

   (e) Some form of group outline or discussion plan (simple, short, flexible).

3. *Procedure.*

   (a) Chairman opens discussion by introduction of the subject problem and the panel members.

(b) Chairman secures interest of audience and prepares for following discussion.

(c) Chairman explains the procedure to be followed, indicating whether or not the audience will have opportunity to participate.

(d) Chairman opens the discussion with a question or statement.

(e) After the panel's discussion period, discussion opens up to the audience.

(f) Finally, chairman summarizes the conclusions of the total discussion period.

4. *Principles to follow.* Since participants in panel discussions speak to the audience as well as to each other, their language should be more precise and explicit than it would be in a private committee discussion. They must speak more deliberately and fully, avoiding verbal short cuts and technical language. Simple and direct language is always appropriate. It must be suited to the basic aim of problem-solving.

The chairman should lead off at the beginning and at junctures of the discussion by asking appropriate questions or making transitional statements. At every point in the advancing of group ideas, clear statements of belief accompanied by reasons should be made. Relevance to the problem is essential at every stage of the discussion.

Limitations to Panel Discussions

Beware of the tendency of some members to monopolize time. There are some teenagers who know it all and they tend to have an opinion on everything that comes up. Use tact in guiding these teens out of the discussion. At the same time, use tact to bring all teenagers into the discussion.

Another weakness of the panel discussion is the tendency of some members to ramble from subject to subject and make speeches instead of discussing. Well-prepared speeches may be enlightening but may not contribute to the point of the discussion. Also, in panel discussion, memmers tend to ignore the audience. They may discuss among themselves, attack one another, quibble over points, or tend to follow personal tangents. The point of a panel discussion is to communicate to the group.

FORUM

The forum has not been used much in the evangelical church, but it is an effective method of communication. A forum is a period of audience (or class) participation. It may follow a lecture, a panel discussion, a conference, or another form of public discussion. Usually, it is a lecture followed by a question-and-discussion period. In the class-room it would follow the lecture, taking the form of class questions and discussion.

Why Use a Forum?

1. It enables the audience to gain supplementary information from experts on points not fully developed.

2. A forum helps to give final form and organization to knowledge gained in the pre-forum period.

3. It provides an opportunity for correcting any distortion of facts or misunderstandings.

4. It provides opportunity for verbal expression by the audience as a supplement to their silent thinking and serves to review the ma-terial covered.

How to Use the Forum Method

The forum must be guided by a chairman. He may be the lecturer, the panel moderator, the conference leader, or someone designated for the task. It is important that he be skilled in the art of guiding discus-sion. His duties are:

1. To instruct the teens as to the mode of participation desired, i.e., informal discussion, questions and answers, comments from the floor, or a combination of these.

2. To stimulate participation by the use of leading questions, strik-ing statements which draw comment, posing issues previously discussed, etc.

3. To restate questions whenever there is a doubt that they have been heard or clearly understood.

4. To advise beforehand of any limitations on questioning or speak-ing so as to keep the discussion within reasonable bounds in regards to time and relevance.

5. To bring the forum to a satisfying conclusion by summarizing aptly and briefly while there is still interest in the subject.

The effective use of this method will depend, in a large measure, upon the teacher, lecturer, or expert who provides the pre-forum infor-mation. The best teacher will be free from contention and dogmatism. He will be frank and enthusiastic in advocating his position, yet co-operative in providing data and advice needed for full understanding. Further effectiveness can be attained if the audience is instructed to ask questions useful to others as well as to themselves, to phrase their questions and comments clearly, briefly and interestingly, and to maintain good taste and temper no matter how controversial the issues.

When to Use the Forum Method

It is best to use the forum method with questions of a controversial and contemporary nature, i.e., the type which would stimulate audience participation. Its primary purpose is to stimulate thinking and provide information—not to solve problems, although it may be used to explore problems with a view to gaining a tentative solution. It is best used with adult and college age groups. With a skillful chairman it may be effective with high school adolescents.

THE DEBATE

The debate is a technique of communication to teenagers that has not been used much in the church. Debates are better adapted to youth groups than the Sunday School class.

The minimum age for the use of the debate should be the senior high level. This group is just beginning to think in terms of issues rather than of pure emotional response. It should be a selected group because of the demand of time and effort involved in building a good case. A good maxim for debate is: "Read, read much, read very much," and "Think, think much, think very much."

The place of a leader in fostering debate is that of a guide, not a coach. He should make research material available to both sides in planning for the first few debates. The building of the case, however, must be left up to the members of the teams with occasional assistance, where needed, for special problems. He must strive for absolute justice on each side, making sure that no debater holds the opposite position from that which he is proposing.

The students must have a real desire to find the true solution to the problem. This means that the subject should hold vital interest in their minds and be closely related to their interest span.

The material should be controversial in nature and a practical problem facing the age group utilizing the method. Furthermore, the subject must be non-technical enough to be of interest to the team's members and the average audience, thus stimulating involvement in the issues and their implications.

The debate method should be used where there is a definite attempt to get the audience or group to see the full implications of a problem, to see the other or both sides of a question for perspective. It should always be in the form of a resolution in the affirmative, placing the burden of proof on the affirmative. Sample propositions might be: "Resolved: Christian Colleges give the finest preparation for life to the Christian student." "Resolved: All Christians should try to go to the mission field." "Resolved: A Christian should participate in labor unions."

What Is a Debate?

Debate is a form of argumentation which has the following features:

1. It is the analysis of a problem with both sides defended.

2. It is a logical argument based upon evidence bearing upon the subject presented by each side, out of their independent research and study.

3. It is a brief persuasive composition created with a view to winning acceptance of the listeners that its view is true.

4. In the delivery it involves all phases of the public-speaking science.

5. Debate differs from argument in that it involves a definite time limit for each speaker; it is governed by parliamentary rules; there is an equality of speakers on each side; and it is couched in resolution form.

6. The review is accomplished through rebuttal by both sides in an equal amount of time.

7. A vote decides the case, either by the audience or by a judge.

Why Use Debate?

The debate brings the teenager to recognize a definite standard of achievement. This demands a thorough knowledge of the subject and develops a wholesome analytical attitude, reliability and resourcefulness through sustained and rigorous thinking. Debate fosters genuine humility in learning and brings the debater and audience a keen awareness of the disparity between finite and infinite knowledge. Debate engenders objectivity in thinking, and enables the participant to make a genuine contribution to his home, church and community life.

THE DEMONSTRATION METHOD

One of the favorite methods of teaching used by Christ was demonstration. When teenagers see a truth demonstrated, they remember much more than if they are told. Demonstration as a teaching method is the re-enactment of a given situation, scene or sequence of facts before a class.

The demonstration is pupil-centered and therefore gives maximum involvement to the student in learning. Also, involvement sustains the interest of the teenager, creating and holding maximum motivation. Demonstration also gives variety to the teaching process and affords opportunity for the pupil to learn by example and experience. All things considered, demonstration can become the most effective means of communication to the teenager. Who would try to teach a course in swimming by correspondence, or instruct a teenager in driving a car over the phone? Demonstration is indispensable to instruction of many subjects. (See demonstrations on counseling at the end of the sections on counseling.)

Demonstration is adaptable to all age groups but works especially well with young people and adults. It must of necessity be adapted to the particular situation and course.

Teenagers involved in the demonstration should be given ample time beforehand to prepare sufficiently so that the demonstration will be effective. In some cases, especially with young people, the participants should not be allowed to converse with each other before the actual demonstration—to add a real-life flavor as well as aid in negative and positive teaching. This is most important in soul-winning procedures and counseling demonstrations.

1. *Demonstration of Bible truth.*

(a) The re-enactment of the religious and civil trials of Christ, using students to portray the individuals involved.

2. *Soul-winning and counseling demonstrations.*

(a) Selected students re-enact, before the class, a meeting of two high school students trying to win a friend to Christ. The scene could be in a school lunchroom.

(b) A pastor can deal with a teenage problem. The youth would then have a chance to view their problem from two points of view.

3. *Church training programs.*

(a) Defective and effective teaching methods may be enacted before the class.

(b) The rights and wrongs of church ushering can be taught through this method.

(c) Visitation procedure can be effectively taught as a mock situation.

(d) Conduct a mock divorce hearing in which both sides of the case are presented. A judge (properly dressed) would preside over the hearing, with lawyers presenting the case.

(e) Song leading is an action that can be taught effectively through demonstration.

4. *Secular subjects demonstrated.* Areas of usage are as multiple as there are subjects. Brief historical scenes and events can be enacted. Scientific demonstrations are most effective and perhaps most common.

Language demonstrations, such as those used by Wycliffe Bible Translators, are also effective and valuable.

THE BUZZ SESSION METHOD OF TEACHING

The buzz session method of teaching is a comparatively new method for instructing and teaching others. This method has been called "discussion groups" or "the sixty-six method." It was called the "sixty-six method" because the room was divided into groups of six who were given six minutes to discuss a problem. When using the buzz session method of teaching, the group is divided into groups from four to ten persons to discuss or solve problems introduced by the teacher. Many times the teacher will begin with the lecture or some other form of instructing. Then at a set time, and according to the needs, the larger group is divided into discussion groups. The smaller groups usually do not leave the larger classroom or auditorium. When several groups are discussing at the same time, there is usually little distraction between the groups. (When two groups are in the same room, pupils hear one other distinct conversation in the room. When there are three or more groups discussing a problem, pupils hear a diffused sound rather than a distinct voice.)

When the larger group is divided, each smaller group should be given direct and clear guidance. Perhaps each buzz group is given the same problem; or, to cover more ground, each buzz group is given a different set of problems. The directions to each group should be written, either on paper or on the chalkboard.

When the buzz group first assembles, a leader should be chosen. He should then direct, not monopolize, the conversation. A reporter or secretary should be chosen for the group. The pertinent points and group conclusions should be recorded for the report later on.

Each person should be allowed to take part in the discussion. This is one of the advantages of the buzz group. Teenagers will enlarge their capacity according to their involvement in the learning situation. However, some teens who like to monopolize the conversation will have to be courteously "muzzled," while the bashful youth are encouraged to speak.

After a suitable length of time, the teacher should call the entire class to attention. Each group should be called upon for a report of their discussion. The report and summary by the teacher is as important as the investigation and discussion by the buzz group.

Those leading the buzz session should read the section on leading group discussion. Apply those principles in the buzz session.

There are limitations to teaching through the buzz session. When the teacher desires to communicate content or give inspiration, another method should be used. Buzz session should be used when the teacher desires to get student expression or involvement. Also, the buzz session should be used when exploration or problem solving is needed.

DYADS OR NEIGHBOR NUDGE

A *dyad* is a technique of teaching where a large class of students are arranged in pairs and assigned a topic for discussion. This method has also been called *Neighbor Nudge* because students carry on a discussion with the person next to them. The topic for dyad is usually a discussion of a lecture they have just heard. Also dyads can be used to introduce a new subject when students share opinions or experiences at the beginning of a class period.

Divide the class into pairs. Start at the left side of each row, and have the students number off for discussion. If the room is crowded. have the partners turn their chairs toward each other. This will help to minimize the sound of the discussions in the classroom.

Have each individual share with his partner one particular practical application gleaned from the exposition just presented by the teacher. Ask the students to project themselves into the near future and to try to determine how today's Scripture can relate to their lives in the coming week.

Set aside approximately three minutes for Neighbor Nudge after each presentation by the teacher. Remind the students that every person should contribute during the times of discussion. Since teens like to "rap," this is an excellent teaching method for young people. Dyads give them a chance to share their opinion either before or after a lecture.

If your class period is long, ask the students to take some notes during their discussions for a sharing time later with the whole class. The teacher should be flexible and use whatever time is available to encourage a maximum number of contributions by the students.

LISTENING TEAMS

Listening teams are an innovation in teaching, whereby the class is divided into teams at the beginning of a class. The teams of students are then given a question to answer and they must listen to the lecture to find their answer. After the lecture, the listening team gathers for discussion, after which a report is made to the larger class.

Listening teams usually have from four to six people on each team. Divide your class into groups. Try to have one question for each listening team. If not, more than one listening team will have to be working on the same question. Appoint a captain for each team. The captain will make a report to the entire class after the lecture.

Before the beginning of the lesson, have each team assemble at a specified place in the classroom. A good way to divide the class into teams would be to number the students (by fours, if four to a team, and so on) and then instruct them to sit together according to the designation of their numbers. This way, teams are not made up of social cliques, and there can be more interaction in the group; thus you produce fellowship among your young people.

Each team is given a listening assignment. Each listening assignment (question) can be typed out on a file card and handed to the team before the lecture begins. The value of a listening team is that *all* of the class gives close atention to *all* of the lecture, even though each team reports on only a part of the lecture. This is because a person doesn't know when the information concerning his assignment will be given, so he listens throughout the entire class session.

The lecture or oral presentation of the lesson should not take more than half of the class time. If you do not leave enough time for student discussion, class members will feel cheated and feel that you are just presenting another lecture. Therefore, the teacher must discipline himself to stop lecturing and give the students time to discuss.

Give the small listening teams five or six minutes to discuss the answers to their assigned questions. Someone in each listening team should write a summary of the discussion.

These small listening teams do not have to leave the room or seek another place in the building to have quiet. A number of small group discussions can be carried on in one classroom at the same time without disturbance.

As the small groups are having their discussions, write the four questions on the chalkboard. Then when each listening team is making its report, the other students in the class can see the question toward which the discussion is directed. Let the spokesman from each listening team give his report. There may be others on the team who would like to amplify or contribute additional information to what the spokesman has said. Such discussion can edify the whole class. However, divide the discussion time, allowing equal time for each assigned question.

CIRCULAR RESPONSE

When *circular response* is used as a technique of teaching, pupils are usually seated in a circle; however, circular response can be used when they sit in auditorium style. A topic is announced and each person is given an opportunity to respond. Circular response will give all your students an opportunity to make contributions on the announced topic. If possible, have the class seated in a semicircle. Then proceed around the group clockwise, giving each person opportunity to contribute. If the class is seated in auditorium style, have each person in a row contribute, going from left to right, until each row has had opportunity.

Ask each student to contribute the first thing that comes to mind on the topic of the lesson. Remember, many teens are reticent to speak before a group, so encourage them. Remind the teen that his contribution may be (1) an illustration from life, (2) a question regarding the lesson, (3) a fact from the Bible, (4) a verse from the Scriptures pertaining to the lesson, (5) a question based on a previous contribution by another member, or (6) a personal insight regarding the lesson.

Do not make evaluative comments on the contributions of class members as the contributions are being made. The teacher who points out the more significant contributions may embarrass the shy person who has only asked a question or read a verse of Scripture.

The teacher should stand by the chalkboard, and be prepared to write down questions which students may ask during the circular response. Do not try to answer the questions at this time, for this would only discourage contributions by others. Simply list the questions on the chalkboard. After each person in the group has had opportunity to contribute, stop and discuss the questions that have been raised.

Some teachers may feel that a circular response takes away from class time. They may believe that students are not learning because specific lesson content is not being presented. However, teachers should think in terms of meeting the needs of students. Perhaps the contributions of the students may not be as substantial as those of the teacher, who has studied the lesson in detail. But discussion and involvement by individual members of the class may provide just the needed motivation to make them consider their Christian faith more seriously. Involvement in the class by students is the key to personal growth.

BRAINSTORMING

Brainstorming is a technique of teaching that is also used in problem-solving. A problem or question is introduced to a group of people or a class of students. The teacher steps out of his traditional role. He does not assume that he has the answer nor does he try to lead the class to an answer. The topic may be written on the chalkboard or printed and distributed. Each student is allowed to share his thoughts and solutions to the problem. In the initial stage of brainstorming, the purpose is not to analyze the ideas, but to get as many thoughts as possible on the table. When the flow of ideas dries up, then the group can begin to fit the ideas together.

Another approach to brainstorming is to give each student a three-by-five-inch card on which you have written the topic for discussion. Have each one write down the first thing that comes to his mind concerning the topic. You can discuss these contributions later. Right now you are interested in getting students to think creatively.

After each class member has written something on his card, give him the opportunity to share his ideas with the class. The reason you have him write his ideas out, is to clarify his thoughts and later the teacher can call on each student to read what is on his card. The ground rules for brainstorming are simple. Each person says what is on his card or whatever comes to his mind that he may not have written down. As he reacts to what is said by others, he should not question the validity of their contributions. When such questioning and refutation begin, creativity generally stops; and the aim of brainstorming is creativity.

Encourage your class members to amplify what is said by other students. This is called "hitchhiking" on someone else's thoughts. The contribution of one student may bring to another person's mind a further thought on the topic. This person simply shares his new or expanded thought.

PARAPHRASING

Paraphrasing is an effective teaching tool with teenagers. Students are guided into the learning activity of rephrasing verses of Scripture. Many classes have found that restating the truths of Scripture in modern idiom is a helpful learning procedure. When this technique is used, each Scripture verse under consideration is rewritten. Care is taken to avoid using the original words of the text; yet the paraphrase must communicate the true meaning of the text. Paraphrasing yields new understanding to youth who are seriously seeking to study the Scriptures.

The student's ability to paraphrase a passage depends upon his grasp of the initial idea in the passage. Many times the King James Version expresses thoughts in a language that is now considered archaic. However, it must be noted that any person who honestly seeks to find the true meaning of Scripture can do so. Perhaps the need of twentieth-century Christians is not for modern translations, but for the healing of their own spiritual blindness, so that they can perceive God's Word. Occasional archaic language is not the main obstacle that keeps people from understanding God's Word, though modern translations do have a place in the Christian's library.

Using paraphrasing as a technique of teaching is different from using a modern version. Paraphrasing is used to place emphasis on study by the student. Modern versions are used when emphasis is to be placed on the final product.

Paraphrasing is not an attempt to change the meaning of Scripture. In fact, if students change the meaning of Scripture, they have missed the point of paraphrasing. The purpose is to express the meaning of the Scripture passage in a way that will give clarity and understanding to each student.

Supply paper and pencils for each student. If possible, it is best to work at one or more tables where your students can spread out their Bibles and notepaper. Students can work as a team on a verse. They learn as they discuss the Scripture and arrive at a finished topic. Also, students may work individually on a Scripture assignment.

Class members will get more out of the Scripture passage if they are given ample opportunity to discuss their written material. Misunderstanding and lack of clarity in thinking show up quickly in such an exercise. Have several student paraphrases read aloud.

In paraphrasing Scriptures, a variety of tools for Bible study will be helpful. Have several copies of Bible dictionaries on hand to which students can refer. Two or three copies of a regular English dictionary will also be helpful. There are some archaic words for which the dictionary gives good definitions, though some of them may not be familiar to your class members. A book of synonyms and antonyms may also prove useful.

COLLOQUY

"The colloquy is a learning-group method usually used by groups of from 25 to 75 persons. Basically the colloquy is a pattern of purposeful, cooperative interaction between three units of participants—an audience, a panel of resource persons, and a panel of audience representatives. The interaction is controlled by a moderator. The audience representatives present a problem or initiate questions which originated in the audience. The resource persons present information designed to help answer the questions, and members of the audience participate actively whenever feasible, under the direction of the moderator." The aim of a colloquy is to secure information from experts on the problem or issue under consideration, by allowing representatives of the larger group to question the authority.

When to use Colloquy

1. It can be used in many cases as an effective method of following up a speech, a symposium, or a panel presentation.

2. It can be used effectively by a group which has been studying some problem or need area and has accumulated a fund of questions or issues they need to clarify with trained resource persons.

3. It can be used effectively to arouse interest in a problem area and in a series of follow-up meetings.

4. It can be used to illustrate the value of two educational principles:

    a. molding a program to the problems and needs recognized by the participants.

    b. using resource persons at the moment they are needed.

How to use Colloquy

The leader—

1. Places two tables facing one another diagonally in the front of the room, and places the appropriate number of chairs behind each table. Group representatives will sit at one table, and resource persons at the other.

2. Selects resource persons in advance and gives them instructions about their responsibilities.

3. Introduces the problem or issue to the entire group.

4. Requests suggestions from the group members that might solve the problem, clarify the issues, or answer the question.

5. Selects three to four persons from the group to act as group representatives.

6. Acts as moderator of the colloquy as the group representatives ask questions of the resource persons.

7. Requests additional questions from the group as a whole if the time or occasion permits.

8. Summarizes the contributions of the resource persons.

9. Proposes additional study or a course of action.

10. Evaluates the learning experience.

Strengths of the colloquy. It combines the virtues of the forum, the lecture, and the panel. Like the forum, the colloquy encourages questions from the audience; like the lecture, it seeks to bring out evidence bearing on the questions raised; from the panel it borrows a technique of drawing an audience into a discussion and a weighing of the evidence.

The colloquy not only is an efficient way of utilizing experts and meeting the needs of the audience, but also the colloquy is a stimulating and intellectually exciting large-group discussion method.

Weaknesses of the Colloquy. One main disadvantage of the colloquy is its need for trained or highly prepared personnel to man the experts' panel. These people not only need to be knowledgeable in the topic at hand, but must also be able to respond to the needs of the group.

Because the size of the group is usually most effective when from 25 to 75 in number, there are situations where its use would be a disadvantage. The vital part of the colloquy is not so much the questions asked by the audience representatives, or the answers handed down by the authorities: the most vital contribution is the *active clarification* by the audience of the *significance* of the informational material they receive from the authorities. In an effective colloquy the audience often does as much talking as the resource experts. This is desirable, since it is the participants' job actively to discover personal meaning and obstacles to understanding.

CONCLUSION

This chapter has attempted to give only a brief introduction to methods of teaching teens. Not only were some methods neglected, but those methods which were mentioned are abbreviated because of space and purpose. The conscientious teacher should consult a book on teaching methods and principles. Since entire volumes are given over to one method of teaching, it would be impossible to be complete in this chapter.

Note that many of the new techniques of teaching are built around social groupings. These are especially effective with teens since they seek social interaction. The lecture is still the best method to communicate biblical content, but these new methods will support the lecture and give the teenager insight, understanding, stimulation, practical application and growth.

THOUGHT QUESTIONS

Section Six

(Covers Chapter 14, "What Goes on in a Sunday School Class"; Chapter 15, "Learning and the Young Person"; Chapter 16, "Methods of Teaching Young People.")

1. A logical definition of learning is given and explained in Chapter 15. Suggest several wrong concepts of learning. Why are they wrong?

2. Is an experience necessary to conversion? Can a teen learn in a Sunday School class without an experience? What is an experience?

3. Seven principles of motivation are given in Chapter 15. On the basis of these, explain how you would motivate teens in the following situations:

    a. Getting a teen to take part in a youth program

    b. Convincing a reluctant teenage girl to atend a social

    c. Getting a teenage boy to read his Bible daily

    d. Convincing a teen to attend prayer meeting

    e. Getting a teen who is continually late to come to Sunday School on time

    4. Define and describe communication. Can you teach without communication?

    5. Why is the Bible an essential element for teenage spiritual growth?

    6. Why is Bible teaching most effective in an informal atmosphere?

    7. Suggest how you would arrange a classroom for the best teaching. How could you rearrange your youth classroom at church for more effective Bible teaching?

    8. What should be your attitude when teenagers give the wrong answer to your question?

    9. Should an invitation to accept Christ be used to close every class lesson? Why?

    10. What method of teaching would you use as a basic approach to teach the following?

    a. John 21:14

    b. How to become a better witness in high school

    c. Helping a teenager find his spiritual gifts

    d. Why we believe the Bible is the Word of God

    e. How to overcome the temptation of evil thoughts

    f. Should all Christian young people go to a Christian college?

    g. Why the heathen are lost

    h. The scripturel teaching on hell

    i. How to get the most benefit out of devotions

    j. Creating in teenagers a desire for Bible study and knowledge

    11. In choosing a method of teaching, which is more important: noting the needs of a class or noting the needs of an individual? Why?

    12. Do you agree with the statement, "The spiritual level of the class should help determine the method of teaching?" Why?

    13. Think through the Gospels: Which method of teaching did Christ use most frequently?

    14. Why is the lecture method of teaching used most in youth work? How can you improve it?

    15. How would you answer the objection to paraphrasing, that it distorts the words of Scripture?

    16. Suggest a topic for a panel discussion in your church. Also suggest four people to serve on this panel. Why did you choose these people? What leading questions would you use to stimulate discussion?

17. Why don't most churches use the forum as a method of teaching?

18. Which of the methods suggested in this section will be most effective in communicating content? Changing attitudes? Improving skills?

19. Why does the use of dyads or circular response appeal to teens?

20. On what occasions would you choose colloquy over other methods of teaching?

SECTION SEVEN

COUNSELING YOUNG PEOPLE

Who can counsel teenagers?

What is the difference between counseling and teaching?

What goes on in an effective counseling situation?

How accurate are our opinions about teenagers?

When should counselors give advice?

Do youth have within themselves resources to solve their problems?

Can church counselors use "talk therapy"?

How can the Bible be used in counseling?

17

THE FOUNDATION OF COUNSELING YOUNG PEOPLE

Jim Peterson, a Sunday School teacher of high school boys, walked into his pastor's office. After a few minutes of conversation, Jim opened up with a problem.

"Pastor, those boys in my class are extremely difficult to teach. I'm afraid that maybe I should give up the class."

"Why do you say that?"

"I just can't seem to get through to them. Instead of wanting to talk about the Bible lesson, they just want to talk about their own interests and problems."

"Perhaps your answer is to spend more time with them during the week. That way you could get to know them, see why they have these problems, and then counsel with them."

"*Counsel* with them? Oh, not me, Pastor. I'm no counselor. I have enough problems of my own without trying to counsel others—and especially *teenagers*. Besides, I wouldn't have the slightest idea of how to counsel. I've never had any training in it. I'm afraid I'd have to leave that to the psychiatrists and psychologists."

Do *you* feel like Jim? Do you feel as if you don't know much about counseling young people on their numerous problems? Is counseling a task that should be left entirely to professionally trained personnel? What is counseling, anyway? What problems are teens facing today that suggest the need for a stronger counseling ministry by pastors and lay workers in

259

local churches? How may a pastor, youth worker, or Sunday School teacher counsel young people?

This section attempts to help you answer these and other questions about counseling.

Counseling has become one of the greatest ministries in the church because our society has become *problem*-centered. Counseling has grown in importance and will continue to grow. The church must continue to meet the needs of its young people. Church teaching is said to be effective when it is meeting needs and solving problems. Since the greatest ministry of counseling is helping people solve their problems and meet their needs, we can see why counseling has become a great ministry in the church.

Counseling has become prominent in our society. Our larger high schools employ a counselor. Glancing through the phone book will reveal marriage counselors, investment counselors, guidance counselors, psychiatrists, psychologists, psychiatric social workers, welfare counselors, etc. Why not the church?

The church has been counseling and meeting needs since its inception. Recent developments and trends of guidance and counseling have made the church take stock of its basic ministry to individuals. As our society has organized and refined its techniques of counseling, so must the church.

Our basic approach to counseling is Bible-centered. There are no new discoveries pertaining to the field of counseling. The Word of God has been applied to modern counseling techniques. Where the latest techniques of counseling are in opposition to the Word of God, the techniques are sacrificed. Where the Word of God is silent, principles governed by reason are applied in harmony with the principles of God's Word.

A Bible-centered approach to counseling has been taken. The extremes of a strict Freudian approach to counseling has been avoided. The opposite extreme of "advice giving" has also been avoided. The *inductive approach* to counseling is the biblical approach.

This section is slanted to the *lay* youth counselor. There are many Sunday School teachers, youth sponsors, camp counselors and parents who counsel teenagers. Many of them are doing an acceptable job. However, if given better techniques they can do a better job.

The aim of this section is to produce a Bible-centered concept of counseling that will give skills, understandings and techniques to lay workers in the church so that they may help average teenagers solve average problems.

Who Can Counsel?

"When I was a young man, we didn't have anyone to counsel us and we got by all right."

This was the response of a deacon to the Board of Christian Education when the need for individual counseling was discussed. The implication is that young people can grow up naturally without any help. This may be true. But, since the Christian church exists to help individuals, we should take advantage of every opportunity to minister to teens.

The entire organization of the twentieth century church—the physical plant, nurseries, classrooms, visual aids, music program, and well-trained ministers—exists for the purpose of ministry. Those who work in the church as Sunday School teachers, youth sponsors, directors of Christian education, and parents can give help to the teenagers. Many people who need help, including the teenager, turn very naturally to the church. The already overworked pastor cannot meet every demand that comes to him.

Many in the church have the potential of being a counselor. The ministry of counseling is open to any Christian in the church. One of the tests that you should ask yourself before beginning counseling is, "How constructive is my counseling?" If God has used you to help other people, you can be a counselor. Even those who have never been used in the lives of others can learn to be counselors. Counseling does not necessarily take a great amount of knowledge about techniques. Perhaps you have the gift of counseling, and the principles presented in this section will help you become a better counselor.

If you can help yourself spiritually, you can help others. Helping yourself may be simply analyzing problems in your life and finding solutions. A primary criterion for being an effective counselor is personal adjustment to the will of God.

What Is Counseling?

Counseling is not limited to professional full-time workers. Mature adults in the local church *can* help young people face and solve their problems. The dictionary defines the word "counsel" as "opinion, advice, direction, instruction, or recommendation given especially as a result of consultation." Counseling, then, is guiding a person to a better understanding of his potentialities and problems. Another teacher has defined counseling as "the use of techniques to help a person solve a conflict or better his life adjustment." There is a technical sense in which counseling is given by the person professionally trained to give therapy. But the definition of this section centers around helping average young people with average problems. Ninety-five percent of the problems facing teenagers can be solved with help from the counselors already ministering in their church.

What, then, is counseling? Simply stated, it is helping another person analyze and solve his problems. Counseling is nothing new. As a science (in which laws, principles, and techniques are studied and presented), counseling may be a relatively new field. But as an art, counseling is an ancient practice. Whenever a father has helped his son with a personal problem, counseling has taken place. Whenever a teacher has helped a novice learn a skill, there has been counseling.

Common Attitudes Toward Counseling

You will meet many kinds of people in your counseling ministry. First there are those teens, like the ostrich with its head in the sand, who deny that they have problems, yet their lives are unhappy and unproductive for God. These young people are basically unsatisfied and their lives are purposeless. Even though these young people do not enjoy a life of happiness, they refuse to admit they have a problem.

Also in your counseling ministry you will meet these kids who realize they have problems. Some of these people take the "fire escape route." They seek to run from their problems without really facing them. But running from a problem never solves the problem. If a young person runs from his problem, eventually he will find that the problem has increased in proportions. Each time we meet the same unsolved problem it has an uglier face. It is childish to run from problems. The mature approach is to face the problem, learn from the experience, and make a satisfactory adjustment.

Other teens who have problems won't seek a solution. These Christians follow the "grin and bear it" route. There are many young people today who feel they are doing God a service by disciplining themselves and becoming martyrs. These Christians feel if they are living a happy, satisfied, well-adjusted life, something is wrong. This may be called "Bible fatalism." There is no merit in living a miserable life. Christians are told to rejoice and live happy lives. "Thou wilt shew me the path of life: in thy presence is fulness of joy; at thy right hand there are pleasures for evermore" (Psalm 16:11). "I am come that they might have life, and that they might have it more abundantly" (John 10:10).

Then there are Christian teens who feel that they can go directly to the Lord and the Bible to solve their own problems. The impression is given that youth counselors are unnecessary. It is true that God speaks through prayer and the Word of God. However, the Bible also tells us that we should go to others for counsel. "Where no counsel is, the people fall: but in the multitude of counselors there is safety" (Prov. 11:14).

Christ exercised the office of Counselor. The Scriptures are adequate, but they need interpretation. The blind reading of the Scriptures without understanding will not bring satisfaction nor will they solve a problem. Sometimes the ministry of a youth counselor is to get the teenager to understand the problem, and then lead him into a correct understanding of the Word of God.

Foundation Stones of Counseling

The general aims of counseling are as broad as the aims of the Christian church. These goals are (1) to bring teenagers to know Christ and the fellowship of the Christian church; (2) to help them acknowledge and repent of sin and to accept God's freely offered salvation in Jesus Christ; (3) to help them live a victorious Christian life; (4) to lead them to serve Christ. Through counseling you can help Christian teens live in faith and confidence instead of doubt and anxiety, in peace instead of discord. In another sense, however, counseling has specific purposes. Counseling consists of many implicit and self-contained goals. These short-term goals are like the rungs on a ladder which, when taken in order, will lead to the general aims of the Word of God.

Broadly speaking, counseling is the attempt of the counselor to help teenagers help themselves through gaining an understanding of their inner conflicts.

You must help the teenager see himself as he really is—as God sees him. Sometimes counseling is referred to as emotional re-education. In addition to counseling and helping the youth with an immediate problem, counseling should enable them to help themselves with other problems. As a youth counselor you will have to guard against being blinded by the immediate situation and losing sight of the future. For if the method of solving the problem will not at the same time prepare the youth to face the future and the next problem, you may have left him no farther along on life's road than where you found him.

1. *Counseling is a relationship between two people.* The teen who has a problem and is seeking help is the counselee. The one to whom he goes for help is the counselor. The counselee comes to the counselor and together they seek for the answer. This is the counseling situation. The counselee must have confidence in the counselor to receive help. The youth counselor must be thoroughly interested in the counselee and make him aware that he desires to and will do all he can to be of help. From this mutual interest arises a mutual relationship between the two. This relationship has often developed into lifelong friendship. Counseling is a relationship between two people.

2. *Counseling is a ministry to the individual.* The Lord had genuine

compassion for the needs of people. Many such incidents are recorded in the Gospels, including Jesus' concern for Nicodemus, the Samaritan woman, the woman with the issue of blood, and Peter. The Lord was vitally concerned with the needs of each of these counselees.

Much is said concerning the preaching and teaching ministry of the Lord. However, his greatest sermons were preached to individuals. These sermons were communicated in counseling situations in which the Lord led the person to whom He was talking to a better understanding of God the Father in heaven and his relationship to Him.

Counseling is a ministry of meeting needs. When you regard ministering in terms of meeting needs, you readily see how it applies to the counseling situation. Essentially, a counselee comes to you because there is a need in his life. So when we think of counseling, we must think in terms of meeting individual needs.

3. *Counseling is a process of education.* Counseling is, in every sense of the word, education. Christian education is the process of transmitting the truth of God to teens in such a way as to bring wholehearted response and obedience to the nature and will of God. The aims of Christian education are like the aims of counseling.

They consist of bringing pupils to Christ, bringing them up in Christ, and sending them forth in Christ. Maturity is the goal of both education and counseling. Christian teaching is guiding pupils to solve life problems. Counseling is guiding youth's experience through questioning, dialogue, and sharing the Word of God. This kind of teaching and counseling demands a leader who is an example of the Christian life and is a mature leader. He should use many techniques such as telling, showing, questioning, helping students to discuss, exploring, research, etc., in order to provide opportunities for teenagers to live out God's Word.

Christian teaching is successful only when constructive change has taken place in pupils' lives. In the same way counseling is successful only as it meets needs and changes the lives of teenagers. This change may be inner, with a long-range plan of action. The change may be outer and result in immediate adjustment.

Christian teaching must be structured according to the problem-solving process. In the same way effective counseling is structured toward solving the problems of teenagers. As teenagers gain insights and solve their own problems, they mature in life. Using words that are unknown to the youth must be avoided both in the teaching and counseling situation.

The Word of God is a living Book that was written for living people. Teenagers must have an opportunity in teaching and counseling to see living truth and to make that truth an inner conviction.

Christian teaching begins where the pupils are—mentally, culturally, socially, emotionally, and spiritually—and takes them where they should be. Christian counseling has the same purpose and goal. Teenagers will develop as they see the relationship between the directives of God, their current need, and their environment. This relationship must constantly reflect emphasis consistent with the whole Word of God. Therefore, you must continually evaluate the pupils' current stage of development.

Christian teaching and counseling are based on experience. This experience is Bible-based, life-related, and Christ-centered. All learning, whether in the classroom or counseling session, takes place through experience. Experience is necessary in order to confirm the truth of God's Word and provide contemporary interpretation to life's problems. True Christian experience involves both scriptural content and living responsibility.

Christian experience is unique in that the Holy Spirit works upon and within the teenager to illumine the written Word of God. Scriptural authority sets standards and provides divine power that makes genuine discipleship and discipline possible for teens.

Through personal experience teachers and counselors help their pupils form adequate concepts of life, adjustment, and maturity. Young people who have developed a scriptural concept of life can live to the glory of God.

4. *Counseling involves interaction.* Knowledge, facts, and understanding cannot be passed from mind to mind like apples from one basket to another. They must in every case be recognized, rethought, and assimilated by the receiving mind. It may be unfortunate, but nevertheless true, that a teenager may listen to a lecture from an adult without "hearing" anything. Picture the youth listening to his parent. He is looking at the ground and digging in his pockets. Is he learning? Has the parent communicated? Is he listening? Does meaning pass from one to another? If so, what must be present? The answer is *interaction.* Interaction is activity and response on the part of the youth counselor and the teen. The teenager must reproduce (in his own mind) the truth to be learned, then express it in his own words.

Counseling, then, is not giving something to a listless, inactive pupil; it is exciting the teenager to definite, purposeful self-activity. Thus, the true counseling situation must be a reciprocal action called interaction. Interaction in counseling is absolutely necessary if any help is to be given.

Various Types of Counseling*

There are many types of counseling. The youth leader should not be content to use only one medium in dealing with teens. He must be acquainted with these various approaches to counseling if he is to meet adequately the needs of his youth.

1. *Preventive versus curative counseling.*

Counseling can take place before and after the problem arises. If the counselor knows that the young person is having a problem, it is his responsibility to seek out the young person, counsel with him, show him principles from the Word of God, and attempt to lead him to adjustment before the problem actually arises. A good counselor will detect danger signals from dating and social relationships. Watch for the loner in a crowd; this may be a danger signal. There are times when the problem has happened and only a cure can help. It is best to prevent, but better to cure than to give no help at all.

2. *Formal versus informal counseling.*

Formal counseling takes place when a youth counselor has scheduled office hours for counseling and does it by appointment. Usually the counselee initiates the session and asks for the appointment.

This type of counselor is warned to be careful about being too formal. Sometimes the desk itself becomes a "barrier" to effective communication. The position of the counselor on one side of the desk and the youth on the other side is a disadvantage. Sometimes the most effective counseling is done not in the office, but on the athletic field or in the locker room. The formal situation can help in many situations, but it has its barriers.

Informal counseling includes those non-scheduled conversations that go on at the lunch counter, in the park, or on the ride home after a youth activity. This is sometimes called "shirt sleeve" counseling. The barriers are down. A question is approached, and you are asked for an opinion. Many times the question is not the deep problem but only a surface question. The counselor must take advantage of this situation and determine what answer is to be given. A wise youth counselor will make an informal situation lead into a friendship and perhaps into a future time of counseling the teenager.

3. *Single interview versus a series of interviews.*

In the single interview the young person may drop in and ask you about some help on the young people's program. The teen may ask you to help him decide an answer to a problem that is facing him. The

---

* Dr. Howard Hendricks. Unpublished class notes. This outline was adopted and printed by permission.

counselor should look at single interview sessions with real anticipation and realize he is there to help teens all he can.

In a series of counseling sessions the youth counselor should realize that as the teenager returns, the youth is being educated. Perhaps the teenager needs to be helped gradually. As the youth's capacity grows, he can be fed more, until he comes to a time of complete adjustment.

4. *Personal versus group counseling.*

Personal counseling is primarily the kind of counseling discussed in this section. The ministry of the speaker with the group has been emphasized throughout the years. The Christian counselor should work closely with youth committees and youth activities. When the youth leader solves problems on the group level, he is counseling. However, there are many disadvantages. Interaction is poor. The youth will not confide in the leader in a group situation. In group counseling, problems are solved but there is little personalized help.

Preaching and teaching may be forms of group counseling. This is especially true when the session is structured in a problem-solving approach. In group counseling you should have the same goal as you would in individual counseling—to help individuals face and solve their problems.

In group counseling you may have a family conference when you deal with a family problem. Premarital counseling falls under this title.

5. *Face-to-face counseling versus absentee counseling.*

Face-to-face counseling is the best type. You are dealing with an individual young person. There is no danger of warping or misrepresenting the truth. Genuine communication is possible and can be experienced both by the counselor and the counselee so that clear understanding will result.

Absentee counseling is sometimes the only route. Correspondence, to be sure, is helpful but it can be only relative. In writing, don't make bold statements. Be careful of trying to diagnose too much through letters. Do that counseling which has to be done through letters but keep it limited.

CONCLUSION

We can conclude that counseling is an important ministry. As defined in this section, counseling is not the professional approach of the psychiatrist or psychologist. Church youth counseling does not have as its aim special therapy. Counseling is helping average young people with average problems.

Many leaders in the church have been counseling teenagers. If they are given some technical help, these youth counselors can do a better job. Counseling is simply a ministry and as such it meets needs. Counseling is much like teaching; as such, teenagers are guided into the solution of their problems. Counseling is a relationship of interaction in which both counselor and counselee seek the solution from the Word of God.

18

PRINCIPLES OF COUNSELING YOUNG PEOPLE

"Find me two people and I will show you two different philosophies of life." This statement has more truth than meets the eye. Because of different environments, everyone views life differently. So is the case in counseling. There are many philosophies in counseling.

If you were to view two counseling situations, you would perhaps notice different techniques being used. In one session you would find a permissive atmosphere of interaction. There is freedom of expression by the teenager. The next session would resemble a lecture. The teenager is being told what he must do. Both approaches may be effective. Different philosophies of counseling dictate different techniques of counseling. The use of the question may be a technique of producing motivation in one session, while the question in the next session may be a diagnostic instrument.

Non-Directive Counseling

The nondirective counselor believes that the pupil has within himself resources for solving his own problems. He believes that through counseling he can help the teenager remove the emotional blocks which prevent him from solving his own problem. The counselor also affirms that since the teenager has such strong drive to become well adjusted in every area of life, he will strive to become independent and to accomplish for himself the changes that are necessary to achieve full maturity.

269

Carl Rogers has set out the nondirective form of counseling in characteristic steps. These are as follows:

1. The individual comes for help.

2. The helping situation is usually defined.

3. The counselor encourages free expression of feelings in regard to the problem.

4. The counselor accepts, recognizes, and clarifies these negative feelings.

5. When the individual's negative feelings have been quite fully expressed, they are followed by the faint and tentative expressions of the positive impulses which make for growth.

6. The counselor accepts and recognizes the positive feelings which are expressed in the same manner in which he has accepted and recognized the negative feeling.

7. This insight, this understanding of the self and acceptance of the self, is the next important aspect of the whole process.

8. Intermingled in this process of insight (there is no rigid order) is a process of clarification of possible decisions, possible courses of action.

9. Then comes the initiation of minute, but highly significant, positive actions.

10. There is a development of further insight, more complete and accurate self-understanding as the individual gains courage to see more deeply into his own actions.

11. There is increasingly integrated positive action on the part of the client.

12. There is a feeling of decreasing need for help, and a recognition on the part of the client that the relationship must end.[1]

This philosophy of counseling is called the "Talk Therapy" method of counseling. Therefore, the teenager is not only permitted but encouraged to focus attention on the issues that are important to him.

There is no direction given by the counselor. The teenager is permitted to talk at will about what is interesting to him. The conversation jumps from sports, to school, to social activities of the church. Many times at the end of such a counseling session the counselor may feel that nothing has been accomplished, yet at the same time the teenager may have been helped a great deal.

When a pupil seeks the nondirective counselor's help, he soon discovers that the counselor will accept him for what he is and he will believe in his ability to solve his problems in his own way. The teenager

[1] Carl R. Rogers, *Counselling and Psychotherapy* (Boston: Houghton Mifflin Co., 1942), pp. 30–44.

believes by previous experience that counselors are ones to "give advice." He now finds that he is talking with a person who is trying to understand him, trying to follow what he is saying and feeling, trying to help him understand himself. He finds that this counselor neither gives advice nor attempts to manipulate him into making a decision which the counselor believes is best. Many times the teenager will restate or attempt to clarify something which the counselor does not understand. The teenager can make a contradictory or inconsistent statement without being challenged. He also may reveal something of a terrible nature without the counselor's being shocked. The teenager should feel that the counselor understands why he sees things differently at different times.

There are times when the teenager may become aggressive and want to attack the counselor verbally. He tells the counselor what he thinks of life, the church, and the Sunday School teacher. In return he does not receive a scolding but the counselor accepts these aggressive feelings and helps the pupil express them. If the teenager is truthful in admissions of feelings of aggression, the counselor can expect the teenager to be truthful in other admissions.

When the youth finds expression difficult, the counselor helps him tell why he is finding it difficult. Some of the questions that the counselor might use are: "Is this what you are trying to say?" "Am I following you?" "You feel this?" or "Is this what you mean?" These types of responses by the counselor will help to pull the answer out of the teenager. A good response may be, "Then you are bothered over what your parents think about you?" or "You are wondering whether you have what it takes to go to Bible College?" Or "You would very much like to know how those in your Sunday School class feel about you?" In assisting the pupil to express his feelings, the counselor helps the pupil realize that he may discuss whatever bothers him.

The nondirective counselor gives full attention to the counselee during such a session. He puts aside all his own needs and enters into the world of the pupil. Indeed, he tries to be "another self." Only then can he comprehend the teenage view of life and the problems which he faces. As a result he does not give advice or force information on the pupil. The nondirective counselor's task is to free the pupil from emotional blocks or inhibitions which impede his use of his own potentialities. By creating a situation in which there are no tensions, the counselor helps to build maturity in the teenager. The teenager approaches maturity as he unfolds his own life, seeks his own problem, finds his own way to the Lord and ultimately stands on his own two spiritual feet. Hence his growth is accelerated toward adulthood.

Occasionally the teenager wants advice and resents not getting it.

At such times he may feel that he is alone with his problem just when he wants someone to lean upon. There are times in which the teenager should feel that there is someone on whom to lean. At this time the counselor will want to take a directive approach. More will be said about this in subsequent paragraphs. On these occasions the counselor and the teenager should talk about the facts on which the pupil wants advice, why he wants the advice, and the effect which giving advice may have on him.

Directive Counseling

Whereas the nondirective counselor is primarily interested in helping the teenager learn to cope with himself, the directive counselor appears to be primarily interested in helping the pupil solve the immediate problem. The directive counselor is also interested in helping the pupil achieve a better overall adjustment. This adjustment is made by solving problems one at a time. Large problems must be broken down into small segments. In seeking answers, the counselor relates the problem back to the youth's background and experience. This solution is then discussed with the teenager. As he finds an answer, it is applied and as a result the youth is helped.

The directive counselor believes that the persistent unsolved problems account for the pupil's present behavior. As a pupil solves immediate problems he will gradually acquire better adjustment. Also, it is believed that the pupil's satisfaction which comes from solving the immediate problem will increase the teenager's confidence in himself and in his counselor. As this confidence grows, the teenager will attack his less obvious problems with increasing success.

In directive counseling relationships, the counselor has a much larger emphasis. Stress is given to the diagnoses of the problems, questioning whether the pupil has within himself the power first of all to see and then to solve his problems. Information is given to the teenager only when it is meaningful to him and he realizes that he needs it. The Word of God is used as a direction sign pointing young people to the true answer. It is at these times that we cannot become overconscientious as to the feelings of the teenager. The counselor must speak, determine the direction and cause the teenager to surrender and accept the will of God. Directive counselors believe that counselors may give advice. They also feel that it is their duty to question the pupil's inappropriate decisions and to take the initiative in helping him re-examine the implications involved in questionable choices. Nevertheless, it should be noticed that the pupil should select the alternatives. This is done with the counselor's help.

Before the interview the directive counselor studies the story of the counselee's life and pertinent details. He reviews counseling notes and looks for possible solutions to the problem which the pupil faces at the moment. The better he knows the pupil the more helpful he can be in interpreting for the pupil the forces which are creating his problem.

Before the counseling situation the counselor plans ways to help the teenager see the relationship between his immediate problem and any other problem which the counselor may have discovered. At the beginning of the interview the counselee and the counselor get acquainted. The directive counselor may discuss a variety of topics. Sometimes they do not begin by talking about the problem at all. The pupil is made to enjoy this interview. Sometimes the counselee doubts if all of the "small talk" is helping him. Nevertheless, the teenager will find that the counselor is usually very friendly. He has confidence that the counselor must know much about people and how to help him solve his problem.

During this counseling situation the counselor asks questions to bring out points which the pupil usually forgets to mention. Nothing can be overlooked. The counselor must secure the complete picture before he can provide his best help. The teenager usually realizes that he must be cooperative and does not have much difficulty accepting this fact. The youth must provide the counselor with all of the information that the counselor requests. The counselor usually asks questions concerning his happiest moments of life and his feelings of rebellion towards God, the unhappy moments of Sunday School, questions concerning his home, members of his family, and how he feels about his friends, the things he likes, the things he does not like, how he stands with God at the present. This conversation usually runs along so smoothly at times the pupil hardly realizes that he is answering very personal questions.

When the teenager has gained confidence in the counselor's ability, he does not worry about providing the counselor with the information requested. Usually the counselor does the worrying for the teenager. Usually the youth feels good about knowing his counselor is making it possible to know himself better, and the counselor is also not going to let him make any other mistakes.

Eventually, however, the teenager must make some decisions. If he cannot identify any acceptable alternatives, he can always count on the counselor to identify the solution to his problem. Though the counselor believes that the pupil should make the decision, he also feels that it is appropriate for him to supply the needed information which the two of them need for defining alternative solutions. If the teenager should choose an alternative with which the counselor disagrees and he believes to be an unwise decision, the counselor raises questions to cause the pupil to re-evaluate the choice.

Most directive counselors take very complete notes either at the time of the interview or immediately after the interview. The counselor who does not take notes during the interview usually believes that the note-taking may interfere with the building and maintaining of good rapport and thus he prefers to run the risk of losing pertinent facts.

Because the directive counselor assumes the responsibility for diagnosis, he must create a friendly climate in which the pupil will tell his own story, reveal his own feelings and those values which he most cherishes in life. The release of the pupil's feelings is very important. The nondirective counselor tries to help the pupil clarify his feelings by expressing them. The directive counselor tries to free the pupil of emotional tensions so the pupil can attack his problem from his own point of view.

Inductive Counseling

Inductive counseling is taken from the phrase "inductive Bible study," where the Bible is approached objectively to allow its message to speak for itself. Inductive Bible study applies the scientific method of inquiry to the Word of God, which is also called inductive logic. Since the Bible has the answer to life, the Scripture must be applied objectively to the problem. Also, inductive counseling applies the same methodology to the teen. The counselor applies inductive reason to determine the problem as it exists, not as his prejudice directs.

Inductive counseling selects the best technique from both the directive and nondirective counseling. Some tend to be nondirective, others tend to be directive, depending on their basic attitude toward pupils and the amount of responsibility which they assume.

Since we have already considered the relationship of nondirective and directive counselors, we shall not attempt to repeat them in discussing the relationships of the inductive counselor; instead we shall consider only the unique features of inductive counseling. In attempting to do this we must consider two basically different points of view held by the inductive counselor.

One claims that he uses nondirective methods at some time and directive methods at other times, adapting his technique to the pupil and the problem. There are varying opinions as to why we use one method over the other.

The second point of view held by the inductive counselor is that while he can choose his techniques from both nondirective and directive counseling, he cannot adapt his techniques to the particular pupil and his problem because his basic value and especially his attitude toward his pupils will determine the way in which he works with them. The inductive counselor believes that he should select the appropriate technique on the basis of the pupil's needs and problems. He believes that it is inappropriate for the counselor to make certain diagnostic judgments beforehand. Some inductive counselors function in a nondirective capacity while they are classifying a pupil's problem and then function as a directive counselor in the solution of the pupil's problem.

This is not quite the picture as it should be. The inductive counselor has a goal and a solution. However, it is not his desire to force this solution on the teenager but to cause the teenager to see the solution for himself. It is the attempt of the inductive counselor to introduce into the life and thinking of the teenager the facts, the information, the problem, the relationship and the Word of God. The teenager, having all of these facts, makes his own decision, ultimately and is led to maturity.

In nondirective counseling there appears to be no standard or criterion. It seems to be an aimless wandering, searching, following at the leading of the counselee. In directive counseling there is a goal, an aim, and the counselor leads the teenager by the hand to the solution of his problem. This solution may be correct and the problem may be solved. This is a short-term solution with no overall solution to life's problem. The directive counselor tends to be problem-centered rather than pupil-centered. The ultimate life of the teenager is not usually changed in this manner.

In inductive counseling there is a goal, a criterion and a standard. The goal is perfect maturity in Jesus Christ. The criterion is the Word of God. The duty of the counselor is to guide the pupil and his problem to the Word of God. Then, an open-face relationship between the pupil and the Word of God will be established and maintained for the present as well as future help of the pupil.

Inductive counseling is sometimes called "eclectic counseling." Thorne's concepts are adapted, giving a general approach:

1. In general, nondirective methods should be used whenever possible.

2. Directive methods should be used only when special conditions obtain, and then with caution.

3. Nondirective techniques should generally be used at the beginning stages of counseling when the counselee is telling his story and also to permit emotional release.

4. The simplest techniques are the best and the counselor should never become involved in complicated techniques until the simple methods have been tried and found unsuitable.

5. It is desirable to let the counselee have an opportunity to resolve his problems nondirectively. If a counselee is not making progress when nondirective methods are being used, it may be an indication that more directive methods should be utilized.

6. Directive methods are usually indicated when the counselee is surrounded by circumstances that must be changed or the cooperation of other people sought.[2]

Inductive counseling has a two-way relationship and communication. This is the basic concept of counseling. Counseling is a process rather than a lecture or advice-giving session. It is a process in which there is a mutual quest for the solution of the problem. The teenager's problem is often too deep to be solved in one easy advisory session. So it becomes a process as the counselor and the teenager search for the answer. Notice the difference between directive and inductive counseling in the following illustration.[3]

A. The teenager brings his problem to the counselor. The sharing of this problem may be formal or informal, but the youth indicates he needs help. The first line of communication is from the counselee to counselor.

B. The counselor considers the problem and goes to the Word of God for the answer. This is the second line of communication. This assumes the counselor has access to and understands the Word of God. In the Word of God the counselor finds certain directives from God. The counselor must understand the problem and the relationship of the problem and God's will.

C. The counselor finds the answers in the Word of God. Now the Bible must communicate to him. Principles of life must "leap" from printed page into everyday meaning.

---

[2] Frederick C. Thorne, "Principles of Personality Counselling," *Journal of Clinical Psychology*, pp. 88–89.
[3] Dr. Howard Hendricks, Unpublished class notes, Dallas Theological Seminary, used by permission.

Word of God

Counselee ● ◄──────── Counselor

D. The last form of communication is from the counselor to the teen-ager. The communication of these answers from the counselor to the teenager may be in the form of a conversation as they talk out the problem, or it may be in the form of a lecture. However, the insights are the counselor's, and the solution to the problem may be temporary. The youth has found the answer to his problem. It is now his prerogative either to accept the advice and follow the solution or to ignore the advice and go his own way.

The major weakness is that the teenager has found the answer for his own problem but has not learned the secret of finding his own answer to future problems. The next time a problem may arise, the counselor may not be available. The youth, having no source of advice, may flounder. As a result he may fail in his Christian life. If the teenager had access into the Word of God and discovered his own answer, the next time there was a problem he might have had a means of solution. This solution is an access to God, filling out the third leg of the triangle.

"Advice-giving" fills only two legs of the triangle. The law of mathematics indicates this triangle cannot stand, so our youth who are "brought up" on advice-giving cannot stand. Advice-giving when exercised by itself is against the concept of spiritual maturity as taught in the Word of God.

Advice-giving such as we have seen above in directive counseling is sometimes called "spiritual apron-strings." As the young child is tied to his mother's apron strings so the teenager is tied to the counselor. He never thinks for himself, makes decisions for himself, or grows to be an independent person walking before God. In the same way the teen-ager becomes dependent upon the counselor for advice in life and never establishes his own roots. The mature concept of counseling may be seen in the illustration below. In this process the teenager comes with his problem to the counselor:

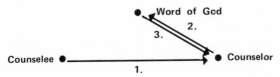

E. Inductive counseling will follow the first three steps as seen above. (1) The counselee will come to the counselor for help. (2) The counselor will have access to the Word of God as the source for the problem.

(3) There is a communication from the Word of God to the counselor. This communication involves *understanding* and *meaning* on the part of the counselor. He gives *meaning* to the words of the Scripture and *understands* the relationship between God's principles and everyday life.

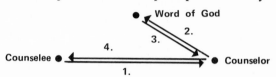

F. However, his method of communication is different. This time he doesn't give the answer "ready mixed" to the teenager and send him on his way. But instead he guides the teenager into the Word of God. Steps (4) and (5) occur simultaneously. The counselor is the agent guiding the teenager to the solution. By guiding him into the Word of God he helps him to find the answer.

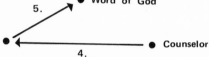

G. The Bible must be understood and must have meaning to the teenager, as to the counselor. The teen must see the Word of God as a living Book, with principles for living teens. God has a will for teenagers in the twentieth century and the teenager must see the *meaning* of the Bible as well as *understand* the relationship to his life.

The Bible must be discovered rather than declared. The Bible must be examined rather than explained. Therefore, the role of the counselor is that of a guide.

H. As the counselor and counselee get into the Word of God, they find that God speaks to the counselee. Only as the youth understands the meaning of God's Word, can eternal perspective be thrown on the problem.

In this way the counselee has established the third link of the triangle and God speaks to him. This has been called "independent-dependence." The youth is independent of man, yet dependent upon God. The teenager will thus become dependent upon the Lord and His Word rather than upon the counselor and will eventually develop true spiritual maturity.

The critics of inductive counseling, contend that the switching of the role of the counselor confuses the pupil and interferes with his experiencing a successful counseling session. Many believe that, instead of changing roles, the counselor should clearly define himself from a point of view. Then he should select only those techniques from both directive and nondirective schools which will allow him to practice within his principal frame of reference. Thus the counselor can maintain one relationship with the pupil rather than changing roles from a "fellow searcher" to one who "gives advice."

From what has been written it should not be implied or inferred that directive or nondirective counselors fail and that only inductive counselors are successful. Counselors must always maintain an effort to communicate their attitudes toward the teenager. As youth become aware of possible variance between attitudes and counseling behavior, they are able to help the counselor. The inductive counselor does not force his diagnosis into the pupil's thinking. Instead, he uses his understanding of the problem and the pupil to have rapport with the youth and to help the pupil answer his own questions. The counselor lets the pupil lead the way. He knows where they are going and he constantly checks to determine whether he is following what the pupil is saying. He tries to make sure that he is seeing the situation as the pupil does. At the same time he is leading the teenager to understand himself as he really is. The inductive counselor reflects the pupil's feelings back to him in order to force the pupil to look at himself. The inductive counselor makes sure that their communication channels are always functioning properly. He believes that when the pupil expresses himself so that his words are meaningful, the pupil probably is improving his understanding of himself. The inductive counselor knows that the ultimate aim of the teenager is full maturity in Jesus Christ as seen in Ephesians 4:12-15. Therefore, he has a goal but at the same time he realizes that every teenager is different. The gifts of God to every person are different; the calling of God to every individual is different; and the capacity, the background, and the environment of every individual are different. The youth must be allowed to unfold from within his own limited spheres of capacity into the man that God would have him to become.

Inductive counseling involves the uniting of two apparently contradictory approaches to counseling. The methods, results, and attitudes of nondirective counseling are assumed, while the direction, authority, and criteria of the directive method are embraced.

CONCLUSION

There is no one best method of counseling. At times the directive method of counseling is all the counselor can use. This may be the result of circumstances, time or personality. Other times the nondirective counseling is the only method possible. Problems are complex and personalities are interrelated. Times are demanding and problems have varied implications. The method that will become most effective in solving immediate problems and producing long-lasting results is the inductive method. Whenever possible the counselor should attempt to employ this approach, guiding the teenager to the solution of his problem. Even though the inductive method is recommended, the counselor will have to determine the best method to use. His judgment should be made after a careful consideration of all aspects of the situation, personalities, backgrounds and factors. In the last analysis, the best method is that which produces the adjustment and maturity of the teenager.

19

STRUCTURING THE ACTUAL COUNSELING SITUATION

The counseling approach will be considered in this chapter. What shall be the modus operandi? How will we proceed to help our youth with their problems? There are certain basic attitudes the counselor should have in his mind before the counseling situation ever comes into existence. This is true whether the counselor will use the nondirective, directive or inductive type of counseling situation. There are universal laws and methods of attacking a problem which should be followed in every situation.

There are times when informal guidance will have to be the rule of the day. This has sometimes been called "shirt sleeve" counseling. This method of informal counseling may be used any time and at any place by the counselor. Perhaps he will be having lunch with a young person or discussing sports after a game. During this informal discussion the young person may approach the counselor with a problem. At this time a formal counseling situation cannot be structured, but the counselor will learn to give what help he can at the time and meet the immediate need without going into the involved session. It should be the duty of the counselor to draw out the young person and let him express his problem. Then the counselor's advice should be given. It should not be a self-talk, therapeutic type of counseling situation. The successful young people's worker will do 90 percent of his counseling in this informal method.

The counseling situation under consideration in this chapter is the formal one in which the young person comes to you with his problem. This counseling session is worthy of a definite appointment. The young person who brings his problems to the counselor is expecting help. At this time you should have those basic rules in mind with which you will attack the problems that are brought to you. Here you must structure the actual counseling situation. The old saying, "For want of a nail . . . a kingdom was lost," points out the significance of details in life. Just so in counseling, details are very important. To be an effective counselor you must be conscious of all details.

For example, teenagers will come to you with problems of how to choose the right college, how to know the will of God concerning marriage, how to get along better with teachers in school or how to have a better personality. By knowing more about proper techniques you are provided with increased effectiveness in all of the guidance services for which you are responsible.

On the other hand, you should not think that you are expected to give therapy. Therapy requires a complex understanding which should be reserved for the specialist. In most churches those who give counsel are not trained to go beyond helping "normal" pupils with their disturbing problems. Therapy involves serious personality disorders and should be reserved for the counseling physiologist or psychologist. However, the average Christian counselor is a needed individual; he must understand and give understanding to those who come to him for help. There are several reasons young people come to you:

REFERRALS

1. *Self-referral.* Self-referral is when the teenager seeks the service of a counselor. Perhaps he has heard through other young people that a certain individual in the church understands young people and has good advice to give or can help them. When this young person comes and asks for some time to meet with the counselor and talk with him, this is commonly called self-referral.

2. *Teacher referral.* This is when a teacher, youth worker or other person in the church refers a young person to you for help. It may be that the teenager would rather not come, but is coming to please the one who is sending him. Perhaps the teenager comes with confidence in you. Those who come because of "teacher referral" may not have the same rapport as those who come because of "self-referral."

3. *Call them in.* Many times you will find that you must call the teenager into your office. At this stage, perhaps you have seen some problem or apparent disorder in the life of the young person and want to help him. You usually begin by "small talk." Use real discern-

STRUCTURING THE COUNSELING SITUATION

PREPARATION	RELAXATION	EXPLORATION	RECONSTRUCTION	FOLLOW-UP

1. Referrals
  a. Self-referral
  b. Teacher referral
  c. Call them in
    1) With threats
    2) Convince
    3) No clearance
2. File
	1. Chat "small talk"
	2. Admission to teen
	  a. Don't know all
	  b. Work together
	  c. Normal to have problems
	3. Rapport
	4. Permissive atmosphere
		1. Making notes
		2. Helping teens talk (question)
		3. Creative listening
		4. Pauses
			1. Clarify Summarization of problems
			2. Diagnosis Determine the alternatives
			3. Scriptural insight
			4. Confession of sin (catharsis)
			5. Resist efforts to place you in role of adviser
			6. Draw solution out of teenager
				1. Don't leak
				2. Remain the counselor-friend no matter what the decision
				3. Continued concern

ment in such a case. Some young people have tremendous and deep problems. They are looking for someone to help them. And yet because of reluctance on their part, they will not seek out the counselor. When you come to them and offer them help, usually they are very thankful and in return respond.

However, some young people are rebellious toward older adults' prying into their lives and hence consider the counseling situation as nothing more than an "inquisition" or the "third degree." Use common sense and discernment in dealing with the "call them in" approach.

One of the most common questions facing new counselors is, "When are you justified in taking the initiative in counseling?" It may be that the initial question is too simple. Instead, you may ask, what do you mean by initiative? The conclusion is that the psychological task implies that you may approach the subject by raising the question or going to call on someone. In short, you may take a geographic or factual approach but not the psychological initiative.

Attempt to establish a good relationship with the young people to whom you minister so that they will trust you and readily come to you for help. Also, attempt to create an accepting attitude among the young people for counseling. Instilling this attitude in the young people will make for better acceptance of help by students—both spiritually, socially and intellectually.

There are three warnings to be left with the church at large when it comes to referral for counseling:

1. *Referrals with the implication of threat.* Sometimes an unwise Sunday School teacher may tell a teenager, "If you don't go and talk to the pastor, I'll tell your parents." This type of threat may cause the young person to go but the counselor's hands are tied and there can be no real counseling relationship established.

2. *Convince the teenager that counseling is the thing to do.* The attitude is sometimes given by an unwise Sunday School teacher, "I'll send you to the Youth Director and he will convince you this thing is right." The attitude is that the counselor will talk them into doing that which they should do.

3. *Referring the teenagers to the pastor or counselor without prior clearance.* When you do not know the teenager is coming, this can destroy any relationship that you might have. The teenager unexpectedly knocks at the pastor's study door or shows up at the counselor's home and says, "I'm sent by my Sunday School teacher." The pastor or counselor, not knowing the background, immediately says, "Oh, I didn't realize." The rapport that might be established is thereby broken and any help that the young person might have received is lost.

There are many occasions when the average Sunday School teacher acting in the role of counselor should refer the teenager on to a more specialized counselor—a pastor, youth director, or someone who can give the exact information. This is not interpreted as need for psychological therapy, but help for normal teenagers with normal problems. Some of these are as follows:

1. An unusual amount of aggressive behavior by the teenager.

2. The student is maintaining a record of underachievement and disinterest in the Sunday School class.

3. The student is undecided as to his future vocation or plan of life or he constantly changes his life's goal from one type of vocation to another.

4. Students or teenagers who do not participate in the normal activities of the church group.

5. A teenager whose aspiration is not in accordance with his ability. Either the aspirations are beyond his ability or his aspirations are below his God-given gifts.

6. When the teenager needs special types of information which the counselor cannot give.

7. When the Sunday School teacher recognizes that the problem is beyond his or her limitations.

It should be noted that the acceptance of a referral by the counselor is an obligation to report back to the person making the referral. The action taken or accomplishments should be reported to the one giving the referral, so that together they may continue to help the individual. The establishment of good communications makes for better teamwork for the church to accomplish the goals to which God has called them.

RELAXATION

The second step in counseling is relaxation. The youth who comes to you must be put "at ease." A young person may come "all keyed up" and be very uncommunicative. Other teens will come to you and will enter into small talk. Some do not feel at home in the presence of a counselor. The counselor may not build this barrier, but he must tear it down if he is to be successful. The counselor must get the teenager to have confidence in him.

First, make the young person feel at home in your presence. He must feel that you are really interested in him and want to help him. Relaxation often comes when the young person has the inner confidence that you understand his problems. If the young person realizes that you have a heart for God and a heart for young people, he is more likely to open up.

There are many embarrassing moments in life, but one of the most humiliating comes to the counselor when he is caught short because he has failed to give the young person his undivided attention. His mind wanders and a few minutes later he is guessing what the young person has or has not said. You must forget what is on your own mind and enter into the experience of the young person. To do this you must listen well and put the young person at ease.

Beginning the Interview

When you have the chance to study the teenager's folder or the accumulative data gathered on the student, you will find it easier to understand the pupil and to see his situation as he does. However, sometimes the teenager is faced with an emergency and therefore cannot wait to talk with you at a later time. In such cases you should talk with the pupil, even though you have not had an opportunity to study the background of the pupil. You should listen and encourage the pupil to talk about those things which bother him.

When the teenager comes to you because he himself recognizes that he needs help, he is actually motivated to do something about those problems which are bothering him. Usually he will assume more responsibility for solving his problems than those pupils who are not sure why they are seeing the counselor.

Even when a teenager comes to the counselor on his own accord, it will not always be immediately clear to the counselor why the pupil wants help. With whom has the teenager already discussed these problems? Why did he come to you? Did he come because some friend told him you had helped them? What does the teenager expect of you?

First Few Minutes

When the teenager first approaches you as counselor, it is your job to make him feel welcome and to help him get comfortably seated or to be in a comfortable position in which you can talk. There are no set ways to accomplish these aims because counselors differ and teenagers differ. Some counselors find it natural to open the conversation, "Hi, Jim, pull up a chair" and proceed with the conversation. Other counselors would be out of role if they did not use a formal approach. To make the teenager feel truly trusted and welcome is the duty of each counselor and the method must be your natural approach.

Since the teenager comes to talk to the counselor about something, he will usually start talking after greetings are exchanged. Of course, he may not start talking about what is bothering him most. Many times teenagers will bring up something of an alternative pattern rather than the real problem. He may try you out first, before sharing his most important problem with you. If he comes to feel that he can trust you and you are trying to understand him, he will sense that it is all right for him to talk about anything which is important to him. Should the young person not start talking, you may help him start: "What is on your mind today?" or "What is it you wanted to see me about?" With such a remark you indicate that the teenager knows better than you what should be discussed in the session.

Naturally it makes a difference how you say what you say, even though you may use the right words. Your tone of voice may reflect an attitude. The young person may feel threatened by the tone, or a different young person may feel that he must fight that which he believes to be a harsh comment. Neither situation has helped create a friendly and permissive attitude in which the young person feels that he can talk about his problem.

Some counselors feel that they must use "small talk" at the beginning of the interview with the young person or build up a good rapport in an informal counseling situation. This may be a technique used by the counselor to lead the pupil out into the open, but at the same time it may lead a young person away from the problem which he has just barely developed the courage to face.

Beware of making it too easy for the young person to talk about something other than his problems. When the young person comes for help, you should help him talk about his problems rather than encourage conversation about social activities, school life or church life in general.

Under no circumstances should the counselor encourage gossip. If the young person cannot face his problem, assist him by use of the question in talking out why he cannot face his own problem.

Admission to the Teenager

The teenager usually admits that he has a problem and wants to do something about it. This is usually very difficult, but it is the first step toward solving a problem. You must then define your helping role to the youth. Let him know what you intend to do. Convey to the teenager that it is his responsibility to work with you so you both can solve his problem. There are a few basic points of clarification.

1. *The counselor must admit that he does not know all the answers.* Here you must not play God. Be very slow to give an answer, especially until you know both sides of the issue. Sometimes the teenager may be very frank and very honest; however, you have only one side of the picture.

To give an answer immediately would only be encouraging immaturity because you do not know both sides of the picture. As you admit that you do not have all of the answers, you break down a "counselor superiority attitude." This breaking down of a "counselor superiority attitude" helps get the counseling off to a Christ-centered start, rather than a counselor-centered or counselee-centered start. Point out to the counselee that only the Lord has the solution to all problems. Then the counselee and the counselor can begin working on the problem together.

2. *The counselor and the teenager must be informed that they will work on problems together.* Your role is that of a guide and a participant. You are not to solve problems. You are not to give all answers. You are not to give your own opinion. Together you will work out the details, define the problem, determine the alternatives, but the counselee applies the solution.

3. *The teenager must be told that it is only normal to have problems.* Many teenagers feel that something is wrong if they are having problems. Modern advertisement and publicity from the television, magazines and other media of communication have portrayed a problemless way of life. This is not true.

The teenager must be told that it is only normal to have problems. As long as he is in the flesh and attempting to live the will of God, he is attempting to do the impossible. He will have problems as long as he seeks God's will—for the flesh, the devil and the power of the world are against him. But there is victory in Jesus Christ; this is the hope of the Christian counselor.

RAPPORT

You must have rapport with teens to help them. Rapport means "a relation characterized by harmony, conformity, accord or affinity" (Webster). It is an intimate harmonious relation as applied to people having close understanding.

Rapport is gained in much the same way that you get youth to relax. However, there is a difference between rapport and relaxation. Through relaxation the youth merely relaxes and tells his story, but in rapport you must think along with the youth as he is telling his problem. You must forget what is on your own mind and enter into his experience. To do this, you must listen well. You must have warmth in understanding but control in your emotions. Be patient with the youth and help him talk, and be careful not to embarrass him if he cries or just cannot seem to say what he wants to.

When a student comes to you with a problem about dates and realizes that you are not a judge but that you understand, this is rapport.

If you come to an immediate solution or call this "puppy love" or unimportant, you have lost contact and destroyed rapport. You gain rapport by getting the youth to relax.

Rapport is distinguished from relaxation in that through relaxation the young person is merely feeling at home. This is a subjective experience to the young person. Rapport is a reciprocal reaction; both the counselor and counselee feel this. Relaxation is a method of gaining rapport. Often young people hesitate to divulge their basic problem when they first talk with the counselor. They begin with one problem or a surface struggle when actually they came to talk about something quite different. The wise counselor is conscious of this tendency and willing to wait for the real problem to arise to the surface. It is unwise for any counselor to jump to conclusions.

Creating a Permissive Atmosphere

What you do outside your office does much to direct your counseling and effectiveness inside your office. Your reputation is very important. What you do in social activities, in after-church get-togethers, makes a difference.

Your impressions as a teacher count; spending extra time helping the pupils with their work attracts a pupil's attention. Wherever the young person meets you or works with you, he should find the personal qualities that indicate a mature Christian attitude toward life. Your everyday life should lead the young person to believe in you and accept you as a person able to give him help.

The building of a good counseling relationship is interfered with when you fail to sense the importance of the pupil's problems. A remark like, "Oh, don't let this bother you," or "You'll forget all about her in a couple of days," insults the pupil's good judgment and makes him feel that you don't understand him. When you try to reassure the pupil with such a comment instead of causing him to see the problem, you become a problem. The young person says to himself, "This guy doesn't understand me; he doesn't know how it hurts to have a girl drop you."

Responding to Feelings

The feelings of the young person are of utmost importance in the counseling situation. All of us have said at one time or another, "I know what I should do, but I don't feel like doing it," or "I know I should do this but I want to do something else." We must help the young person understand his feelings. Many times he has feelings within himself that he doesn't understand, and to these he cannot respond.

At the same time you should neither agree or disagree with the attitude or feelings expressed by the young person. When the youth says, "My father is the lowest drunkard in our town," he should not expect you to say, "Right—I think so too." He should expect the counselor to accept these views. When the young girl says, "Our Sunday School teacher is the poorest teacher that I have ever heard," you should not condone or condemn the statement but should accept it.

Concentrate on how the teenager feels, and help the young person to discover that he can talk freely. This is not the place to give a lecture on respect for parents or respect for the teacher. Until the problem is properly diagnosed a lecture should be withheld. The young person may express his feelings and ultimately help himself to accept himself, his father or his teacher. The release of the feelings is important in the counseling situation, but this in itself is not enough. The teenager must be led to understand why he feels as he does and learn what he can do to achieve the positive adjustment and happiness that he seeks.

Pauses

There are times when the teenager wants to talk about something but he finds it difficult to express himself. He may approach a problem, or he may speak about a related problem and then abandon it for some reason or another. There are uncomfortable pauses as he struggles to tell about his inner feelings. Pauses are awkward in social conversation and they are also difficult in counseling. Badly handled problems are frustrating, both to the young person and to the counselor. If the young person does not understand the significance of the pause, he may be distracted from the problem with which he is struggling and lose his whole train of thought.

When the young person is struggling with the problem, be watchful not to break into the pupil's personal struggle, even though there is a pause. It may be that the young person is making satisfactory progress by himself. Interrupting the pupil's thinking when he is making satisfactory progress from his point of view may lead the pupil away from his important issue at hand.

If you are distracted or bothered about the period of silence, your uneasiness may distract the pupil's thinking about the issue facing him. Pauses of only fifteen or twenty seconds may seem to be long and prove embarrassing because you do not know what to do. Rather than break these pauses with probing questions, try to make the youth realize that it is all right to take time to think about these things and that some topics are difficult to discuss. Pauses are not disturbing when the counselor and the young person know that it is normal for them to occur.

Making Notes

Some writers in the field of counseling believe that taking notes during the actual interview interferes with the building of a good counseling relationship. Other writers feel that taking notes during an interview helps to obtain an accurate report. The taking of notes should be examined in light of attitude of the counselor to this problem. Some counselors feel that they cannot follow the problem without expressing themselves on paper; other counselors feel guilty about taking notes; they recognize that they need the information but do not feel that they can justify their notes to the pupil. If making notes interferes with your ability to follow the conversation or detracts from rapport with the young person, then notes should not be taken. If you do not feel right about what you are doing, the young person will detect these feelings. The young person may not know what you are concerned about, but he will sense it; consequently it becomes difficult for him to tell his story.

This author feels that it is best not to take notes during the counseling situation. Counseling should be a heart-to-heart relationship. The counselor and the young person should explore the truth of God's Word together. Notes are in bad taste and become too professional for the church-related scene. It may be that after the counseling session is over you will want a complete written report of what was said. At this time makes notes of what was said.

Answering the Pupil's Question

When the young person asks a question, look beyond the question to determine whether the pupil is expressing feelings of inadequacy or simply requesting facts. It may be that the question is showing a feeling of great inadequacy. The answer is not so much the factual information but the student facing himself. He may be inadequate in this situation.

Sometimes the facts that are desired are sought only to fortify a decision which the young person has already made in life. The trained counselor will learn to look beyond the question to the reason that motivates such questions.

REVELATION

The principle of revelation indicates that the counselor should take all the information obtained and analyze it, to come up with the problem which is really bothering the youth. Revelation does not deal with the solution of the problem but the clear understanding of the problem.

Guide the counselee to tell his whole story. Before you can help the counselee you must know the need. Before the doctor treats his patient he must first diagnose the case. A problem well defined is a problem half solved.

Helping the Pupil Talk

Helping the pupil talk is sometimes difficult. There are emotional blocks and the teenager cannot verbalize his problem. These blocks may arise out of conflict within the pupil, or these blocks may arise out of conflict between the pupil and the counselor. Sometimes the young person is approaching a problem that is personal and he is not quite sure that he can trust the counselor. Assure the young person that you will keep his trust in that which is shared, then the teenager will have more freedom to express himself. It may be something which he has never discussed with anyone. The teenager may not be sure that he can or cares to share his problem with anyone.

The use of the question should come naturally. Be careful of using too many stereotyped questions. Be careful of using the question with the pause that implies guilt. Use the question that comes naturally. The use of the question is an art—something that comes from within and is expressed—rather than a science, that which follows rules and orders.

You should be alert continually to the possibility that you may be talking too much. Some counselors immediately upon hearing of a problem say, "I went through that," or "I'm in that situation now." The teenager is not primarily interested in the feeling of the counselor; he is interested in his own problems. Therefore, resist the temptation to share your own feelings. The feelings of the teenager are what is important at this time.

The following questions will help the counselor evaluate himself:

1. *Did I help the teenager say what he wanted to say?*
2. *Was I trying to follow the young person?*
3. *Was I trying to get him to talk about those things which I wanted him to talk about?*
4. *How often did I interrupt the boy?*
5. *Did I give him a chance to say what he wanted to say when I interrupted him?*
6. *Did he try to interrupt me and fail?*
7. *What was he trying to say?*
8. *Did he ever try to say it again?*
9. *Did I really understand what he said?*
10. *What did I do to help him clarify how he felt?*

Creative Listening

Creative listening is a wise procedure which you can learn to employ. Counseling is not mere advice-giving. It is more than employing information or answering questions. To tell another person what to do is to assume that you know all the answers and that you are willing to assume the responsibilities for the direction given. Surely no youth director, no matter how well educated or mature, is willing to assume this responsibility for teenagers today. Be a sympathetic, understanding listener. By listening, you gain insight and make progress toward a successful solution of the problem of the young person.

How can you know what the problem is unless you hear it expressed? How can you know what is in the young person's mind unless you hear him out? How can you uncover the real emotional difficulties and the basic disturbances unless skillful questioning and creative listening take place?

As the skillful listener you should not talk about your own experiences and convictions. Rather you should speak only to maintain a friendly atmosphere and to draw the young person out. This requires self-restraint, patience, mental flexibility, and discipline. In an unhurried interview the youth will express himself.

The young person will not reveal his innermost feelings unless you are an attentive person who seems to understand. You must express confidence in the young person so that the young person may in return express confidence in you. In a permissive, relaxed atmosphere the young person will share and will reveal his heart.

The simple "talking out" of a problem may be a major step in helping the young person. Many young persons have come away from a counseling situation indicating that real help has been received. The counselor has not given any direction. He has not given any advice and in essence has not solved the problem. What has happened? The counselor has become a sounding board. Problems are subjective. As the teenager has the problems within himself he cannot see the situation objectively. To put it in an old phrase, "You can't see the forest for the trees." As the teenager talks the problem out, he is hanging his questions on the clothesline, then he steps back and looks at the problem. As he sees the problem, many times he knows what the solution is. The mere talking out of the problem may be a major step in helping the teenager solve his own problem.

Summarization of the Problem

When you feel you understand the problem, determine if the youth understands the problem. Questions, restatement of facts, and introduction of other material should be used to make sure the youth understands the problem. Once you feel the teenager understands the problem, then a clear statement of the problem should be made.

Take the counselee back to the beginning for a review. This is not a time of rehashing, but of hitting salient points, separating the wheat from the chaff. The problem must be once again brought to the point of view of the teenager.

Try to establish progress during the summarization. This is not just a feedback-look for insight; look for the solution and try to better understand the problem. The teenager is not just rehearsing the situation. This is an excellent chance to objectify or review the case as he once again sees the problem out before him.

He is helping himself to understand himself.

You must do more than take all the information obtained and analyze the problem within your own mind. You must share with the young person the problem and together determine the courses of action. What alternatives are there? Guard against helping the young person too much. Naturally, it is easy to presume we are showing love by doing as much as we can for them. But is this truly an act of kindness when we tie the apron strings to ourselves? Actually we may be weakening the young person by not encouraging self-reliance and independent growth. If at all possible, do not show the possible solutions to the young person. If the young person can see the solutions for himself and then choose the solution that is best, he will grow to Christian maturity.

During this summarization period, possible areas for future exploration might be suggested. You might pave the way for growth while saying, "Have you thought of—?" or "You might have—" Never close the door of help to the teenager.

RESULTS

After all is said and done, the true test of counseling is results. Have you helped teenagers?

Results are not always the solution they want or you want. Results may not always be the choice of an action, sometimes they must refrain from action. Results may not always be seen, but nevertheless they are there.

The climax of the counseling situation is crucial. All the progress up to this point may be lost if the counselor does not display wisdom.

There are no dogmatic rules to obtain results. What may work in one situation will fail in the next. Use your inner feeling of rapport rather than follow a prescribed pattern. Even though you cannot always follow a rigid mold, there are some suggestions to follow. These general principles are applicable in most situations. They are not, however, chronological.

Determine the Alternatives

The youth should understand the problem before a solution is attempted. There are no easy solutions to life's problems. You should realize that there are many possible solutions. Problems are complex and solutions are complex. The first solution in the teenager's mind is not necessarily the best or right solution.

The counselor and the youth should attempt to explore all possible solutions before making any decisions. As you discuss possible solutions, these could be listed on paper for examination at a later time. When listing all the possible solutions, both the counselor and youth should suggest all that come to mind.

It may be best at this point for the possible solutions to be written either by the youth or counselor. The listing of the solutions will help to objectify the situation in the youth's mind. The simple writing out of a possible solution with its problem will indicate to the youth the validity of the solution.

These courses of action should be listed together with the implications. The young person should know what are the alternatives facing him. As he sees the alternatives, it should be brought continually to his attention that it is his decision to make. The decision is not yet the issue. The understanding of the alternatives is the present problem.

There are three pitfalls to note for the counselor who pushes his solution to the problem on the youth.

1. *If the result or decision is not as anticipated, the young person will not come back.* You should recognize that you don't know the will of God for his life. Therefore, it is best that you do not push the decision on him at this time. If the decision is the youth's and the results are not as expected, you will have left the door open for him to come back with a future problem.

2. *The teenager decides against the recommended cure.* If he decides against what you think is best, he feels that you are against him so he will not return to you. Be aware of pushing your decision on the teenager.

3. *If the teenager gets results, he becomes increasingly dependent upon you.* You may have helped his immediate problem but have started a long-range pattern of life. You become his Ouija board. When he has a problem, he comes to you and expects you to solve it for him.

Scriptural Insight Phase

The most certain and helpful phase of counseling is found here. This is where you present Christ and the revelation of His Word. You must remove those things that are blocking adjustment so that the soul may heal. Doctors remove the blocks and God does the physical healing. At this stage the teenager is to the point where he comes to accept himself and his position in life.

Interject Scripture at points of insight. This interjection of Scripture brings divine perspective to the human problem. The greatest use of the Bible comes in this phase of counseling, but it should not be excluded at other phases. Just as soil must be prepared before the planting of the seed, so the heart should be tilled before the sowing of the Word of God. The Word of God is not a substitute for counseling; it is a supplement to counseling. It is not the amount of reading of Scripture but the meaningful reading of Scripture which must be emphasized. The teenager must understand what is being read.

Readiness is important. The timing of the introduction of the Word of God is very crucial. It may determine the entire outcome of the counseling situation. Do not give the teenager too much Bible so that he cannot understand it. A principle of life is to introduce revelation in proportion to the teenager's receptivity.

Take the teenager through the actual process of discovering for himself the answer in the Word of God. This is done by adhering to the following principles:

1. *Do not read the Scripture to the teenager.* The youth should read the Scripture for himself. The counselor is a resource individual. He ought to know the Word of God and the teenager. Then the counselor should get the youth into the Word of God and the Word of God into the youth. This is called double transference.

2. *Ask the teenager for the meaning.* Don't assume that the teenager understands what he has read. Assumption here might be a false step. If the teenager does not understand the Word of God, he cannot apply it to his heart. Therefore, if he does not understand the meaning, go to step 3.

3. *Make sure the teenager can determine the relationship between the passage and his problem.* Raise questions that will point out insights and relationships.

If the teenager continues in his inability to see the relationships, guide him into an understanding by every means of education available. It is now that the counselor assumes the role of a teacher.

Avoid engaging in preaching and exposition. Forget "If I were you." The Word of God is alive; use it that way.

Confession of Sins to God

The confession of sin is the admission of failure in a responsibility. Confession must be self-motivated; it must come from the heart. Confession must be a personal admission of failure and a self-confessed guilt. This is the first step in deliverance from sin. As long as sin is secret, it must be repressed and guarded. Such repression of sin increases tension and anxiety. This results in a disturbed personality.

There is no cure for guilt apart from a verbalized self-admission. The teenager must say, "I am wrong." The psychologist sometimes calls this an inner catharsis.

This purging and releasing of guilt tensions from the heart of the teenager results in happiness. Only the person who knows the forgiveness of God that comes through the cleansing of the blood of Jesus Christ can have true happiness. "If we confess our sins, He is faithful and just to forgive us our sins and to cleanse us from all unrighteousness" (I John 1:9). To reveal the secrets of the heart and confess sin, leads to peace of soul. As the young person confesses his sin, talks it over with you and objectifies the situation, he enters into the way of release.

The Roman Catholic Church has made the confession of sin a required practice. The priest who receives the confession has been delegated the authority to allay the parishioner's conscience and to absolve his guilt. Protestant churches have not given this sense of release to its members. Pastors assume no authority to forgive sins. This authority is in the Word of God. The Protestant principle is that each man has a direct access to God for the forgiveness of sins. (I Timothy 2:5.)

Making Decisions

Young people grow with each correct decision they make. Direct the young person toward the climax of the counseling situation in which he will make a decision. Remember that great decisions are not made halfheartedly. Many small decisions made correctly enable the youth to make great decisions for God.

Young people seek help because they are faced with problems which appear too difficult for them to solve alone. These decisions are too great for them to make. Sometimes they need to recognize the tensions which prevent them from using their own resources to solve their own problems and to make their own decisions. At other times young people need facts about themselves and the conditions of their surroundings which can be used to achieve the necessary basis for a choice. Decisions come hard. Although you help the pupil achieve all of these goals, in the final analysis the young person is responsible for defining the alternatives and making the decision which he feels is best for him.

Young people learn to make independent decisions gradually, and they need the help of the human teacher as well as the divine teacher in this capacity. Young people learn to make decisions through solving problems which are important to them. When the young person comes to you seeking help, use every means at your disposal to guide him through the solving of his problems to the decision that he must make.

Sometimes the young person may seek your help and define the alternatives but, as far as you know, may never reach a decision. A young person may stop coming to you for help before reaching the decision. Be able to accept such behavior. It is unwise to press a young person into a decision before he is ready to make such a choice. Nevertheless, there are times when, because of the obligations of eternity and the commands of God's Word, you should use every pressure at your disposal to cause the young person to choose the path of righteousness and the will of God. Young people should be warned concerning the serious consequences of making decisions that are wrong. The ideal is when the young person concludes the problem, examines the alternatives, and decides the will of God for his life. This is best, but this is not always the case in a counseling situation.

RESPONSIBILITY

After the young person has made his decision, the problem is not yet solved. The problem will be solved as it is worked out in the life. It is best for you to pray with the counselee. After this, map out an attack on the problem; a daily plan of Bible reading, Scripture memorizing, suggested books to read, and quiet time can be planned. Help the young person select activities which will help him become strong in his decision. There may be opportunities to witness and fellowship with other believers. But the young person must be aware that just because he has told you his problem it is not automatically solved.

The responsibility of change is upon the young person. The only problems that are really solved are the ones we solve ourselves. Remember that your goal is for the counselee to become autonomous. Some counselors have a strange feeling of disappointment in discovering that the youth is able to solve his own problems.

Follow-up

You still have a role to play in prayer and interest for the youth. From time to time ask the youth, "How goes it?" When the young person realizes that someone else knows of the problem and is interested in the progress, this added incentive helps the progress of adjustment. It is good for the youth to realize someone is anxious for him to overcome his problem.

Even though the responsibility belongs to the youth, you must assume some responsibility, for you have had an investment in the direction and solution of the problem. The responsibility of applying the solution to the problem belongs to the young person, but the responsibility of teenagers belongs to you.

Confidence

The counselor must have a heart like a "graveyard." Many problems will be buried there. Resist the temptation to tell another person the problems of a young person. If the teens find out that the counselor "spills the beans," they will stop coming to the counselor. Once a counselor loses respect from the teens, it will be almost imposssible to win it back. Betraying confidence is nothing more than gossip. Be careful of sharing "juicy bits" of information about your youth as prayer requests. This spiritual cover-up is deadly. If you don't have the confidence of your youth, you might as well close up shop.

CONCLUSION

Every counseling situation will take a different shape. Problems are different, people are different, circumstances are varied, and solutions are complex. The general approach suggested in this chapter can be used in an ideal situation, but there are no ideal situations. Even though this structured approach cannot be employed fully in each situation, the general guidelines and attitudes of approach can be used in every situation. In some counseling situations the problem is evident and *realization* can be skipped. In the next situation the counselor and counselee will have to give attention to *relaxation* and *rapport*. A further counseling situation will find *results* receiving all the attention.

In any situation the goal of counseling is adjustment and maturity. The application of the several principles in "Structuring the Actual Counseling Situation" will accomplish these goals. However, the goal— not the technique—must be kept in sight. Be counselee-centered, not technique-centered. The wise counselor will choose those techniques in the required order to lead teenagers to a solution of their problems and a proper adjustment in life.

COUNSELING DYNAMICS

This is a demonstration in counseling dynamics. Use this in a classroom or workshop situation. Choose two persons for role playing.

Choose an older man, perhaps a pastor or someone who has leadership ability in the local church, to be Reverend Frank. Choose a younger girl who can act the role of Mary Lou.

1. Give out sheets of paper explaining Rev. Frank and Mary Lou to all of the class. Give the sheet of paper explaining Rev. Frank only to the person doing the role-playing of Rev. Frank, and the same to the person playing Mary Lou.

2. Send Mary Lou out of the room. Go over the role of Rev. Frank with the class and the person playing Rev. Frank.

3. Send Rev. Frank out of the room to study his sheet of paper and call Mary Lou in. Go over the role of Mary Lou with the class and the person who is going to play the role of Mary Lou. Send Mary Lou out of the room to a place scheduled from Rev. Frank so she may study her role.

4. Distribute the set of five questions to the class only. (The persons playing Rev. Frank and Mary Lou should not have a set of the questions.) Go over the questions with the class, pointing out to them certain things they should look for in the counseling situation.

The effectiveness of this counseling dynamics is ñot the successfulness of the counselor but the learning of the class as they observe the counseling situation.

5. Divide the class into study groups (buzz sessions). Give the class five minutes to study the problem and to indicate what each person in the study group would do to solve the problem.

6. Call in Rev. Frank and Mary Lou. Indicate to them that the setting is the pastor's office. It is after the Sunday evening church service and Mary Lou has asked to talk with the pastor. Rev. Frank arrives at the office one minute before Mary Lou knocks on the door.

Questions

1. Did Rev. Frank listen to all of the facts before he drew a conclusion? What "clues" (among those which Mary Lou gave that she needed help) did Rev. Frank miss? Where did he begin preaching at Mary Lou? Does the pastor consider himself "God's gift" to young people?

2. What should Mary Lou have told her pastor? Where did Mary Lou start drawing into her shell? If you were Mary Lou would you have done the same thing?

3. What is Mary Lou's main problem? List all of her problems on a sheet of paper. What is Mary Lou's most important problem? List the problems in order of priority.

4. Now that you know both sides of the problem, what help can

Rev. Frank give to Mary Lou? What should he help her do first? What should be Rev. Frank's attitude towards Mary Lou's parents. What should Rev. Frank tell Jim?

5. What spiritual help does Mary Lou need? What Scripture portion would you use with Mary Lou? Would you advise them to remain married or to get an annulment?

COUNSELING DYNAMICS
Rev. Dwayne Frank

Dwayne Frank graduated from Seminary last year. He has been in the pastorate of Elmdale Church for six months. Dwayne pastored the church during his last year in Seminary as a student pastor and is now the full-time minister. Since Frank is young, he works with the young people. The church has many young people and an aggressive youth program. Rev. Frank teaches the high school Sunday School class and is the chaperon on all of the youth outings.

Rev. Frank is married, and his wife is expecting their first child. Mary Frank graduated with her husband from Bible college and has a real desire that the young people in the church grow in Christ. She also attends many of the young people's outings but is limited in participation because she is pregnant.

Pastor Frank was converted during his high school years and became an active worker in the high school Bible club. He is a good song leader and the young people like for him to lead singing. Since Frank was a class leader in Bible college, the young people like to hang around him to hear his jokes and stories. He also has a good selection of games to play at the church parties. Since Frank has come to the church the attendance has doubled.

The adults in the church support Rev. Frank in the youth work. They feel that he is doing with their young people what they cannot do.

Even though Rev. Frank has the young people's support, he has not "buddied" with them to an extreme. Rev. Frank always is dressed conservatively and does not hang out at teenage spots. Frank was good in sports at college and spends time with the boys playing football, basketball, and golf. The young people admire his ability in sports.

Rev. Frank has a keen desire that the young people be separated from worldly amusements. On occasions he has spoken against commercial novels, ballroom dancing, and drinking. But he has not stopped there. He has had many discussions giving the young people reasons that they should abstain from worldly practices. Many of the young people have abstained from worldly practices and the adults in the church appreciate Rev. Frank's stand.

Rev. Frank considers Mary Lou a borderline case. She has great potential and at times shows real desire in spiritual things. Dr. Frank feels that Mary Lou has an overt desire to be popular among the boys so he cautions her against seeking out unsaved boys and dating them. Rev. Frank also mentions that she will harm her testimony by dancing. Mary Lou answers that she already knows this.

It's not that Mary Lou is rebellious against her pastor and the Lord; she is having a difficult time yielding this area of her life because she sincerely enjoys musical expression through dance. On previous occasions Mary Lou has talked to her minister about dancing, and she knows why she should not dance. She has told him that she is a weak-willed girl and just can't seem to control herself. She can't say no.

Rev. Frank has been successful in counseling other teenagers, and he feels if he had enough time to talk to Mary Lou he could help her grow in Christ and become a stable Christian girl.

Mary Lou

Mary Lou comes from a non-Christian home, and her parents are quite apathetic about spiritual things. They know that she goes to church, but they do not care. Rev. Frank has been in the home to talk to the parents about the Lord, but they have not been responsive. However, they are quite willing for Mary Lou to go to church and be a Christian.

Mary Lou has three older sisters. The oldest sister finished high school and is now working evenings in an all-night diner. She is not interested in spiritual things. The other two older sisters quit high school to get married. Both girls married laborers. One lives in a housing project and the other lives in West Elmdale, considered the slums of the town.

Mary Lou has been getting $D's$ and $F's$ in school ever since she can remember. Her parents never pushed her in school, and she feels that school is a waste of time. Mary Lou feels that high school will not help her be a better wife and mother. Her aim in life is to get married.

For two months Mary Lou has been going secretly with a Catholic fellow. Since this is condemned at church, she has not told anyone at church she has been going with Jim. When Jim picks up Mary Lou for a date, he never comes in; therefore, Jim and Mary Lou's father have met only briefly. Jim and Mary Lou like to go dancing in taverns; although Mary Lou doesn't drink, Jim sees nothing wrong with a bottle of beer.

Mary Lou thought she was pregnant, but she felt that she couldn't tell anyone. She began telling her older sister but ended up telling her that the church was against her going with Jim because he was a Catholic.

Mary Lou lost her nerve when telling her sister. Since she was not very close to her parents, she couldn't tell them.

When Mary Lou told Jim that she was pregnant, he talked her into running off and getting married. They did this but decided not to tell anyone at home or school. The high school had a rule that if any of the kids got married they had to drop out. Mary Lou wants to drop out of high school but Jim wants her to finish high school. Now after being married for three weeks Mary Lou finds out she is not pregnant. She knows that Catholics can annul their marriage but she knows nothing about the procedure.

Mary Lou goes to see Rev. Frank. She feels that he understands young people and can help her with her problem. So she begins by explaining to her pastor that she is going with Jim. She tells Rev. Frank that she wants to drop out of high school, work and save money to get married. Since Mary Lou doesn't have much courage, she figures if she can get Rev. Frank to tell her what's involved first in getting married, then she can ask what's involved in getting a divorce or annulment. She asks him if he can perform marriages and how much it costs. She asks how old you have to be to get married and if she needs parents' approval.

THOUGHT QUESTIONS

Section Seven

(Covers Chapter 17, "The Foundation of Counseling Young People"; Chapter 18, "Principles of Counseling Young People"; and Chapter 19, "Structuring the Actual Counseling Situation.")

1. Can all Christians counsel youth? Do you feel you can give spiritual help to teenagers?

2. Why has counseling demanded more attention in the church in the past ten years?

3. What is the difference between counseling and teaching?

4. What should a teenager learn about himself in a counseling interview?

5. Do you believe teenagers have within themselves resources for solving their problems?

6. In counseling with teens, many times you will find they share the surface problem rather than the real problem. Why do teens do this? How can you get to the real problem?

7. Are there times when you should give advice rather than just listen? When? Why?

8. How can you put teens at ease when they come to you?

9. What is inductive counseling? What does the word "induct" mean? How does this apply to your counseling?

10. What kind of referral is best, and what should be the correct attitude of referrals? How can you improve the referrals in your church?

11. What are some basic admissions that you must make to a teenager in a counseling session?

12. What is rapport? How do you establish this relationship with teenagers?

13. Should counselors take notes during sessions? Explain your answer.

14. Do you agree with the two statements: "A teenager must understand his problem before he can solve his problem"; "A teenager must determine the alternatives before choosing an answer to his problem"?

15. What happens if you give advice and the teen does not heed your advice?

16. How can you use the Bible in counseling? Doesn't use of the Bible hinder free discussion because it amounts to preaching?

Use the following questions with buzz groups, dyads, circular response or brainstorming. See Chapter 17 for a discussion of using these techniques.

17. How would you deal with the following problems?

   (a) A boy asks your opinion of rock and roll music during refreshments at a party.

   (b) An unmarried girl in church becomes pregnant.

   (c) A boy away at university has problems with evolution.

   (d) A teen needs help in preparing a talk for school.

   (e) Several teens question the use of television.

   (f) You note several unexplained absences of a teen who usually attends regularly.

   (g) A teenage boy has a problem with immoral thoughts.

18. Make a list of twelve people or officers in the church who can assist you in counseling youth.

19. Think through a description of one teenager you know. Don't explain or analyze his action; just describe him.

20. Note the illustration of inductive counseling as portrayed by a triangle. Think through the six steps to the following problem:

   A teenage girl has been elected homecoming queen by the high school. She is to reign over the annual dance, yet the other Christian girls won't attend because of Christian convictions. The girl comes to you as a counselor. Describe the six steps of the triangle you would use in dealing with her.

SECTION EIGHT

THE TOTAL YOUTH PROGRAM

Do teenagers desire quiet meditation when they worship God?

How can a youth meeting be effectively advertised?

Who is responsible for advertisement?

Why does God want youth to sing?

Is entertainment a valid goal in church music?

Why does camping affect Christian youth more than any other agency in the church?

Who is the most important leader at camp—the director, the speaker or the counselors?

What is the primary purpose of a recreation program?

20

WORSHIP AND THE YOUNG PERSON

Worship is a little-known entity in the teenage program. Most fundamental churches are centered about activity, programming, organization, involvement, interaction, and service. There is very little place for worship. This is probably a reaction to churches which substitute worship for personal experience with Christ.

Teenagers today need the worship experience. Basically they are insecure and unstable. In worship their needs are met in a face-to-face relationship with God. When instability meets stability there is *an experience*. Christianity embraces every area of the teenage experience. So worship should embrace every area of the teen's experience.

Worship is both corporate and private, teens can worship in personal devotions or in a youth meeting. Also worship is both structured and spontaneous; teens can worship God at a singspiration after evening church, or as they serve God. Dr. Jerry Falwell, pastor of Thomas Road Baptist Church, Lynchburg, Virginia, states, "We begin worshiping God when the first Sunday School bus driver leaves at 8:00 A.M. to pick up children, and we continue worshiping God all day long, by all we do."

Worship is not the primary aim of a youth program, but it cannot be left out. A well-balanced youth ministry should allow for worship, both corporate and private. Also it should provoke spontaneous worship by planned meetings.

What Is Worship?

Worship should be an emotional, intellectual, volitional, and moral response. Worship is a face-to-face involvement with a living God, based on a regeneration experience, prompted by the Holy Spirit, and resulting in the exaltation of God's glory.

Because of this, worship is a growing thing and is a dynamic entity. Worship is personal. True worship cannot be divorced from the worshiper. Worship, we might say, is an earnest effort to re-create the conditions and experiences that have been found to deepen man's relationship to God.

Worship is not just an intellectual process, it involves more than knowledge and fact; worship must stir the emotions and result in activity. It begins with a knowledge of the Word of God. The heart moves upon biblical facts to re-create a fundamental experience, simply and dramatically to help the person gain a personal understanding of the Lord. Then the teenager can give back to God and magnify Him for what He is. The roots of worship are knowledge, emotions, and will. Worship is not a mystical experience; it is at best a spiritual experience. Teenagers do not automatically worship because they have Christian knowledge. Worship must be learned, and some teenagers never do have the stirring experience of genuine worship of God.

Psychology teaches us that emotions or inner drives control our lives. Only as we display every emotion of love in approbation to God do we truly worship. As a volitional process, worship focuses all of our ideas, actions, and feeling in effective tones on a specific center which is God Himself. All of the teenager's thinking and action must be wrapped up in worship. Worship can be said to be an emotional and volitional response to an intellectual evaluation.

Too often worship in young people's societies has been neglected because it has not been understood. At this point we ought to distinguish between worshiping and learning to worship. Teenagers need to learn how to worship God as well as participate in the actual act of worship.

How Do You Worship?

Learning to worship is one of the basic processes in the Christian education of young people. Because the nature of teenagers is different from that of adults, their expression of worship will be different. Some of the following principles will help in planning a worship service for teenagers.

1. *Preparation.* When a speaker addresses the young people's society, this is not worship. Worship must include involvement by the youth. However, teenagers may worship God during a message. The

Lord is lifted up and magnified in the hearts of the teens. When hearts are correctly prepared in five minutes, a fifty-minute message may be effective, but only if the teen's heart has been prepared. The first prayer of the teenager is more important than the leader's first prayer. A poorly prepared youth sponsor will make poorly prepared teenage worshipers. Preparation is essential to worship.

First, make sure that the worship service is centered around a specific aim or purpose. As was seen in the program planning section, this should be directly related to central objectives which the youth director and his youth committee have planned for a whole year and divided into sections and subdivisions. Make sure this theme is written down on paper so that it is precise and clear to all who plan and participate in the program.

Second, you should gather the materials for a worship period, following the planning suggested in the programming section. The teenager who is responsible should gather such materials as music, hymns, Scripture, prayers, inspirational quotations, pictures, and posters. What may be a splendid program for one worship service may not be useful in another.

2. *Examination.* Sincere worship begins by an examination of the teenager's heart motives. Why am I attending church? What am I looking for in this service? Am I content with myself? What do I need? How can the Lord speak to me? What do I owe God?

As the teenager examines his own heart's needs before the Lord, he sees himself as he really is. The teenager must objectify his needs, then the Lord can meet these needs.

Note several of the worship experiences in the Bible. In each occasion the man involved examined himself before he worshiped God.

(a) Isaiah in the temple (Isaiah 6:1-13). When Isaiah saw the holiness of God he cried out, "Woe is me! for I am undone; because I am a man of unclean lips" (Isaiah 6:5). Note that the praise of the greatness of God is tied to the humility of examining the heart.

(b) Moses before the burning bush (Exodus 3:1-17). In the natural surroundings of nature, God met Moses. After a revelation of the holiness of God in the midst of the bush which burned with fire and was not consumed, Moses examined himself. He cried out, "Who am I, that I should go unto Pharoah" (Exodus 3:11). In God's challenge to service, Moses saw his own uselessness.

(c) Worship through the communion table (Matthew 26:20-30). Teenagers can worship God through the communion service. Whether the service is simple or elaborate, the element of examination should be there. At the actual last supper the question rang out from the hearts of the disciples, "Master, is it I?" (Matthew 26:25).

Later the apostle Paul exhorted those who would worship through the Lord's table, "Let a man examine himself, and so let him eat" (I Corinthians 11:28). When the teenager participates in the Lord's Supper, it is not a time of mystical experience. It is a time when his heart in true worship and praise can render unto God the glory and adoration that are due to Him.

(d) Paul's experience on the Damascus road (Acts 9:1-9). This experience contains the elements of worship, even though it is a time of intense emotion. Here was a man zealously following his conviction, persecuting Christians, when suddenly his whole life is threatened. Paul meets God. In light of a true revelation of God Paul falls to his face and examines himself. "Who art thou, Lord?" And, "Lord, what will thou have me to do?" (Acts 9:5-6). As the young man Paul met God and responded, so may teenagers today.

3. *Expectation*. Only as the teenager comes expecting to meet God can he have a true worship experience. The human spirit inevitably reaches out to the Lord. You as the youth sponsor will have to create an atmosphere of expectancy. If the teenager comes to youth meetings and through many worship experiences his needs are ignored and denied, he will not come to the next worship experience expecting to meet God.

"My soul, wait thou only upon God; for my expectation is from him" (Psalm 62:5). God does not need the apostle Paul to speak to the young people. God needs open hearts among the young people and then they can respond and meet Him. Expectation is the vital element of faith, and faith is needed in a worship experience.

4. *Appropriation*. Worship is a form of human activity. The teenager is an active individual and as such needs activity in worship. A person doesn't participate in a hike unless he walks. A person doesn't participate in a meal unless he eats. A teenager doesn't participate in worship unless he appropriates the presence of God.

One of the faults of true worship is that we do not appropriate what is offered. We do not take what God gives. Worship is not overcoming the acquiescence of God. Worship is laying hold of His willingness. "The Father seeketh such to worship Him" (John 4:23). The Father makes available all we need in worship. We do not worship because we have not taken what He has offered.

5. *Meditation*. True worship involves quietness, meditation, and thinking. The average person's concept of the teenage is one of hustle,

bustle, and activity. This image of the teen is not a correct one. The teenager can and will participate in deep thought. The teenager can and will participate in meditation and worship.

Teenagers often have a thin veneer of sham and self-sufficiency. Underneath they have deep and searching questions. Their frustrations and lack of ability to perform the demands of an adult society produce fears and self-distrust. They think, grope for answers, seek meanings and search for reality. They desire quietness to think. Exploit this desire in your worship service. Provide abundant opportunities for meditation.

The teenager, like the adult, receives understanding only with mental effort. Therefore, it takes work to worship. Worship is not coming to an end of activity and effort. It is not just quietness. But quietness that is filled with reflection, interpretation and integration can produce a spiritual dynamic in the life of the teenager.

6. *Consummation.* Just as a mountain must have a peak, so the worship experience must come to an end, but not merely through a benediction or closing prayer. The worship service must end in a complete and fitting close. The peak of the worship experience is a dedicated life. The revelation of God demands a response in the life. God has revealed truth to produce an experience. The worship of the teenager is the deepest experience in life.

If this worship experience does not overhaul his thinking and change his life, it is meaningless and empty.

7. *Transformation.* The teenager must have more than just a dedicated life. He can be dedicated to a cause but without strength and ability to carry out the demands of the cause. The enemy, the nature of the world, and sin are all against his living for Christ. Therefore, the youth needs a supernatural transformation. He needs divine enablement to help him to live his life for the glory of God.

In a true worship experience the teenager examines himself. He meets God. He expects that God can do for him what only God can do. The teenager appropriates the power and person of the Lord for his life. Through deep meditation he dedicates his life, the only result of this experience. With this dedicated life the youth can go out and live for God. His life is transformed.

Moses was in the presence of God on the top of Mount Sinai. From this experience he walked again among people. The people saw the presence of God in his life for his face shone. "The children of Israel saw the face of Moses, that the skin of Moses' face shone" (Exodus 34:35). Thus, true worship will meet needs and transform lives.

Media Through Which Teenagers Worship

Christianity is concerned not only with the end (worship experience and transformed life) but with the means to an end (media of worship). There are scriptural patterns for both manner and the instruments of worship. Some organizations claim they worship God, but apart from the New Testament means of worship, only an emotional subjective experience is felt and if a change in the life results, it is a self-inflicted change. God invades the life through divinely set instruments and means.

The following list of media are not all needed in a worship experience. The list may not be complete but is suggestive. A complete list of media for worship would be as complete as the Bible itself.

1. *The Word of God.* The Bible is the primary resource for Christian worship. The Bible contains the revelation of God, and worship is the response of the willing heart. The Bible can be used in many ways to bring about worship. There can be collections of Scriptures that are read by the teenagers. These can be from many versions of the Bible. Responsive reading is effective. Call for favorite verses from the teenagers. Choral readings have their place. Visiting teenagers should recognize that the Bible is appealed to as the authority in your teenage worship service.

2. *Prayer.* Prayer is the heart of communion with God. It is the expression of man's aspirations toward the Lord. Teenagers can pray. They can offer public prayers as well as intercede privately. Call on teenagers to lead in prayer. Beware of printed prayers that do not come from the heart, even though they may be grammatically and theologically correct. Have the teens spend time in silent prayer. During quiet prayer the teenagers can have meditation, reflection, and examination.

Instruct the teenager how to pray. Give him an example of how to pray and praise God. Also give him instruction in how to pray and ask God for specific requests. In some cases prayer can be intermeshed with meditation and listening. All types of prayer can be of value in worship.

3. *Music.* Music is the soul of the church and the universal language. It has an important place in the worship service as well as the informal devotional service. Can you imagine a young people's service without a piano, choruses or singing?

Some churches have fallen into the snare of using only the music of two or three hundred years ago. This was great and in the past met needs of the heart. However, it may not reach the heart need of the teenager today.

Other churches have fallen into the snare of using only the light choruses and gospel "ditties" that are sung in youth services. There must be balance in music. The selection of music for a teenage program should not be a matter of personal taste, but rather a careful analysis of the quality of the music needed to bring out a young person's heart worship to God and result in the magnifying of God's person.

Sacred anthems and hymns can be an important part of our worship service. Teenagers respond to depth and a challenge. Teach them the great hymns of our Christian tradition. At the same time sing the choruses of praise and testimony. These are written to modern music appealing to modern youth. Use instrumental music. Many teenagers have talent on musical instruments, learned at the public school and at home. Vocal music can lead others into a worship experience. Use solos and group ensembles. Have music with accompaniment or a cappella.

4. *The Lord's table.* When teens correctly participate in the Lord's table, they worship God. Make sure you instruct the teens in the biblical meaning of communion. The Lord's table is a church ordinance and youth leaders should not plan such a service, if it is not an extension of the church and approved by church leaders.

The Lord's table can produce the experience of worship. It can be a simple or elaborate ceremony. It can be quiet or accompanied by an explanation of the occasion. Here the teenager must not think only in terms of being ministered to but of his ministering to God.

5. *Testimony.* The fundamental church today commonly thinks of testimonies as a time of helping a weaker Christian. Teenagers may give a testimony in which others who are afraid may be encouraged. Also, testimonies are a time of sharing what God had done for us to encourage others that God will do the same for them.

The testimony should mean something to the heart of God. In a true worship service the teenager can give a testimony and encourage other teenagers. At the same time the testimony has worshiped God, magnified His person, and exalted His name. Use planned testimonies that are assigned weeks in advance. Also call for spontaneous testimonies that come from a heart that expresses what God has done.

6. *Atmosphere.* Many fundamental churches do not provide atmosphere for worship. They expect teenagers to worship in a church basement or converted gymnasium. At the same time their church sanctuary is a beautiful house structured to re-create a response in their minds and hearts.

Atmosphere can be the charm of a lovely chapel or the quietness of a devotional on the mountainside at camp. Since worship is an emotional and volitional response, anything that will add to this response should be used. You as the youth director should make sure that the room is prepared. The mechanical details of the service need to be hidden. Clumsy introductions of people, as well as obvious blunders, should be eliminated. Needless movement on the platform should be avoided. Coordinate the people on the program and others in the service to make sure of a smooth-running program. The ushers need to understand when people can and cannot be seated. They need to understand when the service should not be interrupted. Watch for the placing of announcements in the program. Do not let them become time-consuming without a purpose. Radio and TV programs run well and are executed precisely because of planning and practice. Just so, the Lord's work needs exact planning and practice. These little things will make the difference in a meaningful worship experience.

7. *Visual aids, art, and interpretation.* A good worship service should certainly include inspirational and challenging literature, art, and visual aids. There are many excellent poems, readings, and stories that can cause the heart to respond to God. These may demand a challenge, response, emotion, or attitude of mind.

A word of warning is in order. Beware of idolatry. A symbol can blot out or be substituted for the source — God Himself. Some visuals become the purpose rather than means to an end.

21

ADVERTISING THE YOUTH PROGRAM

Two junior high boys were going into business—shoveling snow. Elaborate plans were made. They bought shovels, made preparations, decided who was boss, and even went so far as to give their business a name. When the first big snow of the year came, two disappointed boys didn't have any business. No one knew they were in business.

Many youth functions in the church are planned and organized in just such a fashion. Good programs, fine organizations and terrific planning, but no one comes! Usually publicity for the average youth programs is "too little and too late." Here are a few suggestions.

Consider the Product

What do you have to offer? The youth group specializes in a product needed by all—Christ, the Word of God. Through Christ are offered the joy of salvation, the peace that satisfies, the answer to the problem of life, and direction for life. Promote with confidence, assurance and enthusiasm.

While our product is the best in the world, the average non-Christian teen doesn't know it. As a result, you will find a great deal of sales resistance. You must create a desire for the product. Remember, Christianity is unpopular in the eyes of the non-Christian youth, but Christ is what they need. Unknown to young people, Christ is what they search for.

What is your market? To many, the only market is the few teens who now attend the church. True advertising begins at home but doesn't end there. First, you must determine your source of potential or your market.

Divide your young people into natural groupings and appeal to each on the basis of their needs and desire. Some of the following potential will start you thinking:

1. The youth who already attend
2. Youth in the church who don't attend
3. Youth who came to church, but stopped attending
4. Youth related to church members
5. The friends of youth in the church
6. Youth who live in the neighborhood
7. All other youth in the total area

Not only do you consider the potential youth as your market. Good promotion reaches to other areas. These groups also are the different publics to which you will minister:

1. The parents of youth
2. Smaller children
3. The church clientele
4. The non-Christian public

As you promote the youth group in these broader areas, you will be eventually helping your immediate group. As you reach parents, they may encourage their kids to come. Don't forget to sell younger children on the youth group; they will be teenagers one day. Also the church clientele must be aware of your activities. They may have contact with other teenagers you can never reach.

Be concerned about the *image* of the youth in your church. What does the average person think of your organization? It's dead? Too worldly? Always busy, but never producing? The *image* of the youth group is the sum total of the impressions created in the mind of the public. You want people to have a positive attitude when they think of young people in the church. Too often, people think of teens as juvenile delinquents or unstable persons. When people think of the youth in the church, they should think of dedication, spiritual life, energy for God, growth, and vitality.

Attitudes Toward Advertising

The announcements or posters might reflect your attitude toward advertising. Since the total impression or the image of the youth is dependent upon the method of advertisement, your philosophy or attitude toward advertising should be correct.

1. *Advertising should be truthful.* In the secular world it is well known that some advertising is untruthful and dishonest. It is often exaggerated to the extent of being entirely false in relaying to the public its worth.

Advertising in the Lord's work must produce good after-effects. Young people do not like to be fooled, so when advertising, keep the results in mind. When the evening is over and the program has been tested and tried, the effects should verify what was promised.

2. *Advertising should publicize something worthwhile.* Needless to say, we have the best product in the world. We should be so sold on Jesus Christ and what He is able to do, that we want to share Him with the world.

Be careful of over-advertising some smaller event. When a worthy event needs the prayers, support and attendance of many, perhaps the effect has been lost and many do not respond. Advertisement should be commensurate with the product.

3. *Adequate advertisement requires adequate individuals.* Use the available talent for the jobs best suited to them. Make sure the individuals who are affiliated with the advertising are sold on what they are promoting. Push your promotion after you see the Lord's will and use the individuals God would desire in this position. There are some individuals who do better at ushering than advertising; if so, use them in this manner. Be sure that those on the advertising committee are enthusiastic, sold on the product, and willing to help.

4. *Advertisement leads to personal contact.* Good publicity cannot be realized from a poster or announcement alone. People are individuals and good advertisement contacts individuals. A phone call, personal letter, or personal chat will usually do the job and sell a teen. Even though the youth are already attending regularly, give them personal invitations and make sure of their presence at the special meeting. Adequate advertisement must preview a personal visit.

5. *Advertising begins at home.* Many times in the church, the advertising campaign is aimed at those who never heard of the work. This is valid and necessary but not primary. Begin with those closest to the group. Sell the executive committee and officers. If they aren't ready to support the program, don't expect the youth on the fringes to get excited. Advertising is like waves in a pond. Once you throw the stone in the water, the waves are highest near the splash. Therefore, concentrate your advertisement on those closest home.

6. *Advertising gets all youth involved.* If you want to get fifty teens out to a special meeting, get fifty teens *"in"* on the special push. The world gets the market involved and hence becomes effective. Contests

where you listen, guess, find, draw, predict, judge, explore or participate are successful. The advertiser knows if he can get a person to make up a "jingle" about a soap, the person will probably start using the soap.

Involvement is the key to learning, growth and spirituality. *Involvement* is also the key word to advertisement. How can you get twenty-five kids involved? Simple:

Two on posters
Three on advertising committee
Four making phone calls
Four writing letters or post cards
Three making personal invitations
One contact the pastor to announce
Five responsible for announcement skit in the youth group
One responsible for announcement in the church bulletin
Two put on skit to make announcement

However, the best way to get 25 kids involved, is to get 25 kids to an organized soul-winning campaign. Getting 25 kids to go visiting will guarantee 25 kids at your program, probably more.

7. *Best advertisement is a satisfied customer.* When a youth receives a blessing or has a good time, he will tell others. Adults, the pastor, or the youth leader can invite teens to a youth program and they may or may not respond. When young people invite other young people, they will be more successful in getting results.

One of the basic philosophies of this volume is that the youth sponsor or teacher is not to be the main evangelist to unsaved kids. The effective youth sponsor must work through the Christian youth to effectively reach the unsaved.

8. *Advertising should not call attention to itself but to the thing advertised.* Be careful of a high-powered program that becomes more important than people. It is possible for publicity to be an end, rather than a means to an end. The pastor should not make such an elaborate announcement that the message is forgotten. Announcements in youth meetings should not be so spectacular that the *method* of announcement is remembered but the *message* forgotten.

9. *Advertising should glorify God.* Although last on the list, it is not least. Advertising for Christ calls forth several basic and vital criteria.

In Christian advertising those involved must seek to be led by the Holy Spirit and rely upon Him for direction. The Spirit guides men in various ways. Prayer is a powerful and effective way of knowing God's will and of being led of the Spirit. A good way to begin an advertising campaign is with a prayer meeting in which all in attendance display one desire: to let the Holy Spirit do the leading.

Study of the Word of God can also be a means of showing the way in which God desires that you go. All advertising should be kept within limits of the Word of God.

Circumstances play a large part in determining the leadership of the Spirit. If the group in charge is sure that a certain method is the Lord's will and yet all doors seem to be closed, they might humbly concede that it was their will and not God's will. God often uses circumstances, and more often than not, when things don't work out, it is because God has said "no" in an indirect way. Always seek to glorify God.

Principles for Attracting Youth

In the previous section, attention was given to inner attitudes; now outer principles will be considered. Apply these principles to posters, announcements, direct mailing, personal invitations, brochures, radio and press coverage.

1. *Make advertising appeal to youth.* This should be kept in mind in every detail. Take into consideration their interests and their desire to have things a little different from the general everyday elements and the fast pace at which they live and move. Youth think differently from adults; therefore, advertisement to youth will have to be different to appeal to them.

2. *Be brief.* Don't try to put the sixth chapter of Matthew on a postcard and expect kids to take it all in. They are usually in too much of a hurry to take that much time. Select a striking Scripture motto or theme and put it down in as few words as possible. Stick to the point. Why use twenty to say what can be written in four?

3. *Be different!* If there is anything that appeals to youth it is something out of the ordinary. Make the letter sideways, upside down, slanting or crooked; anything to make it eye-catching, yet readable. Be sure it's different, and youth will love it and read it too!

4. *Be personal.* In the Lord's work many methods can be utilized successfully if used prayerfully and thoughtfully. But one of the most important aspects of advertising is to make it personal. The youth must feel personally wanted at the youth meeting. "You" becomes a magic word in selling because it's personal.

5. *Advertise well in advance.* No matter how well you advertise, if it is not in sufficient amount of time, your advertising will be of no avail. Advertising should be done under the assumption that it will be early enough for all to build their schedules around the event. In this busy age many very interesting activities occupy a young person's mind

and interest. Youth will display a very positive response when your program meets their needs—early enough.

6. *Be neat and attractive.* In advertising for your youth programs, you can't always display professional work, but you can and should display neat and attractive work. Many times a neat and well-organized poster is indicative of a neat and well-rounded program.

7. *Be informative.* The information on the poster should contain all the information but should be done in as little space as possible. You should always make your program posters informative but brief.

8. *Be colorful and attractive.* Use color, as this will catch the youth's eye and they will want to look at it twice. Use illustrations wherever possible. Modern comedy and cartoons appeal to youth.

9. *Be creative.* A poor poster is one that follows the same pattern each time. Use new ideas. Watch magazines, TV, newspapers and other announcements for new ideas. Sit around with a committee and brainstorm, accepting each idea until all new thoughts are exhausted. Then try to organize a new approach that will be in keeping with accepted criteria for advertising.

Media for Advertising

The general principles of advertising must be correct, but they are not effective unless they are put to work. Selling teenagers on a program or idea needs more than one medium of approach. Just the use of postcards or the exclusive use of announcements is not enough. Use many "avenues" of selling to kids.

1. *Advertising through teenagers.* One of the best mediums for advertisement is the *personal testimony.* This can be spontaneous or organized, appointing the kids to give testimonies to certain individuals or at specified places. *Personal invitations* are effective. Divide the members of the youth group and assign to each youth a certain person. Then each person in the gang gets a personal invitation and feels included.

Skits at meetings or opening exercises of Sunday School are effective in making announcements. Let the teens use their imaginations in creating an original skit. This way you accomplish a double duty. The announcement is made, and the youth are trained in leadership creativity.

Phoning is effective. Even though all the kids heard the announcement at the meeting, phone them to check up. Polling the members by phone is an effective medium of advertising. If the youth commits himself early to attendance, then he is not faced with last-minute decisions of attendance. He will probably show up.

Another effective medium for advertisement is to distribute *handbills* at school or in a shopping center. This not only advertises the meeting to strangers but sells the kids who are doing the distribution of the handbills.

There are many other ways to advertise through using the teenager. This list is only suggestive. However, using the young people will be the most effective means of advertising a youth project.

2. *Advertising through church resources.* You should begin far in advance by informing the leaders of the church. This can be done through the *Church Planning Calendar.* Then there should be no conflicts in the schedule of the church. Use of the *church bulletin* is effective, for almost everyone reads this. Don't forget the *church newspaper* or the *pastor's newsletter.* Another medium for advertising in the church is the *bulletin board.* Use small typed announcements as well as colored posters. These posters, however, need not be limited to bulletin boards. Place them on windows, in stairwells, in the church bus, and on doors. Make sure they can be seen by the people.

Use *announcements* by other church leaders. The pastor can make an announcement in the morning service, or the Sunday School superintendent may call attention to youth meetings in the opening exercises of the Sunday School. Another voice pushing the youth activities is effective. If the church has a *radio broadcast* or *TV program,* don't forget to include a well-worded announcement in this medium of communication.

3. *Advertising through direct mail.* People always laugh about getting extra mail and placing it in "file 13" which is the trash can. In spite of the laughter 47 percent of all money spent in advertising in the United States is spent on direct mail advertising. People look forward to getting mail. There is curiosity in most people that makes them open and read every piece of mail. According to some advertisers, direct mail gives the best return for investment of money on publicity.

Use *post cards* announcing the meeting. Sometimes the second mailing is more effective than the first. Even though kids know about a meeting, send a second post card. If it's important to you, it will become important to them.

A *personally typed letter* is sure to be read. Amazing responses have been recorded from neat, informative, *handwritten* letters. Try it.

4. *Advertising through communication media.* There are several media of public communications that should be used. The *radio* and *TV* have programs of public service. They will be happy to include your announcement if it is brief, to the point, and includes all the vital information. Make sure the announcement is typed for easy reading.

The *newspapers* are important. Don't neglect this medium of communication. *Purchase advertising* for the church page. This is the spot your prime reading public will not miss. Informative articles can make news columns if they are well written, include all of the facts, and are delivered ahead of time. Make sure these news articles are delivered in person to the church news editor.

5. *Advertising through community resources.* There are many avenues of advertising available to your youth group in the community. *Posters* in store windows are effective. Organize the kids into a group to go and place posters in stores. Make sure to get permission from the store owner first. *Community bulletin boards* may be used. These are found in shopping centers, community clubs or local stores. *Bumper stickers* on cars are effective and inexpensive. Once again, make sure you get the permission of the car owner before you attach the bumper sticker.

CONCLUSION

These suggestions for advertising are not exhaustive but are included to start you thinking. If you have something worthy to advertise and a great desire to let people know, you can and will communicate. In advertising as in all phases of the Lord's work, we should seek daily the Lord's guidance in all we do, and remember in all things, to God be the glory.

22

CHURCH MUSIC AND THE TEENAGER

Frank, age 16, likes to sing rousing choruses. Shirley has taken piano lessons since the first grade and she likes classical music. The youth sponsor likes the solid theological hymns of a century ago. Some of the kids like folk music played with guitar.

What type of music should a church provide for its young people? You can't please them all. What they want may not be best. What music do young people *need?* What type of music fulfills the aims of the New Testament church? The young people of any church must be acquainted with the best type of music possible. It is your responsibility as youth sponsor to take the initiative to guide your young people into a well-balanced diet of Christian music.

The Scriptures show music and singing as prominent in the life of the early church. The apostle Paul, under divine inspiration, gives us the following admonition: "Let the word of Christ dwell in you richly in all wisdom; teaching and admonishing one another in psalms and hymns and spiritual songs, singing with grace in your hearts to the Lord" (Colossians 3:16). The importance of singing can be proven by the fact that it is closely linked with prayer. Paul says in I Corinthians 14:15, "I will pray with the spirit, and I will pray with the understanding also: I will sing with the spirit, and I will sing with the understanding also."

You, as youth sponsor, should be aware of the purpose of music, the kinds of music, and the use of music in the youth program.

323

THE PURPOSE OF CHURCH MUSIC

The ultimate purpose of all church music should be to glorify God. The primary emphasis of the book of Psalms, the songbook of the Old Testament Jew, was to glorify God. The question remains, "How can God be glorified?" The answer is simple: carry out His commandment (John 14:23, 15:14). The ultimate command for Christians and for the local church is the Great Commission (see chapter on Aims of Youth Work). Since evangelism is the first aim of a Christian, our music should carry out that aim. The Reverend Lindsay Terry states, "We sing to save." By that he means proper music is evangelistically slanted. We believe conversion is an experience that affects the whole man: intellect, emotion and will. Therefore, Christian music should communicate biblical content to the mind, should provoke an emotional experience and should get a commitment of the will. It is difficult for teens to identify with church anthems and be stirred to an experience affecting the total man. At the same time, the contemporary rock sound does not move teens to a wholesome positive response to Jesus Christ. The nature of our Christian conversion and daily walk with God should be expressed in church music. The words, melody, and rhythm of a song (hymn or chorus) are therefore very important when viewed in this light. The words, phrases, and sentences of all church music should be true to the Word of God. Do not sing that which clearly contradicts what God has revealed in His Word. Young people, and indeed all Christians, ought to sing only those hymns and choruses which are doctrinally sound as pertaining to major Bible themes (such as the Trinity, sin, salvation, and the Christian life).

The Purpose of Group or Congregational Singing

Your young people will engage in group or congregational singing more than in any other type. They participate in group singing during Sunday School and the morning and evening worship services, during their regular weekly meeting, and on other special occasions, like socials. The purpose of group music and music in general is basically fourfold:

1. *Singing is a musical outlet.* Every individual, and especially a teenager, has a desire to express himself through music. Not every young person can sing well enough to be a soloist or sing in a trio or quartet, so group singing is especially appealing. But everyone can participate.

2. *Singing is an emotional outlet.* When a person is happy, he will probably sing a song which depicts his mood. The same is true when a person is unhappy. The songs the young people sing in the church will express one of these moods—joy or sadness. The majority of the songs which young people sing display joy and gladness. The Word of God

has instructed the Christian to be joyful and has provided the necessary elements to make all Christians—young and old—happy.

3. *Singing is a social experience.* Singing produces an atmosphere of fellowship. Group participation levels barriers and gives to all those participating a sense of belonging, sharing in the true Christian experience. Singing can produce this experience among non-Christians, and infinitely more so among Christians who have fellowship with God the Father, God the Son, and other Christians through the Holy Spirit.

4. *Singing is a spiritual necessity.* Teenagers can worship God through singing. If the music during a service has produced worship, there will be (a) a realization of the presence of God; (b) a consciousness of one's dependence upon God; (c) a contemplation of the ideal or Christian way of living, and (d) a dedication or commitment of one's life to the Christian way of living.

The Purpose of Special Church Music

The purpose of special music is the same as that which has already been stated—that of bringing glory to God. Special music is designed to bring the unsaved to conversion or to encourage the believer. However, it must be admitted that special music in church has a certain amount of entertainment value. The quality of this entertainment depends, of course, on how well the teenagers perform. You should help the young people to realize that other people want to see and hear a special number done well, whether that special number be singing or instrumental. Teenagers not only glorify God by what they sing or play but also by how well they do it.

The Purpose of Melody and Rhythm

If the purpose is accepted as stated above, then the melody and rhythm of the music must be such as to make this possible. God has blessed most young people, to a greater or lesser degree, with a sense of rhythm and melody. These should be fitted to the words of the hymn or chorus. For example, you would expect a song like "In My Heart There Rings a Melody" to have a fast and lively rhythm with a melody to match. On the other hand, a song like "The Old Rugged Cross" is sung slowly and in a more reverent manner. But as youth sponsor you will find that teenagers prefer hymns and choruses that will allow them to "let loose." This is fine, provided the message of the song is not buried in the rhythm. Be careful that your singing does not become too "jazzy." Frequently ask yourself the following questions: Do the young people mean what they are singing? Is God being glorified in what the young people are singing? Are the young people applying the message of the songs to their lives?

KINDS OF CHURCH MUSIC

All church music—whether a hymn, chorus, group singing, or special numbers—falls into three broad divisions: testimony, worship, and devotional.

Testimony

The testimony song is the expression of the young person's personal experience, either of his salvation or of his Christian walk after the time of his conversion. This type of music is an essential element in any Christian's life. It gives the teenager an opportunity to put into words and song what Christ has done and is doing in his life. These are usually songs which express the feeling of joy as the young person walks in communion with his Saviour. Very often when checking how such a song was written, one will discover that the author was experiencing some outstanding blessing from God. Then he wrote his feelings in poetry and music. A testimonial song is therefore a product of the heart, brought about by a deep experience with Christ. Because such songs find their basis in an experience, they express varying moods or temperaments. A song such as "Come Thou Fount" is quite light and joyful. The writer realized God's grace and mercy toward him and this created within him a feeling of praise and dedication. A song like "It Is Well with My Soul" reveals the author's state of peace and safety amid the turmoil and conflicts of daily living.

A word of caution is in place here. It is highly possible that songs of testimony can become merely mechanical; that is, the young people can drift through a song and miss its message or not even be aware that the song has a message. Encourage teenagers to think of what they are singing. If a Christian young person is heartily singing a song like "Jesus Is a Wonderful Saviour" and yet is unhappy and miserable in his personal life, he is a hypocrite. The singing of testimony songs can be a time of dedication for the teenager who is not yielded. The unsaved young person may be led to a saving knowledge of Christ through such songs. You must show by your general attitude and outward expressions that this type of song means much to you and comes from your heart.

Worship

The worship song differs from the testimonial and devotional song in that it usually expresses one's adoration and praise to God, especially to God the Father. In this type of song, God is praised for what He is and does. Worship does not revolve so much around a person's individual experience as he walks from day to day with the Lord. Worship revolves around the person of God. One example of a worship song is "Holy, Holy, Holy."

Worship is giving back to God the "worth-ship" due unto His most holy name. Through the worship song the young person recognizes God as Creator, Ruler, Redeemer, and personal Lord.

There is an essential difference between the worship hymn and the testimonial song or chorus. The worship hymn usually has a "heavier" style of music or music which is on a higher plane. This is due mainly to the fact that the worship song expresses an exalted emotion which requires a more majestic form of music.

Some Christians hold the view that worship songs should be sung only on Sunday morning during what is generally called the worship service. However, this is an erroneous and narrow outlook. God desires all Christians—young and old alike—to honor Him and sing praises to His matchless name. The young people can do this at their weekly meetings and indeed ought to do so. Through the singing of such hymns, the teenager becomes aware of God as a personal Being, vitally concerned with Him as an individual. They can feel exceptionally close to God when pouring out their hearts in songs of praise and adoration. Most worship songs convey in a graphic way the inner feeling of the young person in a more picturesque way than he himself could express.

Devotional

Devotional music does not differ greatly from testimonial music. Instead of being based on experience, however, it is usually concerned with one's consecration to Christ. Naturally, this type of song, as is the case with testimonial and worship songs, is more meaningful to teenagers who have accepted Christ as their personal Saviour and who are experiencing genuine fellowship with their Father and with Christ through the Holy Spirit.

The actual melody and rhythm of the devotional song is usually quite reserved and meditative. This type of music creates a solemn and reverent atmosphere. It may noticeably affect the emotions of the young person as he is drawn close to Christ his Saviour and as he recognizes Him as Lord and Master of his life. This type of song may motivate the young person to be a better witness for Christ. Devotional hymns may also stimulate him to live a life more separated unto Christ.

THE PLACE OF ENTERTAINMENT IN CHURCH MUSIC

A certain amount of entertainment is involved in church music, especially in special numbers. But it should also be emphasized that no church music (and by this is meant songs and choruses based on the Word of God or the Christian life) should be presented solely for the purpose of entertainment. However, there are many songs which one would not classify as "Christian" which may be sung by teenagers. Folk songs and light ditties would fall into this classification. These songs are usually humorous and sometimes entertaining in the way they are sung and in the words employed. Entertainment songs are perfectly in order as long as they are clean and wholesome. They should be sung only at socials and usually not as part of the regular young people's service.

THE USE OF MUSIC IN THE YOUTH PROGRAM
Sunday School

Good music is an integral part of praise and worship. It will help build and maintain a successful Sunday School. But good music does not just happen. You must train your people to appreciate the best in music. Your long-range program will include the best hymns and gospel songs. Some Sunday School songs and choruses may be used, but these should not be the constant musical diet of the church. Remember, the aim of the Sunday School is to instruct in the Word. Expression is interwoven. The songs used should be of teaching value. There are some songs which shouldn't be used, not because they are wrong, but because they just are not worthwhile.

Young People's Meetings

The youth meeting contributes to the total youth program. It builds upon the effectiveness of the Sunday School and contributes to the evangelistic outreach. Most, if not all, of your young people enjoy good music. Therefore, let them have a part in planning the music to be used in their youth meetings. They should have variety in the music, but it should generally be of spiritual value.

Have a talent file of the members in the group. In this way, you have information close at hand concerning what each teenager is capable of doing in the line of music, and how willing he is to use his talents. Such information can easily be gathered by having all the teenagers fill in a mimeographed survey sheet.

In the youth programs always correlate your music with the theme of the program and the Scripture to be used. Choruses can be used more in the regular youth meetings than in congregational gatherings, for in the former the group is made up primarily of young people who like enthusiastic, joyful singing.

When using musicians, don't have a group that muddles through or has to start over. They should spend time practicing. (Warn them a couple of weeks in advance.) Don't feature the same kind of music every time. Try a vocal solo and a brass quartet once, a small choir and an instrumental duet the next time, a girls' chorus or a string trio and a male quartet, depending on the musical abilities of the group.

Try using a talent contest sometime or a Hymn Hit Parade. For the latter, take a survey of the ten favorite gospel songs, hymns, or choruses. Then use records, solos or instrumentals to present them. Have many young people take part. At the youth activities there is opportunity to use fun songs—those sung just for entertainment, if the activities are held outside the church. Examples of such songs would be spirituals, folk songs and rounds.

Congregational

Young people participate in group singing as in the form of congregational songs. There is an attitude of release and a feeling of unity in group singing. Such an activity helps to create receptivity of heart in preparation for the spoken word. Singing should be regarded as a phase of Christian stewardship. Of course the usual excuse is that the individual is not musical and cannot sing. But all should be reminded of a significant fact concerning human voices—that a group of people, not one of whom would be qualified to sing a solo, can join their voices and produce quite beautiful music.

Encourage your young people to pay attention to what they are singing and to relate the truths to their own lives. Cause your young people to realize that while participating in group singing they are singing individual messages and are singing as individuals. Each person should be just as truthful in the words he sings as in those which he speaks.

Choir

Teenager choirs or church choirs in which teenagers may sing offer excellent opportunities for securing the interest, participation, and loyalty of the youth in the church. Such choirs can add much variety and appeal to the life and outreach of the church.

The purpose of using youth in your church choir or teenage choir is not just to display their talent or to entertain the listeners; you are striving to win unsaved young people to Christ and to help believers mature as Christians. In organizing the choir, you should give a sample voice test, even though you might plan to use the whole group. Trying out for a choir makes the teen realize the importance of choir. The director learns who can read music, for what part the teen is suited, and which voices will need help. The male voice is stronger and therefore not as many are needed, so don't despair if you lack male members.

Set forth the purpose of the choir. In this respect impress upon the members the fact that singing in the choir is a service unto the Lord. The young person should put forth his best and do it for Christ, and not for the glory of other people. You should give the choir an idea of the music which will be used.

Plan your practice carefully. Pick out music which suits the age level of the choir. Mark out in advance approximately how much time you plan to spend on each song. Start on time. Right from the outset demand promptness and full attention. Have the music out on the chairs. The type of music they find on their chairs the first night will make a difference. If they feel that choir practice will be an easy time, they'll fool around. They need a challenge to give their best attention. Elect or appoint a secretary to take attendance. This will save you valuable time. Start the practice with Scripture concerning music and prayer. Spend one hour in strict rehearsal. Master a song, piece by piece, not the whole thing at once. If you try mastering the whole song it will take much longer and the members will soon get tired of the song. Insist on pitch, timing, and attention. Stress the importance of a choir, setting atmosphere for the church service. Insist that there be no talking or chewing of gum.

The qualifications of the music director are as follows: (1) He must have a working knowledge of music; (2) he must be liked by the young people; and (3) he must demonstrate spiritual maturity.

Camp Work

Camp is a time of education and evangelism. It is a time for definite decisions. You must present Christ and His claims even in your music program. The songs should also express true Christian living—the joy and reality of living for Christ. Here, songs of testimony can be very useful.

It is good to teach your young people new songs at camp. Often expressing a truth in different words and music means more to the young person than singing the trite, worn songs and choruses. Songs for fun and games involving music are useful tools in breaking down barriers among campers. You can use a choir made up of campers at the evening services. The campers enjoy presenting special numbers, though they may be too shy to volunteer for such programs.

The natural beauty of campsites is advantageous to the camp program. The beauty of creation can easily be the basis of worship and drawing close to God. You can have singing by a lake or around a camp-fire, using songs which are favorites of the campers.

Song Leading

Song leading is a spiritual ministry. The song service should prepare the hearts of the people for the service in general and for the ministry of the Word of God in particular. As a song leader, you must get the participation of the people. Capture their attention. Be enthusiastic; enthusiasm is contagious. As a song leader you should have a sense of authority and of assurance. Have a thorough mastery of the song. Be definite as to directing the opening notes. You have the responsibility of teaching the congregation new songs. In choosing the songs, consider the words: are they true to the Word, and are they worthwhile to sing? Keep the beat of the song simple. Do not direct a congregation as if they were a choir. Congregational singing is to be congregation-centered and never director-centered. Do not engage in lengthy exhortations or the telling of favorite stories. Never direct a song at such a speed that it is beyond the average person. The other extreme of going too slow must also be avoided.

As a song leader, you must use the gestures which are understandable to both the audience and the accompanist; you must be consistent in your gesture patterns. You should be in good command of both the up-and-down beat and the looping beat. The former is used especially for dignified singing and the latter is ideal for informal singing.

The pattern of beating time must be simple and should not be complicated by extra arm and hand motions. The hand and the forearm are to move together, though the wrist should be flexible. Downward motions should end at the waist. Motions coming inward and upward should bring your hand within your shoulder line.

The song leader's actions produce psychological effects upon the audience. For example, if your outward motions are free and sweeping, relaxation is suggested and the audience gives forth volume. You may at times want to use both hands to direct. This is permitted, but you should usually not let your hands cross. In songleading, use clear-cut angles to end and to begin beats. Ragged beating produces similar singing. The downward beats are always the accented beats of the song.

To bring the song to a close, bring the hand in smartly, below the chest, while forming a clenched fist. You do not always have to beat out the time of a song. You may want to change the tempo, convey the correct mood of the song, change the volume, or make the rhythm more distinct. The basic techniques of song leading are really quite simple. You, as a song leader, have the responsibility to teach the technique to the young people in your church. It is an art which holds a unique spirit of enjoyment, especially for music lovers. Train your young people now to be leaders. Although such training is not limited to fellows, the majority of song leaders are fellows.

Special Singing

Use your teenagers to participate in special singing. It will give them enjoyment and at the same time give them confidence to appear before the public. The total message of the song is the important thing in special music. "Unless a message of truth and significance gets to the people, the time and effort involved are wasted. It is for this reason that, if a choice is possible or necessary, it is better to have a relatively rough performance that brings a response from the hearts and minds of the people than a polished, technically excellent performance that leaves the hearers cold and indifferent."*

Soloists have a large field of music to choose from. It is refreshing to hear them sing a new song from time to time. In trios and quartets there are also many excellent opportunities. Where the voices are not strong enough to sing solos, these smaller groups are excellent.

Instrumental Music

Teenagers are often competent in the use of some instrument. You may have enough young people playing instruments so that an orchestra can be formed which could play for fifteen minutes before the evening service. Participation in such a group is a means of helping the young person to see that his life can be useful in practical Christian service.

It is very likely that you have teenagers who are not capable of singing well, but they do play instruments. Use them in instrumental ensembles or as solos. Your social get-togethers are excellent times for using instrumental selections.

The pianist or organist of your church has an important role to play. She may be a teenager but she must be able to play the music as written and she should refrain from "running all over the keyboard." The choir director and pianist must work in smooth cooperation with each other.

CONCLUSION

How can you as a youth sponsor use the young people in your church's program of music? The avenues of opportunity are many—in the Sunday School, in the young people's meetings, in congregational singing, in the choir, camp work, song leading, special singing, and

---

* Benner, High C. *Singing Disciples—Toward Better Church Music.* Kansas City, Missouri: Lillenas Publishing Company, 1959, p. 43.

instrumental music. Many a young person is talented in the area of music and such talents can and ought to be used for the glory of God. Aim to win your young people to Christ and exhort them to present their whole time, talents, and treasures to Him. Use them in the church in the area of music. Give them the responsibility and the satisfaction of serving their Lord in this way.

23

GUIDING PRINCIPLES FOR THE YOUTH CAMP

Youth camps, conferences, retreats and seminars are being greatly used by the church today. In the past the church made a limited use of the out-of-doors experience for its young people, but now more than ever before the church is moving into the outdoors to reach, win and train young people and give them a place to serve. The United States is experiencing a renaissance of outdoor living, and with it the church is experiencing a camp revival. Camping is no longer merely taking the young people out to the state park for Bible classes. Camping has become diversified, with many goals and schedules of activities. Camping in its own right has become an integral and important part of the growth and maturity of the young people within the church.

TYPES OF CAMPING
Retreat

The retreat concept of camping is growing in effectiveness. Young people are taken from the church to a camping site, usually within a quarter- or half-day drive away from the city. The leadership is usually indigenous to the church and sometimes the young people may return that night to their homes. Other times the retreat takes the form of a weekend jaunt. Retreats are a semi-living situation and not intended to be a school. The young people are transported by bus or cars, and the time of the retreat is arranged to best suit the climate and availability of facilities. The activities of the retreat usually involve sports, study exhortation and/or preaching, research groups, and/or handcraft.

Youth Conferences

The conference-assembly has been used by denominations and other interdenominational agencies to bring young people together from many places. The number of participants may be as few as 50 or as many as 1500. These groups are coeducational and usually provide inspirational speakers. Youth leaders are increasingly seeing the emphasis on education. Therefore, many of the conference-type ministries are including smaller group studies and educational ministries. The conference-type ministry for young people may or may not include an overnight lodging. The sports program usually is not as elaborate as at the retreat but the recreation may be vigorous with more indoor games played. The conference ministry may or may not be situated out of doors. Some conferences are held in churches which may be located in a city or suburban situation. Other conferences are held at specially designed conference grounds, while some are held at resort hotels or motels.

Summer Camps

Camping is usually thought of as the church-sponsored experience for youth in the summertime. Usually these camps last for one or two weeks with a daily schedule. The schedule is regimented according to the needs of the group. Some of these experiences are structured to lead the camper through learning, sharing, experiencing, and participating. Some camps are given over to indoctrination, whereas others are given over to experiences and participation. The leadership of the camp has usually been indigenous to the local church or denomination. Now camps attempt to secure personnel for the entire summer. Usually additional experienced teachers and speakers are added to establish and deepen the life of the young person. The unique feature of the camp is that it is a living situation and is not intended to be a school.

THE AIMS OF CHRISTIAN CAMPING

Camping in the secular world is built around this practical aim: Endeavor to give the camper a rounded personality through social interaction, creativity, and education in camp craft and leadership skills. Christian camps have that aim also, but their leaders believe it should be related to the campers' personal experience with Jesus Christ.

General Aim

The general aim of Christian camping is the same as that of Christian education. It is to bring a person to know Christ, then to grow to full maturity in Jesus Christ. The Christian camp, by exposing campers to the Word of God, seeks that the man of God may be perfect, or mature (II Timothy 3:17). In the outworking of the aims there are two major tasks involved:

1. To win individuals to a personal acceptance of Jesus Christ.

2. To guide them in those experiences and habits which will develop maturity in Christ.

Specific Aims

The general aim of camping meets its fulfillment in the specific aims of the camp program. Some of these aims are as follows:

1. To provide opportunity to deal with campers as individuals, and to counsel them personally in the areas of their spiritual need.

2. To encourage definite spiritual decisions at the level of the camper's readiness. This requires a thorough knowledge of the campers and a patient dependency on the Holy Spirit. A premature decision may not be a healthy decision.

3. To help establish good habits of Christian living, such as prayer, Bible reading and study, personal devotions, and witnessing.

4. To provide practical experience in leadership, service, witnessing and application of spiritual truths to daily living.

In addition to these specific aims the Christian camp should also have aims which relate to the total development of the camper. These aims would correspond to the aims of most secular camps.

1. The camp should provide for the establishment of sound health habits such as cleanliness, adequate rest, proper diet, wholesome exercise, and good attitudes toward the body as God's temple (I Corinthians 6:19, 20).

2. The camper should learn the profitable and wise use of leisure time, independent of amusements such as television (Ephesians 5:15, 16).

3. The camper should have opportunities for use of outdoor skills to develop his character and to train him for possible missionary work.

4. The camper should develop the ability to get along with others.

5. Each camper should learn to take a share of responsibility.

These goals must seek to relate the ministry of the camp to the total educational program of the church and home. The camp program and counselor must be used in an effective way in order to bring the camper into a vital relationship with Jesus Christ as Saviour and Lord of his life.

PHILOSOPHY OF CAMPING

The aims of Christian camping are similar to those of the church, but the philosophies pertaining to the accomplishment of these aims are varied. In dealing with the philosophy of Christian camping we will look at the two basic philosophies: centralized and decentralized camping. Most camp programs fall under one of these.

Centralized

The centralized camping philosophy emphasizes the mass meeting. This is also called the conference-type camp and has grown out of the traditional Bible conference. The key to this program is a strong preaching ministry. This is followed up by a counseling staff which uses the message of the speaker as a jumping-off point for making person-to-person contact with the members of their group. This type of camp is characterized by Bible study classes, somewhat formal in nature, and a recreational program of athletic activities. This approach serves well for an adult or family camp as it gives opportunity for all. The larger camps are organized on this basis and have proved quite successful in many areas. The disadvantage of this program is that there are unplanned gaps which tend to counteract the influence of the preaching program. It also has a tendency to create an atmosphere which becomes a crutch in the life of the camper and does not prepare the camper for life as it is in reality.

Decentralized

The decentralized camping philosophy emphasizes the needs, aims and desires of the individual. The key words are *individual differences,* where the camper learns as he interacts with nature and with his counselor. Emphasis is on freedom, away from the regimental program. Those who advocate decentralized camping might say, "Why bring kids to the outdoors, then coop them up in a building to listen to a speech?" This type has also been called the outdoor adventuring camp. The emphasis here is on utilization of the great outdoors and the development of camping skills such as nature lore and woodcraft.

The key to the effectiveness of an outdoor adventure camp is the counselor. The program is designed to keep camper and counselor together day and night. Every possible opportunity is utilized to bring the counselor's Christian testimony and personality to bear on the camper. The counselor becomes the teacher, companion, evangelist and guide.

CAMPSITES

When planning the camp program the importance of the setting and site must be realized. The setting of the camp determines the program. It also affects the camper greatly. Selection and development are of great importance in attaining the objectives of Christian camping. In no other agency of Christian education does the environment itself play as large a role in shaping the total program.

The natural setting of the camp is also important because if the camp does not have an appropriate setting, then exposure of the campers to the beauty of God's handiwork will be neglected and so will the camper's appreciation for God's creation.

It is also important to locate the camp away from the large centers of population. This makes for a more relaxed type of camp. It is important to turn thoughts away from rush and hurry to a time of relaxed meditation. This is best fostered by a proper campsite.

There are several specific things to look for in an ideal campsite:

1. A rustic spot near a lake or river
2. A place conducive to hikes and outdoor activities
3. A place for outdoor services near the lake
4. A place accessible to fuel, milk, fresh fruits and vegetables, water and other supplies
5. A central location for all churches to send campers to camp

In developing a campsite, it is a good idea to use the campers. This gives them a sense of value for the property.

Another aspect in relation to the campsite which must be considered is whether to rent or to buy the site.

1. *The advantages of renting:* The upkeep is less expensive, and it is easier to move the location for a growing camp.

2. *The advantages of buying:* Camp improvements can be made, future plans can be made with the interest of the groups in mind, and the camp can become the focal point of group activity.

In most cases, ownership of the campsite is preferable; however, this is not a hard-and-fast rule. Circumstances will guide the final decisions.

THE CAMP PROGRAM

The camp program includes the spiritual, secular and physical factors, all of which are to be effectively coordinated. The aim of the camp program is to demonstrate spiritual values through the total camp program. The spiritual instruction time and opportunities to work out the Christian principles are all-important. The successful Christian camp has a topnotch program with a wide variety of activities based on campers' needs and interests.

Structure of the Program

There are three choices of camp program structure:

1. Lay out a structured outline for every hour of the day so that no free time is allowed. Often this type of camp structure is seen in camps where there is insufficient staff, or a program that is so full of activities that a structured program is necessary to accomplish all that is planned.

2. The program may be completely free, where the campers choose their activities daily, according to their interests. Here the camper must choose wisely.

3. In the third type, a camp is set up to include aspects from both the above programs. The camp has some elements of regimentation and some of freedom. This basis makes provisions for individual campers' needs, interests, and abilities.

Camper Participation

The more the camper becomes involved in helping plan and carry out camp activities, the more effectively he will absorb the values of camping. The campers must participate under guidance at first before they are motivated to work on their own. They should also be allowed responsibilities. But this does not mean handing the camp over to the campers to run.

Content of the Camp Program

Camp life in its natural setting is creative, simple, informal, and relaxed. In comparison with a one-hour Sunday School period, the camp setting presents a good means of educating the camper. The program content should be indigenous to the site. We must use natural environment as much as possible. The program should be simple so that important values can be emphasized. It should be flexible, thus allowing for individual abilities. The whole program should be geared to meeting the needs of the individual and graded according to the ability and interests of the varying ages.

Spiritual Life in Camp

The spiritual life should permeate the entire program. Camp is in an ideal position to affect the camper's whole life and personality. Spiritual emphasis should never be segregated from the rest of camp life. This setting is an ideal place to encourage youth to have a quiet time—where

the atmosphere is conducive to worship and devotion. Bible memorization, devotional time, worship time should all be a part of the spiritual
life of the camper. The influence of these should radiate throughout
every camp activity.

1. *Use of evangelistic methods.* Evangelism and nurture are the
main purposes of Christian living. Often the concentrated spiritual emphasis of camp creates a readiness for decisions. The decisions made
should be on an individual basis, usually dealt with by the counselor.

An invitation and opportunity provided to talk to the counselor may
help sift out campers who are in earnest about spiritual matters. Always
beware of quick decisions, and ascertain that they fully understand what
is happening.

The camper looks for an example in the counselor in Christian
living. We all teach by what we are.

The camper must be encouraged to *do* as well as to *hear.* He should
be given opportunity to express his desire to serve the Lord.

2. *Use of the Bible.* The camper should be encouraged to look into
God's Word on his own. Bible studies should encourage camper involvement.

3. *Relation to the local church.* Camp should be keyed to produce
in young people a spiritual life and leadership which can be used in the
local church. There should be a communication between camp personnel
and the local church.

4. *Music.* The Bible exhorts the believer to sing and make melody
in his heart to the Lord. In camp work it is very important to have trained
personnel in the field of music; singing will add greatly to the benefit and
blessing of camp experiences. Next to preaching, music affects the camp
more than anything else.

Planning a good song service which is Spirit-led demands prayer
and preparation. Besides a qualified music leader, the pianist should be
qualified for her position. The whole camp theme should include the
hymns and choruses to be sung.

Music provides a means of expression. Through song we give
testimony of what God has done for us. Often the young camper places
his whole feeling into the worship and testimony of the songs he sings.

As campers come from various backgrounds, music is a means of
unifying the camp, breaking down barriers and building up group spirit.

One principle to follow is that fun songs should be kept separate
from spiritual songs, for fear of handling the things of God carelessly.
Fun songs should be kept for recreation.

RECREATION

Aims

Recreation is both a large and important part of the total camp program. The aim of recreation should have more than the good time of the camper in view. A good recreational program will include these features:

1. Help round out personalities and show the need of a Christ-centered social life.

2. Develop wholesome friendships in group activities and break down cliques.

3. Provide opportunities for developing leadership and self-confidence

4. Provide wholesome emotional outlets for pent-up energy, and release tension

5. Be a direct and indirect means of winning souls

Selection

Recreational activities should be selected within the abilities of the group and the ability of the leader. They should be well-adapted to the degree of motor skill, and emotional and social maturity of the camper. They should be within the interests of the age group. They should show a certain amount of progress from simple to more difficult feats (teens always respond to a challenge). Allow the teens a part in selection and planning.

Participation

Participation in the recreational program is an important aspect of the recreation and should receive careful attention from the leaders. Be sure that each camper has an opportunity to participate in activities that require leadership. Youth lose interest if the same campers are used as leaders all the time. Do not continue the activity after interest has waned.

CAMP PERSONNEL

The success of the camp depends to a great extent on the counselors and other personnel. They are the instruments for bringing the campers to a saving knowledge of Jesus Christ. It is, therefore, important that the staff be united in goals and methods. The entire staff should be a unit.

Qualities which need to be evidenced in lives of those chosen to be camping personnel are: a vital experience with the Lord, love of youth, patience, maturity in age as well as spirituality, skill in some capacity, and a knowledge of counseling techniques.

You may ask, "Where can we find staff with these qualities?" Some sources would be Bible schools, Christian colleges, secular colleges, schoolteachers, and former campers. There should be a pre-camp session for training workers. This will help to make them more effeective in the camp program. The following personnel are necessary in managing a camp program:

1. *Camp director.* Without this person you would likely have a camp without any organization. The camp director is responsible to the organization operating the camp. He coordinates the year-round program, hires salaried personnel, and directs their activity. He looks after business management and grounds maintenance. This person is the key person to the whole camp program and therefore needs good leadership qualities.

2. *Program director.* This person is responsible to the camp director and coordinates the activities of a given week. He looks after details not assigned to the camp director. When preparing the program it is important to keep in mind the likes and dislikes of the age groups. Staff members are responsible to the program director.

3. *Camp pastor.* He is the speaker at chapel sessions and is responsible for arranging the devotional activities for the campers. He considers the spiritual needs of staff and campers. He also can be effective in assisting with counseling.

4. *Chief counselor.* There should be one person who is responsible for the other counselors. Discipline problems should be channeled through him. He should be responsible for the daily staff meetings to discover and strengthen the camp program.

5. *Counselors.* The number of counselors needed will depend on the number of campers. There should be one counselor for every eight campers. The teaching task of the counselor is a 24-hour-day job. His unconscious influence is more potent than his planned teaching session. Can he open God's Word skillfully and help campers develop spiritual wholesome attitudes toward the practical duties of everyday life such as cabin-clean-up, taking turns on riflery range, or sharing equipment? Campers are quick to see the Lord in a counselor and to desire Him because of the life of the leader. Therefore, every act of the counselor is important. The counselor is responsible to the chief counselor. He looks after the health, safety and spiritual welfare of his cabin group, and helps his campers to gain the maximum benefit from the program. The counselor leads in cabin devotions and remains alert to opportunities for personal guidance.

6. *Athletic director.* The recreation program is under this person's supervision. He must be one who enjoys recreational sports and is a good

athlete himself. He will need those to help him who are specialists in water activities, field sports, etc. It will be his responsibility to insure safety in all athletic activity.

7. *Craft director.* This must be a person interested in handcraft activities and capable of teaching the campers.

8. *Cooks.* They play an important part in the camping activity as far as the campers are concerned. There should be a chief cook to draw up the menus and supervise the preparation of the meals. In choosing the cooking staff the director must keep in mind experience and cleanliness.

9. *Maintenance manager.* His responsibility is the upkeep of the grounds and buildings. Any items which need repair should be directed to the attention of this person. He must maintain the camping site in such a way that it is as free of hazardous conditions as possible.

10. *Camp nurse.* This person is necessary at every camp. She should be equipped with adequate supplies for first aid. Any illness or injury, no matter how slight, should be reported to her.

AGE GROUPINGS

An important factor in a successful camping program is the grouping of the age levels. In order to have the most effective program, certain age levels should attend camp at different times. Titles for these groupings may vary, but the age brackets usually are basic in an ideal camping situation. By ideal situation it should be understood that there are adequate counselors, workers, and facilities. Let us consider each group individually.

1. *Junior high camp.* Young people in the 12-14 age group are fond of activity and enjoy a full schedule. However, since they are above children's age they can absorb more from classes and open sessions. They are at the age where it is common for each to have his idol or hero, and here again the camp counselors and helpers play an important part. Any inconsistency in their lives will be noted by these young people and the effectiveness of their leadership will be weakened. They should "belong" and be one of the group, thus making group activities more effective.

2. *Young people's camp.* Young people in this age group, 15-18 years, are in senior high. These fellows and girls enjoy a good time but also are interested in the serious side of life. They are looking for answers to their problems concerning their vocation and problems connected with everyday life. They sense quickly whether or not there is a genuine interest and concern for them. Counselors once again may have an effective ministry here.

3. *College and career camp.* These young people have been away from home and are now seeking "reasons why" and are realizing that, as individuals, they must stand firm spiritually.

CAMP RULES AND DISCIPLINE

Camps are fun, even though they do have rules. Camp life wouldn't be the same without rules, as they do have their place. If properly enforced they will provide a better all-round camp for everyone.

Camp life imposes restrictions on campers that are essential if the goals of Christian camping are to be realized. There has to be some standard of conduct, dress, and conversation which may be quite different from those the camper sees in his everyday life, but on the other hand are essential to a good camp. We find that certain aspects of the daily schedule appeal more to some campers than to others. .

Rules are necessary and often many problems can be avoided if the campers know beforehand what is expected. Reasonable regulations clearly understood eliminate many discipline problems that normally arise early in the week, and in spite of all the grumbling about rules, campers do appreciate the need for orderly procedure.

On the first day of camp the camp director should discuss the rules with the entire camp, followed with cabin discussions directed by the counselor. This will give them a chance to clarify anything that may not be clearly understood and also gives opportunity for questions. The schedule should be posted where all can see it and each procedure should be carefully explained.

The rules for each camp are different, depending upon the purpose and aims of the camp, although some areas are stressed by all camps. Magazines, comic books, and books of questionable taste have no place at a Christian camp. To retain a wholesome atmosphere many camps do not permit the use of radios. Campers should be reminded that off-color stories and comments will not be tolerated. Those who are troubled with smoking must be asked to refrain. Car keys should be turned in to the camp director until camp is over. Standards in clothing for both boys and girls should be clearly defined. An objective straightforward approach to problem areas will be well received by the campers. A list of don'ts or authoritarian attitudes will accomplish little.

The counselor must set the pace for the campers. The campers should know that he expects their cooperation and should understand that they are under authority. Point out the discipline policy so that they understand it and know that the maximum penalty for infraction is expulsion from camp. If the counselor comes out on top after the first night, he is pretty well set for the rest of the week. If he doesn't assert his authority the first night, he may just as well give up. Rules and authority, if properly enforced, will be adhered to willingly by all and will insure an effective camp.

Cabin Life

Cabin life is often the best part of camp. This is often the biggest adjustment the camper must make in learning to get along and share with others. The counselor should encourage campers to draw up their own rules to meet their various needs. The campers should respect the personal property of one another. They should be responsible for keeping their beds and immediate area clean. Clothing should be neatly packed and neatly hung, and all wet towels and swimsuits belong outside. Everyone must cooperate in keeping the cabin tidy and in observing the schedule. Friendly relationships should develop between cabin mates.

Safety Regulations

The safety regulations at camp must conform to those laid down by the state in which the camp is held. Nothing should be considered that falls short of these standards. Everything possible must be done to insure the safety of campers and the proficiency of the camp.

PROBLEMS

To avoid problems in maintaining schedules everyone should report promptly at the designated hour for cabin activity.

Often camp gossip can present a problem. Never discuss another staff member with a camper except to speak well of him. Silence or quick change of subject will discourage another staff member who begins to discuss fellow staff or camp policy in an improper manner.

Sometimes there may be homesickness even among teens. From the outset determine that sending a camper home will be the last resort. Homesickness can be contagious, so it is wise to remember that affection, understanding and capturing interests help overcome homesickness.

The many problems that arise in a camp and their solutions cannot all be mentioned in this chapter. Stable, dedicated staff, good organization, understanding of teenagers, and Christian love will eliminate most difficulties. Remember that the camp program is also God's program and He will undertake for your success at camp if you put God first and follow His commandments.

24

RECREATION FOR YOUNG PEOPLE

The church ministers to every area of the young person—spiritual, social, emotional, mental and physical. This includes the recreational life of teenagers. We must provide recreation for all of our young people at every stage of their development as an integral part of our program. Of course, recreation should be in keeping with the aims of the church and provide variety and balance.

However, there are those who would oppose a recreational program. They would say the aim of the church is to provide spiritual food. "Recreation is beyond the aims of the New Testament."

The following section, "Why the Church Should Provide Recreation for Teenagers," answers this criticism. It also gives a sound basis for adding recreation to your program. The activity program does not "keep 'em busy" but has a positive ministry to the teenager.

Why the Church Should Provide Recreation for Teenagers

1. *Because recreation satisfies a normal need in teenagers.* Teenagers need recreation. Their bodies demand that they have movement, activity, and life. Their social nature demands fellowship and companionship. Their spiritual nature demands involvement and interaction.

We as Christian leaders have no right to prohibit unless we can provide. Many youth leaders tell young people what they cannot do but never provide for their recreation. It should be said here that entertainment is not recreation. Many young people are entertained and become observers, but true recreation includes participation. Some teenagers feel that "Christianity robs life of all of its pleasures." Christ promised a new quality of life: "I am come that they might have life and, that they might have it more abundantly" (John 10:10). "In thy presence is fulness of joy; at thy right hand there are pleasures for evermore" (Psalm 16:11). Recreation helps provide an abundant victorious life for the Christian teenager.

2. *Because recreation builds values in the teenager.* Values are learned as young people put into practice rules and requirements, social interaction, and reactions of judgment and responsibility. A good recreation program can fulfill this in the life of the young person. A teenager who can play by the rules of the game, can live by the rules of life. If you as a youth leader want to learn whether your teenage boys have spiritual victory, play basketball or touch football with them.

The teenager who can control his temper when the umpire makes a close call against him in baseball can control his spiritual life when he is tempted and tried.

Never lose your poise in leading young people in recreation. If you exhibit poor sportsmanship, if you tolerate shoddy or mediocre performances, if you use destructive criticism, you will destroy all you are trying to build up. Your example sets the pattern for those you direct. This is why you as a leader have a very important part in the character education of the young people you lead. There should be systematic procedure regarding the use of tools and equipment in play as well as cleanup. Sharing develops good habits in the teenager.

Through well-directed games and activities teenagers learn the satisfaction that comes from good social behavior. Their demand for belonging is satisfied. They overcome self-consciousness and they learn how to easily meet people and enjoy their company. Such learning is basic to character growth.

Check periodically your total program of education, including recreation. Note the results that you are having in developing Christian character. If you are not making satisfactory progress, examine your program to see where the fault lies.

3. *Because recreation builds strong personalities.* Personality is the sum total of all of our personal attributes—mental, emotional, social, spiritual, and psychological. These are expressed from the inward man. Personality may be stated as the total impression or effect which we make upon others—or simply "you." As the youth sponsor you will want to build and develop personality. This is a matter of building up habits. We are the sum total of all of our decisions. What we do becomes a part

of us. Sloppy habits reveal a sloppy character. A good character and a fine personality are best insured by establishing good habits. Recreation does much to insure character in the teenager with whom we work.

Loyalty and cooperation can be developed through team games and through united effort in a recreational sport. The teenager can grow and develop a strong personality by participating wholeheartedly in a game or in activity planning.

Competition has its place in recreation. Many of the best games are competitive. There are important lessons to be learned from competition—how to lose without bitterness, how to win without gloating, how to bring about improvement, how mistakes bring penalties, and that "he who hesitates is lost."

At the same time competition has another advantage to the teenager. He learns unselfishness when the main motivation is a group-wide endeavor.

As a recreational leader you must display good habits and strong personality to build this into the teenagers. You must meet engagements promptly, always be courteous, kind, accommodating, methodical, and systematic. You must always start everything on time, stay with the engagement to the finish, and be scrupulously fair and honest. Be wholehearted.

Personality can be cultivated and developed. He who will set himself determinedly and intellectually to the task of self-improvement is bound to make progress.

4. *Because recreation relieves the pressures of life for the teenager.* The true nature of recreation is to *re-create*. Recreation is to re-create in our bodies new values and life. It has been said that the church must re-create or the teenagers will "wreck-create." Recreation is a safety valve in which the pressures of life are relieved.

Some have said that it is better to *burn out* for God. This person indicates that the Christian should have no release from tension but should be working at all times. This is an approach of ignorance. It is better to work out our life for God. There is a time when the Christian young person should have recreation. Then he can serve God better at another time. "For bodily exercise profiteth little" (I Timothy 4:8).

There are many social and personal tensions that recreation relieves. Some of these are: unconscious cravings, hidden motivations, frustrations, insecurity, self-depreciation, lack of self-assertion, inadequate creative expression, or excessive pressure of work. Some of these have a direct bearing on spiritual growth. Recreation will compensate for an unbalanced life. The redirection and sublimation of drives that may hinder normal or healthy character growth is a function that recreation can perform when properly chosen and directed.

5. *Because recreation trains teenagers in creativity.* Adults who are most active are those who were most active as youth. Adults who serve best in the church are those who served best as teenagers. Teenagers today are caught in the drive of modern high-pressure living and they suffer from a poverty of creativity. They do not know what is required in making a satisfactory life. Much of their free time becomes entertainment rather than creativity. Entertainment alone cannot satisfy and bring out the best from the youth. Young people learn creativity as they express themselves. Cheapness is the high price that is paid for entertainment.

Teenagers often are confused. They need help. They do not only need preaching sessions or to become spectators. They need opportunities to experience, to practice, to do, to learn, to follow, to obey, and to act. Only in this manner will they be able to tell what is good. The church that prepares teenagers for intelligent living is the church that makes good use of leisure time.

6. *Because recreation provides a sense of "belonging" for the teenager.* Good recreation is a fortification of Christian fellowship. One of the criteria for spiritual growth is spiritual fellowship. There is nothing that unites and gives security to the Christian teenager more than social recreation. The young person needs a sense of "I belong." This is one of the strongest drives in the teenager. If the teen feels a part of your group, he will serve the Lord better. If he feels that the young people of your group are rejecting him or giving him the "cold shoulder," he will not have the opportunity to grow in Christ.

7. *Because recreation gives teenagers an opportunity to meet the opposite sex.* The first criticism we face is "The church is not a matchmaking factory." This is very true; however, you must recognize that there is no better place for teenagers to find their mates than in the church.

It has been suggested that there isn't too much love in the world, but there is too much love-making. The sex drive is strong, and if steadily pushed it generates more emotion and tension than can be safely handled. Through recreation, sex drives can be sublimated and redirected into socially acceptable expression. The youth who is bashful can meet, be on the same team, and share with the opposite sex. Those who are overly motivated can be sublimated and held in check. When Christian boys and girls play games together, have cooperation, competition, laugh and joke together, this can be a very wholesome satisfaction of the sex drive.

Many Christian young people are at a loss to know what to do on a date. They should be encouraged to date at church gatherings. At some of the church gatherings games for twosomes can be played. Those who are dating can be paired off, and other young people who are not dating can be put together. The church has a responsibility for training young people in a wide variety of recreational interests so that they will not become victims of cheap behavior patterns. Romance and recreation are twins.

8. *Because recreation attracts and holds young people.* Many churches are opposed to a progressive recreational program. Their main opposition is that recreation is used only to attract young people, and they feel that this type of attraction is wrong. If we have recreation only to attract young people, it is a very shallow goal. However, strong positive reasons have been stated in this section as to why recreation should be in the church program.

The church which has a progressive recreational program will attract other young people. This is because the teenager who is enjoying his experience in Christ will bring along other teenagers who are outside of Christ. The teenager who has an unsatisfying experience at his church will not bring his friends.

Recreation is more than playing games, having parties, and being active. It includes the entire program of leisure-time guidance. Recreation includes reading in the church lounge and listening to records. It includes art, drama, and a chance to converse with friends. Recreation includes the creative experience of a hobby. Recreation can be the enjoyment of a nature hike, a quiet moment of worship, working in the garden, the fellowship of a friendly game, or the athletic competitive program. Recreation is writing a play, carving an animal out of a block of soap, painting a landscape, making a belt. Recreation can set free the creative powers of the teenager.

The acid test of church-centered recreation is not, "What does the teenager do?" but "What does the recreation do to the teenager?"

It should be pointed out that recreation is no "cure-all." Perhaps this fact needs to be emphasized. Exaggerated claims for the efficiency of recreation in achieving changes in behavior patterns do not help the cause of recreation. Some churches which have great recreational programs are not necessarily changing lives. Recreation must be integrated into the total program of character and spiritual development. It is the wholesomeness of the whole program that makes the whole Christian. Evangelism, worship, Bible study, service, learning, and recreation are all teammates.

Structuring the Activity Time

The activity that is planned well is enjoyed by all. Recreation never just happens; it takes time, planning, and work to be successful.

1. *First meeting of recreation committee.* At the first meeting of the recreation committee several things will need to be decided. First of all, when planning an activity or a time of recreation you will have to decide the following:

a. Place

b. Time

c. The type of party or recreation

d. The theme of activity or recreation

e. The games to be played or recreational events

f. Food, refreshments, and/or meal

g. Devotions

h. Assign members to committees to plan details

(1) Committee on food

(2) Committee on games

(3) Committee on clean-up

(4) Committee on publicity

The party or recreation that is planned thoroughly will be enjoyed immensely. John Ruskin said, "If you want food, you have to toil for it. If you want knowledge, you have to toil for it. If you want enjoyment or pleasure, you must toil for it." The young people's leader will have to work diligently in order that the teenagers will enjoy themselves in church-sponsored activities.

2. *Check the day before the event.* At this time you should make sure that the place of the meeting is secured against possible conflicting arrangements. Check the alternate plans in case of bad weather (for outside activities). Check to see if the personnel and committees are definitely ready and committed. Note if the properties and equipment are ready. Try to determine what will be the probable attendance. Note the other details of the party.

3. *Be on hand at least thirty minutes before the event begins.* You as the youth director should be there to check on the physical arrangements and to get yourself in tune. The youth leader who comes dashing in at the last moment and tries to look after details will get the activities off to a slow and faltering start.

By arriving early you should check your assistants, the equipment, the ventilation, the seating arrangement, the food and the order of program. Is everything in place? Are the balls there? Are the nets up? Is the piano in place for singing? Are there lights, chairs and tables? The efficient leader will make a list for a final check; then as he checks on these things on arrival, he will have the confidence that everything is ready to go.

4. *Recreation begins when the first person arrives and ends when the last person leaves.* An activity or good time can be ruined by letting the first few people arrive and sit around with nothing to do. A good time should be arranged for those who come early as well as for those who are the last ones to leave.

Individual competition or "ice breakers" can be planned for those who come early. The activity does not begin when everyone has arrived and you stand in the middle of the room and say, "All right, let's get started!" The good time begins when the first person arrives. If the few minutes before the beginning of the first game are dull and unattractive, this sets the pattern for the entire evening. Plan a good time for those who come first.

5. *Know your program by heart.* If you as the youth director are planning and directing the good time, know what you are going to do. Put the outline of the games and activities on a card or slip of paper as an aid to memory. Have an aim for the recreation and point everything towards that aim.

6. *Stand where you can be seen by all.* You as the leader should be in a place where you can be seen and heard by all. If the group is in a circle, it is usually bad to stand in the center. Half of the group would be behind you. Stand at the side where all can see you and look into their faces. This commands attention.

7. *Secure attention before giving directions.* Avoid repeated blows on a whistle, if possible. Speak softly but firmly. Use a piano chord, a hand raised, or any other means, but make sure you have attention.

By all means avoid the attitude of a dictator. Never bluster, boss, or blame. Be sold on the crowd and the program. If you as the youth director note any sign of disinterest in the games that are being played, move on to the next activity. Disinterest is contagious. The teens can tell if you feel that the games are childish. If you reflect your attitude, they will surely rebel at playing such a game. Be absolutely sold on the good time that you are having. Be an enthusiastic participant.

8. *Be your age.* Young people expect you to be fun as well as fun to be with. However, don't be juvenile. Don't insult the intelligence of the teenager with cheap and childish behavior. Teenagers do not expect their adult leaders to act like teenagers. They may laugh *at* you, but you want them to laugh *with* you. The teenager has sincere respect for the adult who acts his age and who respects teens for acting their age.

9. *Speak in a normal tone of voice when giving directions.* Be courteous, enthusiastic, and responsive no matter what the response is.

You have the responsibility to set the pace and tone for the recreation period. There is no place for sarcasm and discourtesy. Never try to shout over the noise of the group. You only add to the confusion. Always make sure that people are listening and attentive before giving directions.

10. *Get all to participate.* This is easy to say and difficult to do. Invariably a group of teenage girls will run off into the hall or to the rest rooms to discuss some matter that has come up. Then the group is divided and there is no esprit de corps.

Make sure that all teens participate in a game. There must be good group interaction and dynamics. At this place you will have to anticipate the possible problems and difficulties by carefully thinking through every angle of the program. Consider carefully the groups, the young people, and any possible problems. Be ready to face whatever situation comes up. To do this, you must develop resourcefulness.

11. *Stop each phase of recreation at the peak of enjoyment.* Sometimes the youth will want to carry a game on and on and on and on. Note lagging signs of activity. When you have the "feel" of the group and it seems as though enjoyment is at a peak, stop. A game may be entertaining and enlightening if played twice, but played the third time it becomes a bore and a drag on the evening.

12. *Plan your program in detail and sequence.* Sequence is important so that the same types of recreation follow one another. Set the mood by the type of games you play. For instance, a relay game should ordinarily be followed by another relay game. Mental activity games that are played sitting in a circle should be followed by the same type of game. Setting of the mood is important. Active games should be phased together. Team games should be put together. Music activities should be planned according to their mood as well as linguistic games.

13. *Bring good times to a climax.* The teenager should feel that the closing game, song, event, is just the thing to top off the evening. Games should be started slow with little activity and the momentum carried throughout the evening. The games may get progressively more active, or the opposite can be planned. The games may start off fast and active with the evening ending with quiet games, preparing for the devotional. The sequence of games should be in keeping with the aim of the evening activities.

14. *Use maximum help in clean-up.* Many times a youth activity has been a big success. The youth leader and council have gone to much work. The activity is over. The teens have gone except for the three or four faithful left to clean up. This is wrong. Enlist volunteers to help make an investment of time. The more teenagers who have a direct investment in the recreation or party, the more successful the event.

Teenagers can grow spiritually and culturally as they apply themselves in helping to plan a successful social or recreation period. Therefore the teenager should be used to a maximum in helping with preparation, program and clean-up of a social.

Guiding Principles for the Recreational Program of the Church

1. *Provide recreation for all teenagers.* The needs, interests, and capacities of each teenager and each youth group within the church should be considered. All teenagers are not the same. Therefore, the recreational programs should consider the junior high as well as the college and career age groups. Consider all of the needs of the young people in providing for recreation.

2. *The recreational program should be an integral part of the youth program.* Too often the recreation is considered a sideline of the youth program. Many church leaders feel that Bible study, prayer meetings, and planning sessions are vital to the life of the church and that recreation is an unneeded commodity. It is tolerated only because the kids want it. This view sells short the true nature of the Scripture, the church, the young people, and the purpose for which the church is operating. Recreation can and does minister to the aim and makeup of the local church and young people's group.

3. *Follow democratic participation of the teenagers in all aspects of the recreational program.* Good organizational and administrative principles should be followed. Involve as many teenagers as possible in selecting, planning, promoting, and executing the recreational activities of the young people's program. Teenagers are like adults. They have reached an age of independent choice, and they are likely to rebel at having a program administered to them in dictatorial fashion. You as the youth leader cannot tell them what to do. You must work with them. If you do not observe this principle, you will bring failure to other aspects of your ministry to young people.

4. *Choose those activities which are in keeping with your group's aim and purpose.* Choosing the recreational and social life will depend on the attitudes and capacities of the teenagers in your group. This will also depend on the available funds, facilities, and leadership. Some churches may have gymnasiums; others may have a small multipurpose room. Some country churches have no place for recreation at all. Some churches will have softball diamonds. Other churches have access to recreational fields and city parks. Therefore, the activities that are chosen will have to be in keeping with the resources that are available.

5. *Do not begin with a full-grown recreational program.* Recreation should begin with one or more activities that will promise to give suc-

cess. As a few activities are successful, others may be added to an ever-growing range of interests. As your youth group grows in its total maturity and capacity, it may add organized recreational facilities, music facilities, drama, forums, book clubs, arts, craft clubs, etc. Thus in time your youth group will serve all ages and all kinds of teenagers. It will give them opportunities for training in a variety of leisure-time skills as well as leisure-time activities.

6. *The recreational program should contain variety and balance.* Activities that are satisfying and are self-expressive for one teenager may hold no interest for the next. People are different, needs are different, and life is different. It is a mistake to try to regiment all teenagers into the same program. Opportunities should be afforded for each teenager to express his individual makeup as well as to have his own enjoyment.

One teenager may enjoy sitting in the lounge of the church playing checkers, table games, reading, painting, or just talking. The next teenager is full of life and enjoys track, running, basketball and contact sports. The program should be geared to all youth. No program should be so grooved and limited as to encourage only limited participation. Life is too broad for this. Variety and balance in the program make it possible for all individuals to be reached. Also, variety and balance make it possible for all individuals to mature in their own development.

All young people should specialize in more skills, knowledge, and rewarding recreations than they now have. Growing and expanding interests will lead teenagers to other interests, each filled with the promise of a satisfying and rewarding life. You as the youth leader can help them to grow spiritually and culturally as you lead them into many new areas and avenues of experience.

7. *Community recreational projects should be considered.* There is a place in the total recreational program of the young people to consider such activities. Consideration should be given to church-sponsored softball leagues, basketball teams, and bowling tournaments. Other recreational departments of the city as well as park boards should be considered.

8. *Recreation should be anchored to the aims of the New Testament.* After every social or recreational feature has been concluded, you should thoughtfully test and evaluate the results of the event. Have wholesome fun and fellowship been experienced by all the teenagers? Are the teenagers more unified in spirit? Were all in attendance impressed with the fact that Christians have the best times together after all? Were cliques overcome? Did the total recreational experience strengthen or weaken the youth work and the program? Did the social period conclude with the teenagers carrying away a deep appreciation

for Christ, who alone can give true happiness? Did the visitors and prospective members realize that Christ is the center of our life? Was the recreation reflective of the entire church program?

There are many points by which we can evaluate the recreation and good times of a local church. These become reflective, some become critical, because of bias and prejudice against teenagers. There are some in the church who feel that good times, leisure times, and recreation are a waste of time and therefore border on sinfulness. There are many tests for recreation. Some of the following tests can be applied to the recreational program in your church.*

TEST FOR CHURCH ACTIVITIES

1. Testimony test: what will it do for others?
2. Spirituality test: what will it do for me?
3. Health test: what will it do for my body?
4. Sociability test: does it foster unsocial attitudes or does it develop a spirit of friendliness and appreciation of others?
5. Fun test: is it as profitable in retrospect and participation as in prospect?
6. Value test: does it crowd out the better and the best?
7. Time test: does it have durability? Is it passing or permanent?
8. Self-expression test: does it allow opportunity for creative activity or is it simply a dictated action?
9. Aesthetic test: does it lift your level of appreciation or pull it down?
10. Budget test: can you afford it?

SUMMARY

The purpose of this chapter is not to be an encyclopedia or source book of games and ideas on recreation. Therefore, we have not included a list of games, activities and recreation that may be played in a church or church related situation. We have not suggested party outlines. If this were done, you would only have a small resource of what could be done. Once this chapter had been read and applied, it would be useless to you as a youth leader. But the opposite has been attempted. Principles and practices of leading recreation have been suggested. You will find that these principles will become true in every party or activity which you plan. The principle of leading young people in recreation can become permanent because principles and practices are suggested in this chapter

---

*Unpublished class notes. Professor Howard Hendricks, Christian Education of Youth, Dallas Theological Seminary, 1956.

that become a way of life. It is felt that the principles of this chapter, if applied, will build maturity in the young people of your church.

THOUGHT QUESTIONS

Section Eight

(Covers Chapter 20, "Worship and the Young Person"; Chapter 21, "Advertising the Youth Program"; Chapter 22, "Church Music and the Teenager"; Chapter 23, "Guiding Principles for the Youth Camp"; Chapter 24, "Recreation for Young People".)

1. What is worship? Is it important in your church?

2. What is the main contribution that worship makes to teenagers?

3. Does faith on the part of the young person help the worship experience?

4. Refute or defend this statement: "Teenagers are life, activity, and movement; they don't like quiet meditation."

5. What is the ultimate purpose or climax of a worship experience?

6. The chapter on advertising indicates that a youth group should be concerned about its *image*. What would you want the image of your youth group to be? What ideas would you want people to have when they think of your youth group?

7. Did the advertising of the early church in the book of Acts follow the principles set down in this chapter? Prove your answer.

8. What specific principles of advertising would appeal more to youth than to other ages?

9. Suggest the one best medium for advertising each of the following activities. Give one sentence explaining your reason.

   a. Halloween party

   b. Public installation of youth officers

   c. Weekly program

   d. Spring banquet

   e. Weekend retreat

   f. Summer camp

   g. Youth rally in another city

   h. Sunday School

   i. Missions program

10. What is the purpose of church music? How can the words, rhythm, and melody express the purpose?

11. What is the difference between the worship, devotional and testimony hymn?

12. Does entertainment music have a place in the church music program? If so, when should it be used?

13. Would your church use a centralized or a decentralized camping program more effectively?

14. Why does camp affect the life of youth more than any other church agency?

15. What person on the camp staff will make the greatest impact on the campers—the director, the speaker or the counselors? Why? Who in your church would you choose to be camp director, counselors, speaker?

16. Why does your church have recreation for its youth? How could you improve the recreation program in your church?

17. What is the strongest biblical argument for having a recreation program in the church?

18. Think through a game file. It might be a good idea to write out five games for each of the following:

   a. Relay games
   b. Mental games
   c. Ice breakers
   d. Group competition
   e. Skill competition

19. If you had to plan one recreational activity for each month in the year for your youth group, what would they be? How can you make the activities varied and reflect the season of the year?

20. How much money should your church spend on the recreational budget for young people this year? Think through a budget to include the events you suggested in the previous question.

SECTION NINE

SUMMARY AND CONCLUSION

Where do we go from here?
Can we get there?
When do we begin?

25

RETROSPECT AND PERSPECTIVE

I am sure this book has succeeded in overstepping the limits. First of all, this book is too long. If you have read the entire manuscript—congratulations. I realize it has taken many words to say what I have said about youth. But I have written what was upon my heart. Second, this book is too short. No one in a few chapters can hope to cover all of the aspects, problems, approaches, and potentialities of youth work. An entire book could be written on what I have covered in one chapter. My intent was not to be exhaustive, but to give you an introduction to youth work. Thirdly, this book is too simple. Youth work is profound. The problems in a single teenager are more complex than can be examined in one book. When the sum total of problems of teenagers is considered, these difficulties are as incomprehensible as the problems of theology. Fourthly, the book is too exhaustive. Youth problems that are very simple have been made to seem impossible. Actually, adolescence is as simple as growing up. Every person on earth either has been, shall be, or is now in adolescence.

Be careful. You are not now an expert on adolescence. You may have a few more insights and a few more ideas, but no one in his right mind will consider himself an expert on adolescence. Now you are prepared to learn about adolescence. Learn from the youth in your church and home. Take every opportunity to grow with them. Learn from your experience. If you quit growing, there is no hope for you or for the young people to whom you minister. Learn from God's presence. If you have a heart for teenagers and attempt to work with them, they will drive you to the presence of God. In God's presence, learn those things that will make you a better worker with young people.

You probably haven't heard all I have said in this book. If you are an average reader, you will bring your background to a book. This background becomes a screen or grid through which you view the contents of a book; as a result you don't actually hear what the book says. Therefore, I challenge you to read the book again, to see what it says for itself.

I don't consider this book a final word on youth work. I consider this book a tool to help you in your work with youth. During the original writing of this manuscript, I edited and changed it six times. After the book was in the bookstores for six years, I once again edited and changed it. The more I work with teenagers, the more I grow and realize I must grow. Growth produces change. My ideas on youth work will probably change again—I hope yours will. I trust our continual change will produce spiritual growth to maturity in the lives of teenagers with whom we work.

In the final analysis the product, which is the young person, is the determining factor of our work. Can you see in his life the outgrowth of your work? Is he winning others to Jesus Christ? Is he a maturing youth who reveals Jesus Christ in his life? If so, you are doing a good job of training teens.

It is almost midnight; tomorrow morning this book is due at the publishers. Clocks, expectations, and deadlines are a part of our life, but especially the life of the teenager. This afternoon a teenage girl named Mary Elizabeth gave me a challenge. May this spur us to action. She said:

"I'm not quite somebody.

"I would rather be nobody, or somebody bad, or dead, but to be not quite somebody is hell."

Jesus Christ makes everybody, somebody.

GLOSSARY

Accumulative records: a file or collection of information about persons, groups, activities, etc., which is continually increasing as new information is added to keep the file up to date.

Adjustment: the establishment of a satisfactory relationship, as representing harmony, conformity, adaptation, or the like, with the desire of experiencing a minimum of conflict involving a proper relationship to every area of life.

Administration: the persons collectively who are entrusted with leadership in the managing of affairs.

Adolescence: that period of life between puberty and adulthood usually characterized as one of the least understood, but one of the most determinative areas of life. Involves the social, mental, physical, and sexual areas of life.

Advisory: having or exercising the power to advise; to give advice, recommendations, information, warning or counsel.

Aim: the ultimate purpose toward the achievement of one's endeavor or toward which effort is directed.

Anecdotal: that which is characteristic of or containing brief narratives or meaningful, interesting (often amusing) incidents or events called anecdotes.

Approbation: act of approving; approval; sanction; commendation.

Audiovisual: that which is used to attract and to teach through the ear and the eyes of the audience. Physical objects, materials, or representations to be seen and/or heard in order to impress the mind, stimulate interest, and explain facts.

Autonomous: independent; self-governing; also, without outside control.

Average: the usual, typical, or most-often-encountered thing, happening, or person of a considerable number.

Behavior reaction: activity or response aroused in an organism by a stimulus and demonstrated by conduct.

Brainstorming: A conference technique of solving specific problems, amassing information, stimulating creative thinking, developing new ideas by unrestrained and spontaneous participation in discussion.

Catharsis: elimination of a complex idea or problem by bringing it to consciousness and affording or allowing it expression. (The healthful "talking out" of painful ideas to an understanding listener.)

Chronic absentee: one who is continuously or habitually not present.

Church: A group of baptized believers, in whom Christ dwells, under the discipline of the Word of God, organized for evangelism, education, worship, fellowship and the administration of the ordinances.

Church morals: behavior or conduct, and/or principles which are affected and influenced by a house of worship and those who worship there.

Circular response: a teaching technique whereby each person in the circle (or auditorium) is given opportunity to contribute spontaneously his ideas on an announced topic of consideration.

Clientele: those who take advantage of the services of a person, group, or institution.

Clinical: the treatment of a disorder rather than the investigation of it.

Clinical psychiatry: the medical specialty dealing with mental disorders through observation, investigation, and case study into the inner thinking of man.

363

Cliques: small, exclusive, intimate sets of persons, usually made up of pupils from the same socio-economic background. These groups are relatively stable and furnish "belongness" and prestige to those who join.

Colloquy: a learning-group method whereby audience representatives present questions which are first considered by resource persons. Members of the audience participate actively whenever feasible, under direction of the moderator.

Counsel: advice, especially that given as the result of consultation; opinion, advice, direction, instruction, or recommendation given especially as a result of consultation; that which is offered in order to help another person analyze and solve his problems.

Counselee: one who goes to a counselor for help and advice because he has a conflict or difficulty in adjusting to life.

Counselor: one who uses various techniques to help people solve conflicts or better their life adjustment.

Counselor involvement: when a counselor occupies himself absorbingly or engrossingly with the counselee's problem; when the counselor's feeling about a person affects him to the extent that he cannot accept the counselee as he is and allow the counselee the opportunity to make his own decision—thus creating unwholesome relationship in which the counselor has a strong personal investment in the choices being made by the other person.

Communication: interchange of thoughts, opinions, ideas or information. Making something common to two persons.

Concept: a thought; an opinion; an idea of what a thing in general should be.

Conversion: a spiritual and moral change attending belief in Jesus Christ, changing one's ultimate destiny from hell to heaven, and the receiving of a new divine nature.

Conviction: a strong persuasion or belief.

Creative listening: the sympathetic, understanding listening of a person, in an unhurried interview, to the innermost feeling of another person as the first person becomes a sounding board and the second person is drawn out and given the opportunity to see his situation objectively.

Criterion: a standard of judging; a rule or test by which anything is tried in forming a correct judgment respecting it.

Curriculum: a course of study; a planned and guided pattern of objectives, experiences, and content through which God may act and confront persons.

Developmental tasks: those abilities—whether physical, mental, emotional, sexual, or social—that a youth must successfully experience in a progressive, orderly, coherent nature, leading to the goal of maturity.

Diagnostic techniques: methods used in order critically to scrutinize, recognize and make judgments concerning the reasons for certain actions, attitudes and behaviors, the application of the scientific method (figuring the probability that certain things will happen) to the prediction of human behavior.

Dialogue: an interaction, a giving and receiving of information, experiences, and desires. In the process of dialogue two people unfold the nature of and together pursue a common solution to the problems of life.

Disciple: a learner.

Dogmatic: asserting a matter of opinion as if it were fact; positive in manner or utterance; seeking to put over one's viewpoint by the force of presentation.

Domineering: to rule with insolence or arbitrary sway; to be overbearing, to run everything.

Double transference: occurs when the counselor acts as a resource person; and because he knows the Word of God and the teenager, he is able to put the youth into the Word of God and the Word of God into the youth.

Drives: attempts to restore equilibrium in a life, the basis for activity; psychologically produced desires to restore balance (equilibrium) in a life.

Dyads: neighbor-nudge. A class or group is divided into pairs. Each pair discusses a topic to be introduced or a lecture just heard, to form conclusions.

Dynamics: the force behind a change or process.

Ecclesiology: theological doctrine relating to the church.

Eclectic counseling: that counseling in which the counselor selects from various systems what methods seem best—depending on his counselee and the individual situation.

Education: the knowledge and development resulting from an educational process; training; the field of study that deals mainly with methods of learning and teaching.

Ego-ideal: the positive standards, ideals, and ambitions assimilated into the total personality, the sum total of what a person wants to become.

Ego-strength: a firm or confident view one has of his personality, a strong self-image.

Empathy: intellectual (objective) awareness and understanding of the feelings, emotions and behavior of another person. Differs from sympathy which is the emotional (subjective) identification with the feelings and behavior of another.

Equilibrium: a state of balance, or even adjustment, between opposing influences, interests and attractions.

Evaluation: the ascertaining of the value of a program, purpose, or idea; an appraisal.

Evangelicalism: an evangelical represents the theological position between fundamentalism and liberalism. The evangelical agrees with the fundamentalist in theology but is relevant in methodology, giving attention to a sympathetic attitude toward science, a willingness to re-examine beliefs concerning the work of the Holy Spirit, a more tolerant attitude toward varying attitudes on eschatology, an increased emphasis on scholarship, a growing recognition of social responsibility, a deep concern to make the gospel relevant to society, a willingness to converse with liberal theologians, and a shift away from indoctrination.

Evangelism: witnessing the gospel to the total personality of man in his sinful condition, motivating him to respond to the gospel.

Experience: the actual living through an event or events; the sum total of the conscious events which compose an individual life; observed facts and events in contrast with what is supplied by thought.

Fellowship: companionship; friendliness, comradeship; association.

Freudian: relating to, or according with, the theories or practices of Sigmund Freud, especially in regard to the causes and treatment of hysteria and other psychopathic phenomena, and the interpretation of dreams and other mental products, as based upon a psychology of the unconscious; using the directive counseling approach in which the counselor is primarily interested in helping the pupil solve the immediate problems one at a time and in helping him achieve a better overall adjustment; and, in doing so, the counselor relates the problem back to the person's background and experience and then comes up with an answer.

Frustration: thwarting of a need or desire; the blocking of a person's efforts to satisfy basic needs and drives; prevention of attaining a purpose.

Goals: the end toward which educational effort is directed.

Gospel: the good news concerning Christ and salvation. The gospel includes the death, burial and resurrection of Jesus Christ.

Grading curve: the pattern which follows, charts, or measures the procedure of grading or sorting.

Guidance: the direction, training of others, implies that those offering the direction, training, information, or advice have intimate knowledge of the course or way and of all its difficulties or dangers.

Heredity: the pattern of characteristics and potentials which a person receives from his parents; the passing on or down of the physical and psychical characteristics of parents to their offspring.

Hero: a man admired for his achievements and qualities.

Heterogeneous: that group or thing which is composed of that which differs in kind, has unlike qualities, or is dissimilar to each other.

Homogeneous: that which is composed of similar persons or elements; composed of that which is of the same kind or nature.

Idealistic: that which is dreamed or imagined to occupy a more important place in the mind than in real life; visionary.

Identification: orientation of the self in regard to something (as to a person or group) with the resulting feeling of close emotional association.

Identity crisis: a search for self-identity, usually associated with adolescence.

Image: a form, aspect, likeness; a mental representation of anything not actually present to the senses.

Independent dependency: the state or occasion when a person is independent of man, but yet is dependent upon the Lord and His Word—this state will eventually develop true spiritual maturity.

Individual differences: the areas in which persons are not alike or similar; variation, distinctions between persons.

Inductive: the process of reasoning from a part to a whole.

Inductive counseling: the selection of the best techniques from both directive and nondirective counseling on the basis of the individual's needs and problems, leading the counselee to an answer in the Word of God. Coming to a problem with no preconceived plan of solution but selecting the technique and plan from the most appropriate method or methods and applying it to the situation in the manner most suitable to the individual and his particular needs; no generalized solution or method to fit every person, every situation, and every problem.

Insight: self-understanding; the ability to see and understand clearly the inner nature of things; the extent to which a person understands his real motives and conflicts; to see the relationship between two ideas, parts or things.

Integration: oneness; the organization of various traits or tendencies into one harmonious personality; the absence of conflict; harmony within the personality; a generally harmonious relationship with others; a relationship or real meaning between what is learned and how life is lived.

Interaction: mutual or reciprocal action or influence between two or more persons.

Intrinsic: belonging to the constitution, nature, or essence of a thing; that which is inherent or part of the nature of a thing rather than that which is caused by influence from without.

Learning: a change in the use of abilities that comes through experience drawn from the curriculum, reflecting a continuous pattern in the life.

Lecture: the procedure that includes all oral presentation by the teacher— whether it be by way of remarks made to clarify issues, to elaborate upon pupils' answers to questions, to supplement facts already at hand; or whether it be by way of extended formal exposition, or to indicate how something is to be done. A discourse delivered on any subject, especially a formal discourse intended for instruction.

Liberalism: a movement in modern Protestantism emphasizing intellectual liberty, humanism, a relevant approach to truth, and the ethical content of Christianity.

Listening teams: teams of students are given a question to answer and must listen to the lecture to find the answer. (See buzz groups.)

Logical: in accordance with the inferences reasonably to be drawn from events or circumstances.

Maturity: (as a static concept) is viewed as an unchanging goal of development toward which all growth is aimed, usually reached in the late teens or early twenties and synonymous with adulthood; (as a sliding scale—relative concept) is viewed as the average rate of development expected for those who perform at that age; a relative concept; the display of a level of life equal to the person's chronological age.

Medium: that through or by which anything is accomplished; the means used to attain a purpose; the means to an end.

Motivation: the conscious experience or subconscious condition which serves as a factor in determining an individual's behavior. The inner force which disposes a person to act in a certain way.

Negative ego: a person's inner knowledge of who he is not and what he does not want to become.

Novice: an inexperienced person; a beginner.

Officers: an elected group responsible for the actual administration of an organization.

Organization: that which is arranged, systematized, or constituted into a whole of interdependent parts, each having a special function or relation with respect to the whole. The executive structure of a business. The entire body of officials and committees of a certain group.

Paraphrasing: rephrasing verses of Scripture according to the true meaning as understood by the students.

Peer pressure: a constraining force, influence, or impulse exerted by an equal, or one of the same rank, quality, by equals in age group and status.

Perception: an immediate or intuitive cognition, knowledge or judgment, often implying nice observation or subtle discrimination, in most cases influenced by previous background experiences; understanding of an experience and material, as well as the interpretation of its meaning; insight into relationships.

Permissive atmosphere: a surrounding or pervading influence which is non-restrictive, non-prohibitive; which is encouraging for individual freedom and initiative; which causes a person to feel accepted, at ease, comfortable.

Persuasion: opinion, belief; a system of religious beliefs.

Presession: that which occurs with a group just previous in time or prior to their actually scheduled period of classes or instruction.

Pride: an unreasonable or unjustifiable self-respect; delight or elation arising from some act of possession.

Program planning: the method or scheme of action, procedure or arrangement for forthcoming classes, activities, public exercises, or performances.

Projective tests: tests or measures which reveal the inner or subjective feelings of the person tested.

Puberty: the beginning of adolescence. The time when the sex organs begin to mature; the state or quality of being first capable of begetting or bearing offspring. (It may be a time of increased psychological stress for the boy or girl, a time when they need the guidance of adults in understanding what is happening to them. Adequate prior and current information about sex will help boys and girls pass through pubescent years with wholesome, desirable attitudes.)

Punitive: that which inflicts or is concerned with punishment or penalties.

Rapport: a relationship characterized by harmony, conformity, accord, or affinity—which must be so in order for one member of the relationship to help another; an intimate, harmonious relationship as applied to people having close understanding, an interpersonal relationship characterized by a spirit of cooperation, confidence, and harmony, usually between counselor and counselee.

Reaching: using every acceptable means to get the listener under the hearing of the gospel.

Reciprocal: mutual, shared, felt, shown or the like by both sides; shared, experienced, or the like, by each; implies a return in due measure by each of two sides, courtesies, duties, etc.; corresponding to each other as by being equivalent or complementary.

Referral: the act of sending or directing (yourself or another) (to some person or place), as for treatment, aid, decisions; the act of pointing to or directing attention toward.

Reorientate: to acquaint again concerning the awareness of a situation or existing situation, with reference to time, place, and identity of persons.

Response: any activity resulting from stimulation, a reaction; a desired outcome of our teaching.

Reticence: quality, state, or an instance of being inclined to keep silent or be uncommunicative.

Retrogress: to move backwards; to revert to an earlier state or condition.

Role diffusion: the different roles assumed by a teenager in the course of his home, school, church, and community life.

Sanctification: being separate from sin, set apart to God. Position sanctification, "I was separated from sin, my standing in heaven is perfect;" practical sanctification, "I am daily being separated from sin or I grow in Christ;" Future sanctification, "I shall be completely separated from sin by the return of Christ."

Sect: a group; an organized ecclesiastical body; a dissenting or schismatic religious body.

Self-concept: See Self-identity.

Self-identity: the view that a person has of his personality or ego. The self is the sum total of all that a person calls "his." This internal perspective forms an external frame of reference by which the person gives direction to his life.

Self-image: See Self-identity.

Self-values: the values or goals which seem important to a person, according to his self-identity.

Sensation: (sensationalism) that which results from stimulation by the use of certain means calculated to arouse excited interest and emotional response.

Sensitivity: the capacity to sense, to respond, primarily to stimulation.

Small talk: informal chatting for the purpose of putting one at ease in a counseling situation.

Spiritual schizophrenia: a confusion of roles and appropriateness of exercising these roles in the religious realm; the result of the conflicting and diversified roles and behavior expected of a person in the religious realm.

Statistical: pertaining to classified facts respecting any particular class of interest; especially, those facts which can be stated in numbers.

Stimulus: that which incites to activity; any agent or environmental change capable of influencing activity, as exciting the activity of a muscle or inner desire.
An impulse in a nerve or of exciting a specific end organ of sensation.

Subjective: exhibiting or affected by personal emotional background; belonging to reality as perceived or known.

Suggestibility: easily influenced.

Supervising: overseeing for direction.

Tangent: departure or deviation from a subject, aims, or goals; digression from a theme or main topic.

Test-oriented: having the main focus of attention on tests—their scores and their implications; to be guided mainly by test facts and principles.

Theme: a central idea or thought around which something is built. A subject or topic; the characteristic part.

Therapeutic: to serve, take care of, to heat, to heal; to apply remedies for the purpose of healing or curing.

Thermatic apperception test: a personality measurement test which reveals the inner or subjective feelings, needs, drives of the person tested on the basis of judgment and decision.

Total depravity: completely depraved or corrupted; bearing no trace of good or bent toward that direction; the complete lack of original righteousness by which man gains merit with God.

Underachiever: one who does not or who cannot accomplish, or perform, according to his own innate ability or according to the average standards of his group.

Units: a single thing or person, or a group regarded as an individual member of a number of groups.

Worship: a face-to-face involvement with a living God based on a regeneration experience, prompted by the Holy Spirit, and resulting in the exaltation of God's glory; an earnest effort to recreate the conditions and experiences that have been found to deepen man's relationship to God; it focuses all of our ideas, actions, and feelings in effective tones on a specific center which is God Himself; an emotional, personal and volitional response to an intellectual evaluation.

BIBLIOGRAPHY

Adams, James F. *Problems in Counseling, A Case Study Approach.* New York: The Macmillan Company, 1962.

Aultman, Donald S. *Guiding Youth.* Cleveland, Tennessee: Pathway Press, 1965.

Babin, Pierre. *Adolescents in Search of a New Church.* New York: Herder and Herder, 1969.

_____. *Crisis of Faith.* New York: Herder and Herder, 1963.

Baruch, Dorothy W. *How to Live With Your Teenager.* McGraw-Hill, 1953.

Bier, William C., ed. *The Adolescent: His Search for Understanding.* New York: Fordham University Press, 1963.

Bowman, Clarice M. *Ways Youth Learn.* New York: Harper and Row, 1952.

Bowman, Locke E., Jr. *How to Teach Senior Highs.* Philadelphia: The Westminster Press, 1963.

Boyer, Claude F. *Counseling Youth.* Winona Lake, Indiana: Light and Life Press, 1959.

Brunk, Ada Zimmerman and Metzler, Ethel Yake. *The Christian Nurture of Youth.* Scottsdale, Pa.: Herald Press, 1960.

Carlsen, G. Robert. *Books and the Teen-age Reader.* New York: Harper and Row, 1967.

Clemmons, Robert S. *Young Adults in the Church.* New York: Abingdon Press, 1959, 138 pp.

Cole, Luella. *Psychology of Adolescence.* New York: Farrar & Rinehart, Inc., 1942.

Culley, Kendig Brubaker. *The Westminster Dictionary of Christian Education.* Philadelphia: The Westminster Press, 1964.

Ellis, Howard W. *Evangelism for Teen Agers.* New York: Abingdon Press, 1958.

Erb, F. O. *The Development of the Young People's Movement.* Chicago: University of Chicago Press, 1917.

Ferguson, Rowena. *The Church's Ministry with Senior Highs.* Nashville: The Graded Press, 1963.

_____. *Youth and the Christian Community.* Nashville: Abingdon Press, 1960.

Focus on Youth. Vols. III-IV. Colorado Springs, Colorado: Young Life, 1969-1970.

Friedenberg, Edgar Z. *The Dignity of Youth & Other Atavisms.* Boston: Beacon Press, 1965.

_____. The Vanishing Adolescent. New York: Dell Publishing Company, Inc., 1959.

Gallagher, J. Roswell and Harris, Herbert I. *Emotional Problems of Adolescents.* New York: Oxford University Press, 1964.

Garrison, Karl C. *Before You Teach Teen-Agers.* Philadelphia: The Lutheran Church Press, 1962.

Ginott, Haim. *Between Parent and Teenager.* New York: The Macmillan Company, 1969.

371

372

Glueck, Sheldon and Eleanor. *Delinquents in the Making.* New York: Harper and Row, 1954.

Goldman, Ronald. *Religious Thinking from Childhood to Adolescence.* London: Routledge and Kegan Paul, 1964.

Goodman, Paul. *Growing Up Absurd.* New York: Random House, Inc., 1960.

Gottlieb, David and Reeves, John. *Adolescent Behavior in Urban Areas.* New York: Free Press of Glencoe and Macmillan Company, 1963.

Hakes, J. Edward. *An Introduction to Evangelical Christian Education.* Chicago: Moody Press.

Harbin, O. E. *The Recreation Leader.* New York: Abingdon Press, 1952.

Harris, Thomas Allen. *Counseling the Serviceman and His Family.* Englewood Cliffs, N. J.: Prentice-Hall, 1964.

Havighurst, Robert. *Development Task and Education,* Second Edition. New York: Longman, Green and Co., 1952.

Hechinger, Grace and Fred M. *Teen-age Tyranny.* New York: William Morrow & Company, Inc., 1963.

Hoglund, Gunnar and Grabill, Virginia. *Youth Leader's Handbook.* Grand Rapids: Zondervan Publishing House, 1958.

Irving, Roy G. and Zuck, Roy B., ed. *Youth and the Church.* Chicago: Moody Press, 1968.

Jenkins, W. L. *The Young Adolescent in the Church.* "A Guide for Workers with Junior Highs." Philadelphia: The Geneva Press, 1964.

Kemp, Charles F. *Counseling with College Students.* Englewood Cliffs, N. J.: Prentice-Hall, 1964.

Laymon, Charles M. *The Use of the Bible in Teaching Youth.* Nashville: Abingdon Press, 1962.

Little, Sara. *Youth, World, and Church.* Richmond: John Knox Press, 1968.

Leuke, Harold. *Teenage Religion.* London: SCM Press, 1961.

Miller, Haskell M. *Understanding and Preventing Juvenile Delinquency.* New York: Abingdon Press, 1958.

Moore, Allen J. *The Young Adult Generation.* Nashville: Abingdon Press, 1969, p. 16.

Moore, Peter C., ed. *Youth in Crisis.* New York: The Seabury Press, 1966.

Morris, C. Eugene. *Counseling with Young People.* New York: The Association Press, 1954.

Muuss, Rolf E. *Theories of Adolescence.* New York: Random House, Inc., 1966.

Nelson, Donald E. "Causal Factors Relating to Failures in Youth Programming in the Local Church of the New Testament and Suggested Biblical Solutions." Unpublished Master's dissertation, Department of Christian Education, Pillsbury Conservative Baptist Bible College, 1960.

Omega Advisor. Chicago: Success with Youth, Inc., 1970.

Person, Peter P. *The Church and Modern Youth.* Grand Rapids: Zondervan Publishing House, 1963.

Peters, Clarence. "Developments of the Youth Programs of the Lutheran Churches in America." A thesis presented to the faculty of Concordia Seminary, St. Louis, Missouri, Department of Practical Theology in partial fulfillment of the requirements for the degree of Doctor of Theology, June 1951.

Pike, James A. *If You Marry Outside Your Faith.* New York: Harper and Row, 1954.

_____. *Teen-Agers and Sex.* Englewood Cliffs: Prentice-Hall, 1965.

Riesman, David; Glazer, Nathan; and Denney, Reuel. *The Lonely Crowd.* Garden City, New York: Doubleday & Company, Inc., 1956.

Roberts, Dorothy M. *Leading Teenage Church Groups.* New York: The Association Press, 1963.

Roberts, Guy L. *How the Church Can Help Where Delinquency Begins.* Richmond: The John Knox Press, 1958.

Rosenberg, Morris. *Society and the Adolescent Self-Image.* Princeton, N. J.: Princeton University Press, 1965.

Rusten, E. Michael. "Factors Associated with Success in the Senior High School Youth Programs of Selected Evangelical Churches." Unpublished Master of Theology thesis, submitted in partial fulfillment of the requirements for a Master's of Theology at Trinity Evangelical Divinity School, 1968.

Ryrie, Charles R. *Patterns for Christian Youth.* Chicago: Moody Press, 1966.

Senter, Mark H., III. "An Analysis of a Project-Based Approach to Youth Work in the Local Church." A thesis submitted to the faculty in partial fulfillment of the requirements for the degree of Master of Arts with a Major in Christian Education at Trinity Evangelical Divinity School, June 1971.

Shaver, Erwin L. and Stock, Harry T. *Training Young People in Worship.* Boston: The Pilgrim Press, 1929.

Snyder, Ross. *Young People and Their Culture.* New York: Abingdon Press, 1969.

Staton, Thomas F. *Dynamics of Adolescent Adjustment.* New York: The Macmillan Company, 1963.

Steimel, Raymond J. *Psychological Counseling of Adolescents.* Washington, D. C.: The Catholic University Press, 1962.

Stromen, Merton P. *Profiles of Church Youth.* St. Louis: Concordia Publishing House, 1963.

Tani, Henry N. *Ventures in Youth Work.* Philadelphia: The Christian Education Press, 1957.

Walker, Paul L. *Counseling Youth.* Cleveland, Tennessee: Pathway Press, 1967.

Whitam, Frederic L. "Adolescence and Mass Persuasion: A study of Teen-Age Decision Making at a Billy Graham Crusade." Unpublished, microfilm Ph.D. dissertation, Indiana University, 1965.

Winter, David. *Old Faith, Young World.* London: Hodder and Stoughton, 1965.

Zuck, Roy B. and Getz, Gene A. *Christian Youth, An In-Depth Study.* Chicago: Moody Press, 1968.

Zuck, Roy B. and Robertson, Fern. *How to be a Youth Sponsor.* Wheaton, Illinois: Scripture Press, 1960, pp. 19, 20.

INDEX